Visual Basic .NET Developer's Guide to ASP.NET, XML, and ADO.NET

Jeffrey P. McManus and Chris Kinsman

♦Addison-Wesley

Boston • San Francisco • New York • Toronto • Montreal
London • Munich • Paris • Madrid
Capetown • Sydney • Tokyo • Singapore • Mexico City

Many of the designations used by manufacturers and sellers to distinguish their products are claimed as trademarks. Where those designations appear in this book, and Addison-Wesley were aware of a trademark claim, the designations have been printed in initial capital letters or in all capitals.

The author and publisher have taken care in the preparation of this book, but make no expressed or implied warranty of any kind and assume no responsibility for errors or omissions. No liability is assumed for incidental or consequential damages in connection with or arising out of the use of the information or programs contained herein.

The publisher offers discounts on this book when ordered in quantity for special sales.

For more information, please contact:

Pearson Education Corporate Sales Division
201 W. 103rd Street
Indianapolis, IN 46290
(800) 428-5331
corpsales@pearsoned.com

Visit AW on the Web: www.awl.com/cseng/

Copyright © 2002 by Pearson Education

ISBN 0-672-32131-9

05   04   03   02   4   3   2   1

First printing, February 2002

ASSOCIATE PUBLISHER
Linda Engelman

ACQUISITIONS EDITOR
Sondra Scott

DEVELOPMENT EDITOR
Angela Allen

MANAGING EDITOR
Charlotte Clapp

PROJECT EDITOR
Carol Bowers

COPY EDITOR
Barbara Hacha

INDEXER
Tim Tate

PROOFREADER
Plan-It Publishing

TECHNICAL EDITORS
Phil Syme, Jawahar Puvvala, and Chris Thibodeaux

TEAM COORDINATOR
Lynne Williams

MEDIA DEVELOPER
Dan Scherf

INTERIOR DESIGNER
Anne Jones

COVER DESIGNER
Aren Howell

Contents at a Glance

Table of Contents

4   Debugging ASP.NET Applications   149

About the Author

Jeffrey P. McManus is a developer and speaker specializing in Microsoft tools. As a developer, he has specialized in online application development using Internet and client/server technologies. He is the author of four books on database and component technologies, including the best-selling *Database Access with Visual Basic 6*. Jeffrey regularly speaks at the VBITS/VSLive, European DevWeek, and VBConnections conferences.

Chris Kinsman is a developer and speaker specializing in Microsoft tools. As a developer, he has been responsible for several high-traffic sites based entirely on Microsoft tools and has served as Vice President of Technology at DevX.com. In addition, Chris spent 10 years consulting with Fortune 500 companies throughout the world to solve their needs by utilizing a variety of Microsoft Visual Studio and Back Office technologies. Chris regularly speaks at the VBITS/VSLive, Web Builder, and SQL2TheMax conferences.

Dedication

FOR CELESTE—Jeffrey P. McManus

This book is dedicated to my dad, who supported and encouraged me in everything I did.—Chris Kinsman

About the Technical Editors

Jawahar Puvvala (JP) is currently working as a senior developer with Synapse Integrated Technology. JP has gained a lot of exposure to Microsoft and Java technologies through designing and developing several systems. He has two master's degrees, and he currently holds MCSD, MCSE, and MCDBA certifications. He has a great deal of research experience and has published several conference and journal papers.

Phil Syme has been programming with C++ and Visual Basic since the release of Windows 3.1. He has contributed to the development of several projects for Fortune 100 companies that use Microsoft technologies and has coauthored two articles published in IEEE symposiums. In 1995, Phil graduated from Carnegie Mellon University with a bachelor's degree in computer science. Phil recently coauthored *Sams Teach Yourself C# Web Programming in 21 Days* (2002, ISBN 0-672-32235-8) and *Sams Teach Yourself Visual Basic .NET Web Programming in 21 Days* (2002, ISBN 0-672-32236-6).

Chris Thibodeaux, MCSE+I, MCDBA, MCSD, is the principal consultant of Empowering Solutions, Inc., a management and technology consultancy in Southern California. His primary expertise is in both systems architecture and databases. Chris teaches both Internet/intranet security and SQL Architecture classes at a community college near his home. You can reach Chris via his e-mail at chris@empowering-solutions.com.

Introduction

IN THIS CHAPTER

Problems with ASP Today

When Active Server Pages (ASP) was first introduced almost five years ago, it was seen as an answer to the awkward techniques used at that time for creating dynamic content on the Web. At the time, Common Gateway Interface programs or proprietary server plug-ins were the way that most of the Web's dynamic content was created. With the release of ASP 1.0, Microsoft changed all that. ASP 1.0 provided a flexible, robust scripting architecture that enabled developers to rapidly create dynamic Web applications. Developers could write in VBScript or JScript, and Microsoft provided a number of services to make development easy. At the time, it was just what developers needed. As Web development matured, several shortcomings of the platform became evident and persist until today.

Separation of Code and Design

As the Web grew in popularity in the early '90s, developers experienced three distinct waves of development paradigms. In the first wave, Web developers created static HTML documents and linked them. This was the era of the "brochure" Web site and was more about looks than anything else. The second wave brought the concept of dynamic content to the fore. Developers started creating registration forms and various small pieces of functionality and adding them to existing Web sites. The third wave was when the first and second waves came together. Web sites were being designed from the ground up to be interactive; they were treated more like an application and less like a magazine with a subscription card in it. In most instances, this type of interactive page design created a development paradigm that went like so:

- Designers created page mockups in HTML.
- Developers added code to the pages.
- When designers needed to change their design, they copied and pasted the existing code into the new page, butchering it and destroying its functionality.

The severity of this problem typically depended on the size of the site, the smarts of the designers, and the techniques that developers used to guard against this mangling.

With the release of Visual Studio 6 in September of 1998, it was clear that Microsoft recognized this burgeoning problem and attempted to resolve it with a new feature in Visual Basic 6—Web Classes. Web Classes made an attempt to separate the design of a page from the code that interacted with it. It enabled this separation by using an HTML template and providing a facility for doing tag replacement in the template. However, a number of problems occurred with Web Classes. Although a great idea, they suffered from two main issues. First, the Web Classes were implemented entirely in Visual Basic, which required traditional ASP developers to shift their thinking patterns for creating applications. Second, Microsoft had scalability issues related to the threading models of ASP and Visual Basic. Because of the previously stated reasons and many other smaller ones, Web Classes never really gained any traction among developers.

Scripting Language Based

When ASP 1.0 was first released, the fact that all development was done using scripting languages was a big plus. It meant that developers didn't have to go through a painful restart/ compile process that they might have been accustomed to with CGI or ISAPI style applications. As applications grew larger, numbers of users increased, and developers were using ASP for increasingly difficult problems. The fact that all code was interpreted became a potential performance bottleneck. With VBScript, limited support existed for error handling.

Many developers sidestepped this issue by moving code into compiled COM objects. Although this move solved some of the performance problems, it created new ones in deployment and scalability.

State Management

One of the most frustrating aspects that new Web developers faced early was dealing with the stateless nature of Web development. With ASP 1.0, Microsoft introduced the concept of a Session object, which was designed to make associating state with a particular user easy. This addition was arguably one of the most compelling features of ASP 1.0. Scalability and reliability started to become important as developers began creating larger applications. To address this need, developers started deploying their applications to *Web farms*. Web farms use multiple servers and spread the request for pages across the servers somewhat equally. This makes for a great scalability story… unless the developer is using that cool Session object. This object is specific to a particular machine in a Web farm and will not work if a user gets bounced to another server. Therefore, an application that was deployed to a Web farm could not use the Session object.

Introducing ASP.NET

ASP.NET is Microsoft's answer to the aforementioned problems and many others that were not explicitly stated. It is a fundamental rewrite of ASP that has been in process for more than two years. The ASP team took a close look at the problems facing Web developers and created a brand-new platform in the spirit of traditional ASP to solve those problems. Having used ASP.NET for a considerable amount of time, we can conclusively say they hit a home run with this release.

Platform Architecture

ASP.OLD was an Internet Server Application Programming Interface (ISAPI) filter that was written specifically to interact with Internet Information Server (IIS). It was monolithic in nature and relied very little on external services.

> **NOTE**
>
> In the IIS 5.0 time frame, ASP did use Microsoft Transaction Server (MTS) as an external service.

ASP.NET is still an ISAPI filter. However, unlike ASP.old, ASP.NET relies on a large number of "external" services—the .NET framework. ASP.NET and the .NET framework are so tightly coupled that it is difficult to consider the .NET framework as an external service. However, because it is accessible from applications outside the scope of ASP.NET, it should be considered an external service. As it turns out, this is a huge win for the ASP.NET developer. No longer must the developer write everything from scratch. Instead the .NET framework provides a large library of prewritten functionality.

The .NET framework redistributable consists of three main parts: the Common Language Runtime, the .NET framework base classes, and ASP.NET.

Common Language Runtime

The Common Language Runtime (CLR) is the execution engine for .NET framework applications. However, despite the common misconception, it is not an interpreter. The .NET applications are fully compiled applications that use the CLR to provide a number of services at execution. These services include the following:

- Code management (loading and execution)
- Application memory isolation
- Verification of type safety
- Conversion of IL to native code
- Access to metadata
- Garbage collection
- Enforcement of code access security
- Exception handling
- Interoperability
- Automation of object layout
- Support for debugging and profiling

The CLR is a platform that abstracts functionality from the operating system. In this sense, code written to target the CLR is "platform independent," provided that an implementation of the CLR is on the destination platform.

Managed Execution

The CLR isn't just a library or framework of functions that an executing program can call on. It interacts with running code on a number of levels. The loader provided by the CLR performs validation, security checks, and a number of other tasks each time a piece of code is loaded. Memory allocation and access are also controlled by the CLR. When you hear about "managed execution," this is what folks are speaking about—the interaction between the CLR and the executing code to produce reliable applications.

Cross-Language Interoperability

One of the most frustrating things with current COM or API-based development practices is that interfaces are usually written with a particular language consumer in mind. When writing a component to be consumed by a Visual Basic program, a developer will typically create the interfaces in a different fashion than if the component is intended to be consumed by a C++ program. This means that to reach both audiences, the developer must either use a least-common-denominator approach to developing the interface or must develop an interface for each consumer. This is clearly not the most productive way to write components. A second problem that most developers merely accept as normal today is that most components need to be written in a single language. If you create a component in C++ that exposes an employee object, you can't then inherit from that object in Visual Basic to create a Developer object. This means that typically a single language is chosen for most development projects to enable reuse.

.NET changes all this. Cross-language interoperability was built in from the start. All .NET languages must adhere to the Common Language Specification (CLS) that specifies the base level of functionality that each language must implement to play well with others. The CLS is written in such a way that each language can keep its unique flavor but still operate correctly with other languages within the CLR. The CLS includes a number of data types that all conforming languages must support. This restriction works to eliminate a common problem for developers: creating an interface that utilizes data types that another language doesn't support. It also supports both Binary as well as Source code inheritance, enabling the developer to create an Employee object in C# and inherit from it in Visual Basic.

What this means to you as a developer is that code reuse has become much simpler. As long as the code was written for .NET, you don't need to worry what language it was written in. In fact, the choice of language becomes more of a lifestyle choice than a capability choice. All languages in .NET are theoretically created equal, so you gain no performance or functionality benefit by using C# instead of VB. Use the language in which you are the most productive.

New Features in ASP.NET

Up to this point, all the features mentioned are gained because of the hosting of ASP.NET on top of the .NET framework. However, these features are just the tip of the iceberg. As mentioned previously, ASP.NET is a total rewrite, with significant features aside from the intrinsic .NET ones. We are going to give you an overview of the new features in ASP.NET and show how these features address the problems of separation of code and design, scripting languages, and state management.

Web Forms

Web Forms are Microsoft's attempt to solve the problem of the separation of code and design. ASP.NET now offers a code-behind model reminiscent of the forms designer in Visual Basic. This means that you can now place your code in a separate file and still interact with the page. This separation is done by providing a new event-driven model on top of page execution, as well as providing an object model on top of the HTML in the page. Instead of a top-to-bottom linear execution model, events are raised during the execution of a page. Your code sinks those events and responds to them by interacting with the object model that sits on top of the HTML. This quite neatly solves the issue of designers modifying the HTML and breaking code.

In addition to the new execution model, Microsoft has also created a new server-side control model. Unlike the lame Design Time Controls in Visual Interdev, these new models are incredibly useful encapsulations of common display paradigms. They do not introduce any browser dependencies and they run on the server, not the client. In the few cases where they emit browser-dependent code, they sniff the browser and degrade gracefully. More information on Web Forms can be found in Chapter 3, "Page Framework."

Web Services

As we move beyond the first and second generations of Web applications, it has become apparent that the paradigm of the Web can be extended to solve problems that predate it. In the past, businesses exchanged information using Electronic Data Interchange (EDI) over Value Added Networks (VANs). This worked well enough, but the cost of gaining access to a VAN as well as the complexity of implementing various industry specific EDI protocols excluded all but the largest companies from participating in the exchange of information.

Web services are a way to transfer the same types of information over the Internet (instead of expensive VANs) using industry standard protocols such as HTTP, XML, and TCP/IP. Web services are now so easy to create in .NET that individuals or businesses of any size should be able to play in this space. Web services aren't limited to replacing traditional EDI protocols. They open up many opportunities that EDI has never made inroads into. Jump ahead to Chapter 7, "Web Services," for more information.

Data Access

When ASP 1.0 first shipped, the data access story at Microsoft was in a state of flux. At the time, Remote Data Objects (RDO) was the technology of choice for Visual Basic developers. ActiveX Data Objects (ADO) was introduced with the shipment of Visual Basic 5.0 in

February of 1997. It was intended to be a new data access model for all types of data and was paired with another new technology—OLE DB.

Although ADO was great for what it was designed for—connected data access—it fell short in the disconnected arena. Features were added in successive versions to allow it to work in a disconnected fashion. ADO 1.0 had no support for XML. ADO 1.0 could not predict the success of XML as a data description language when it was shipped, and XML support was cobbled onto later versions. Neither of these features were designed in from the beginning.

ADO.NET is a new data access technology taking advantage of all the things Microsoft learned with ADO, RDO, OLEDB, ODBC, and other preceding data-access implementations. It was designed from the beginning to be coupled very tightly to XML and work effectively in a disconnected fashion. For more information, see Chapter 12, "Creating Database Applications with ADO.NET."

Deployment

One of the perennial arguments among ASP developers was how much code to migrate into COM objects. Some writers advocated that all code living in COM objects and ASP should contain only a single-method call to invoke the COM object. Although this might have been great in theory, it eliminated one of the biggest strengths of ASP: the capability to rapidly create an application and make changes on-the-fly. With all the logic and HTML tied up in COM objects, a simple HTML tag change meant recompiling and redeploying the COM objects. The biggest problem in our minds lies with using this approach. COM objects are Dynamic Link Libraries (DLL) that are dynamically loaded by IIS. While loaded they cannot be replaced. To deploy a COM object, the developer needed to shut down IIS, shut down the MTS packages the COM object lived in, replace it, and then restart IIS. This summary is actually a simplification of the process, but you can see the problems that this technique brings to the fore. Each time a new version is deployed, the Web server must go down! The downtime this technique causes can be handled by creating Web farms and doing rolling upgrades; however, in a large Web farm this means a simple change can take literally hours to deploy as the new objects are rolled out.

With the code-behind model inherent in ASP.NET, this situation could have been exacerbated. Instead, Microsoft vastly simplified the deployment model. Components, now called assemblies, no longer require registration on a machine for deployment. Assemblies are the .NET equivalent of a COM object. They are self describing and contain a manifest that contains metadata about the assembly. The metadata includes the version, the assemblies it depends on, and potentially its security identity.

Deployment is as easy as copying the assemblies into a /bin directory in the application root. ASP.NET will notice that a new version has been copied over, and it will unload the old version and load the new version! Deployment becomes as simple as an XCOPY /S or a recursive

FTP to upload the new files to the Web server. For more information, see Chapter 6, "Configuration and Deployment."

Configuration

In the past, all configuration information for ASP was stored as part of the IIS metabase. This was a binary file analogous to the registry that held all settings for IIS and ASP. The only ways to affect changes were to use the Internet Services Manager or to write scripts that utilized the Active Directory Services Interfaces (ADSI) to automate the changes. This process made it very difficult to synchronize the settings of multiple servers in a Web farm.

ASP.NET introduces a new paradigm for all settings. Instead of being stored in the opaque metabase, they are now stored as a hierarchical set of XML configuration files. These files live in the application root and subdirectories. Therefore, now as a developer uses XCOPY to deploy source files, the settings are also deployed! Developers no longer need to write a bunch of configuration scripts. For more information, see Chapter 6.

State Management

State management has been vastly improved in ASP.NET. Now three options exist for maintaining state on the server. The classic ASP 3.0 method of in-memory state on a single server still exists. In addition, an out-of-process state server and a durable state option is stored in SQL Server.

The other limitation of state services in ASP.old was the reliance on cookies for connecting users back to their state. ASP.NET introduces a new option for a cookieless state that performs URL munging to connect a user to state information. For more information, see Chapter 5, "State Management and Caching."

Caching

The reason most developers use ASP is to lend a dynamic nature to the Web. This could mean accessing back-end databases for data or perhaps pulling it in from nontraditional back ends. The problem with this dynamic content is that although developers can easily scale the Web tier using a scale-out methodology of multiple Web servers, this scaling is not as easily done in the data tier. Scale-out approaches for databases are just beginning to appear. Until these approaches are perfected, how can Web developers scale applications?

For data that changes infrequently, caching is a great solution. ASP.NET offers two forms of caching. Output caching takes an entire page and stores the executed results in memory for later delivery. Data caching takes items that were expensive to create, such as DataSets, and caches them on the server side. For more information see Chapter 5.

Debugging

Debugging ASP applications has always been difficult. Although remote debugging solutions were offered in previous versions of Visual Studio, precious few developers were able to get them to work consistently. Consequently, most debugging consisted of Response.Write statements littered throughout code or some type of logging mechanism that the developer created.

ASP.NET not only improves remote debugging and makes it consistent, it also offers a new Trace facility that is great for handling the types of things that logging or Response.Write were used for in the past. For more information see Chapter 4, "Debugging ASP.NET Applications."

Availability

Anybody that currently has a site on the Web knows that availability is key. If your site is down, a visitor can turn to a million others. Problem is—they might not come back!

ASP.NET has introduced a number of process controls that are aimed directly at improving availability. Now the ASP.NET process can restart automatically based on things such as memory utilization, time up, or even the number of requests handled, which helps cope with situations where ASP used to get jammed up. For more information see Chapter 6.

Migrating from ASP to ASP.NET

IN THIS CHAPTER

ASP.NET is a very exciting step in the evolution of Active Server Pages. If you are a long-time user of Active Server Pages, you are probably wondering how your existing code will run in ASP.NET. Will it run unchanged? Can you continue to use COM objects? How will the much publicized changes to the Visual Basic language affect your code? This chapter answers each of these questions in detail and gives you a roadmap to converting your existing code to ASP.NET.

First the Bad News—ASP 3.0 Code Will Not Run Unchanged in ASP.NET

We might as well get it out of the way right off the bat. Very little of your code will run unchanged in ASP.NET. You might be wondering if you read that right. *Very little of your code will run unchanged in ASP.NET.* Your initial gut reaction is probably, "What the heck was Microsoft thinking—breaking all my code? Doesn't Microsoft care about backward compatibility?"

Rest assured, backward compatibility was high on the feature list for ASP.NET. In adding the enormous number of features in ASP.NET, new features occasionally conflicted with old features. Old features as implemented sometimes used different conventions than newer features. The grafting of the Common Language Runtime onto ASP.NET produced many of these inconsistencies.

After thinking long and hard about maintaining 100% compatibility versus moving Active Server Pages into the future, Microsoft chose the latter. Given the tremendous advantage of the .NET framework with its thousands of base classes, we think they made the right choice.

Now the Good News—The Changes Aren't Rocket Science

As developers who have created thousands of Active Server Pages over the years, the idea of all that code crashing and burning is a thought too terrible to contemplate. What if you want all the features that ASP.NET offers right now, but don't have the time to port all those pages?

Luckily, Microsoft realized that if it was going to break compatibility, there had to be a way to let existing code continue to run. ASP.NET is designed to run side by side with ASP 3.0. No DLLs or dependencies are shared between the products, so you can install ASP.NET on a server that is currently serving ASP 3.0 pages without any worry of breaking the old applications. To get started with ASP.NET, you don't need to isolate your ASP.NET installation by purchasing additional hardware. It will coexist nicely on your existing servers.

New Filename Extensions

ASP.NET gets along with Active Server Pages by defining a whole new set of filename extensions. Filename extensions are used by IIS to determine which Internet Server API (ISAPI) filters will be called to handle a particular request. ASP 3.0 is set up to handle one set of extensions, and ASP.NET is set up to handle an entirely new set of extensions. Table 2.1 shows the mappings used by each.

TABLE 2.1   Filename Extensions for ASP 3.0 and ASP.NET

ASP 3.0	ASP.NET	Description
.ASP	.ASPX	Active Server Pages
.CER, .CDX		Certificate
.ASA	.ASAX	Global
	.ASCX	User control
	.ASHX	Http handler
	.ASMX	Web service
	.AXD	Trace extension
	.CONFIG	Configuration file
	.VSDISCO	Web services discovery file
	.REM	Remoting configuration file
	.CONFIG	Configuration file
	.SOAP	Web services schema file
	.WEBINFO	Web information file
	.CS	C# source
	.CSPROJ	C# project
	.VB	Visual Basic source
	.VBPROJ	Visual Basic project

2

MIGRATING FROM
ASP TO
ASP.NET

NOTE

The last four rows of the table represent file extensions that are mapped to ASP.NET, to prevent their download from the server.

Because each version of Active Server Pages has a unique set of filename extensions mapped to it, don't worry about ASP.NET ever executing a page that was originally designed for ASP 3.0. All your existing code will continue to run while you start writing new ASP.NET based code.

Changes in ASP.NET

The changes in ASP.NET can be divided into three categories: object model changes, semantic changes, and language changes.

ASP Object Model

The previous ASP object model was fairly small compared to what you are getting with ASP.NET. Consequently, the ASP object model received the smallest number of changes (but the greatest number of additions) of the three categories.

QueryString and Forms Collections Have Changed

The QueryString and Forms collections have changed their behavior in ASP.NET. With either collection, any repeated name/value pair becomes a two-dimensional array. Under ASP 3.0, a page called by http://localhost/querystring.asp?Hobby=Skiing&Hobby=Motorcycling would use code like that in Listing 2.1 to read the values. The QueryString collection places another collection inside the Hobby entry. This collection can then be iterated to read each value assigned to Hobby.

LISTING 2.1 Reading Repeated Values

```
<html>
<head>
<title>QueryString</title>
</head>
<body bgcolor="#FFFFFF" text="#000000">
Call this page using querystring.asp?Hobby=Skiing&Hobby=Motorcycling<BR><Br>
<%
    For iCount = 1 To Request.QueryString("Hobby").Count
        Response.Write("Hobby: " + Request.QueryString("Hobby")(iCount) +
"<BR>")
    Next
%>
</body>
</html>
```

In ASP.NET, the QueryString is a NameValueCollection and does not embed a second NameValueCollection inside it. Instead, the values for Hobby are placed into the appropriate name/value key pair as a comma-separated string. Then `String.Split()` is used to break them apart and iterate through them. Listing 2.2 shows this approach.

> **NOTE**
>
> A NameValueCollection in .NET is a specialized type of collection that associates a name or key with a value. A NameValueCollection can retrieve individual items by name or can be iterated to look at each value.

LISTING 2.2 ASP.NET Reading Repeated Values

```
<html>
<head>
<title>QueryString</title>
</head>
<body bgcolor="#FFFFFF" text="#000000">
Call this page using QueryString.aspx?Hobby=Skiing&Hobby=Motorcycling<BR><Br>
<%
     Dim iCount as Integer
     Dim astrHobby() As String


     ' Break the Hobbies apart
     astrHobby = Request.QueryString("Hobby").Split(",")

     For iCount = 0 To uBound(astrHobby)
          Response.Write("Hobby: " + astrHobby(iCount) + "<BR>")
     Next
%>
</body>
</html>
```

The `Forms` collection yields the same problems and can be solved using the same approach. Listing 2.3 shows the solution to reading values from a multiple select.

LISTING 2.3 ASP.NET Reading Multiple Select List Boxes

```
<html>
<head>
<title>Form</title>
</head>
<body bgcolor="#FFFFFF" text="#000000">
<form method=post>
```

LISTING 2.3 Continued

```
    <select name=Hobby multiple>
        <option>Skiing
        <option>Motorcycling
        <option>Shooting
    </select>
    <input type=submit>
</form>

<%
    Dim iCount as Integer
    Dim astrHobby() As String

    If Request.Form("Hobby") <> "" Then
        ' Break the Hobbies apart
        astrHobby = Request.Form("Hobby").Split(",")

        For iCount = 0 To uBound(astrHobby)
            Response.Write("Hobby: " + astrHobby(iCount) + "<BR>")
        Next
    End If
%>
</body>
</html>
```

The code above shows how to get your ASP 3.0 code running with the fewest number of changes. ASP.NET provides new methods for reading form data that offer a much better approach for this if you are writing new pages from scratch or are willing to rewrite significant portions of existing pages. Skip ahead to Chapter 3, "Page Framework," for more information.

The preceding changes in behavior are bad enough for your script-based ASP 3.0 pages. They can be deadly if you are using COM objects that integrate tightly with ASP 3.0 by accessing the ASP object model directly. If you don't have the source for these objects, you would be out of luck. Consequently, Microsoft introduced a page directive that preserves the old versions of the interfaces for COM objects that use GetObjectContext to access the ASP object model. When you specify <%@ Page aspcompat=true %>, ASP.NET places the old unmanaged server objects into the ObjectContext. An example of using aspcompat can be seen in Listing 2.6. For more information on calling old-style COM objects, skip ahead to the section "COM Objects." Listing 2.5 shows an example of a Visual Basic 6.0 COM object that utilizes the ASP 3.0 style of accessing the QueryString. Listing 2.4 shows the ASP 3.0 page that calls the COM object in Listing 2.5.

LISTING 2.4   ASP 3.0 Page Calling Visual Basic COM Object Shown in Listing 2.5

```
<html>
<head>
     <title>Call COM Object</title>
</head>

<body>
<font face="Verdana" size="+3">
<%
     Set obj = Server.CreateObject("ASPCom.cTest")
     obj.Output
     Set obj = Nothing
%>
</font>
</body>
</html>
```

LISTING 2.5   Visual Basic COM Object Using `GetObjectContext`

```
Public Sub Output()
     Dim octx As ObjectContext
     Dim Response As ASPTypeLibrary.Response

     Set octx = GetObjectContext()

     Set Response = octx("Response")

     Response.Write "Made it!"

     Response.Write octx("Request")("Name")

     Set Response = Nothing
     Set octx = Nothing
End Sub
```

Listing 2.6 is an ASP.NET page that uses aspcompat to instantiate a COM object and call a method on it.

LISTING 2.6   Page That Uses the AspCompat Attribute to Instantiate an Apartment
Threaded COM Object

```
<% @Page Language=VB Explicit=True Strict=False AspCompat=True %>
<html>
<head>
```

LISTING 2.6 Continued

```
    <title>Call COM Object</title>
</head>

<body>
<font face="Verdana" size="+3">
<%
    Dim obj
    obj = Server.CreateObject("ASPCom.cTest")
    obj.Output
    obj = Nothing
%>
</font>
</body>
</html>
```

Semantic Changes

In addition to changes to the underlying ASP object model, some changes have been made to what constitutes a valid ASP page.

Single Language Per Page

ASP.NET limits the developer to a single language per page. In the past, you could easily mix JavaScript and VBScript on the same page. Going forward, all code on the page must be in the same language.

If you think about what ASP.NET is doing behind the scenes, this limitation makes a little more sense. When a browser first accesses a page, all the code is stripped out of the page and placed into a temporary file. This temporary file is then compiled using the appropriate compiler, and the resulting module is wired to the page to become the "code behind" the page.

You might think it wouldn't be that hard to create two temporary files (one for each page) and then create two assemblies. But start thinking about such things as variable scoping. How would you make sure that page-level variables are shared across the separate modules? It becomes very difficult to intuit the correct way to separate the code.

Server Versus Client

What if you write all your server-side code in Visual Basic and your client-side code in JavaScript? This is a pretty common scenario, intended to give your client-side code a chance of executing correctly in other browsers. This still works. Any code in a script block that is not marked runat=server is transferred directly down to the client with no alterations. The single language per page rule becomes a single language *executing on the server* per page.

Bending the Rules

A single language per page still might feel a little awkward. Perhaps you want to reuse C# code, integrating it into your ASP.NET page written in Visual Basic. Voila—a way exists to bend the rules. Although you are limited to a single server-side language per page, you can break your page up into smaller chunks called *user controls*. Each user control stands on its own and can use a different language from the rest of the page. Therefore, a Visual Basic page can integrate a user control written in C#. For more information on user controls, skip ahead to Chapter 3, "Page Framework."

Functions Must Reside in Script Blocks

Going back to the earlier discussion of what ASP.NET does behind the scenes, you can probably get a glimmer of the reasoning behind the requirement for functions to reside in script blocks. By forcing all functions into script blocks, it's easy for Microsoft to bake them into assemblies at compile time. Let's compare the way it was done in ASP 3.0 and the way it is now done in ASP.NET. Listing 2.7 shows an ASP 3.0 page with a function inline.

LISTING 2.7   An ASP 3.0 Page with an Inline Function

```
<html>
<head>
<title>Inline Function</title>
</head>
<%
Function SayMyName()
     Response.Write("Chris")
End Function
%>
<body bgcolor="#FFFFFF" text="#000000">
     <% SayMyName %>
</body>
</html>
```

For this syntax to work in ASP.NET, the function must be enclosed in a set of <SCRIPT> tags with the runat=server attribute. Listing 2.8 shows the proper way to declare functions in ASP.NET.

LISTING 2.8   ASP.NET Page with a Function

```
<html>
<head>
<title>Inline Function</title>
</head>
```

LISTING 2.8   Continued

```
<SCRIPT LANGUAGE="VB" runat=server>
Function SayMyName()
     Response.Write("Chris")
End Function
</SCRIPT>
<body bgcolor="#FFFFFF" text="#000000">
     <% SayMyName %>
</body>
</html>
```

The addition of the script tag is all that is required for most functions.

Render Functions No Longer Supported

You might be wondering, "What is a render function?" Many developers didn't even know that render functions existed in ASP 3.0. A render function mixes a function with embedded HTML. This combination provides a quick way for a piece of HTML—for example, a table row—to be used as a template. It is easier to show than to explain. Listing 2.9 shows an example of an ASP 3.0 render function. This code creates a table containing the numbers 1 through 10. It does this by embedding the HTML for a table row inside a standard For...Next loop.

LISTING 2.9   ASP 3.0 Render Function

```
<%
Function RenderTable(iLimit)
     Dim iCount
%>
     <table border=1>
<%
     For iCount = 1 to iLimit
%>
          <TR>
               <td>
                    <% = iCount %>
               </td>
          </tr>
<%
     Next
%>
     </table>
<%
End Function
%>
```

LISTING 2.9 Continued

```
<html>
<head>
     <title>Untitled</title>
</head>
<body>
<% RenderTable 10%>
</body>
</html>
```

This code won't run under ASP.NET. HTML isn't valid inside script blocks, and all functions must now reside in script blocks. To migrate this code to ASP.NET, all the embedded chunks of HTML must be converted into Response.Write() statements. The Response.Write() statements will output the same HTML that was previously embedded. Listing 2.10 shows the migrated code.

LISTING 2.10 Migrated Render Function

```
<%@ Page Language="vb"%>
<SCRIPT runat=server>
     Function RenderTable(iLimit)
          Dim iCount
          Response.Write("<table border=1>")
          For iCount = 1 to iLimit
               Response.Write("<TR>")
               Response.Write("<td>")
               Response.Write(iCount)
               Response.Write("</td>")
               Response.Write("</tr>")
          Next
          Response.Write("</table>")
     End Function
</script>
<html>
<head>
     <title>Untitled</title>
</head>

<body>
<% RenderTable(10) %>

</body>
</html>
```

Maintaining the indent levels of your HTML is a little more difficult, but the original intent of the function is maintained.

Type Libraries No Longer Supported

ASP 3.0 introduced the capability to reference type libraries, such as ADOVBS.INC, instead of having to create your own lists of constants and then include them on each page. Type libraries were capable of being referenced on a page basis or in the global.asa. By referencing them in the global.asa, the constants were made available to all pages in an application. Listing 2.11 shows an ASP 3.0 page that imports a type library.

LISTING 2.11   ASP 3.0 Page That Imports a Type Library

```
<!-- METADATA TYPE="TypeLib" Name="ADO"
     UUID="00000200-0000-0010-8000-00AA006D2EA4" VERSION="2.0"-->
<html>
<head>
    <title>Type Library</title>
</head>
<body>
<% Dim cn, rs

Set cn = Server.CreateObject("ADODB.Connection")
cn.Open "Provider=SQLOLEDB;User ID=sa;Initial Catalog=pubs;Password=;"

Set rs = Server.CreateObject("ADODB.Recordset")
rs.Open "SELECT * FROM Authors", cn, adOpenForwardOnly, adLockReadOnly

If rs.EOF Then
    Response.Write "No Records"
Else
    Response.write "Got some"
End If
rs.Close
cn.Close
%>
</body>
</html>
```

In ASP.NET, the capability to reference type libraries in either the page or the global.asa has been removed. We believe this is part of the move away from COM objects toward .NET assemblies. This change offers you two choices:

- Return to using include files
- Fully port the code to .NET

Given the previous example using ADO, the first option would mean adding back includes for ADOVBS.INC. Listing 2.12 shows what this would look like.

LISTING 2.12   Type Library Replaced by Include

```
<%@ Page aspcompat=true %>
<!-- #include file="adovbs.inc" -->
<html>
<head>
    <title>Type Library</title>
</head>
<body>
<% Dim cn, rs

cn = Server.CreateObject("ADODB.Connection")
cn.Open("Provider=SQLOLEDB;User ID=sa;Initial Catalog=pubs;Password=;")

rs = Server.CreateObject("ADODB.Recordset")
rs.Open("SELECT * FROM Authors", cn, adOpenForwardOnly, adLockReadOnly)

If rs.EOF Then
    Response.Write("No Records")
Else
    Response.write("Got some")
End If
rs.Close()
cn.Close()
%>
</body>
</html>
```

The other option would be to port all the database access code to ADO.NET. See Chapter 12, "Creating Database Applications with ADO.NET," for more information on ADO.NET.

Option Explicit

In ASP 3.0, code written in VBScript could use Option Explicit to force declaration of all variables before use. Option Explicit had to be declared before any ASP directives or HTML. Listing 2.13 shows the proper way to use Option Explicit in ASP 3.0.

LISTING 2.13   Using Option Explicit in ASP 3.0

```
<% Option Explicit %>
<html>
<head>
```

2

MIGRATING FROM ASP TO ASP.NET

LISTING 2.13   Continued

```
<title>Option Explicit</title>
</head>
<body bgcolor="#FFFFFF" text="#000000">
<table border1>
<%
Dim iCount

For iCount = 1 to 10
     Response.Write("<tr><td>" + CStr(iCount) + "</td></tr>")
Next
%>
</table>
</body>
</html>
```

In ASP.NET, the usage of Option Explicit has changed. In addition to being defined inline, it is now part of the @Page directive. The @Page directive replaces the old @Language directive in ASP 3.0 and adds a number of new features. For more discussion of the @Page directive, see Chapter 3. Explicit=True gives you the old VBScript behavior from ASP 3.0. Listing 2.14 shows the new way to use Explicit in ASP.NET.

LISTING 2.14   Using Explicit in ASP.NET

```
<%@Page Explicit=true %>
<html>
<head>
<title>Explicit</title>
</head>
<body bgcolor="#FFFFFF" text="#000000">
<table border1>
<%
Dim iCount

For iCount = 1 to 10
     Response.Write("<tr><td>" + CStr(iCount) + "</td></tr>")
Next
%>
</table>
</body>
</html>
```

In addition to Explicit, a new option, Strict, is available. Strict controls how data type conversions are allowed to happen. If Strict is on, only widening conversions are allowed. A widening conversion is the conversion of data from a smaller data type to a larger data type. An example of this is the conversion of an Integer to a Long. The Long is a larger data type with more precision. A narrowing conversion would be the opposite. Converting a Long to an Integer is considered a narrowing conversion and will throw an error if Strict=True. Table 2.2 documents the typical widening conversions you will encounter. Strict defaults to on and implies Option Explicit. This behavior can cause problems with code migrated from ASP 3.0. Typically, you will set Explicit=True and Strict=False for most pages that you are converting.

TABLE 2.2   Widening Conversions

Type	Widens To
Byte	Byte, Short, Integer, Long, Decimal, Single, Double, Object
Char	Char, Integer, Long, Decimal, Single, Double, String, Object
Short	Short, Integer, Long, Decimal, Single, Double, Object
Integer	Integer, Long, Decimal, Single, Double, Object
Long	Long, Single, Decimal, Double, Object
Single	Single, Double, Object
Double	Double, Object
Date	Date, String, Object
String	String, Object
Nothing	Byte, Short, Integer, Long, Decimal, Single, Double, String, Object
Fixed-length String	String, Object
Class	Object; any of the classes that it inherits from; any of the interfaces that it implements (for .NET runtime defined classes, this will include only the interfaces listed in the class's definition within its type library)
Interface	Object; any of the interfaces that it inherits from
Structure	Object
Array	Object

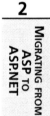

Language Changes

Some of the compatibility issues with migrating ASP 3.0 code to ASP.NET code are related to the elimination of scripting. ASP.NET no longer runs any scripting languages on the server.

Instead, all code is now fully compiled using the appropriate compiler. This change from VBScript to Visual Basic .NET means that many of the language changes in VB .NET will also affect ASP code. This one change introduces numerous compatibility issues.

Array Basing

In ASP.NET, all arrays are 0 based. This means that if you declare an array with 10 elements, you get an array with elements 0–9. In ASP 3.0, this was never consistent. Some things required 0-based arrays and others required 1-based arrays. At the very least, ASP.NET has made this consistent regardless of your religious beliefs on whether arrays should be 0-or 1-based.

No Default Properties

Most ASP 3.0 pages use default properties implicitly. Default properties enable you to write less code by not having to fully specify the particular property that you want to access. Default properties have a few downsides. When reading someone else's code, unless you are very familiar with the object model, default properties can become very confusing. Take a look at the code in Listing 2.15.

LISTING 2.15   ASP 3.0 Default Property Access

```
Set cmd1 = Server.CreateObject("ADO.Command")
Set cmd2 = Server.CreateObject("ADO.Command")
Cmd1  = Cmd2
```

Does this code set cmd1 equal to cmd2 or does it assign the ConnectionString of cmd2 to the ActiveConnection of cmd1? Unless you know the object model for ADO, it isn't clear what the operation is attempting to do.

Default properties have been removed from Visual Basic .NET with one exception. Parameterized or overloaded default properties are still allowed. The method signature provided by the parameters allows the compiler to differentiate among the default properties.

This change is probably one of the most pernicious things to root out of old code. We have found that certain styles of code, especially code that uses ADO, uses literally hundreds of default properties in a standard page. Take a look at the code snippet in Listing 2.16.

LISTING 2.16   ASP 3.0 Example of Using Default Properties

```
<%
' Get the list of miles
rsList.Open "SELECT * FROM Miles m, MileageAccounts ma, Airlines a
    ➥WHERE m.MileageAccountID = ma.MileageAccountID AND
    ➥ma.AirlineID = a.AirlineID AND ma.UserID = " & Request("UserID") &
    ➥" ORDER BY Name, AccountNumber, FlightDate", cn, adOpenForwardOnly,
    ➥adLockReadOnly
' Did we get an empty list?
If rsList.EOF Then
    ' Write out a notice
    Response.Write "No mileage entered."
    Response.End
End If

' Loop through miles
Do While Not rsList.EOF
    ' Is this a new account?
    If szLastAccountNumber <> rsList("AccountNumber") Then
        If szLastAccountNumber <> "" Then
            ' Close the last table
            Response.Write "</table><BR><BR>"
        End If

        ' Save off the account number
        szLastAccountNumber = rsList("AccountNumber")
        ' Output the description
        Response.Write "<font face=Verdana size=3 color=Maroon><B>" & _
            rsList("Description") & "</b></font><BR>"
        Response.Write "<font face=Verdana size=3 color=Maroon><B>" & _
            rsList("Name") & " - " & rsList("AccountNumber") &
"</b></font><BR>"
        Response.Write "<table border=1>"
        Response.Write "<tr>"
        Response.Write "          <Td><b>Date</b></td>"
        Response.Write "          <td><b>Flight #</b></td>"
        Response.Write "          <td><b>Description</b></td>"
        Response.Write "          <td><b>Departure</b></td>"
        Response.Write "          <td><b>Destination</b></td>"
        Response.Write "          <Td><b>Miles</b></td>"
        Response.Write "          <td align=center>Action</td>"
        Response.Write "</tr>"
    End If

    ' Output the miles
    Response.Write "<tr>"
```

LISTING 2.16   Continued

```
Response.Write "          <td>" & rsList("FlightDate") & "</td>"
Response.Write "          <td align=center>" & rsList("FlightNumber") & _
    "</td>"
Response.Write "          <td>" & rsList("Description") & "</td>"
Response.Write "          <td align=center>" & rsList("Departure") & _
    "</td>"
Response.Write "          <td align=center>" & rsList("Destination") & _
    "</td>"
Response.Write "          <td align=center>" & rsList("Miles") & "</td>"
Response.Write "          <td> <a href=modifymiles.asp?" & _
    "Action=Edit&MilesID=" & rsList("MilesID") & ">[Edit]</a> " & _
    " <a href=modifymiles.asp?Action=Delete&MilesID=" & _
    rsList("MilesID") &">[Delete]</a> </td>"
Response.Write "</tr>"

    ' Get the next record
    rsList.MoveNext
Loop
' Close the table
Response.Write "</table>"
rsList.Close
cn.Close
%>
```

This snippet uses ADO to retrieve a list of mileage values from SQL Server. Can you spot all the places where default properties are used? We have found that it typically takes two to three passes through the code before most are found. Rewriting this snippet to eliminate default properties yields the snippet shown in Listing 2.17.

LISTING 2.17   Default Properties Eliminated

```
<%
' Get the list of miles
rsList.Open "SELECT * FROM Miles m, MileageAccounts ma, Airlines a
    ➡WHERE m.MileageAccountID = ma.MileageAccountID AND
    ➡ma.AirlineID = a.AirlineID AND ma.UserID = " &
    ➡Request("UserID") & " ORDER BY Name, AccountNumber,
    ➡FlightDate", cn, adOpenForwardOnly, adLockReadOnly
' Did we get an empty list?
If rsList.EOF Then
    ' Write out a notice
    Response.Write "No mileage entered."
```

LISTING 2.17   Continued

```
        Response.End
End If

' Loop through miles
Do While Not rsList.EOF
      ' Is this a new account?
      If szLastAccountNumber <> rsList("AccountNumber").Value Then
          If szLastAccountNumber <> "" Then
              ' Close the last table
              Response.Write "</table><BR><BR>"
          End If

          ' Save off the account number
          szLastAccountNumber = rsList("AccountNumber").Value
          ' Output the description
          Response.Write "<font face=Verdana size=3 color=Maroon><B>" & _
              rsList("Description").Value & "</b></font><BR>"
          Response.Write "<font face=Verdana size=3 color=Maroon><B>" & _
              rsList("Name").Value & " - " & rsList("AccountNumber").Value &
"</b></font><BR>"
          Response.Write "<table border=1>"
          Response.Write "<tr>"
          Response.Write "          <Td><b>Date</b></td>"
          Response.Write "          <td><b>Flight #</b></td>"
          Response.Write "          <td><b>Description</b></td>"
          Response.Write "          <td><b>Departure</b></td>"
          Response.Write "          <td><b>Destination</b></td>"
          Response.Write "          <Td><b>Miles</b></td>"
          Response.Write "          <td align=center>Action</td>"
          Response.Write "</tr>"
      End If

      ' Output the miles
      Response.Write "<tr>"
      Response.Write "          <td>" & rsList("FlightDate").Value & "</td>"
      Response.Write "          <td align=center>" & _
          rsList("FlightNumber").Value & "</td>"
      Response.Write "          <td>" & rsList("Description").Value & "</td>"
      Response.Write "          <td align=center>" & _
          rsList("Departure").Value & "</td>"
      Response.Write "          <td align=center>" & _
          rsList("Destination").Value & "</td>"
```

2

MIGRATING FROM
ASP TO
ASP.NET

LISTING 2.17 Continued

```
      Response.Write "             <td align=center>" & _
          rsList("Miles").Value & "</td>"
      Response.Write "             <td> <a href=modifymiles.asp?" & _
          "Action=Edit&MilesID=" & rsList("MilesID").Value & ">[Edit]" & _
          "</a>  <a href=modifymiles.asp?Action=Delete&MilesID=" & _
          rsList("MilesID").Value &">[Delete]</a> </td>"
      Response.Write "</tr>"

      ' Get the next record
      rsList.MoveNext
Loop
' Close the table
Response.Write "</table>"
rsList.Close
cn.Close
  %>
```

No More Set

Default properties required the introduction of a new keyword to Visual Basic and VBScript to differentiate between value assignments and object assignments. The Set keyword is used to differentiate whether a value assignment or an object assignment should be performed. Let's run through a VBScript example of why this is the case. There is an object called MyObject. It has a default property, Value, which returns the value of the object. With code such as C = MyObject, the Value of MyObject will be assigned to C. With code such as Set C = MyObject, C is assigned a reference to the instance of MyObject. These two very different results are produced by a small difference—the presence of the Set keyword.

In VB .NET all operations are a Let. Set has been eliminated. It is possible to do this because of the removal of default properties. Let's run through the preceding example again in VB .NET with a small change: The Value property of MyObject is no longer a default property. Instead, it is just a normal property. Now when code says C = MyObject, C receives a reference to MyObject. When C = MyObject.Value, C receives a copy of the value contained in the value property of MyObject. With the removal of the default property, ambiguity of the Let assignment is gone and the compiler can determine the operation to perform based on the return type.

After removing all default property use, eliminate all instances of the Set statement. Listing 2.18 shows a snippet of ASP 3.0 code that creates instances of several objects.

LISTING 2.18   ASP 3.0 Code Using Set

```
Dim cn, rsList, szLastAccountNumber

' Create the ADO objects
Set cn = Server.CreateObject("ADODB.Connection")
Set rsList = Server.CreateObject("ADODB.Recordset")

' Open the database
cn.Open Application("DSN")
```

To port this code to ASP.NET, just remove the Set statements. Listing 2.19 shows the modified code.

LISTING 2.19   ASP.NET Code Eliminating Set

```
Dim cn, rsList, szLastAccountNumber

' Create the ADO objects
cn = Server.CreateObject("ADODB.Connection")
rsList = Server.CreateObject("ADODB.Recordset")

' Open the database
cn.Open Application("DSN")
```

Parentheses Required for Subroutine Calls

In VB .NET, parentheses are required around all subroutine calls. In previous versions of Visual Basic and VBScript, parentheses were required for function calls but were optional for subroutine calls. The syntax for subroutine calls had a number of options. Listing 2.20 shows an example of three legal ways to call a subroutine in ASP 3.0. The first is with no parentheses. The second uses parentheses with a single argument. The third makes use of the Call statement, which calls a subroutine using a syntax that is identical to a function call.

LISTING 2.20   ASP 3.0 Showing Subroutine Calling Syntax

```
<html>
<head>
<title>Subroutine Calling</title>
</head>
<%
    public sub onearg(x)
```

2

MIGRATING FROM
ASP TO
ASP.NET

LISTING 2.20   Continued

```
        Response.write "OneArg x = " + CStr(x)
    End   sub

    sub twoarg(x, y)
        Response.Write "TwoArg x = " + x + ", y = " + y
    end sub

    public sub test()
        Response.Write "Test"
    end sub
%>
<body bgcolor="#FFFFFF" text="#000000">
One argument without parenthesis: <BR>
<%        onearg 2 %>
<BR><BR>
One argument with parenthesis: <BR>
<% onearg(3) %>
<BR><BR>
Two Arguments with parenthesis: <BR>
<% call twoarg("4","5") %>
<BR><BR>
</body>
</html>
```

VB .NET has cleared up this morass. All subroutine calls now require parentheses, regardless of the number of arguments. The `Call` statement is optional. Continued use of `Call` is now a stylistic choice. Listing 2.21 shows the code from Listing 2.20 updated to work in ASP.NET. The sample of one argument without parentheses has been removed because this construction does not work in ASP.NET. Parentheses have also been added to the `Response.Write` statement. This is a subroutine or method call also, even though that's not explicit in the code.

LISTING 2.21   Listing 2.20 Ported to ASP.NET

```
<html>
<head>
<title>Subroutine Calling</title>
</head>
<SCRIPT LANGUAGE=VB runat=server>
    public sub onearg(x)
        Response.write("OneArg x = " + CStr(x))
    End   sub
```

LISTING 2.21   Continued

```
    sub twoarg(x, y)
        Response.Write("TwoArg x = " + x + ", y = " + y)
    end sub

    public sub test()
        Response.Write("Test")
    end sub
</SCRIPT>
<body bgcolor="#FFFFFF" text="#000000">
One argument with parenthesis: <BR>
<% onearg(3) %>
<BR><BR>
Two Arguments with parenthesis: <BR>
<% call twoarg("4","5") %>
<BR><BR>
</body>
</html>
```

This is the thing that has to be changed in almost every ported page. It is also one of the easiest things to miss on the first pass through code.

ByVal Versus ByRef

VBScript defaults to passing variables to subroutines and functions by reference (ByRef). VB .NET defaults to passing variables to subroutines and functions by value (ByVal). This is one change that can seriously affect functioning code just because of the use of a different language. This change can be a tough one to catch unless you have treated arguments in ASP 3.0 as ByVal by convention.

One little interesting gotcha exists here. Look at the code in Listing 2.22. What would you expect this code to do?

LISTING 2.22   What Does This Code Do?

```
<SCRIPT LANGUAGE="VBScript" runat=server>
    Sub ModValue(iValue)
        iValue = 4
        Response.Write "Value In Call: " + CStr(iValue) + "<BR>"
    End Sub
</script>
<html>
<head>
```

LISTING 2.22   Continued

```
        <title>ByVal</title>
</head>

<body>
<%
    Dim iValue
    iValue = 2
    Response.Write "Value Before Call: " + CStr(iValue) + "<BR>"
    ModValue(iValue)
    Response.Write "Value After Call: " + CStr(iValue)
%>
</body>
</html>
```

We just stated that VBScript passes arguments by reference. This would mean that the code in Listing 2.22 passes a 2 into the subroutine, the subroutine sets the passed-in value to 4, and when the subroutine returns, the caller would expect a 4. In this case, we used one of the optional syntaxes for calling a subroutine. It has an interesting side effect, however. Whenever you enclose an argument being passed to a ByRef routine and enclose it within parentheses, you cause VBScript to create a copy of the variable and pass the copy ByRef! So in this code example, the value after the call remains 2 because we passed a copy of the 2 into the subroutine to start with.

Block Scoping

ASP.NET changes the rules for variable scoping. In ASP 3.0, variables declared anywhere within a routine were available throughout that routine. Listing 2.23 shows a variable declared within the scope of a For...Next loop. This variable is available throughout the page as evidenced by the capability to write it to the page after the loop is completed.

LISTING 2.23   A Variable Defined Inside a For...Next Loop Is Available Outside It

```
<html>
<head>
    <title>Scoping</title>
</head>

<body>
<%
    Dim iCount
```

LISTING 2.23   Continued

```
    For iCount = 1 to 10
        Dim iValue

        iValue = iCount + 10
    Next

    Response.Write("iValue = " + CStr(iValue))
%>
</body>
</html>
```

In ASP.NET this code will not work. Variables are scoped to the block they are defined within. The code in Listing 2.23 will throw an error indicating that `iValue` is undefined.

If you have consistently defined variables at the top of a routine, your code should require little updating. If you habitually define variables just prior to using them, you might have to move the declarations out of any enclosing block statements.

COM Objects

For the most part, COM objects continue to work with few changes in ASP.NET. However, there are a few exceptions. The ASP.NET thread pool has been changed from a single threaded apartment (STA) thread pool to a multiple threaded apartment (MTA) thread pool. This has some implications when calling objects written with an STA model in mind.

Visual Basic creates components based on an STA model. To call these types of components from an ASP.NET page, the page calling the STA object must use an STA model; placing `<%@ Page AspCompat="true" %>` on the page will accomplish this.

Using the new `AspCompat` attribute, you can call a Visual Basic object from ASP.NET. Although this approach is fine for a quick-and-dirty port, it doesn't take advantage of the scalability improvements that an MTA provides. If you want the scalability improvements, it is time to rewrite your component in .NET. See Listing 2.24 for an example.

LISTING 2.24   Using the AspCompat Attribute to Call an STA COM Component

```
<% @Page Language=VB Explicit=True Strict=False AspCompat=True %>
<html>
<head>
    <title>Call COM Object</title>
</head>
```

LISTING 2.24   Continued

```
<body>
<font face="Verdana" size="+3">
<%
    Dim obj
    obj = Server.CreateObject("ASPCom.cTest")
    obj.Output
    obj = Nothing
%>
</font>
</body>
</html>
```

Late Bound Access

If you like using late bound access for your COM objects, you can do this in ASP.NET by using `Server.CreateObject`. Be very careful with the data types that are passed back and forth, however. As you can see in Listing 2.25, `VBCom.Add()` is expecting to be passed two arguments of type integer. Integer in Visual Basic 6.0 maps to Int16 in VB .NET. Consequently, attempting to call `VBCom.Add()` and passing it ASP.NET integers will yield an error. To make this work correctly, pass two Int16 variables to `VBCom.Add()`. Listing 2.25 shows this technique.

LISTING 2.25   Late Bound Access to COM Objects

```
<%@ Page AspCompat=true debug=true %>
<html>
<head>
<title>COM Integration</title>
</head>

<body bgcolor="#FFFFFF" text="#000000">

<%
    Dim co
    Dim x, y, z as int16
    Dim iCount as integer
    Dim iStart, iEnd as integer


    ' Create the com object
    Response.Write("Creating ASPNET.VBCom...<BR>")
    co = Server.CreateObject("ASPNET.VBCom")
```

LISTING 2.25 Continued

```
' Call Method1
Response.Write("Calling Method1<BR>")
co.Method1()

' Call the Add method
Response.Write("Adding...<BR>")
x = 1
y = 5
z = co.Add(x, y)

co = nothing

Response.Write("Starting timings<BR>")
iStart = Environment.TickCount()
' Call it 1000 times and time it
for iCount = 0 to 10000
    co = Server.CreateObject("ASPNET.VBCom")
    z = co.Add(x,y)
    co = nothing
next
iEnd = Environment.TickCount()
Response.Write("Finished timings<BR>")
Response.Write(((iEnd-iStart)/1000).ToString() + "s")
%>

</body>
</html>
```

Create a Runtime Callable Wrapper

You can use TLBIMP.EXE to import the type information from a COM object and create a .NET assembly that contains a namespace and all the metadata for the object. This assembly can then be used like any other .NET assembly. The runtime handles the instantiation of the COM object and the creation of the runtime callable wrapper. This method of accessing an object can be four to five times faster than accessing COM objects late bound. Using TLBIMP.EXE to import the ASPNET.VBCom object used in Listing 2.25 looks like this:

```
tlbimp aspnet.dll /out:aspnetrcw.dll
```

When you run this command, be sure to specify the out parameter, perhaps changing the name of the output assembly so that you can differentiate it from the original DLL. Aspnetrcw.dll now contains a namespace called aspnetrcw, which contains a class VBCom. Now you can utilize this assembly as though it were built originally in .NET. Listing 2.26 shows the new code that uses the runtime callable wrapper.

LISTING 2.26   COM Access Using a Runtime Callable Wrapper

```
<%@ Page AspCompat=true %>
<%@ Import Namespace="aspnetrcw" %>
<html>
<head>
<title>COM Integration</title>
</head>
<body bgcolor="#FFFFFF" text="#000000">
<%
    Dim co
    Dim x, y, z as int16
    Dim iCount as integer
    Dim iStart, iEnd as integer

    ' Create the com object
    Response.Write("Creating ASPNET.VBCom...<BR>")
    co = new aspnetrcw.VBCom

    ' Call Method1
    Response.Write("Calling Method1<BR>")
    co.Method1()

    ' Call the Add method
    Response.Write("Adding...<BR>")
    x = 1
    y = 5
    z = co.Add(x, y)

    co = nothing

    Response.Write("Starting timings<BR>")
    iStart = Environment.TickCount()
    ' Call it 1000 times and time it
    for iCount = 0 to 10000
        co = new aspnetrcw.VBCom
        z = co.Add(x,y)
        co = nothing
    next
    iEnd = Environment.TickCount()
    Response.Write("Finished timings<BR>")
    Response.Write(((iEnd-iStart)/1000).ToString() + " seconds")
%>
</body>
</html>
```

Although existing COM objects can be used in ASP.NET, a cost exists to marshaling between managed and unmanaged code. This cost can be reduced by minimizing the function calls when interacting with COM objects. The interactions should be "chunky" instead of "chatty." Ideally, the COM objects should make one function call that does the majority of the work (chunky) in contrast to calling a function hundreds of times in a loop (chatty). With a chunky function, the overhead of the marshaling is relatively small compared to the execution time of the function. With a chatty function, the overhead of marshaling increases with the number of times that the function is called.

Migration Strategy

So how do you migrate your application? It is an iterative process. As shown in the previous section, it is not necessarily a one-to-one mapping of functionality, so in some cases a total rewrite might be more appropriate than migration. For applications in which migration is deemed more appropriate, following is a checklist of steps for migrating ASP applications to ASP.NET.

Migration Checklist

1. Resave ASA as ASAX.

    If you are setting `Application` variables in the global.asa or have any application or session initiation code, moving the global.asa over is a first step. Step 2 might have to be performed on the new Global.asax also.

2. Remove TypeLibs. See the section "Type Libraries No Longer Supported."

    Remove any `METADATA TYPE="TypeLib"` statements from the page and replace them with include statements. If you remove a type library from global.asa, you will need to place includes in all files that utilized values from the type library. The most commonly used typelib is ADO, which can usually be replaced by ADOVBS.INC.

3. Change Option Explicit. See the section "Option Explicit."

    Change Option Explicit to `<%@ Page Explicit=True Strict=False %>`. This change is most appropriate for code that you are initially porting but might eventually change to `Strict=True`.

4. Add AspCompat. See the section "COM Objects."

    If the page is using any apartment-threaded COM objects or COM objects that rely on `GetObjectContext()`, add the `AspCompat=true` attribute to the `@Page` tag.

5. Place () on all method calls. See the section "Parentheses Required for Subroutine Calls."

Add () on all method calls that do not already have parentheses or use the `Call` statement. This task is simpler if the code consistently uses `Call` statements, because you can use them as indicators to where method calls exist. But if the code lacks consistent use of `Call` statements, you need to actually read through each line of code and find all the method calls. This is probably the second-toughest step in the migration, and you might need to rely on the compiler to find the method calls that you missed.

6. Eliminate `Set` keyword. See the section "No More Set."

   Eliminate the `Set` keyword. This one is easy—just do a find/replace, searching for "Set" and replacing it with "".

7. Eliminate default property usage. See the section "No Default Properties."

   This is the most difficult part to migrate. Most code uses a large number of default properties, and many developers are so used to reading and writing them that they just look natural. Recordset field usage is one of the most common cases.

8. Change the filename. See the section "New Filename Extensions."

   Resave the file with the appropriate ASP.NET file extension. If the file refers to other files in the application that have been updated, you will need to update these references.

Migration Example

Next, let's take a very simple example that tracks miles in my myriad frequent flyer programs. It first presents the user with a login page to log into the application. It then allows the user to add or view mileage accounts or the miles in the accounts. The entire application consists of 13 files. We'll convert a few pages from ASP 3.0 over to ASP.NET. We will do this in stages so that we can test each step after we are done.

> **NOTE**
>
> The ASP version of this sample is included on the Web site in the `Chapter1\MileageTracker\ASP.old` directory. The completed ASP.NET samples are included in the `Chapter1\MileageTracker\ASP.NET` directory.

The goal of this migration is not to rewrite the code in ASP.NET. That would be a lot of work to replace all the ADO code with ADO.NET, all the table building code with bound DataGrids, and so on. The goal is to do the minimum amount of work necessary to get the pages running in the ASP.NET environment. To this end we will follow the steps in the checklist outlined previously.

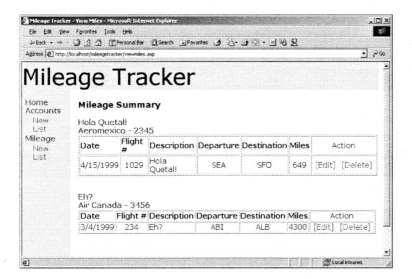

FIGURE 2.1

The original sample MileageTracker *application.*

Migrating global.asa

First, we need to look at the global.asa shown in Listing 2.27.

LISTING 2.27   global.asa for Original Application

```
<!-- METADATA TYPE="TypeLib" Name="ADO"
    UUID="00000200-0000-0010-8000-00AA006D2EA4" VERSION="2.0"-->

<SCRIPT LANGUAGE="VBScript" RUNAT="Server">
Sub Application_OnStart
    Application("DSN") = "Provider=SQLOLEDB;Server=localhost;" & _
        "Application Name=WebServer;Initial Catalog=MileageTracker;" & _
        "Password=mt;User ID=MileageTracker"
End Sub
</SCRIPT>
```

Starting with step 1 in our list, we will resave the global.asa as global.asax.

Step 2 indicates that we need to remove any references to type libraries. This means removing the METADATA tag in the first line, which refers to a type library. The final global.asax doesn't look too different from the original global.asa. It is shown in Listing 2.28.

LISTING 2.28   global.asax After Migration

```
<SCRIPT LANGUAGE="VB" RUNAT="Server">
Sub Application_OnStart
    Application("DSN") = "Provider=SQLOLEDB;Server=localhost;Application
Name=WebServer;Initial Catalog=MileageTracker;Password=mt;User
ID=MileageTracker"
End Sub
</SCRIPT>
```

Migrating the Login Page

Now that the global.asa is converted, it is time to turn our attention to some of the other pages in the application. The next page we need to migrate is the login page. This is the first page the user hits when starting the application; therefore, it is the first page we need to migrate. The login page authenticates the user against the database and sets a session variable to indicate that the user is logged in. This application uses session() to track whether a user is logged in. This means that a gradual migration is not possible because ASP 3.0 and ASP.NET have separate session objects. We can't intermix pages written in ASP 3.0 and ASP.NET in this case. The login page, default.asp, is shown in Listing 2.29.

LISTING 2.29   Default.asp Logs the User In and Sets a Session Variable

```
<%@Language=VBScript%>
<% Option Explicit %>
<%
Dim cn, rsLogin, szError
If Request("Action") <> "" Then
    Set cn = Server.CreateObject("ADODB.Connection")
    Set rsLogin = Server.CreateObject("ADODB.Recordset")

    ' Open a database connection
    cn.Open Application("DSN")

    ' Get the userid and save it into the session
    rsLogin.Open "SELECT UserID FROM Users WHERE Username = '" & _
        Request("Username") & "' AND Password = '" & Request("Password") & _
        "'", cn, adOpenForwardOnly, adLockReadOnly

    ' Did we get one?
    If Not rsLogin.EOF Then
        ' Save the UserID in the session
        Response.Cookies("UserID") = rsLogin("UserID")
        ' Redirect to the main page
```

LISTING 2.29   Continued

```
            Response.Redirect "/mileagetracker/main.asp"
        Else
            szError = "Not a valid login.  Try again."
        End If
End If
%>
<html>
<head>
<title>Login</title>
</head>
<body topmargin="0" leftmargin="0" ONLOAD="SetFocus()">
<script language="javascript">
    <!--
    function SetFocus()
    {
        document.forms[0].Username.focus();
        document.forms[0].Username.select();
    }
    // -->
</script>
<!-- #include file="header.inc" -->
<p>
    <font face="Verdana" size="3">Welcome to the Mileage Tracker demo.</font>
</p>
<p>
    <font face="Verdana" size="3">This demonstration application was created
todemonstrate development and scalability issues.</font></p>
<p> </p>
<%
If szError <> "" Then
    Response.Write "<P><font color=""Red"">" & szError & "</font></p>"
End If
%>
<p><font face="Verdana" size="3">Please Login:</font></p>
<form method="POST" action=default.asp>
  <table border="0" width="28%">
    <tr>
      <td width="10%"><font face="Verdana"><b>Username</b>:</font></td>
      <td width="14%"><font face="Verdana">
          <input type="text" name="Username" size="20"></font></td>
      <td width="76%"><input type="Submit" name="Action" value="Login" notab>
      </td>
    </tr>
    <tr>
```

LISTING 2.29 Continued

```
    <td width="10%"><font face="Verdana"><b>Password</b>:</font></td>
    <td width="14%"><font face="Verdana">
        <input type="password" name="Password" size="20"></font>
    </td>
    <td width="76%"></td>
  </tr>
  </table>
</form>
</body>
</html>
```

Following the checklist, the first step is to add an include for ADOVBS.INC to replace the typelib removed in the global.asa. The second step is to modify the @Language= tag and change it to an @Page tag that includes Explicit=true and AspCompat=true. AspCompat is set in this case to enable the use of ADO.

The next step is to find all the method calls and place parentheses () around their arguments. Then, using find/replace, eliminate all the Set statements.

The final step is to remove any default property usage. In this page, the majority of work here is related to the use of ADO recordsets.

That is all that is required for this page to compile. However, it still has references to other ASP 3.0 pages that need to be updated to ASP.NET. For example, the form tag still points to default.asp and should be updated to reflect the new page name, default.aspx. After a login is completed, the user is redirected to main.asp, which needs to be updated to main.aspx. After the pages that each of these items refers to are updated, the references themselves in default.aspx can be updated. The final code is shown in Listing 2.30.

LISTING 2.30 Default.aspx After Conversion

```
<%@ Page Language=VB AspCompat=True Explicit=True Strict=False%>
<!-- #include virtual="/adovbs.inc" -->
<%
Dim cn, rsLogin, szError
If Request("Action") <> "" Then
    cn = Server.CreateObject("ADODB.Connection")
    rsLogin = Server.CreateObject("ADODB.Recordset")

    ' Open a database connection
    cn.Open(Application("DSN"))

    ' Get the userid and save it into the session
    rsLogin.Open("SELECT UserID FROM Users WHERE Username = '" & _
```

LISTING 2.30   Continued

```
            Request("Username") & "' AND Password = '" & Request("Password") & _
            "'", cn, adOpenForwardOnly, adLockReadOnly)

        ' Did we get one?
        If Not rsLogin.EOF Then
            ' Save the UserID in the session
            Response.Cookies("UserID").Value = rsLogin("UserID").Value
            ' Redirect to the main page
            Response.Redirect("/mileagetracker/main.aspx")
        Else
            szError = "Not a valid login.  Try again."
        End If
End If


%>
<html>

<head>
<title>Login</title>
</head>

<body topmargin="0" leftmargin="0" ONLOAD="SetFocus()">
<script language="javascript">
    <!--
    function SetFocus()
    {
        document.forms[0].Username.focus();
        document.forms[0].Username.select();
    }

    // -->
</script>
<!-- #include file="header.inc" -->
<p><font face="Verdana" size="3">Welcome to the Mileage Tracker demo.
</font></p>
<p><font face="Verdana" size="3">This demonstration application was created to
demonstrate development and scalability issues.</font></p>
<p> </p>
<%
If szError <> "" Then
    Response.Write("<P><font color=""Red"">" & szError & "</font></p>")
```

LISTING 2.30   Continued

```
End If
%>
<p><font face="Verdana" size="3">Please Login:</font></p>
<form method="POST" action=default.aspx>
  <table border="0" width="28%">
    <tr>
      <td width="10%"><font face="Verdana"><b>Username</b>:</font></td>
      <td width="14%"><font face="Verdana">
          <input type="text" name="Username" size="20"></font></td>
      <td width="76%"><input type="Submit" name="Action" value="Login" notab>
          </td>
    </tr>
    <tr>
      <td width="10%"><font face="Verdana"><b>Password</b>:</font></td>
      <td width="14%"><font face="Verdana">
          <input type="password" name="Password" size="20"></font></td>
      <td width="76%"></td>
    </tr>
  </table>
</form>
</body>
</html>
```

Two more pages to convert and we will have a working application. The next page to convert is main.asp to main.aspx. This page shows the main menu of the application, but because it checks the login status of the user, it needs to be an ASP.NET page. However, this is only three lines of code, and it's the only code on the page. It also happens to already be ASP.NET compatible; therefore, after renaming the file, no further changes are needed. The menus in the left navigation bar still point to the old .asp files and need to be updated to point at the new .aspx files. The menu links are in menu.inc. Remember that all this code in its preconversion as well as in its post-conversion state is included on the Web site.

Migrating the Pages That Do Actual Work

After the preceding steps have been done, we have ported enough of the application to start the ASP.NET version of the application and log in. The last step is to port one of the pages that does actual work. ViewAccounts.asp is a good example—it displays a listing of accounts and their numbers. It is shown in Listing 2.31.

LISTING 2.31   ViewAccounts.asp—The Starting Point for Our Migration

```asp
<%@Language=VBScript%>
<% Option Explicit %>
<!-- #include file="checklogin.inc" -->
<%
Dim cn, rsList

' Create the ADO objects
Set cn = Server.CreateObject("ADODB.Connection")
Set rsList = Server.CreateObject("ADODB.Recordset")

' Open the database
cn.Open Application("DSN")
%>
<html>
<head>
<title>Mileage Tracker - View Accounts</title>
</head>
<body topmargin=0 leftmargin=0 style="font-family: Verdana;">
<!-- #include file="header.inc" -->
<table border="0" cellspacing="0" cellpadding="0" height=100%>
    <tr>
        <td width=7 bgcolor="#CCFF66"> </td>
        <td width="100" valign="TOP" bgcolor="#CCFF66">
            <!-- #include file="menu.inc" -->
        </td>
        <td valign=top>
            <table>
                <tr>
                    <td width=10> </td>
                    <td>
                        <BR>
                        <font face="Verdana" size="4"><b>
                            Mileage Accounts</b>
                        </font><BR><BR>
                        <table border=1>
                            <TR>
                                <Td><b>Airline</b></td>
                                <td><b>Description</b></td>
                                <TD><b>Account Number</b></td>
                                <TD ALIGN=center><b>Action</b></td>
                            </tr>
                            <%
                            ' Get the list of items
                            rsList.Open "SELECT * FROM MileageAccounts ma, " & _
```

LISTING 2.31   Continued

```
                            "Airlines a WHERE ma.AirlineID = a.AirlineID AND " & _
                            "UserID = " & Request("UserID") & " ORDER BY Name", _
                            cn, adOpenForwardOnly, adLockReadOnly
                        ' Loop through them
                        Do While Not rsList.EOF

                            %>
                            <tr>
                                <td><% = rsList("Name") %></td>
                                <td><% = rsList("Description") %></td>
                                <td><% = rsList("AccountNumber") %></td>
                                <TD> 
                                 <A href="modifyaccount.asp?
                                 ➥Action=Edit&MileageAccountID=
                                 ➥<% = rsList("MileageAccountID") %>">
                                 [Edit]</a>  
                                 <a href="modifyaccount.asp?Action=
                                 ➥Delete&MileageAccountID=
                                 ➥<% = rsList("MileageAccountID") %>">
                                 [Delete]</a> </td>
                            </tr>
                            <%
                                ' Get the next record
                                rsList.MoveNext
                        Loop
                        ' Close the recordset
                        rsList.Close
                        %>
                    </table>
                </td>
            </tr>

        </table>
    </td>
    </tr>
</table>
</body>
</html>
<%
cn.Close
%>
```

Again we run through the checklist. The first step is to add an include for ADOVBS.INC. Then change the @Language directive to a @Page directive and add Explicit=true and

AspCompat=true. Third, update all the method calls to include parentheses () around their arguments, and then remove all Set statements. Finally, remove all default property usage. The final version of this page is shown in Listing 2.32.

LISTING 2.32 ViewAccounts.aspx—The Migrated Version

```
<%@Page Language=VB Explicit=True Strict=False AspCompat=True %>
<!-- #include virtual="/adovbs.inc" -->
<!-- #include file="checklogin.incx" -->
<%
Dim cn, rsList

' Create the ADO objects
cn = Server.CreateObject("ADODB.Connection")
rsList = Server.CreateObject("ADODB.Recordset")

' Open the database
cn.Open(Application("DSN"))
%>
<html>
<head>
<title>Mileage Tracker - View Accounts</title>
</head>
<body topmargin=0 leftmargin=0 style="font-family: Verdana;">
<!-- #include file="header.inc" -->
<table border="0" cellspacing="0" cellpadding="0" height=100%>
    <tr>
        <td width=7 bgcolor="#CCFF66"> </td>
        <td width="100" valign="TOP" bgcolor="#CCFF66">
            <!-- #include file="menu.inc" -->
        </td>
        <td valign=top>
        <table>
            <tr>
                <td width=10> </td>
                <td>
                  <BR>
                  <font face="Verdana" size="4"><b>Mileage Accounts</b></font>
                  <BR><BR>
                  <table border=1>
                    <TR>
                        <Td><b>Airline</b></td>
                        <td><b>Description</b></td>
                        <TD><b>Account Number</b></td>
                        <TD ALIGN=center><b>Action</b></td>
                    </tr>
```

LISTING 2.32   Continued

```
<%
' Get the list of items
rsList.Open("SELECT * FROM MileageAccounts ma, " & _
        "Airlines a WHERE ma.AirlineID = a.AirlineID AND " & _
        "UserID = " & Request("UserID") & " ORDER BY Name", _
        cn, adOpenForwardOnly, adLockReadOnly)
' Loop through them
Do While Not rsList.EOF

%>
    <tr>
        <td><% = rsList("Name").Value %></td>
        <td><% = rsList("Description").Value %></td>
        <td><% = rsList("AccountNumber").Value %></td>
        <TD> <A href="modifyaccount.asp?
                ➥Action=Edit&MileageAccountID=
                ➥<% = rsList("MileageAccountID").Value %>">
        [Edit]</a>  
        <a href="modifyaccount.asp?
                ➥Action=Delete&MileageAccountID=
                ➥<% = rsList("MileageAccountID").Value %>">
        [Delete]</a> </td>
    </tr>
<%
    ' Get the next record
    rsList.MoveNext()
Loop
' Close the recordset
rsList.Close()
%>
            </table>
        </td>
    </tr>
</table>
</td>
</tr>
</table>
</body>
</html>
<%
cn.Close()
%>
```

That is it. Those are the steps required to take your existing ASP 3.0 applications and move them into the future. Now your applications can start to take advantage of all the cool new features in ASP.NET.

Page Framework

IN THIS CHAPTER

Programming an ASP.NET application is significantly different than programming in ASP.old. The difference can be likened to the change that occurred when moving from QuickBasic programming to Visual Basic programming.

The changes in ASP.NET can be broken down into three categories: the control model, the event model, and the separation of code from presentation.

ASP.NET's Control Model

In QuickBasic, your code dealt with the screen as a long piece of paper to which you sent output. You may have used screen libraries that encapsulated a lot of this functionality and made it a much higher-level operation with better positioning.

With the advent of Visual Basic, you moved into a world of reusable controls. You designed your UI by dragging and dropping controls onto a design surface instead of outputting text to the screen or drawing polygons.

These controls were objects that had methods and properties that were used to customize their display and functionality. ASP.old was in many ways similar to QuickBasic. The entire page was essentially treated as a long piece of paper onto which your code placed content. No object model gives you access to the HTML that surrounds your code—just a way for you to output additional HTML based on the location of your code.

ASP.NET changes this by introducing the concept of server controls. If you used Visual Interdev to create ASP.old Web applications, you may be thinking, "Great! They just renamed those onerous design-time controls!" This is not the case. Server controls are not design-time controls in another guise. Nor do server controls require any particular type of client—in other words, server controls aren't ActiveX Controls or client-side behaviors. Server controls are a high-level abstraction of functionality utilized during page execution to place user-interface elements onto the page.

Let's take a look at this. Listing 3.1 shows the HTML for a traditional ASP.old form.

LISTING 3.1   A Simple ASP.old Page, SimplePage.asp

```
<html>
<head>
    <title>SimplePage.asp</title>
</head>


<body>
    <form name="WebForm1" method="post">
```

LISTING 3.1   Continued

```
<p>
<table border=0>
   <tr>
     <td>Name:</td>        <td><input type=text name=txtName></td>
     <td>
       <input type=submit name=Button1 Value="Send">
     </td>
   </tr>
   <tr>
     <td valign=top>Hobby:</td>
     <td>
       <select name=lbHobbies Multiple>
       <option Value="Ski">Ski</option>
       <option Value="Bike">Bike</option>
       <option Value="Swim">Swim</option>
     </select>
     </td>
     <td> </td>
   </tr>
</table>
</p>
   </form>
</body>
</html>
```

What happens when a user fills in a name, chooses a hobby, and presses the Send button? The page is first posted back to the server. No code is in the form at this point, so all the selections that the user made in the Select tag (information that we'll refer to as *form state*) is lost. The page is then returned back to the browser. In ASP.old, if you want to preserve the form state, you are forced to write code to do that.

Listing 3.2 contains SimplePage2.asp showing the typical code you would write with ASP.old to make this work.

LISTING 3.2   SimplePage2.asp Showing Code to Preserve Form State in ASP.old

```
<html>
<head>
        <title>SimplePage.asp</title>
</head>

<SCRIPT LANGUAGE="VBScript" RUNAT=SERVER>
        function IsOptionSelected(strControlName, strOption)
```

Listing 3.2   Continued

```
                    for iCount = 1 to Request(strControlName).Count
                         if request(strControlName)(iCount) = strOption then
                    response.write " SELECTED "
            end if
        next
    end function

</SCRIPT>

<body>
    <form name="WebForm1" method="post">
        <p>
        <table border=0>
            <tr>
                <td>Name:</td>
                <td><input type=text name=txtName
                    value="<% = Request("txtName") %>"></td>
                <td><input type=submit name=Button1 Value="Send"></td>
            </tr>
            <tr>
                <td valign=top>Hobby:</td>
                <td>
                    <select name=lbHobbies Multiple>
                        <option <% IsOptionSelected "lbHobbies", "Ski" %>
                            Value="Ski">Ski</option>
                        <option <% IsOptionSelected "lbHobbies", "Bike" %>
                            Value="Bike">Bike</option>
                        <option <% IsOptionSelected "lbHobbies", "Swim" %>
                            Value="Swim">Swim</option>
                    </select>
                </td>
                <td> </td>
            </tr>
        </table>
        </p>
    </form>
</body>
</html>
```

With the advent of server controls, ASP.NET adds functionality to HTML's own user-interface controls, making them do what you would expect them to do; that is, save the data that the user just spent time typing in.

You need to do three things to make ASP.NET server controls work.

1. ASP.NET server controls are identified using the ID attribute instead of (or in addition to) the Name attribute. You are allowed to use both. You may want to use the Name attribute if you have client-side script that needs to refer to the control.

2. ASP.NET server controls require you to add the runat=server attribute. This attribute indicates to ASP.NET that the tag is something more than a built-in HTML tag.

3. ASP.NET server controls require a closing tag. Server controls are implemented using XML namespaces and, like XML, require every element to have a matching closing element. You can use XML style syntax as a shortcut creating a tag such as <input type=text runat=server />.

So let's do this to the code that was in Listing 3.1. Listing 3.3 shows simplepage.aspx, an ASP.NET implementation of simplepage.asp.

LISTING 3.3   SimplePage.aspx—A Reworking of Listing 3.1 in ASP.NET

```
<html>
<head>
    <title>SimplePage.aspx</title>
</head>

<body>
    <form id="WebForm1" method="post" runat="server">
<p>
<table border=0>
   <tr>
     <td>Name:</td>
     <td><input type=text id=txtName runat=server /></td>
     <td><input type=submit id=Button1 Value="Send" runat=server />
     </td>
   </tr>
   <tr>
     <td valign=top>Hobby:</td>
     <td>
       <select id=lbHobbies Multiple runat=server>
       <option Value="Ski">Ski</option>
       <option Value="Bike">Bike</option>
       <option Value="Swim">Swim</option>
     </select>
   </td>
   <td> </td>
   </tr>
</table>
```

3

PAGE
FRAMEWORK

LISTING 3.3   Continued

```
</p>
    </form>
</body>
</html>
```

All that's changed is the addition of the runat=server attribute to the form tag, the input tag, and the select tag. We've also changed each of the name attributes to ID attributes. That's it. If you run this page, fill in a name, select a hobby, and then click the Send button. The data that you entered stays there after the page is destroyed and re-created on its round trip to the server. The server controls realize that the desired default behavior is to maintain input; that is, they maintain their state, and they do so automatically.

If you don't want a given server control to maintain its state, you can use a new attribute with any server control called EnableViewState. By setting this to false, you can override the default behavior of maintaining form state across posts.

Two categories of server controls are HTML controls and Web controls. The HTML controls mirror their HTML counterparts. HTML controls include the following:

HTML Control Class	*HTML Tag*
HtmlAnchor	<a href="...">Anchor</a>
HtmlButton	<button />
HtmlContainerControl	Any control that requires a closing tag
HtmlControl	Any Html server control
HtmlForm	<form></form>
HtmlGenericControl	Represents any HTML tag without a specific server control class. For example, <p>.
HtmlImage	<image href="..." />
HtmlInputButton	<input type=Button />
HtmlInputCheckBox	<input type=Checkbox />
HtmlInputControl	Any <input type=* /> control
HtmlInputFile	<input type=file />
HtmlInputHidden	<input type=hidden />
HtmlInputImage	<input type=image />
HtmlInputRadioButton	<input type=Radio />
HtmlInputText	<input type=Text />
HtmlSelect	<select>...</select>

HTML Control Class	HTML Tag
HtmlTable	<table>…</table>
HtmlTableCell	<td>…</td>
HtmlTableCellCollection	All <TD> or <TH> tags within <table>…</table>
HtmlTableRow	<tr>…</tr>
HtmlTableRowCollection	All <TR> tags within <table>…</table>
HtmlTextArea	<textarea>…</textarea>

> **NOTE**
>
> All these tags require the runat=server attribute to make them HTML controls. If you forget to add this attribute, these controls will be treated as normal HTML tags. They will be programmable only via client-side code, which may not be what you want.

These controls wrap the related HTML tag with a complete object model that allows access to all the attributes of the tag via properties or methods. You'll see examples of this later in this chapter.

Web controls don't always map directly to a single HTML tag. In many cases they are composite controls that represent a large number of HTML tags. Let's take a look at an example. Listing 3.4 shows the Calendar Web control.

LISTING 3.4   Calendar.aspx Showing a Single Web Control

```
<html>
<head>
    <title>Calendar.aspx</title>
</head>

<body>
    <form id="WebForm1" method="post" runat="server">
        <asp:calendar id=Calendar1 runat=server />
    </form>
</body>
</html>
```

Save this file as Calendar.aspx, and that's it. But that one HTML tag generates something that looks like Figure 3.1.

FIGURE 3.1

The output of Calendar.aspx from Listing 3.4.

That looks like more than just a single HTML tag. In fact, it is. When the page is "rendered," or sent to the client, the control replaces the `<asp:calendar runat="server" />` with the HTML that represents a monthly calendar. If you think about it, this makes sense. A browser has no idea what to do with the `<asp:calendar>` tag. HTML dictates that browsers ignore tags they don't understand. But you don't want the browser to ignore the tag; you want the browser to display a calendar rendered in HTML. So before the page is sent back to the browser, ASP.NET renders the calendar in HTML for you.

If you view the source of the page after it is rendered in the browser, you should get something that looks like Listing 3.5.

LISTING 3.5   The Rendered HTML Source for the Calendar Control Shown in Figure 3.1

```
<html>
<head>
    <title>Calendar.aspx</title>
</head>

<body>
    <form name="WebForm1" method="post" action="calendar.aspx" id="WebForm1">
<input type="hidden" name="__VIEWSTATE" value="dDw1MzYzNjkxODU7Oz4=" />

        <table id="Calendar1" cellspacing="0" cellpadding="2" border="0"
style="border-width:1px;border-style:solid;border-collapse:collapse;">
```

LISTING 3.5   Continued

```
    <tr><td colspan="7" style="background-color:Silver;">
        <table cellspacing="0" border="0" style="width:100%;border-
collapse:collapse;">
            <tr><td style="width:15%;">
                <a href="javascript:__doPostBack('Calendar1','prevMonth')"
style="color:Black">&lt;</a>
            </td><td align="Center" style="width:70%;">
                August 2001
            </td><td align="Right" style="width:15%;">
                <a href="javascript:__doPostBack('Calendar1','nextMonth')"
style="color:Black">&gt;</a>
            </td></tr>
        </table>
    </td></tr><tr><td align="Center">
    Sun
</td><td align="Center">
    Mon
</td><td align="Center">
    Tue
</td><td align="Center">
    Wed
</td><td align="Center">
    Thu
</td><td align="Center">
    Fri
</td><td align="Center">
    Sat
</td></tr><tr><td align="Center" style="width:14%;">
    <a href="javascript:__doPostBack('Calendar1','selectDay0')"
style="color:Black">29</a>
</td><td align="Center" style="width:14%;">
    <a href="javascript:__doPostBack('Calendar1','selectDay1')"
style="color:Black">30</a>
</td><td align="Center" style="width:14%;">
    <a href="javascript:__doPostBack('Calendar1','selectDay2')"
style="color:Black">31</a>
</td><td align="Center" style="width:14%;">
    <a href="javascript:__doPostBack('Calendar1','selectDay3')"
style="color:Black">1</a>
</td><td align="Center" style="width:14%;">
    <a href="javascript:__doPostBack('Calendar1','selectDay4')"
style="color:Black">2</a>
</td><td align="Center" style="width:14%;">
    <a href="javascript:__doPostBack('Calendar1','selectDay5')"
style="color:Black">3</a>
```

Listing 3.5   Continued

```
</td><td align="Center" style="width:14%;">
    <a href="javascript:__doPostBack('Calendar1','selectDay6')"
style="color:Black">4</a>
</td></tr><tr><td align="Center" style="width:14%;">
    <a href="javascript:__doPostBack('Calendar1','selectDay7')"
style="color:Black">5</a>
</td><td align="Center" style="width:14%;">
    <a href="javascript:__doPostBack('Calendar1','selectDay8')"
style="color:Black">6</a>
</td><td align="Center" style="width:14%;">
    <a href="javascript:__doPostBack('Calendar1','selectDay9')"
style="color:Black">7</a>
</td><td align="Center" style="width:14%;">
    <a href="javascript:__doPostBack('Calendar1','selectDay10')"
style="color:Black">8</a>
</td><td align="Center" style="width:14%;">
    <a href="javascript:__doPostBack('Calendar1','selectDay11')"
style="color:Black">9</a>
</td><td align="Center" style="width:14%;">
    <a href="javascript:__doPostBack('Calendar1','selectDay12')"
style="color:Black">10</a>
</td><td align="Center" style="width:14%;">
    <a href="javascript:__doPostBack('Calendar1','selectDay13')"
style="color:Black">11</a>
</td></tr><tr><td align="Center" style="width:14%;">
    <a href="javascript:__doPostBack('Calendar1','selectDay14')"
style="color:Black">12</a>
</td><td align="Center" style="width:14%;">
    <a href="javascript:__doPostBack('Calendar1','selectDay15')"
style="color:Black">13</a>
</td><td align="Center" style="width:14%;">
    <a href="javascript:__doPostBack('Calendar1','selectDay16')"
style="color:Black">14</a>
</td><td align="Center" style="width:14%;">
    <a href="javascript:__doPostBack('Calendar1','selectDay17')"
style="color:Black">15</a>
</td><td align="Center" style="width:14%;">
    <a href="javascript:__doPostBack('Calendar1','selectDay18')"
style="color:Black">16</a>
</td><td align="Center" style="width:14%;">
    <a href="javascript:__doPostBack('Calendar1','selectDay19')"
style="color:Black">17</a>
</td><td align="Center" style="width:14%;">
    <a href="javascript:__doPostBack('Calendar1','selectDay20')"
```

LISTING 3.5   Continued

```
style="color:Black">18</a>
</td></tr><tr><td align="Center" style="width:14%;">
    <a href="javascript:__doPostBack('Calendar1','selectDay21')"
style="color:Black">19</a>
</td><td align="Center" style="width:14%;">
    <a href="javascript:__doPostBack('Calendar1','selectDay22')"
style="color:Black">20</a>
</td><td align="Center" style="width:14%;">
    <a href="javascript:__doPostBack('Calendar1','selectDay23')"
style="color:Black">21</a>
</td><td align="Center" style="width:14%;">
    <a href="javascript:__doPostBack('Calendar1','selectDay24')"
style="color:Black">22</a>
</td><td align="Center" style="width:14%;">
    <a href="javascript:__doPostBack('Calendar1','selectDay25')"
style="color:Black">23</a>
</td><td align="Center" style="width:14%;">
    <a href="javascript:__doPostBack('Calendar1','selectDay26')"
style="color:Black">24</a>
</td><td align="Center" style="width:14%;">
    <a href="javascript:__doPostBack('Calendar1','selectDay27')"
style="color:Black">25</a>
</td></tr><tr><td align="Center" style="width:14%;">
    <a href="javascript:__doPostBack('Calendar1','selectDay28')"
style="color:Black">26</a>
</td><td align="Center" style="width:14%;">
    <a href="javascript:__doPostBack('Calendar1','selectDay29')"
style="color:Black">27</a>
</td><td align="Center" style="width:14%;">
    <a href="javascript:__doPostBack('Calendar1','selectDay30')"
style="color:Black">28</a>
</td><td align="Center" style="width:14%;">
    <a href="javascript:__doPostBack('Calendar1','selectDay31')"
style="color:Black">29</a>
</td><td align="Center" style="width:14%;">
    <a href="javascript:__doPostBack('Calendar1','selectDay32')"
style="color:Black">30</a>
</td><td align="Center" style="width:14%;">
    <a href="javascript:__doPostBack('Calendar1','selectDay33')"
style="color:Black">31</a>
</td><td align="Center" style="width:14%;">
    <a href="javascript:__doPostBack('Calendar1','selectDay34')"
style="color:Black">1</a>
</td></tr><tr><td align="Center" style="width:14%;">
```

LISTING 3.5   Continued

```
    <a href="javascript:__doPostBack('Calendar1','selectDay35')"
style="color:Black">2</a>
</td><td align="Center" style="width:14%;">
    <a href="javascript:__doPostBack('Calendar1','selectDay36')"
style="color:Black">3</a>
</td><td align="Center" style="width:14%;">
    <a href="javascript:__doPostBack('Calendar1','selectDay37')"
style="color:Black">4</a>
</td><td align="Center" style="width:14%;">
    <a href="javascript:__doPostBack('Calendar1','selectDay38')"
style="color:Black">5</a>
</td><td align="Center" style="width:14%;">
    <a href="javascript:__doPostBack('Calendar1','selectDay39')"
style="color:Black">6</a>
</td><td align="Center" style="width:14%;">
    <a href="javascript:__doPostBack('Calendar1','selectDay40')"
style="color:Black">7</a>
</td><td align="Center" style="width:14%;">
    <a href="javascript:__doPostBack('Calendar1','selectDay41')"
style="color:Black">8</a>
</td></tr>
</table>

<input type="hidden" name="__EVENTTARGET" value="" />
<input type="hidden" name="__EVENTARGUMENT" value="" />
<script language="javascript">
<!--
    function __doPostBack(eventTarget, eventArgument) {
        var theform = document.WebForm1;
        theform.__EVENTTARGET.value = eventTarget;
        theform.__EVENTARGUMENT.value = eventArgument;
        theform.submit();
    }
// -->
</script>
</form>
</body>
</html>
```

Wow! That is quite a change. Notice that in Listing 3.5, you won't find `<asp:calendar>` anywhere. In fact you won't even find a runat=server! This stuff is of interest only to the server, so it is all stripped out of the page during the rendering process. What is rendered in this case is a combination of HTML and JavaScript.

However, the code on the server is concerned only with the Calendar control. You can programmatically access the code using its name (Calendar1). You can also get the date selected by the user by retrieving the SelectedDate property of the control. The developer doesn't care about all the HTML and JavaScript gibberish the control creates; the control is always accessed as an object, with high-level properties and methods. This layer of abstraction is one of the things that makes Web controls so powerful.

ASP.NET ships with a large number of Web controls.

Web Control Class	HTML Tag
AdRotator	<asp:AdRotator …/>
BoundColumn	<asp:BoundColumn …/>
Button	<asp:Button …/>
ButtonColumn	<asp:ButtonColumn …/>
Calendar	<asp:Calendar …/>
CheckBox	<asp:CheckBox …/>
CheckBoxList	<asp:CheckBoxList …/>
CompareValidator	<asp:CompareValidator …/>
CustomValidator	<asp:CustomValidator …/>
DataGrid	<asp:DataGrid …/>
DataList	<asp:DataList …/>
DropDownList	<asp:DropDown …/>
HyperLink	<asp:Hyperlink …/>
Image	<asp:Image …/>
ImageButton	<asp:ImageButton …/>
Label	<asp:Label …/>
LinkButton	<asp:LinkButton …/>
ListBox	<asp:ListBox …/>
ListControl	Any list control
ListItem	<asp:ListItem …/>
Panel	<asp:Panel …/>
PlaceHolder	<asp:PlaceHolder …/>
RadioButton	<asp:RadioButton …/>
RadioButtonList	<asp:RadioButtonList …/>
RangeValidator	<asp:RangeValidator …/>
RegularExpressionValidator	<asp:RegularExpressionValidator …/>

Web Control Class	HTML Tag
`Repeater`	\<asp:Repeater .../>
`RequiredFieldValidator`	\<asp:RequiredFieldValidator .../>
`Table`	\<asp:Table .../>
`TableCell`	\<asp:TableCell .../>
`TableRow`	\<asp:TableRow .../>
`TextBox`	\<asp:TextBox .../>
`Xml`	\<asp:Xml .../>

For more information about each of these individual controls, see the control reference later in the chapter.

ASP.NET Is Event Driven

Prior to Visual Basic, programs were written in a top-down fashion. That is, a program started executing at the top and continued down through the bottom with the potential exception of subroutine or function calls. All that changed with the advent of Visual Basic and the concept of event-driven programming. No longer were programs written in a top–to-bottom fashion. Instead, code was broken up into small blocks that reacted to *events*. These event handlers would then do the work in response to how the user interacted with the UI. Event-driven programming made things much easier for the programmer because it became possible to worry less about the order in which things occurred and more about how they actually worked.

ASP.NET again parallels this change. In ASP.old, programs were written to start execution at the top of the page and continue down to the bottom of the page. Again, a few exceptions existed—for example, calls to subroutines or functions. ASP.NET, however, moves the ASP programmer into the world of event-driven programming. Event handlers are written that correspond to the user's interaction with the UI. These event handlers perform all the work.

Let's use the SimplePage example from the previous section to illustrate this. After the Send button is pressed, we want to output some information about the selected items. Listing 3.6 shows the typical way this would have been done in ASP.old.

LISTING 3.6 SimplePage3.asp—A Typical Way to React to User Interaction in ASP.old

```
<html>
<head>
    <title>SimplePage3.asp</title>
</head>

<SCRIPT LANGUAGE="VBScript" RUNAT=SERVER>
    function IsOptionSelected(strControlName, strOption)
        for iCount = 1 to Request(strControlName).Count
```

LISTING 3.6   Continued

```
            if request(strControlName)(iCount) = strOption then
                response.write " SELECTED "
            end if
        next
    end function

</SCRIPT>

<body>
    <form name="WebForm1" method="post">
        <p>
        <table border=0>
            <tr>
                <td>Name:</td>
                <td><input type=text name=txtName
                    value="<% = Request("txtName") %>"></td>
                <td><input type=submit name=Button1 Value="Send"></td>
            </tr>
            <tr>
                <td valign=top>Hobby:</td>
                <td>
                    <select name=lbHobbies Multiple>
                        <option <% IsOptionSelected "lbHobbies", "Ski" %>
                            Value="Ski">Ski</option>
                        <option <% IsOptionSelected "lbHobbies", "Bike" %>
                            Value="Bike">Bike</option>
                        <option <% IsOptionSelected "lbHobbies", "Swim" %>
                            Value="Swim">Swim</option>
                    </select>
                </td>
                <td> </td>
            </tr>
        </table>
        <% If Request("Button1") ="Send" Then %>
            Name: <% = Request("txtName") %><BR>
            Hobby:
            <%
            For iCount = 1 to Request("lbHobbies").Count
                Response.Write Request("lbHobbies")(iCount) + ", "
            Next
            %>
        <% End If %>
        </p>
    </form>
</body>
</html>
```

At the bottom of the form, the code checks to see if the Send button contributed its value to the form value collection. If the value is there, work needs to be done, so it displays the data that was entered into the form. This code gets quite complex as the number of buttons and other items that the user interacts with increases.

Let's take a look at this same code in ASP.NET. Instead of executing top to bottom, we set up an event handler. Listing 3.7 shows the same page in ASP.NET. The controls have been replaced with Web controls, and an event handler named Button1_Click has been created. The event handler is connected to the code it runs by adding the onclick="…" attribute to the button control. This connects the button to the event handler.

LISTING 3.7   SamplePage2.aspx Showing an Event Handler for Button1

```
<html>
<head>
    <title>SimplePage2.aspx</title>
</head>

<script language="VB" runat=server>
    public sub Button1_Click(ByVal sender as Object, ByVal e as EventArgs)
        Dim strTemp as String
        Dim iCount as Integer

        ' Build up the output
        strTemp = "Name:" + txtName.Text + "<BR>Hobbies: "
        for iCount = 0 to lbHobbies.Items.Count - 1
            if lbHobbies.Items(iCount).Selected Then
                strTemp = strTemp + lbHobbies.Items(iCount).Text + ", "
            end if
        Next

        ' Place it into the label that was waiting for it
        lblOutput.Text = strTemp
    end sub
</script>

<body>
    <form id="WebForm1" method="post" runat="server">
        <p>
        <table border=0>
            <tr>
                <td>Name:</td>
                <td><asp:textbox type=text id=txtName runat=server /></td>
                <td><asp:button id=Button1 Text="Send" runat=server
                        onclick="Button1_Click" /></td>
```

LISTING 3.7   Continued

```
            </tr>
            <tr>
                <td valign=top>Hobby:</td>
                <td>
                    <asp:listbox id=lbHobbies SelectionMode="Multiple"
                        runat=server>
                        <asp:listitem Value="Ski">Ski</asp:listitem>
                        <asp:listitem Value="Bike">Bike</asp:listitem>
                        <asp:listitem Value="Swim">Swim</asp:listitem>
                    </asp:listbox>
                </td>
                <td> </td>
            </tr>
        </table>
        </p>
        <asp:label id=lblOutput runat=server />
    </form>
</body>
</html>
```

The Button control in this example fires only a single event. Some more complex controls such as the Calendar control have the capability to fire several events.

Separating Presentation from Code Using Code Behind

Code in ASP.old was often difficult to maintain because it was interspersed with HTML markup. Even when using a visual development tool such as Visual InterDev or Dreamweaver UltraDev, it could be difficult and time consuming to track down a chunk of ASP code that needed to be debugged.

The solution to this problem is a tactic that developers on many platforms typically use: separating *logic* (the code that you write) from *presentation* (the way the data appears). By separating logic from presentation, you can be assured that all the code is located in the same place, organized the way you want, and easily accessible. Separating logic from presentation also minimizes the possibility that you'll generate new bugs in the presentation code as you debug the core logic of the application.

One tactic for separating code from presentation in ASP.NET is *code behind*. Code behind is a feature that enables you to take most of or all the code out of an ASP.NET page and place it in a separate file. The code is processed normally; the only difference is where the code is located.

Visual Basic actually introduced the concept of code behind. The idea was that the code that dealt with a particular object was in a different layer "behind" the object. Of course, this was only one way to describe it. In reality, code behind was just a separate source file for each form that encapsulated the code related to that form. The code in the file was actually tightly coupled with the form.

ASP.NET has this same concept with a slight twist. If you write a page as shown in Listing 3.7, behind the scenes ASP.NET creates code behind for you—invisibly in the background. A class is created that inherits from System.Web.Page and includes a Dim statement for each runat=server control in your page. This is done by default to enable you to continue programming using the simple model provided in ASP.old.

Alternatively, you can create this class yourself and derive the page from it. This separates the code from the layout of the page. This separation is potentially a huge benefit. In my previous life I worked with a company whose standard development process went something like this: A business process owner would decide that some feature should be Web enabled. The owner would come to a designer with, at best, a couple of sketches of what the Web pages needed to implement this feature should look like. The owner would then work with the designer to create a series of HTML pages that represented the feature. These pages would then be handed off to a developer to "activate" them. The developer would go through the pages, adding the code to actually make the feature work. When the developer was done, the feature was then shown to the business process owner. Inevitably, the owner would realize that several features had been missed and/or additional features were needed…. So the process would start over again. The designer would take the completed pages and start moving the HTML around to meet the needs of the change requests. After the pages were again looking good, the designer would hand off to the developer. The developer would open up the pages and throw his or her hands up in despair. In the process of reformatting and rearranging the HTML, the designer inevitably would have scrambled the ASP.old code that had lived intermixed with the HTML. In many instances, it was easier for the developer to just rip the old code out and re-add it via copy/paste from the first version. This iterative process could continue for dozens of rounds, depending on the complexity of the feature.

I suspect my previous company and I were not the only ones frequently faced with this issue. It begs for a new model that allows the separation of the layout and formatting from the code that operates on it. ASP.NET is not Microsoft's first attempt at this concept. It was tried, as part of Web Classes in Visual Basic 6.0 but was not very successful. I predict that ASP.NET will be a much more successful implementation.

The way that code behind in ASP.NET works is that you create a class that inherits from System.Web.UI.Page. This is the base class for a page.

> **NOTE**
>
> A complete reference to the Page object can be found at the end of this chapter.

The .aspx page then inherits from the class you create. This inheritance is accomplished via the @Page directive that is discussed in further detail in this chapter. The @Page directive Inherits attribute enables you to indicate from which class the page should inherit.

The Src attribute enables you to indicate from which file the source code should be dynamically compiled. This last attribute is not required if the class has already been compiled and is in the Global Assembly Cache. Alternatively, under the directory the page is in, you can create a special directory called /bin. This directory is one of the first places ASP.NET looks for already compiled code. If the code has not already been compiled, the file reference by the Src attribute is compiled and looked at for the class specified in the Inherits attribute. Listing 3.8 shows the aspx page for the sample we have been looking at previously. Note that no code is in this page, just HTML markup.

LISTING 3.8   SimplePage3.aspx Using Code Behind; This Is the .aspx Page.

```
<% @Page src="simplepage3.aspx.vb" Inherits="SimplePage" %>
<html>
<head>
    <title>SimplePage3.aspx</title>
</head>

<script language="VB" runat=server>
</script>

<body>
    <form id="WebForm1" method="post" runat="server">
        <p>
        <table border=0>
            <tr>
                <td>Name:</td>
                <td><asp:textbox id=txtName runat=server /></td>
                <td><asp:button id=Button1 Text="Send" runat=server /></td>
            </tr>
            <tr>
                <td valign=top>Hobby:</td>
                <td>
                    <select id=lbHobbies Multiple runat=server>
                        <option Value="Ski">Ski</option>
```

Listing 3.8 Continued

```
                    <option Value="Bike">Bike</option>
                    <option Value="Swim">Swim</option>
                </select>
            </td>
            <td> </td>
        </tr>
    </table>
    </p>
    <asp:label id=lblOutput runat=server />
    </form>
</body>
</html>
```

Also note the @Page tag that indicates the code for this page is in a file called
SimplePage3.aspx.vb. The class that implements the functionality for this page is called
SimplePage. Listing 3.9 shows SimplePage3.aspx.vb.

Listing 3.9 Simplepage3.aspx.vb Is the Code-Behind File for SimplePage3.aspx

```
public class SimplePage
    Inherits System.Web.UI.Page

    Protected WithEvents Button1 As System.Web.UI.WebControls.Button
    Protected txtName as System.Web.UI.WebControls.TextBox
    Protected lblOutput as System.Web.UI.WebControls.Label
    Protected lbHobbies as System.Web.UI.HtmlControls.HtmlSelect

    private sub Button1_Click(ByVal sender as System.Object, _
        ByVal e as System.EventArgs) Handles Button1.Click
        Dim strTemp as String
        Dim iCount as Integer

        ' Build up the output
        strTemp = "Name:" + txtName.Text + "<BR>Hobbies: "
        for iCount = 0 to lbHobbies.Items.Count - 1
            if lbHobbies.Items(iCount).Selected Then
                strTemp = strTemp + lbHobbies.Items(iCount).Text + ", "
            end if
        Next

        ' Place it into the label that was waiting for it
        lblOutput.Text = strTemp
    End Sub
End Class
```

This looks very similar to the previous example, except that no markup is in the page! It is strictly code. One cool feature is that by altering the Inherits attribute, you can tie more than one aspx page to the same code-behind file.

Code behind gives you an additional way to wire up events. It's best not to make the HTML markup know any more than it needs to about the code. Using the approach shown earlier to wire up events, you're required to know the name of the event procedure in the code behind. An alternative is to use WithEvents. In Listing 3.9, you will notice that Button1 is defined WithEvents. Furthermore, the event handler Button1_Click has a Handles Button1.Click on the end. This is an alternative way to wire up the event handlers for ASP.NET with code behind. With this technique, the HTML markup doesn't have to know anything about the code-behind class.

Programming HTML Controls

In this section we'll take a look, one by one, at the HTML controls provided by ASP.NET and show you examples of some of the more interesting ones.

HtmlAnchor

Member of System.Web.UI.HtmlControls

Assembly: System.Web.Dll

The HtmlAnchor control encapsulates the <a> tag with a server-side control model. You shouldn't use this for every link, but it makes it easy to dynamically generate links as needed.

Properties

Attributes	ClientID	Controls
Disabled	EnableViewState	Href
ID	InnerHtml	InnerText
Name	NamingContainer	Page
Parent	Site	Style
TagName	Target	TemplateSourceDirectory
Title	UniqueID	Visible

Methods

DataBind	Dispose	Equals
FindControl	GetHashCode	GetType
HasControls	RenderControl	ResolveUrl
SetRenderMethodDelegate	ToString	

Events

DataBinding	Disposed	Init
Load	PreRender	ServerClick
Unload		

Listings 3.10 and 3.11 show a page that alters a link based on whether the page containing the link is accessed using HTTPS. This is a frequent requirement when building secure e-commerce Web sites.

LISTING 3.10   The HTML for a Dynamically Generated Anchor Using the HtmlAnchor Control

```
<%@ Page Language="vb" AutoEventWireup="false" Codebehind="Anchor.aspx.vb"
Inherits="HtmlControls.WebForm1"%>
<!DOCTYPE HTML PUBLIC "-//W3C//DTD HTML 4.0 Transitional//EN">
<HTML>
    <HEAD>
        <title>Dynamically Generated Anchor</title>
    </HEAD>
    <body>
        <form id="Form1" method="post" runat="server">
            <a id="AnchorTag" runat="server">Test Anchor</a>
        </form>
    </body>
</HTML>
```

LISTING 3.11   The Code for a Dynamically Generated Anchor Using the HtmlAnchor Control

```
Public Class WebForm1
    Inherits System.Web.UI.Page
    Protected WithEvents AnchorTag As System.Web.UI.HtmlControls.HtmlAnchor

    Private Sub Page_Load(ByVal sender As System.Object, _
ByVal e As System.EventArgs) Handles MyBase.Load
        If Page.Request.IsSecureConnection Then
            AnchorTag.HRef = "https://www.deeptraining.com"
            AnchorTag.InnerText = "Secure Link"
        Else
            AnchorTag.HRef = "http://www.deeptraining.com"
            AnchorTag.InnerText = "Unsecure Link"
        End If
    End Sub
End Class
```

The ServerClick event enables you to optionally process the anchor on the server side instead of the client side. This adds an extra round trip to the action but allows you to treat text just like buttons that invoke server-side actions. The InnerText or InnerHtml properties enable you to alter the content between the <a> and </a> tags, as shown in Listing 3.11. The Title property corresponds to the alt text or ToolTip that pops up for an anchor.

HtmlButton

Member of System.Web.UI.HtmlControls

Assembly: System.Web.dll

The HtmlButton class provides a server-side encapsulation of the HTML 4.0 <button> tag. It works only in Internet Explorer 4.0 and later. If you want to use a button that works in a wider variety of browsers, take a look at HtmlInputButton later in this section.

Properties

Attributes	CausesValidation	ClientID
Controls	Disabled	EnableViewState
ID	InnerHtml	InnerText
NamingContainer	Page	Parent
Site	Style	TagName
TemplateSourceDirectory	UniqueID	Visible

Methods

DataBind	Dispose	Equals
FindControl	GetHashCode	GetType
HasControls	RenderControl	ResolveUrl
SetRenderMethodDelegate	ToString	

Events

DataBinding	Disposed	Init
Load	PreRender	ServerClick
Unload		

This control is primarily used to kick off some server-side processing. This is done through the ServerClick event. Listings 3.12 and 3.13 show a page with an HtmlButton control that fires off some script in the page to write some text to the page.

3

PAGE FRAMEWORK

LISTING 3.12   The HTML for Button.aspx

```
<%@ Page Language="vb" AutoEventWireup="false" Codebehind="Button.aspx.vb"
Inherits="HtmlControls.Button"%>
<!DOCTYPE HTML PUBLIC "-//W3C//DTD HTML 4.0 Transitional//EN">
<HTML>
    <HEAD>
        <title>HtmlButton Class</title>
    </HEAD>
    <body>
        <form id="Form1" method="post" runat="server">
            <button id="btnClick" title="" type="button" runat="server">
              Click Me</button>
        </form>
    </body>
</HTML>
```

LISTING 3.13   The Code for Button.aspx

```
Public Class Button
    Inherits System.Web.UI.Page
    Protected WithEvents btnClick As System.Web.UI.HtmlControls.HtmlButton

    Private Sub Page_Load(ByVal sender As System.Object, _
        ByVal e As System.EventArgs) Handles MyBase.Load
        btnClick.InnerText = "Click Me!"
    End Sub

    Private Sub btnClick_ServerClick(ByVal sender As System.Object, _
        ByVal e As System.EventArgs) Handles btnClick.ServerClick
        Response.Write("You clicked me!")
    End Sub
End Class
```

HtmlForm

Member of System.Web.UI.HtmlControls

Assembly: System.Web.dll

The HtmlForm class allows you to change the properties of a form on the server side. These properties include the target you are posting to as well as the method used to send the data to the server.

Properties

Attributes	ClientID	Controls
Disabled	EnableViewState	EncType
ID	InnerHtml	InnerText
Method	Name	NamingContainer
Page	Parent	Site
Style	TagName	Target
TemplateSourceDirectory	UniqueID	Visible

Methods

DataBind	Dispose	Equals
FindControl	GetHashCode	GetType
HasControls	RenderControl	ResolveUrl
SetRenderMethodDelegate	ToString	

Events

DataBinding	Disposed	Init
Load	PreRender	Unload

3

PAGE FRAMEWORK

The EncType property controls the encoding of the form. Valid encoding types include "multi-part/form-data," "text/plain," and "image/jpeg." Listings 3.14 and 3.15 alter the Method property to determine how the form data is posted to the server.

LISTING 3.14   The HTML for Form.aspx

```
<%@ Page Language="vb" AutoEventWireup="false" Codebehind="Form.aspx.vb"
Inherits="HtmlControls.Form"%>
<!DOCTYPE HTML PUBLIC "-//W3C//DTD HTML 4.0 Transitional//EN">
<HTML>
    <HEAD>
        <title>Dynamically Altering Form Method</title>
    </HEAD>
    <body>
        <form id="Form1" method="post" runat="server">
            <asp:RadioButtonList id="RadioButtonList1" runat="server"
                AutoPostBack="True">
                <asp:ListItem Selected="True" Value="Post">Post</asp:ListItem>
                <asp:ListItem Value="Get">Get</asp:ListItem>
            </asp:RadioButtonList>
        </form>
    </body>
</HTML>
```

LISTING 3.15   The Code for Form.aspx

```
Public Class Form
    Inherits System.Web.UI.Page
    Protected WithEvents RadioButtonList1 As _
        System.Web.UI.WebControls.RadioButtonList
    Protected WithEvents Form1 As System.Web.UI.HtmlControls.HtmlForm

    Private Sub Page_Load(ByVal sender As System.Object, _
        ByVal e As System.EventArgs) Handles MyBase.Load
        Response.Write("Form Method used to Send: " + Form1.Method)
    End Sub

    Private Sub RadioButtonList1_SelectedIndexChanged( _
        ByVal sender As System.Object, _
        ByVal e As System.EventArgs) _
        Handles RadioButtonList1.SelectedIndexChanged
        Form1.Method = RadioButtonList1.SelectedItem.Value
    End Sub
End Class
```

NOTE

In the code example in Listing 3.15, you will have to press the radio button twice to see the results. This is because the procedure that outputs the form method runs prior to the RadioButtonList1_SelectedIndexChanged event that actually alters the way the form works.

HtmlImage

Member of System.Web.UI.HtmlControls

Assembly: System.Web.dll

The HtmlImage class encapsulates the HTML <img> tag. This can be useful for dynamically pointing to multiple images on your site. Note that this does not enable you to send the actual image data. You can alter only where the browser retrieves the image data from.

Properties

Align	Alt	Attributes
Border	ClientID	Controls
Disabled	EnableViewState	Height
ID	NamingContainer	Page

Properties

Parent	Site	Src
Style	TagName	TemplateSourceDirectory
UniqueID	Visible	Width

Methods

DataBind	Dispose	Equals
FindControl	GetHashCode	GetType
HasControls	RenderControl	ResolveUrl
SetRenderMethodDelegate	ToString	

Events

DataBinding	Disposed	Init
Load	PreRender	Unload

Listings 3.16 and 3.17 use the image-specific properties of this server control to allow you to alter how an image is displayed on the page.

LISTING 3.16 The HTML for image.aspx

```
<%@ Page Language="vb" AutoEventWireup="false" Codebehind="Image.aspx.vb"
Inherits="HtmlControls.Image"%>
<!DOCTYPE HTML PUBLIC "-//W3C//DTD HTML 4.0 Transitional//EN">
<HTML>
    <HEAD>
        <title>Image Properties</title>
    </HEAD>
    <body>
        <form id="Form1" method="post" runat="server">
            <table>
                <tr>
                    <td>
                        <img src="deeplogo2.jpg" runat="server" id="IMG1">
                    </td>
                </tr>
                <tr>
                    <td>
                        Alt:  <input type="text" id="txtAlt"
                        runat="server" value="Deep Logo">
                        <br>
                        <input type="checkbox" id="chkBorder" runat="server">
                        Border    
                        <input type="checkbox" id="chkVisible" runat="server"
```

LISTING 3.16   Continued

```
                                Checked="True">Visible
                                <br>
                                Alignment: 
                                <select id="ddAlignment" runat="server">
                                    <option Value="left">
                                        Left</option>
                                    <option Value="center">
                                        Center</option>
                                    <option Value="right">
                                        Right</option>
                                    <option Value="top">
                                        Top</option>
                                    <option Value="middle">
                                        Middle</option>
                                    <option Value="bottom">
                                        Bottom</option>
                                </select>
                                <br>
                                Size: 
                                <input type="text" id="txtWidth" runat="server"
                                    Width="51px" Height="24px">
                                 x
                                <input type="text" id="txtHeight" runat="server"
                                    Width="51px" Height="24px">
                                <br>
                                Src:
                                <input type="text" id="txtSrc" runat="server"
                                    value="deeplogo2.jpg"> </P>
                                <P>
                                     
                                </P>
                                <P>
                                    <input type="submit" id="btnApply"
                                        runat="server" Value="Apply Settings">
                                </P>
                            </td>
                        </tr>
                    </table>
                </form>
            </body>
</HTML>
```

LISTING 3.17   The Code for image.aspx

```
Public Class Image
    Inherits System.Web.UI.Page
    Protected WithEvents txtAlt As System.Web.UI.HtmlControls.HtmlInputText
    Protected WithEvents chkBorder As _
        System.Web.UI.HtmlControls.HtmlInputCheckBox
    Protected WithEvents ddAlignment As System.Web.UI.HtmlControls.HtmlSelect
    Protected WithEvents txtWidth As System.Web.UI.HtmlControls.HtmlInputText
    Protected WithEvents txtSrc As System.Web.UI.HtmlControls.HtmlInputText
    Protected WithEvents chkVisible As _
        System.Web.UI.HtmlControls.HtmlInputCheckBox
    Protected WithEvents btnApply As _
        System.Web.UI.HtmlControls.HtmlInputButton
    Protected WithEvents IMG1 As System.Web.UI.HtmlControls.HtmlImage
    Protected WithEvents txtHeight As System.Web.UI.HtmlControls.HtmlInputText

    Private Sub Button1_ServerClick(ByVal sender As System.Object, _
        ByVal e As System.EventArgs) Handles btnApply.ServerClick
        ' Set the alt text
        IMG1.Alt = txtAlt.Value
        ' If the border is checked set a border width
        If chkBorder.Checked Then
            IMG1.Border = 5
        Else
            IMG1.Border = 0
        End If
        ' Set the image alignment
        IMG1.Align = ddAlignment.Items(ddAlignment.SelectedIndex).Value
        ' If a width is entered then set it
        If txtWidth.Value <> "" Then
            IMG1.Width = txtWidth.Value
        End If
        ' If a height is entered then set it
        If txtHeight.Value <> "" Then
            IMG1.Height = txtHeight.Value
        End If
        ' Set the image to show
        IMG1.Src = txtSrc.Value
        ' Set whether it is visible
        IMG1.Visible = chkVisible.Checked
    End Sub
End Class
```

3

PAGE FRAMEWORK

HtmlInputButton

Member of System.Web.UI.HtmlControls

Assembly: System.Web.dll

The HtmlInputButton class wraps up several HTML tags, including `<input type=button>` `<input type=reset>` and `<input type=submit>`. This class is supported in all browsers (unlike the HtmlButton class).

Properties

Attributes	CausesValidation	ClientID
Controls	Disabled	EnableViewState
ID	Name	NamingContainer
Page	Parent	Site
Style	TagName	TemplateSourceDirectory
Type	UniqueID	Value
Visible		

Methods

DataBind	Dispose	Equals
FindControl	GetHashCode	GetType
HasControls	RenderControl	ResolveUrl
SetRenderMethodDelegate	ToString	

Events

DataBinding	Disposed	Init
Load	PreRender	ServerClick
Unload		

Listings 3.18 and 3.19 show the difference in behavior between the type=submit and type=reset buttons.

LISTING 3.18   The HTML for inputbutton.aspx

```
<%@ Page Language="vb" AutoEventWireup="false" Codebehind="InputButton.aspx.vb"
Inherits="HtmlControls.InputButton"%>
<!DOCTYPE HTML PUBLIC "-//W3C//DTD HTML 4.0 Transitional//EN">
<HTML>
    <HEAD>
        <title>HtmlInputButton Example</title>
```

LISTING 3.18   Continued

```
    </HEAD>
    <body>
        <form id="Form1" method="post" runat="server">
            <asp:TextBox id="TextBox1" runat="server"></asp:TextBox>
            <input type="submit" id="btnSubmit" runat="server" value="Submit">
            <input type="reset" id="btnReset" runat="server" value="Reset">
        </form>
    </body>
</HTML>
```

LISTING 3.19   The Code for inputbutton.aspx

```
Imports System.Web.UI.HtmlControls
Imports System.Web.UI.WebControls

Public Class InputButton
    Inherits System.Web.UI.Page
    Protected WithEvents btnSubmit As HtmlInputButton
    Protected WithEvents TextBox1 As TextBox
    Protected WithEvents btnReset As HtmlInputButton

    Private Sub Page_Load(ByVal sender As System.Object, _
        ByVal e As System.EventArgs) Handles MyBase.Load
        'Put user code to initialize the page here
    End Sub

    Private Sub btnSubmit_ServerClick(ByVal sender As System.Object, _
        ByVal e As System.EventArgs) Handles btnSubmit.ServerClick
        Response.Write("You clicked submit.")
    End Sub

    Private Sub btnReset_ServerClick(ByVal sender As System.Object, _
        ByVal e As System.EventArgs) Handles btnReset.ServerClick
        Response.Write("You clicked reset.")
    End Sub
End Class
```

PAGE FRAMEWORK

HtmlInputCheckBox

Member of System.Web.UI.HtmlControls

Assembly: System.Web.dll

HtmlInputCheckBox encapsulates the <input type=checkbox> tag. The Checked property indicates whether the item was checked. Listing 3.17 uses the HtmlInputCheckbox to indicate the visibility of the image. The ServerChange event can be used to catch the change in value of the control on the server.

Properties

Attributes	Checked	ClientID
Controls	Disabled	EnableViewState
ID	Name	NamingContainer
Page	Parent	Site
Style	TagName	TemplateSourceDirectory
Type	UniqueID	Value
Visible		

Methods

DataBind	Dispose	Equals
FindControl	GetHashCode	GetType
HasControls	RenderControl	ResolveUrl
SetRenderMethodDelegate	ToString	

Events

DataBinding	Disposed	Init
Load	PreRender	ServerChange
Unload		

HtmlInputFile

Member of System.Web.UI.HtmlControls

Assembly: System.Web.dll

Provides a way for you to upload files to the server. This control encapsulates the <input type=file> tag on the client and also provides a way to extract the file information from the posted data. For this control to work, the EncType of the form must be set to multipart/form-data.

Properties

Accept	Attributes	ClientID
Controls	Disabled	EnableViewState
ID	MaxLength	Name
NamingContainer	Page	Parent

Properties

PostedFile	Site	Size
Style	TagName	TemplateSourceDirectory
Type	UniqueID	Value
Visible		

Methods

DataBind	Dispose	Equals
FindControl	GetHashCode	GetType
HasControls	RenderControl	ResolveUrl
SetRenderMethodDelegate	ToString	

Events

DataBinding	Disposed	Init
Load	PreRender	Unload

Listings 3.20 and 3.21 show a page that collects the name of a file from the user and then uploads it to the server. On the server side we grab the content of the posted file and place it into a text area. The Accept property is used to indicate that only files with a MIME type of text are allowed to be uploaded.

LISTING 3.20   The HTML for inputfile.aspx

```
<%@ Page Language="vb" AutoEventWireup="false" Codebehind="InputFile.aspx.vb"
Inherits="HtmlControls.InputFile"%>
<!DOCTYPE HTML PUBLIC "-//W3C//DTD HTML 4.0 Transitional//EN">
<HTML>
    <HEAD>
        <title>Input File Example</title>
    </HEAD>
    <body>
        <form id="Form1" method="post" runat="server"
            enctype="multipart/form-data">
            <input type="file" id="FilePost" runat="server">
            <input type="submit" id="btnSubmit" runat="server"
                value="Send File">
            <br>
            <textarea id="txtOutput" runat="server"
                style="WIDTH: 733px; HEIGHT: 630px" rows="39" cols="89">
            </textarea>
        </form>
    </body>
</HTML>
```

Listing 3.21   The Code for inputfile.aspx

```
Imports System.Web.UI.HtmlControls
Imports System.Web.UI.WebControls

Public Class InputFile
    Inherits System.Web.UI.Page
    Protected WithEvents FilePost As HtmlInputFile
    Protected WithEvents btnSubmit As HtmlInputButton
    Protected WithEvents txtOutput As HtmlTextArea

    Private Sub Page_Load(ByVal sender As System.Object, _
        ByVal e As System.EventArgs) Handles MyBase.Load
        FilePost.Accept = "text/*"
    End Sub

    Private Sub btnSubmit_ServerClick(ByVal sender As System.Object, _
        ByVal e As System.EventArgs) Handles btnSubmit.ServerClick
        Dim pf As HttpPostedFile
        Dim tr As New System.IO.StreamReader(FilePost.PostedFile.InputStream)

        txtOutput.Value = tr.ReadToEnd()
    End Sub
End Class
```

HtmlInputHidden

Member of System.Web.UI.HtmlControls

Assembly: System.Web.dll

The HtmlInputHidden class encapsulates the <input type=hidden> tag. This can be used to put hidden text into the body of a form.

> **Note**
>
> In Web programming, it was common to use a <hidden> control to retain state information from one page reload to the next. It's not as common to use the HtmlInputHidden control for this purpose in ASP.NET because you have so many other options for state management. For example, you might want to use the State bag provided by the ViewState property of the Page object instead.

Properties

Attributes	ClientID	Controls
Disabled	EnableViewState	ID
Name	NamingContainer	Page
Parent	Site	Style
TagName	TemplateSourceDirectory	Type
UniqueID	Value	Visible

Methods

DataBind	Dispose	Equals
FindControl	GetHashCode	GetType
HasControls	RenderControl	ResolveUrl
SetRenderMethodDelegate	ToString	

Events

DataBinding	Disposed	Init
Load	PreRender	ServerChange
Unload		

Listing 3.22 shows an example of using an HtmlInputHidden object to submit additional information along with the form. In this example, you want the form to send the date and time the user accessed the page along with the data the user entered. The hidden control stores and submits this additional information.

LISTING 3.22   Using an HtmlInputHidden Control to Submit Additional Information in a Form

```
<%@ Page language='VB' debug='true' trace='false' %>
<script runat='server'>
  Sub Page_Load(Sender As Object, e As EventArgs)
    If Not(Page.IsPostBack) Then
      CreationDate.Value = Now
    End If
  End Sub

  Sub btnSubmit_Click(Sender As Object, e As EventArgs)
    spnResult.InnerHtml = "This account was created on " & CreationDate.Value
  End Sub
</script>
<html>
<head>
```

LISTING 3.22 Continued

```
<title>ASP.NET Page</title>
</head>

<body bgcolor="#FFFFFF" text="#000000">
<form runat='server'>
  Your Name:
  <input type="text" id="txtValue" value="Jeffrey" runat='server'>
  <input type='submit' id="btnSubmit" OnServerClick='btnSubmit_Click'
      value="Create" runat='server'>
  <br>
  Your Address:
  <input type="text" name="txtAddress" value="4905 Brown Valley Lane">
  <input type="hidden" id="CreationDate" runat='server'>
</form>
<span id='spnResult' runat='server'></span>
</body>
</html>
```

In this code, the current date and time is stored in the hidden control when the page is loaded. When the form is submitted to the server, the value of the date stored in the hidden field is sent to the server where it can be utilized in code. In this case, the date is simply displayed, but you could incorporate it into database insertions and so forth.

There are several alternate ways you can hide information on the page the way a hidden control does. For example, most server controls have a Visible property. Setting this property to false hides the control, enabling you to assign data to the control without the data displaying on the page.

Note that "hiding" information by assigning it to a hidden control doesn't actually prevent the user from accessing the information; if you view the page's source in the browser, it's easy to see the value of the hidden control. It's even conceivable that a user could change the value of the hidden control. For this reason, be careful when using hidden controls to store certain types of sensitive information in your Web applications.

HtmlInputImage

Member of System.Web.UI.HtmlControls

Assembly: System.Web.dll

The HtmlInputImage class encapsulates the <input type=image> tag. Use this tag when you want your button to look like something other than a button. You supply the image. The ServerClick method fires an action on the server.

Properties

Align	Alt	Attributes
Border	CausesValidation	ClientID
Controls	Disabled	EnableViewState
ID	Name	NamingContainer
Page	Parent	Site
Src	Style	TagName
TemplateSourceDirectory	Type	UniqueID
Value	Visible	

Methods

DataBind	Dispose	Equals
FindControl	GetHashCode	GetType
HasControls	RenderControl	ResolveUrl
SetRenderMethodDelegate	ToString	

Events

DataBinding	Disposed	Init
Load	PreRender	ServerClick
Unload		

HtmlInputRadioButton

Member of System.Web.UI.HtmlControls

Assembly: System.Web.dll

The HtmlInputRadioButton class encapsulates the <input type=radio> tag. You group radio buttons together to form a group by assigning the same Name property to each button. The user may select only one member of the group.

Properties

Attributes	ClientID	Controls
Disabled	EnableViewState	ID
Name	NamingContainer	Page
Parent	Site	Style
TagName	TemplateSourceDirectory	Type
UniqueID	Value	Visible

Methods

DataBind	Dispose	Equals
FindControl	GetHashCode	GetType
HasControls	RenderControl	ResolveUrl
SetRenderMethodDelegate	ToString	

Events

DataBinding	Disposed	Init
Load	PreRender	Unload

HtmlInputText

Member of System.Web.UI.HtmlControls

Assembly: System.Web.dll

The HtmlInputText class encapsulates the <input type=text> tag. See Listings 3.16 and 3.17 for an example of this class in use.

Properties

Attributes	ClientID	Controls
Disabled	EnableViewState	ID
MaxLength	Name	NamingContainer
Page	Parent	Site
Size	Style	TagName
TemplateSourceDirectory	Type	UniqueID
Value	Visible	

Methods

DataBind	Dispose	Equals
FindControl	GetHashCode	GetType
HasControls	RenderControl	ResolveUrl
SetRenderMethodDelegate	ToString	

Events

DataBinding	Disposed	Init
Load	PreRender	ServerChange
Unload		

HtmlSelect

Member of System.Web.UI.HtmlControls

Assembly: System.Web.dll

The HtmlSelect class is the ASP.NET HTML control abstraction of the HTML SELECT element. You can set the Multiple property to true to enable the user to select multiple items in the list. The Items collection contains the items. Use
`<controlname>.Items(<controlname>.SelectedIndex).Value` to get the selected items value. See Listing 3.9 for the HtmlSelect class in action.

Properties

Attributes	ClientID	Controls
DataMember	DataSource	DataTextField
DataValueField	Disabled	EnableViewState
ID	InnerHtml	InnerText
Items	Multiple	NamingContainer
Page	Parent	SelectedIndex
Site	Size	Style
TagName	TemplateSourceDirectory	UniqueID
Value	Visible	

Methods

DataBind	Dispose	Equals
FindControl	GetHashCode	GetType
HasControls	RenderControl	ResolveUrl
SetRenderMethodDelegate	ToString	

Events

DataBinding	Disposed	Init
Load	PreRender	ServerChange
Unload		

HtmlTable

Member of System.Web.UI.HtmlControls

Assembly: System.Web.dll

The HtmlTable class encapsulates the `<table>` tag. The Rows property returns a collection of all the `<TR>` tags in the table.

Properties

Align	Attributes	BgColor
Border	BorderColor	CellPadding
CellSpacing	ClientID	Controls
Disabled	EnableViewState	Height
ID	InnerHtml	InnerText
NamingContainer	Page	Parent
Rows	Site	Style
TagName	TemplateSourceDirectory	UniqueID
Visible	Width	

Methods

DataBind	Dispose	Equals
FindControl	GetHashCode	GetType
HasControls	RenderControl	ResolveUrl
SetRenderMethodDelegate	ToString	

Events

DataBinding	Disposed	Init
Load	PreRender	Unload

HtmlTableCell

Member of System.Web.UI.HtmlControls

Assembly: System.Web.dll

The HtmlTableCell class encapsulates the individual cells in an HtmlTableRow. The ColSpan and RowSpan properties can be used to span a number of columns or rows, respectively. The NoWrap property can be used to indicate that a cell shouldn't wrap. The Align and Valign properties can be used to control alignment.

Properties

Align	Attributes	BgColor
BorderColor	ClientID	ColSpan
Controls	Disabled	EnableViewState
Height	ID	InnerHtml

Properties

InnerText	NamingContainer	NoWrap
Page	Parent	RowSpan
Site	Style	TagName
TemplateSourceDirectory	UniqueID	Valign
Visible	Width	

Methods

DataBind	Dispose	Equals
FindControl	GetHashCode	GetType
HasControls	RenderControl	ResolveUrl
SetRenderMethodDelegate	ToString	

Events

DataBinding	Disposed	Init
Load	PreRender	Unload

HtmlTableCellCollection

Member of System.Web.UI.HtmlControls

Assembly: System.Web.dll

This class represents a collection of all HtmlTableCells within an HtmlTable control.

Properties

Count	IsReadOnly	IsSynchronized
Item	SyncRoot	

Methods

Add	Clear	CopyTo
Equal	GetEnumerator	GetHashCode
GetType	Insert	Remove
RemoveAt	ToString	

HtmlTableRow

Member of System.Web.UI.HtmlControls

Assembly: System.Web.dll

3

PAGE
FRAMEWORK

The HtmlTableRow class encapsulates a <tr> tag.

Properties

Align	Attributes	BgColor
BorderColor	Cells	ClientID
Controls	Disabled	EnableViewSTate
Height	ID	InnerHtml
InnerText	NamingContainer	Page
Parent	Site	Style
TagName	TemplateSourceDirectory	UniqueID
Valign	Visible	

Methods

DataBind	Dispose	Equals
FindControl	GetHashCode	GetType
HasControls	RenderControl	ResolveUrl
SetRenderMethodDelegate	ToString	

Events

DataBinding	Disposed	Init
Load	PreRender	Unload

HtmlTableRowCollection

Member of System.Web.UI.HtmlControls

Assembly: System.Web.dll

A collection of the table rows inside the HtmlTable control.

Properties

Count	IsReadOnly	IsSynchronized
Item	SyncRoot	

Methods

Add	Clear	CopyTo
Equal	GetEnumerator	GetHashCode
GetType	Insert	Remove
RemoveAt	ToString	

HtmlTextArea

Member of System.Web.UI.HtmlControls

Assembly: System.Web.dll

The HtmlTextArea class encapsulates the `<textarea>` tag. The Rows and Cols properties can be used to dynamically size the control. See Listing 3.20 for an example of the HtmlTextArea control in action.

Properties

Attributes	ClientID	Cols
Controls	Disabled	EnableViewState
ID	InnerHtml	InnerText
Name	NamingContainer	Page
Parent	Rows	Site
Style	TagName	TemplateSourceDirectory
UniqueID	Value	Visible

Methods

DataBind	Dispose	Equals
FindControl	GetHashCode	GetType
HasControls	RenderControl	ResolveUrl
SetRenderMethodDelegate	ToString	

Events

DataBinding	Disposed	Init
Load	PreRender	ServerChange
Unload		

Attributes of the Page Object

In ASP.old, you wrote the majority of your page-rendering code against five objects (Application, Request, Response, Server, and Session). All these objects exist in ASP.NET, although their relative utility is diminished somewhat by the more structured event-driven paradigm provided by ASP.NET.

For example, in ASP.old you typically built applications based on forms that were submitted to the server and handled in script. The script automatically parsed the elements of the form into members of the Request.Form collection. You could then send data back to the browser as a combination of templated HTML and calls to the Write method of the Response object.

In ASP.NET, you don't have to use Request.Form to read the contents of form controls; instead, you can read the properties of those controls directly. This makes programming much easier, eliminating a conceptual hurdle to building sophisticated user interfaces and ensuring that data handled by your application is strongly typed from end to end. You do not need to use Response.Write to send output to the browser, either. Although you may be accustomed to using this quite frequently in ASP.old, you'll almost never see it in ASP.NET.

The following sections describe elements of the Page object in more depth, including the familiar Request, Response, Server, and Session objects, and adding some new functionality provided by the Page object that's unique to ASP.NET.

Page Directives

Page directives are commands, inserted at the top of an ASP.NET page, that represent a mixed bag of settings pertaining to how the page is rendered and processed.

Table 3.1 shows a complete list of ASP.NET page directives.

TABLE 3.1   ASP.NET Page Directives

Directive	Description
@Page	A mixed bag of settings pertaining to how the page is rendered, buffered, globalized, and so forth.
@Control	Settings specific to how user controls are rendered.
@Import	Imports a namespace.
@Implements	Utilizes a COM interface.
@Register	Registers a server control tag prefix and namespace for use in the page.
@Assembly	Links an assembly to the page.
@OutputCache	Determines how the page caches output.

You insert a page directive at the top of the page. Listing 3.23 shows an example of a typical @Page directive.

LISTING 3.23   Typical @Page Directive

```
<%@ Page language="VB" debug="true" strict="true" trace="true" %>
```

This Page directive instructs ASP.NET to interpret code in the page as Visual Basic .NET, to activate debugging, to execute code in strict mode (a mode unique to the Visual Basic .NET language), and to execute in Trace mode to assist with debugging and performance analysis.

> **NOTE**
>
> The @Page directive is used when you want to change the default settings for a single page in your ASP.NET Web application. However some of the settings in the @Page directive can also be altered for an entire directory (using the Web.config settings file) or an entire server (using the Machine.config settings file). See Chapter 6, "Configuration and Deployment," for more information on how to use these files to configure your server.

The next few sections give examples and scenarios that demonstrate and describe when you would use the various page directives. (The debugging and tracing features of ASP.NET are covered in Chapter 4, "Debugging ASP.NET Applications.")

Setting Single-Thread Compatibility Using the AspCompat Attribute

COM components built with Visual Basic 6.0 use single-threaded apartment (STA) threading. To use an STA component with ASP.NET, your ASP.NET page must also use single threaded apartments.

Setting the AspCompat attribute of the @Page directive to true causes your page to execute on a single thread, ensuring compatibility with STA components.

This attribute should be used sparingly because it degrades ASP.NET performance. Use it only in cases where you are unable to port the STA object to .NET.

Controlling Event Handlers Using the AutoEventWireup Attribute

The AutoEventWireup attribute of the @Page directive is used to override the default event procedures used to handle Page events. This attribute is set to true by default.

In general, most of the time this will have bearing only on the name of the procedure used to handle the Page object's Load event. When AutoEventWireup is true, the event procedure is called Page_Load. If AutoEventWireup is false, you have to create a custom event handler to handle the Page object's events.

This feature is used most often with code behind. Listing 3.24 shows an example of a procedure definition for a code-behind Page_Load event.

LISTING 3.24 Definition of a Code-Behind Page_Load Event Procedure Without AutoEventWireup

```
Private Sub MyPageLoad(ByVal sender As System.Object, _
   ByVal e As System.EventArgs) Handles MyBase.Load
   ' TODO: Enter your event code here
End Sub
```

You can see that this procedure definition differs from a normal Page_Load. It is named differently from what you might expect. It can be named differently because it contains the clause `Handles MyBase.Load`. This associates the event handler with the Load event of the page, which is necessary because AutoEventWireup was set to false. It also allows us to associate a subroutine with any name with a specified event. (You'll see this pattern frequently in Web forms pages you create using Visual Studio .NET.) In this context, MyBase refers to the Page object itself. The class that implements code behind always inherits from the Page object, and MyBase always returns a reference to the class from which the current object inherited.

For more information on how code behind works, see the section "Separating Presentation from Code Using Code Behind" earlier in this chapter.

Deactivating Page Buffering Using the Buffer Attribute

When the Web server is building a page for display in the browser, it can either send the data to the browser a little at a time, or it can store the entire page and send it to the browser in one fell swoop. Sending the data to the browser all at once is called *buffering*. Buffering a page can yield significant performance improvements because it potentially lowers the number of TCP packets that must be sent to return the page to the user. It can also make for a more positive perceived user experience because a buffered page renders all at once instead of progressively painting as data arrives.

In ASP.NET, buffering is turned on by default. Setting the Buffer attribute in the @Page directive to false turns off buffering.

Denoting the Code-Behind Class Using the ClassName Attribute

You use the ClassName attribute to denote the code-behind class used by the page. For more information on how code behind works, see the section "Separating Presentation from Code Using Code Behind" earlier in this chapter.

Specifying the Target Client Using the ClientTarget Attribute

You can use the ClientTarget attribute to specify the user agent (a.k.a. browser type) for which the server controls in your application should render their content. It makes sense to use this option in a situation where you have a captive audience that has standardized on a particular browser (as in an intranet), and you are using server controls that adapt to browser capabilities.

> **NOTE**
>
> The ASP.NET documentation doesn't explicitly state that setting this value produces a performance gain, but presumably it would because server controls would not have to sniff the browser before rendering themselves.

Every browser is supposed to pass a user agent string identifying the type and version number of the browser each time it makes an HTTP request. You can programmatically retrieve the user agent string reported by the browser by inspecting the value of Page.Request.UserAgent.

Note that some browsers try to trick the Web server into thinking that they're a different kind of browser by passing a bogus user-agent string. For example, by default, Opera 5.0 identifies itself to the browser as Internet Explorer 5.0. This is done to ensure that the browser will work with Web applications that sniff the browser in brain-dead ways (for example, by attempting to detect the brand of the browser instead of its underlying capabilities).

Setting the Language Using the CodePage Attribute

A code page is a set of mappings between text characters and numbers.

One common code page in the United States is UTF-8, also known as Unicode, and described in Internet RFC 2279 (see `http://www.ietf.org/rfc/rfc2279.txt` if you're really interested).

It's necessary only to specify the CodePage attribute when the page you've authored was written using a different code page than the Web server it's running on. We're hoping you don't do this too often.

Setting Compiler Options Using the CompilerOptions Attribute

You can use the CompilerOptions attribute to pass additional arguments to the compiler when the page is run. To do this, you'll need to have an excellent handle on how compiler switches work, a page that somehow lacks a capability found in a compiler switch, and fortitude.

We wracked our brains trying to figure out why you would use this feature, but we couldn't come up with much. The documentation isn't much help, either. Many of the compiler switches are already represented in ASP.NET in various ways (for example, /optionstrict), so it's possible that the CompilerOptions is simply a hook that ASP.NET provides for you, enabling you to take advantage of future compiler options that may become available before ASP.NET officially supports them.

Setting the ContentType Attribute

The ContentType attribute maps to an HTTP setting that tells the browser what kind of data to expect as the response to a request. Almost always, the data sent from the Web server will be an HTML page. However, you may want to change this. You can use the ContentType attribute of the Page directive to make this change.

You change the ContentType attribute in situations where your ASP.NET page is designed to send data other than HTML to the browser; one common, real-world situation would be sending XML directly to the browser. To do this, set the content type to "text/xml". If the output of the page contains well-formed XML data (and nothing but XML data), and your browser has the capability to display XML directly (that is, Internet Explorer 5.0 or later), the XML will render directly in the browser.

Specifying International Culture Using the Culture Attribute

You can use the Culture attribute to specify for which culture the content of your Web page is intended. *Culture* in this context means international dialect and language. For example, the culture attribute "en-US" stands for U.S. English, whereas "en-GB" stands for the kind of English that our good friends in the United Kingdom speak.

Certain operations in the .NET framework, such as the formatting of strings, are culture dependent. For example, many European cultures use a comma instead of the decimal point used by Americans and other sensible cultures. (Just kidding.)

Activating Debugging Using the Debug Attribute

Setting the Debug attribute to true activates ASP.NET Debug mode, which provides rich debugging information in the browser to remote machines when an error is encountered in an ASP.NET page.

Debugging is covered in Chapter 4.

Setting the Description Attribute

The Description attribute enables you to append a textual description of your choice to your page. This page isn't accessible programmatically; it's presumably just a way for you to insert a comment describing the page in the @Page directive.

Setting the EnableSessionState Attribute

Session state refers to the capability of a Web application to store information for individual users as the user navigates from page to page. Session state is turned on by default; you may want to consider setting the EnableSessionState attribute to false—that deactivates session state and can increase performance.

See Chapter 5, "State Management and Caching," for a general discussion of how session state works in ASP.NET.

Activating View State Using the EnableViewState and EnableViewStateMac Attribute

View State is the feature of ASP.NET that causes a control's properties to be retained across round trips to the server. It is discussed more fully in the section "Postback and View State," later in this chapter.

View State is enabled in ASP.NET pages by default. Setting the EnableViewState attribute to false enables you to turn View State off. Note that it is also possible to turn View State off on a control-by-control basis, for controls that support it, by setting the control's ViewStateEnabled property to false.

Turning off View State can increase application performance by reducing the amount of data that must be sent to and from the server.

Setting EnableViewStateMac to true enables an additional check to ensure that View State information was not altered between the time it was sent to the browser by the server and the time it was resubmitted to the server (Mac in this context stands for Machine Authentication Check). This is an important security feature that you should employ whenever sensitive data is stored in View State.

Setting the ErrorPage Attribute
The ErrorPage attribute enables you to redirect to a custom error page of your choosing. The value for the attribute can be any URL. This attribute is commonly set in applications where it's likely that the user will enter a bogus value (a long URL, for example, or perhaps a mistyped query string parameter), and you don't want the user to be confronted with a grungy ASP.NET error page.

Setting VB Option Explicit Mode Using the Explicit Attribute
The Option Explicit setting in Visual Basic forces the developer to declare variables before using them. Setting the Explicit attribute of the @Page directive is the same as using Option Explicit in code.

This setting has no meaning in pages written in languages other than Visual Basic.

Inheriting from a Class Using the Inherits Attribute
Each ASP.NET page is treated as a class. You can cause your ASP.NET page to inherit from another class by setting the Inherits attribute.

You typically use the Inherits attribute to take advantage of code-behind functionality. Code-behind functionality is described in more detail in the section "Separating Presentation from Code Using Code Behind" in this chapter.

Setting the Language Attribute
The Language attribute determines the programming language used in the page. By default, you can choose VB, C#, or JScript, although other .NET languages could be used as well. Note that an ASP.NET page can only have one language.

Setting the Locale Identifier Using the LCID Attribute
The locale identifier (LCID) is an integer that corresponds to a national language setting. The idea behind an LCID is to give the client some idea of what national language the application

supports. Because the LCID value is a 32-bit number, the value can be quite granular when describing different dialects of the same language. For example, the LCID value 1033 denotes United States English; the value 2057 denotes the flavour of English spoken in the United Kingdom.

By default, ASP.NET uses your Web server's locale (set in operating system configuration) as the locale for each page. Setting this attribute to a different value overrides the locale setting.

Setting the Src Attribute for Code Behind

The code executed by a particular ASP.NET page can be located in an external file. You use the Src (source) attribute to specify the name of the external file.

You typically use the src attribute to take advantage of code-behind functionality. Code-behind functionality is described in more detail in the section "Separating Presentation from Code Using Code Behind" in this chapter.

Setting the Strict Attribute to Prevent Narrowing Conversions

The Strict attribute sets a Visual Basic-specific attribute. When the option is turned on, you can't perform implicit narrowing conversions; that is, you can't perform data conversions that would cause a loss of precision in Visual Basic. Listing 3.25 shows an example of an implicit narrowing conversion.

LISTING 3.25   An Implicit Narrowing Conversion in Visual Basic; Illegal When Option Strict Is Turned On

```
Dim x As Integer
Dim y As Double
y = 3.14159
x = y
```

If you run this code when Option Strict is turned off, the value of x is 3. When Option Strict is turned on, the code produces an error.

Turning Strict on as an @Page directive attribute is the same as using the Visual Basic directive Option Strict. Option Strict exists because implicit narrowing conversions can be an obscure and difficult-to-debug source of errors in Visual Basic code.

When Option Strict is on, you also can't use variables without first declaring them, and you can't use late binding. (It's rare that you'd want to use these "features" in ASP.NET anyway, so this is generally a good thing.)

Option Strict is set to false by default. Turning on this setting has no meaning for pages written in languages other than VB.

Setting the Trace Attribute to Activate Tracing

Setting the Trace attribute to True activates tracing for the current page. Tracing helps developers debug an ASP.NET application. Your trace code might simply indicate that a particular piece of code executed successfully; trace code can also give you a sense of how control flows as a page executes and how long each operation in the lifetime of a page takes to accomplish.

Tracing is covered in more detail in Chapter 4.

Setting the TraceMode Attribute to Sort Trace Information

The TraceMode attribute determines how trace information is displayed when tracing is turned on. Setting TraceMode to SortByTime displays trace entries from earliest to latest. Setting the attribute to SortByCategory groups trace entries by type.

Tracing is covered in more detail in Chapter 4.

Setting the Transaction Attribute to Support Transactions

You can add support for transactions to your pages by using the Transaction attribute. Transactions are set to NotSupported by default; other settings are Supported, Required, and RequiresNew.

Setting the WarningLevel Attribute

You can force the .NET compiler to treat compiler warnings as errors by setting the WarningLevel attribute of the @Page directive to true.

Five levels of compiler warnings exist, numbered 0 through 4. When the compiler transcends the warning level set by this attribute, compilation fails. The meaning of each warning level is determined by the programming language and compiler you're using; consult the reference specification for your compiler to get more information about the warning levels associated with compiler operations and what triggers compiler warnings.

@Control Directives

You use an @Control directive in place of an @Page directive in a user control (.ASCX) file. User controls are script files that provide programmable user-interface functionality. The @Control directive has many of the same attributes as the @Page directive.

User controls are discussed in Chapter 10, "Building User Controls and Server Controls."

@Import Directives

The @Import directive is used to make classes found in that namespace easier to access. When you import a namespace, you don't have to refer to the full namespace syntax to refer to a class in that namespace; you can, for example, use the name DataSet instead of System.Data.Dataset.

3

PAGE FRAMEWORK

An Import directive looks like this:

```
<@ Import namespace="System.Data" %>
```

You can have as many Import directives in your page as you want; each namespace reference should have its own Import directive.

Note that you can use classes in any namespace loaded into the Global Assembly Cache (GAC); this includes all .NET framework classes and anything else you've stuck in the GAC.

Implementing External Interfaces with the @Implements Directive

You use the @Implements directive to implement an interface. To understand why this feature exists, remember that every ASP.NET page is really a kind of subclass of the Page object. If you want the object to have access to functionality that requires the implementation of an interface, you must use this directive.

For example, you could use @Implements in user-control development to implement the IPostBackEventHandler interface as a way of raising events associated with postback.

You can't use the @Implements directive in a code-behind class (use the normal Implements statement instead).

Registering Controls with the @Register Directive

The @Register directive is used to make your ASP.NET page aware of user controls and server controls. It also gives custom ASP.NET controls a programmer-defined namespace, ensuring that the name of one control doesn't conflict with the name of another control.

Custom ASP.NET user interface controls are discussed in Chapter 10.

@Assembly Directives

The @Assembly directive is used to make your ASP.NET page aware of external components. You can use one of two elements with this directive—Name or Src. Name is the name of a pre-compiled assembly (without the .DLL extension). Src represents the name of a source code file (such as myclass.vb).

@OutputCache Directives

You can use @OutputCache directives to control how page caching works. Page caching is a feature that can improve performance on ASP.NET pages whose content changes infrequently.

Caching is discussed in more detail in Chapter 5.

Events Raised by the Page Object

The Page object raises a set of events that you can respond to in code.

The events raised by the Page object are standard .NET events, which means they receive a minimum of two arguments: a Sender (a reference to the object that raised the event) and a collection that represents arguments passed to that event (inherited from System.EventArgs). The contents of this collection differ, depending on the event procedure.

Table 3.2 shows a list of events supported by the Page object.

TABLE 3.2 Events Supported by the Page Object

Event	Description
AbortTransaction	A transaction was aborted.
CommitTransaction	A transaction was completed.
DataBinding	Data binding was completed.
Disposed	The page has been released from memory. This is the last event.
Error	An unhandled exception was thrown on the page.
Init	The page was first loaded. This is the first event raised by the page.
Load	The page is loaded.
PreRender	The page content is about to be displayed.
Unload	The page is about to be unloaded from memory.

3

PAGE FRAMEWORK

As you've seen in the code examples to this point, the most common event handled in the Page object is Load. Many of the initialization events, such as Init and PreRender, are essentially the same as Load; they exist here only because the Page object and ASP.NET Web controls inherit from the same class (System.Web.UI.Control).

Creating User Interfaces with Web Controls

The .NET framework provides a number of user-interface components you can use.

These components are divided into several categories:

- HTML controls—An object-oriented way of creating standard HTML page elements such as text boxes and buttons
- Web forms controls—Objects that can incorporate standard and dynamic HTML into rich user-interface elements
- Validation controls—A type of Web form control specifically geared toward validating user input on a form, often without causing a round trip to the server. Validation controls are covered in Chapter 12, "Creating Database Applications with ADO.NET."

This section will show you how to use the controls that are included with the .NET framework. You can also create your own Web forms controls; this is covered in Chapter 10.

Programming Web Forms Controls

The first step to using Web forms controls on a page is to create an ASP.NET Web form. You do this by creating a conventional HTML FORM tag with the ASP.NET runat="server" attribute, as shown in Listing 3.26.

LISTING 3.26 Basic ASP.NET Web Form Declaration

```
<form id='myform' method='post' runat='server'>

</form>
```

Control Event Model

Web controls raise events of their own as well as the events of the classes they inherit.

Web controls that inherit from System.Web.UI.WebControl.WebControl raise the events listed in Table 3.3.

TABLE 3.3 Events Raised by Web Controls

Event	Description
DataBinding	Occurs when the control binds to a data source. (For more information on data binding, see Chapter 12.)
Disposed	Occurs when the control is destroyed; this is always the last event raised by the control.
Init	Occurs when the control is first created; this is always the first event raised by the control.
Load	Occurs when the control is loaded on the page.
PreRender	Occurs when the control is about to be rendered (displayed on the screen).
Unload	Occurs when the control is unloaded from memory.

Taking Advantage of Postback and View State

Postback is the ASP.NET feature that enables you to detect whether a form has been submitted to the server. View State is a related concept that causes the contents of a posted-back form to be preserved.

The concepts of postback and View State grew out of a frustration with traditional Web server scripting paradigms. In a Web form, as with most HTTP Web requests, the page is completely destroyed and re-created each time it is submitted to the server. But in many, if not most cases, you want certain values (such as the contents of a Search box or the selection you've made in a list of custom preferences) to remain on the page. Without View State, you'd have to write code to make this happen, and without postback detection, it's tricky to determine whether the existing form data needs to be displayed.

You can determine whether an ASP.NET Web form is being posted back to the server by inspecting the IsPostBack property of the Page object. The first time a user accesses the page, IsPostBack will be false. At this time, you typically perform initialization work in code. This can be as straightforward as setting defaults in controls or as involved as performing a relational database query to serve as the basis for display on the page.

> **NOTE**
>
> It is possible to manipulate postback directly in code. To do this, you implement the IPostBackEventHandler interface in your page.

3

Earlier in this chapter, Listing 3.5 demonstrated the HTML source of an ASP.NET Web page that contains chunks of encoded View State. Listing 3.27 shows a snippet of that voluminous code listing.

LISTING 3.27   HTML Source for an ASP.NET Page Highlighting View State Information

```
    <form name="WebForm1" method="post" action="calendar.aspx" id="WebForm1">
<input type="hidden" name="__VIEWSTATE" value="dDw1MzYzNjkxODU7Oz4=" />

        <table id="Calendar1" cellspacing="0" cellpadding="2" border="0"
        style="border-width:1px;border-style:solid;border-collapse:collapse;">
          <tr>
            <td colspan="7" style="background-color:Silver;">
              <table cellspacing="0" border="0"
                style="width:100%;border-collapse:collapse;">
                <tr>
                  <td style="width:15%;">
                    <a href="javascript:__doPostBack('Calendar1','prevMonth')"
                      style="color:Black">&lt;</a>
```

Note that we've mercifully deleted the majority of the source code for brevity. You won't have to write this code yourself; fortunately, ASP.NET generates it for you from the high-level ASP.NET controls you specify.

You can see that the View State information is embedded in the page as a hidden control with the name __VIEWSTATE. The value is encoded, but not encrypted.

You should also be able to see that a hyperlink (a tag) toward the end of the code snippet is attached to an automatically generated JavaScript procedure called __doPostBack. This procedure parses the contents of View State and submits the form back to the server.

The ultimately cool thing about View State is that you don't have to lift a finger to make it work. You may choose to turn it off, however; getting rid of View State when you don't need it can provide a bit of a performance gain. To turn View State off for a particular control, set the control's ViewState property to false. (View State can also be shut off for a particular page or an entire Web application by using @Page directives, described earlier in this chapter, and Web.config settings, described in Chapter 6.)

Mobile Controls

The Microsoft.NET framework supports devices with small form factors and limited capabilities, such as mobile phones and Pocket PCs. These devices have demands on the user-interface developer that are totally different from the challenges presented by user-interface design on a desktop PC.

An in-depth discussion of mobile Web forms is beyond the scope of this book; however, many of the techniques discussed in this chapter will give you a good foundation for creating applications for mobile devices. Because the technical implementation (involving HTML, Dynamic HTML, WAP, and so forth) is abstracted behind the .NET Base Class Library, you can use similar programming techniques to code for Windows and Windows CE.

Data Binding

It is possible to bind a data source to controls in ASP.NET. This works both for rich Web forms controls and HTML controls.

For more information on data binding, see Chapter 12.

Determining Browser Capabilities

When you're creating a corporate intranet, you can often specify corporate standards for a Web browser. Although this tends to limit user choice, this is useful for the developer because it means you can utilize the capabilities of a specific Web browser. For Web sites that are intended to be used by the general public, though, you can't know ahead of time what kind of browser the users will have. In this case, you may find it useful to have a programmatic way of determining things about the user's browser. For example, does the user's browser support JavaScript (or, perhaps, did the user deactivate JavaScript support)? How about cookies? Even though most modern browsers support them, users can choose to turn those off, too.

The HttpBrowserCapabilities class, found in the System.Web namespace, provides these capabilities in ASP.NET. An instance of an HttpBrowserCapabilities object is contained by the ASP.NET Request object (in this context an instance of the object, called Browser, is created for you automatically when a page is requested from the server). Listing 3.28 shows how to use this pre-created object to display information about the browser.

LISTING 3.28   Complete Listing of All HttpBrowserCapabilities Contained in the Request Object

```
<%@ PAGE language='VB' debug='true' trace='false' %>

<HTML>
<HEAD>
<TITLE>ASP.NET Browser Capabilities</TITLE>
</HEAD>

<BODY>
<table width="350" border="0" cellspacing="1" cellpadding="3"
  bgcolor="#000000">
  <tr bgcolor="#FFFFFF">
    <td>Supports ActiveX Controls</td>
    <td><% =Request.Browser.ActiveXControls %></td>
  </tr>
  <tr bgcolor="#FFFFFF">
    <td>Is an America Online Browser</td>
    <td><% =Request.Browser.AOL %></td>
  </tr>
  <tr bgcolor="#FFFFFF">
    <td>Supports background sounds</td>
    <td><% =Request.Browser.BackgroundSounds %></td>
  </tr>
  <tr bgcolor="#FFFFFF">
    <td>Is a beta version browser</td>
    <td><% =Request.Browser.Beta %></td>
  </tr>
  <tr bgcolor="#FFFFFF">
    <td>Browser name (user-agent)</td>
    <td><% =Request.Browser.Browser %></td>
  </tr>
  <tr bgcolor="#FFFFFF">
    <td>Supports Channel Definition Format</td>
    <td><% =Request.Browser.CDF %></td>
  </tr>
  <tr bgcolor="#FFFFFF">
    <td>Common Language Runtime version</td>
```

LISTING 3.28   Continued

```
    <td><% =Request.Browser.ClrVersion %></td>
  </tr>
  <tr bgcolor="#FFFFFF">
    <td>Cookies available</td>
    <td><% =Request.Browser.Cookies %></td>
  </tr>
  <tr bgcolor="#FFFFFF">
    <td>Is this a Web search engine (&quot;crawler&quot;)?</td>
    <td><% =Request.Browser.Crawler %></td>
  </tr>
  <tr bgcolor="#FFFFFF">
    <td>Version of JavaScript (ECMAScript) supported</td>
    <td><% =Request.Browser.EcmaScriptVersion %></td>
  </tr>
  <tr bgcolor="#FFFFFF">
    <td>Supports frames</td>
    <td><% =Request.Browser.Frames %></td>
  </tr>
  <tr bgcolor="#FFFFFF">
    <td>Supports client-side Java</td>
    <td><% =Request.Browser.JavaApplets %></td>
  </tr>
  <tr bgcolor="#FFFFFF">
    <td>Supports JavaScript (ECMAScript)</td>
    <td><% =Request.Browser.JavaScript %></td>
  </tr>
  <tr bgcolor="#FFFFFF">
    <td>Browser version</td>
    <td>
      <% =Request.Browser.MajorVersion & "." & _
Request.Browser.MinorVersion %>
    </td>
  </tr>
  <tr bgcolor="#FFFFFF">
    <td>Microsoft XML Document Object Model version</td>
    <td><% =Request.Browser.MsDomVersion %></td>
  </tr>
  <tr bgcolor="#FFFFFF">
    <td>Operating system platform</td>
    <td><% =Request.Browser.Platform %></td>
  </tr>
  <tr bgcolor="#FFFFFF">
    <td>Supports HTML tables</td>
```

LISTING 3.28   Continued

```
   <td><% =Request.Browser.Tables %></td>
 </tr>
 <tr bgcolor="#FFFFFF">
   <td>Client browser type</td>
   <td><% =Request.Browser.Type %></td>
 </tr>
 <tr bgcolor="#FFFFFF">
   <td>Browser supports VBScript</td>
   <td><% =Request.Browser.VBScript %></td>
 </tr>
 <tr bgcolor="#FFFFFF">
   <td>Version of client browser</td>
   <td><% =Request.Browser.Version %></td>
 </tr>
 <tr bgcolor="#FFFFFF">
   <td>W3C HTML Document Object Model version</td>
   <td><% =Request.Browser.W3CDomVersion %></td>
 </tr>
 <tr bgcolor="#FFFFFF">
   <td>Running 16-bit Windows?</td>
   <td><% =Request.Browser.Win16 %></td>
 </tr>
 <tr bgcolor="#FFFFFF">
   <td>Running 32-bit Windows?</td>
   <td><% =Request.Browser.Win32 %></td>
 </tr>
</table>
</BODY>
</HTML>
```

I used godless, archaic render blocks to create this page, mainly to make it easier for me to create, but also to make it simpler to read.

If you have more than one kind of browser installed on your computer, you may find it interesting to navigate to this page using both of them to see the different capabilities reported by the Browser object. For example, I found it interesting to learn that JavaScript 1.2 comes with Internet Explorer 6.0 beta, but that Opera 5.0 comes with the (presumably bigger and badder) JavaScript 1.3. Also, Opera doesn't return operating system platform information to the server the way Internet Explorer does. It's just as well; with well-designed Web applications, the server shouldn't need to know what operating system the browser is running on anyway.

3

PAGE FRAMEWORK

Server Controls and Page Object Reference

This section provides a quick reference to the key objects described in this chapter. Space constraints prevent us from documenting every object in the .NET framework in this book. For the sake of brevity and conciseness, we include only the most important objects here. For more information on the other objects in the .NET framework, consult the .NET Framework Reference online help file.

Validation controls are covered in Chapter 12.

This chapter covers the Page framework classes in ASP.NET, including the Page object itself, its children, and user-interface controls (HTML controls and server controls). The following sections provide a brief reference to the properties, methods, and events provided by those classes.

AdRotator Class

Member of System.Web.UI.WebControls.

The AdRotator class enables you to display a graphical advertisement on your Web page, changing (or "rotating") the advertisement from a list of graphical URLs. Because they are stored in the form of URLs, the graphics and the pages they link to can reside anywhere on the Web.

Properties

AccessKey	CssClass	Site
AdvertisementFile	Enabled	Style
BackColor	EnableViewState	TabIndex
BorderColor	Font	Target
BorderStyle	ForeColor	TemplateSourceDirectory
BackWidth	Height	ToolTip
BackColor	ID	UniqueID
ClientID	KeywordFilter	Visible
Controls	NamingContainer	Width
ControlStyle	Page	
ControlStyleCreated	Parent	

Methods

AddAttributesToRender	GetHashCode	OnUnload
AddParsedSubObject	GetType	RaiseBubbleEvent
ApplyStyle	HasControls	Render
ClearChildViewState	IsLiteralContent	RenderBeginTag
CopyBaseAttributes	LoadViewState	RenderChildren
CreateChildControls	MapPathSecure	RenderContents
CreateControlCollection	MemberWiseClone	RenderControl
CreateControlStyle	MergeStyle	RenderEndTag
DataBind	OnAdCreated	ResolveURL
Dispose	OnBubbleEvent	SaveViewState
EnsureChildControls	OnDataBinding	ToString
Equals	OnInit	TrackViewState
Finalize	OnLoad	
FindControl	OnPreRender	

Events

AdCreated	Init	UnLoad
DataBinding	Load	
Disposed	PreRender	

The list of advertisements is stored in an XML file. Listing 3.29 shows an example of an XML file.

LISTING 3.29 Using the AdRotator Class

```xml
<?xml version="1.0" encoding="utf-8" ?>
<Advertisements>
    <Ad>
        <ImageUrl>ad-1.png</ImageUrl>
        <NavigateUrl>http://www.redblazer.com/</NavigateUrl>
        <AlternateText>Advertisement Number One</AlternateText>
    </Ad>
    <Ad>
        <ImageUrl>ad-2.png</ImageUrl>
        <NavigateUrl>http://www.redblazer.com/</NavigateUrl>
        <AlternateText>Advertisement Number Two</AlternateText>
    </Ad>
</Advertisements>
```

The ImageUrl node denotes which image to display. The NavigateUrl note indicates the page to which the advertisement is linked. The value of the AlternateText node is displayed if the browser has graphics turned off in the browser.

You can have as many Ad elements as you want; the AdRotator will randomly switch between them. To see this, reload the page several times. (To avoid viewing a cached version of the page, be sure you press Ctrl+F5 rather than using the View, Refresh menu command in your browser.)

NOTE

The standard dimensions for a Web advertising banner is 468 pixels wide by 60 pixels high. You can, of course, use the AdRotator control to display images of any dimensions you want.

You link an XML file with an instance of an AdRotator control by assigning the name of the file to the AdRotator control's AdvertisementFile property. Listing 3.30 shows an example.

LISTING 3.30   Using an AdRotator Control to Display Various Advertising Banners in an ASP.NET Page

```
<%@ Page Language="vb" debug="False" %>
<HTML>
<HEAD>
  <title>ASP.NET AdRotator Control</title>
</HEAD>

<body>
<form id="Form1" runat="server">
  <asp:AdRotator id="AdRotator1" runat="server" Width="468px"
Height="60px"  AdvertisementFile="ads.xml" />
</form>
</body>
</HTML>
```

As you can see, no event procedure code is necessary to use the AdRotator control (although the control does provide an AdCreated event you can use to intercept and reassign the properties of the advertisement before it is rendered on the page).

Button Class

Member of System.Web.UI.WebControls.

The Button class is the ASP.NET Web control equivalent of the HTML submit and button elements. The class abstracts both elements, adding a number of additional properties and events as well.

Properties

AccessKey	ControlStyle	Page
Attributes	ControlStyleCreated	Parent
BackColor	EnableViewState	Site
BorderColor	CssClass	Style
BorderStyle	Enabled	TabIndex
BorderWidth	EnableViewState	TemplateSourceDirectory
CausesValidation	Font	Text
ClientID	ForeColor	ToolTip
CommandArgument	Height	UniqueID
CommandName	ID	Visible
Controls	NamingContainer	Width

Methods

AddAttributesToRender	GetHashCode	OnPreRender
AddParsedSubObject	GetType	OnUnload
ApplyStyle	HasControls	RaiseBubbleEvent
ClearChildViewState	IsLiteralContent	Render
CopyBaseAttributes	LoadViewState	RenderBeginTag
CreateChildControls	MapPathSecure	RenderContents
CreateControlCollection	MemberwiseClone	RenderControl
CreateControlStyle	MergeStyle	RenderEndTag
DataBind	OnBubbleEvent	ResolveUrl
Dispose	OnClick	SaveViewState
EnsureChildControls	OnCommand	ToString
Equals	OnDataBinding	TrackViewState
Finalize	OnInit	
FindControl	OnLoad	

Events

Click	Disposed	PreRender
Command	Init	UnLoad
DataBinding	Load	

Code examples that use the Button object are given throughout this book. Essentially, only two members of the Button object are used with any regularity: the Text property, to display text on the button face, and the Click event, which generates a form submit.

Calendar Class

Member of System.Web.UI.WebControls.

The Calendar class renders a calendar in HTML. In most cases, you'll want to respond to a user selecting a date in the calendar; do this by handling the control's SelectionChanged event.

Properties

AccessKey	Font	ShowGridLines
Attributes	ForeColor	ShowNextPrevMonth
BackColor	HasChildViewState	ShowTitle
BorderColor	Height	Site
BorderStyle	ID	Style
BorderWidth	IsTrackingViewState	TabIndex
CellPadding	NamingContainer	TagKey
CellSpacing	NextMonthText	TagName
ChildControlsCreated	NextPrevFormat	TemplateSourceDirectory
ClientID	NextPrevStyle	TitleFormat
Context	OtherMonthDayStyle	TitleStyle
Controls	Page	TodayDayStyle
ControlStyle	Parent	TodaysDate
ControlStyleCreated	PrevMonthText	ToolTip
CssClass	SelectedDate	UniqueID
DayHeaderStyle	SelectedDates	ViewState
DayNameFormat	SelectedDayStyle	ViewStateIgnoresCase
DayStyle	SelectionMode	Visible
Enabled	SelectMonthText	VisibleDate
EnableViewState	SelectorStyle	WeekendDayStyle
Events	SelectWeekText	Width
FirstDayOfWeek	ShowDayHeader	

Methods

AddAttributesToRender	FindControl	OnSelectionChanged
AddParsedSubObject	GetHashCode	OnUnload
ApplyStyle	GetType	OnVisibleMonthChanged
BuildProfileTree	HasControls	RaiseBubbleEvent
ClearChildViewState	IsLiteralContent	Render
CopyBaseAttributes	LoadViewState	RenderBeginTag
CreateChildControls	MapPathSecure	RenderChildren
CreateControlCollection	MemberwiseClone	RenderContents
CreateControlStyle	MergeStyle	RenderControl
DataBind	OnBubbleEvent	RenderEndTag
Dispose	OnDataBinding	ResolveUrl
EnsureChildControls	OnDayRender	SaveViewState
Equals	OnInit	SetRenderMethodDelegate
Finalize	OnLoad	ToString
FindControl	OnPreRender	TrackViewState

Events

DataBinding	Init	SelectionChanged
DayRender	Load	Unload
Disposed	PreRender	VisibleMonthChanged

Listing 3.31 shows an example of a page that displays a Calendar control and a label. When the user selects a date in the calendar, the label indicates which date the user selected.

LISTING 3.31   Responding to a User Selection in the Calendar Server Control

```
<%@ Page Language="vb" debug="false"%>
<SCRIPT runat='server'>
    Sub Calendar1_SelectionChanged(ByVal sender As System.Object, _
        ByVal e As System.EventArgs)
        Label1.Text = "The date you selected is " & Calendar1.SelectedDate
    End Sub
</SCRIPT>
<HTML>
<HEAD>
<TITLE>ASP.NET Calendar Control</TITLE>
</HEAD>

<body>
    <form id="Form1" method="post" runat="server">
```

3

PAGE
FRAMEWORK

LISTING 3.31   Continued

```
            <asp:Calendar id="Calendar1"
            OnSelectionChanged="Calendar1_SelectionChanged" runat="server">
            </asp:Calendar>
            <BR>
            <asp:Label id="Label1" runat="server"></asp:Label>
       </form>
</body>
</HTML>
```

CheckBox Class

Member of System.Web.UI.WebControls.

The CheckBox class is the Web control abstraction of the HTML CHECKBOX element, used to enable the user to select a true/false or yes/no condition.

Properties

AccessKey	CssClass	Style
Attributes	Enabled	TabIndex
AutoPostBack	EnableViewState	TagKey
BackColor	Events	TagName
BorderColor	Font	TemplateSourceDirectory
BorderStyle	ForeColor	Text
BorderWidth	HasChildViewState	TextAlign
Checked	Height	ToolTip
ChildControlsCreated	ID	UniqueID
ClientID	IsTrackingViewState	ViewState
Context	NamingContainer	ViewStateIgnoresCase
Controls	Page	Visible
ControlStyle	Parent	Width
ControlStyleCreated	Site	

Methods

AddAttributesToRender	GetHashCode	OnUnload
AddParsedSubObject	GetType	RaiseBubbleEvent
ClearChildViewState	HasControls	Render
CopyBaseAttributes	IsLiteralContent	RenderBeginTag

Methods

CreateChildControls	LoadViewState	RenderChildren
CreateChildCollection	MapPathSecure	RenderContents
CreateControlStyle	MemberwiseClone	RenderControl
DataBind	MergeStyle	RenderEndTag
Dispose	OnBubbleEvent	ResolveUrl
Equals	OnCheckedChanged	SaveViewState
EnsureChildControls	OnDataBinding	ToString
Finalize	OnInit	TrackViewState
FindControl	OnLoad	
GetHashCode	OnPreRender	

Events

CheckedChanged	Init	UnLoad
DataBinding	Load	
Disposed	PreRender	

You can determine whether the check box is checked by inspecting its Boolean Checked property. Setting its Text property assigns a text label to the check box; the TextAlign property determines where the accompanying text label is displayed. Listing 3.32 shows an example.

LISTING 3.32   Reading the Checked Value of an ASP.NET CheckBox Server Control

```
<%@ Page Language="vb" debug="False" %>
<HTML>
<HEAD>
  <title>ASP.NET CheckBox Control</title>
<SCRIPT runat='server'>
  Sub CheckChanged(Sender As Object, e As EventArgs)
    If CheckBox1.Checked Then
      CheckBox1.Text = "Thank you for checking this."
    Else
      CheckBox1.Text = "Check This!"
    End If
  End Sub
</SCRIPT>
</HEAD>

<body>
<form runat="server">
  <asp:CheckBox id="CheckBox1" runat="server" Text="Check This!"
```

3

PAGE FRAMEWORK

Listing 3.32   Continued

```
TextAlign="Left" /><BR>
 <asp:button OnClick="CheckChanged" text="Send" runat="server" />
</form>
</body>
</HTML>
```

Control Class

Member of System.Web.UI.

The Control class serves as the base class for all ASP.NET server controls.

Properties

ChildControlsCreated	HasChildViewState	Site
ClientID	ID	TemplateSourceDirectory
Context	IsTrackingViewState	UniqueID
Controls	NamingContainer	ViewState
EnableViewState	Page	ViewStateIgnoresCase
Events	Parent	Visible

Methods

AddParsedSubObject	GetHashCode	OnUnload
BuildProfileTree	GetType	OnUnload
ClearChildViewState	HasControls	RaiseBubbleEvent
CreateChildControls	IsLiteralContent	Render
CreateControlCollection	LoadViewState	RenderChildren
DataBind	MemberwiseClone	RenderControl
Dispose	OnBubbleEvent	ResolveUrl
EnsureChildControls	OnDataBinding	SaveViewState
Equals	OnInit	SetRenderMethodDelegate
Finalize	OnLoad	ToString
FindControl	OnPreRender	TrackViewState
FindControl	OnPreRender	

Events

DataBinding	Init	PreRender
Disposed	Load	Unload

DataGrid Class

Member of System.Web.UI.WebControls.

The DataGrid class enables you to display data in a tabular (row and column) format. Like all data-bound ASP.NET controls, the DataGrid need not be bound to a traditional relational data source; you can also bind to an array or one of the many collection objects provided in the .NET framework.

The HTML output of this control is a table, but the DataGrid class adds a number of useful additional accoutrements such as data paging and formatting.

Properties

AccessKey	CurrentPageIndex	PageCount
AllowCustomPaging	DataKeys	PagerStyle
AllowPaging	DataMember	PageSize
AllowSorting	DataSource	Parent
AlernativeItemStyle	EditItemIndex	SelectedIndex
Attributes	EditItemStyle	SelectedItem
AutoGenerateColumns	Enabled	SelectedItemStyle
BackColor	EnableViewState	ShowFooter
BackImageUrl	Events	ShowHeader
BorderColor	Font	Site
BorderStyle	FooterStyle	Style
BorderWidth	ForeColor	TabIndex
CellPadding	GridLines	TagKey
CellSpacing	HasChildViewState	TagName
ChildControlsCreated	HeaderStyle	TemplateSourceDirectory
ClientID	HorizontalAlign	ToolTip
Columns	ID	UniqueID
Context	IsTrackingViewState	ViewState
Controls	Items	ViewStateIgnoresCase
ControlStyle	ItemStyle	VirtualItemCount
ControlStyleCreated	NamingContainer	Visible
CssClass	Page	Width

Methods

AddAttributesToRender	HasControls	OnPageIndexChanged
AddParsedSubObject	IsLiteralContent	OnPreRender
ApplyStyle	LoadViewState	OnSelectedIndexChanged
ClearChildViewState	MapPathSecure	OnSortCommand
CopyBaseAttributes	MemberwiseClone	OnUnload
CreateChildControls	MergeStyle	OnUpdateCommand
CreateControlCollection	OnBubbleEvent	Render
CreateControlStyle	OnCancelCommand	RenderBeginTag
DataBind	OnDataBinding	RenderChildren
Dispose	OnDeleteCommand	RenderContents
Equals	OnEditCommand	RenderControl
EnsureChildControls	OnInit	RenderEndTag
Finalize	OnItemCommand	ResolveUrl
FindControl	OnItemCreated	SaveViewState
GetHashCode	OnItemDataBound	ToString
GetType	OnLoad	TrackViewState

Events

CancelCommand	ItemCommand	SelectedIndexChanged
DataBinding	ItemCreated	SortCommand
DeleteCommand	ItemDataBound	Unload
Disposed	Load	UpdateCommand
EditCommand	PageIndexChanged	
Init	PreRender	

You can find a number of code examples that utilize the DataGrid control in Chapter 12.

DataList Class

Member of System.Web.UI.WebControls.

The DataList class enables you to display data in a list. The control is similar to the DataGrid control, but instead of displaying multiple categories of data in a tabular (row-and-column) format, the DataList displays a single list of data in a single row. This row can wrap into multiple columns, however.

The various elements of the DataList (header, footer, and items) are divided up into sections and formatted according to templates. Templates are XML sections embedded in the script declaration of the control.

Properties

AccessKey	EditItemTemplate	RepeatColumns
AlternatingItemStyle	Enabled	RepeatDirection
AlternatingItemTemplate	EnableViewState	RepeatLayout
Attributes	ExtractTemplateRows	SelectedIndex
BackColor	Events	SelectItemStyle
BorderColor	Font	SelectItemTemplate
BorderStyle	FooterStyle	SeparatorStyle
BorderWidth	FooterTemplate	SeparatorTemplate
CellPadding	ForeColor	ShowFooter
CellSpacing	GridLines	ShowHeader
ChildControlsCreated	HasChildViewState	Site
ClientID	HeaderStyle	Style
Context	HeaderTemplate	TabIndex
Controls	Height	TagKey
ControlStyle	HorizontalAlign	TagName
ControlStyleCreated	ID	TemplateSourceDirectory
CssClass	IsTrackingViewState	ToolTip
DataKeyField	Items	UniqueID
DataKeys	ItemStyle	ViewState
DataMember	ItemTemplate	ViewStateIgnoresCase
DataSource	NamingContainer	Visible
EditItemIndex	Page	Width
EditItemStyle	Parent	

Methods

AddAttributesToRender	HasControls	OnPreRender
AddParsedSubObject	IsLiteralContent	OnSelectedIndexChanged
ApplyStyle	LoadViewState	OnUnload
ClearChildViewState	MapPathSecure	OnUpdateCommand
CopyBaseAttributes	MemberwiseClone	RaiseBubbleEvent

Methods

CreateChildControls	MergeStyle	Render
CreateControlCollection	OnBubbleEvent	RenderBeginTag
CreateControlStyle	OnCancelCommand	RenderChildren
DataBind	OnDataBinding	RenderContents
Dispose	OnDeleteCommand	RenderControl
Equals	OnEditCommand	RenderEndTag
EnsureChildControls	OnInit	ResolveUrl
Finalize	OnItemCommand	SaveViewState
FindControl	OnItemCreated	ToString
GetHashCode	OnItemDataBound	TrackViewState
GetType	OnLoad	

Events

CancelCommand	Init	PreRender
DataBinding	ItemCommand	SelectedIndexChanged
DeleteCommand	ItemCreated	Unload
Disposed	ItemDataBound	UpdateCommand
EditCommand	Load	

Listing 3.33 provides an example of a DataList control bound to a Hashtable object.

LISTING 3.33   Displaying Data in a Hashtable Object in a DataList Server Control

```
<% @Page language="VB" debug="true" %>
<html>
<HEAD>
<TITLE>ASP.NET DataList Control</TITLE>

<SCRIPT runat="server">

    Sub Page_Load(sender As Object, e As EventArgs)
      If Not IsPostBack Then
        Dim h As Hashtable = new Hashtable()
        h.Add ("SF", "San Francisco")
        h.Add ("AZ", "Arizona")
        h.Add ("CO", "Colorado")
        h.Add ("SD", "San Diego")
        h.Add ("LA", "Los Angeles")

        DataList1.DataSource = h
        DataList1.DataBind
```

LISTING 3.33   Continued

```
      End If
    End Sub

  </script>

<body>

  <form runat=server>

    <asp:DataList id="DataList1" runat="server"
        BorderColor="black"
        BorderWidth="1"
        CellPadding="3"
        Font-Name="Verdana"
        Font-Size="8pt">

      <HeaderStyle BackColor="#000000" ForeColor="#FFFF99">
      </HeaderStyle>

      <AlternatingItemStyle BackColor="#FFFF99">
      </AlternatingItemStyle>

      <HeaderTemplate>

        National League West

      </HeaderTemplate>

      <ItemTemplate>

        <%# DataBinder.Eval(Container.DataItem, "Value") %>
        [<%# DataBinder.Eval(Container.DataItem, "Key") %>]

      </ItemTemplate>

    </asp:DataList>

  </form>
</body>
</html>
```

Note that, as with all data-bindable objects, you can bind the DataList to a wide variety of objects. We used the Hashtable object in this example for simplicity, but you could bind to an ArrayList, a DataSet, or any other list type.

DropDownList Class

Member of System.Web.UI.WebControls.

The DropDownList class is the server control abstraction of the HTML SELECT. Like most list controls, it can be bound to data.

Properties

AccessKey	DataMember	SelectedIndex
Attributes	DataSource	SelectedItem
AutoPostBack	DataTextField	Site
BackColor	DataTextFormatString	Style
BorderColor	DataValueField	TabIndex
BorderStyle	Enabled	TagKey
BorderWidth	EnabledViewState	TagName
ChildControlsCreated	Font	TemplateSourceDirectory
ClientID	ForeColor	ToolTip
Context	IsTrackingViewState	UniqueID
Controls	Items	ViewState
ControlStyle	NamingContainer	ViewStateIgnoresCase
ControlStyleCreated	Page	Visible
CssClass	Parent	Width

Methods

AddAttributesToRender	GetType	Render
AddParsedSubObject	HasControls	RenderBeginTag
ApplyStyle	IsLiteralContent	RenderChildren
ClearChildViewState	LoadViewState	RenderContents
CopyBaseAttributes	MapPathSecure	RenderControl
CreateChildControls	MemberwiseClone	RenderEndTag
CreateControlCollection	MergeStyle	ResolveUrl
CreateControlStyle	OnBubbleEvent	SaveViewState
DataBind	OnDataBinding	ToString
Dispose	OnInit	TrackViewState
Equals	OnLoad	
EnsureChildControls	OnPreRender	

Methods

Finalize	OnSelectedIndexChanged
FindControl	OnUnload
GetHashCode	RaiseBubbleEvent

Events

CancelCommand	Init	PreRender
DataBinding	ItemCommand	SelectedIndexChanged
DeleteCommand	ItemCreated	Unload
Disposed	ItemDataBound	UpdateCommand
EditCommand	Load	

Listing 3.34 shows an example of a DropDownList object that is bound to an ArrayList object.

LISTING 3.34 Binding a DropDownList Control to Data Contained in an ArrayList Object

```
<% @Page language="VB" debug="true" %>
<html>
<HEAD>
<TITLE>ASP.NET DropDownList Control</TITLE>

<SCRIPT runat="server">

    Sub Page_Load(Sender As Object, e As EventArgs)
      If Not IsPostBack Then
        Dim list As ArrayList = new ArrayList()
        list.Add ("San Francisco")
        list.Add ("Arizona")
        list.Add ("Colorado")
        list.Add ("San Diego")
        list.Add ("Los Angeles")

        DropDownList1.DataSource = list
        DropDownList1.DataBind
      End If
    End Sub

    Sub Pick_Click(Sender As Object, e As EventArgs)
      Label1.Text = "You selected " & DropDownList1.SelectedItem.Text
    End Sub
```

3

PAGE
FRAMEWORK

LISTING 3.34   Continued

```
    </script>

<body>

    <form runat=server>
      <asp:DropDownList id="DropDownList1" runat="server"
          BorderColor="black"
          BorderWidth="1"
          CellPadding="3"
          Font-Name="Verdana"
          Font-Size="8pt">
      </asp:DropDownList>
      <asp:button text="Pick" OnClick="Pick_Click" runat="server" /><BR>
      <asp:label id="Label1" runat="server" />
    </form>
</body>
</html>
```

Use the SelectedItem object contained by the DropDownList control to return information about the item selected by the user. The SelectedItem object (an instance of System.Web.UI.WebControls.ListItem) contains a Text property as well as a Value property, enabling you to retrieve both the displayed value and the key associated with the selected value.

In addition to binding the DropDownList object to a list object such as ArrayList, you can also hard-code the list definitions by using <asp:listitem> subelements in the DropDownList definition.

HttpApplication Class

Member of System.Web.

This object is typically accessed as the Application object contained in the ASP.NET Page object.

The HttpApplication class provides a way to store information that has application scope. The Application object contains instances objects such as Request and Response objects (instances of the HttpRequest and HttpResponse classes, respectively) that you can use to access the contents of conventional HTML forms.

Properties

Application	Request	Site
Context	Response	User
Events	Server	
Modules	Session	

Methods

AddOnAcquireRequestStateAsync	CompleteRequest
AddOnReleaseRequestStateAsync	Dispose
AddOnAuthenticateRequestAsync	Equals
AddOnResolveRequestCacheAsync	Finalize
AddOnAuthenticateRequestAsync	GetHashCode
AddOnUpdateRequestCacheAsync	GetType
AddOnBeginRequestAsync	GetVaryByCustomString
AddOnEndRequestAsync	Init
AddOnPostRequestHandlerExecuteAsync	MemberwiseClone
AddOnPreRequestHandlerExecuteAsync	ToString

HttpRequest Class

Member of System.Web.UI.

The HttpRequest class represents a request made by a client. It is typically accessed by programmers through the Request object contained in the ASP.NET Page object.

You can use the Request object to set or retrieve the value of cookies, read HTTP header information generated by a Web request, get information about the browser that made the request, and poll the client for security related information.

Properties

AcceptTypes	Files	PhysicalApplicationPath
ApplicationPath	Filter	PhysicalPath
Browser	Form	QueryString
ClientCertificate	Headers	RawURL
ContentEncoding	HttpMethod	UrlReferrer
ContentLength	InputStream	UserAgent
ContentType	IsAuthenticated	UserHostAddress
Cookies	IsSecureConnection	UserHostName
CurrentExecutionFilePath	Params	UserLanguages
FilePath	PathInfo	

Methods

BinaryRead	GetType	SaveAs
Equals	MapImageCoordinates	ToString
Finalize	MapPath	
GetHashCode	MemberwiseClone	

HttpResponse Class

Member of System.Web.UI.

The HttpResponse class represents the data sent to a client in reply to a request. This can include the response itself (handled by the Write method) as well as headers and other configuration data (such as page cache expiry and HTTP headers).

Properties

Buffer	ContentType	Output
BufferOutput	Cookies	OutputStream
Cache	Expires	Status
CacheControl	ExpiresAbsolute	StatusCode
Charset	Filter	StatusDescription
ContentEncoding	IsClientConnected	SuppressContent

Methods

AddCacheItemDependencies	Clear	GetType
AddCacheItemDependency	ClearContent	MemberwiseClone
AddFileDependencies	ClearHeaders	Pics
AddFileDependency	Close	Redirect
AddHeader	End	RemoveOutputCacheItem
AppendHeader	Equals	ToString
AppendToLog	Finalize	Write
ApplyAppPathModifier	Flush	WriteFile
BinaryWrite	GetHashCode	

HttpServerUtility Class

Member of System.Web.UI.

The HttpServerUtility class provides a variety of utilities for ASP.NET programmers, such as mapping a file request to the file system of the Web server (the MapPath method) and encoding data for use in a URL (the UrlEncode method). It is typically accessed by ASP.NET developers as the Server object contained by the ASP.NET Page object.

Properties

MachineName	ScriptTimeout

Methods

ClearError	GetHashCode	MemberwiseClone
CreateObject	GetLastError	ToString
CreateObjectFromClsid	GetType	Transfer
Equals	HtmlDecode	UrlDecode
Execute	HtmlEncode	UrlEncode
Finalize	MapPath	UrlPathEncode

HttpSessionState Class

Member of System.Web.UI.

The HttpSessionState class is used to store and retrieve session state in an ASP.NET application. It is typically accessed by ASP.NET developers in the form of the Session object, contained by the ASP.NET Page object.

Properties

CodePage	IsReadOnly	Mode
Contents	isSyncronized	SessionID
Counts	Item	StaticObjects
IsCookieless	Keys	SyncRoot
IsNewSession	LCID	Timeout

Methods

Abandon	Finalize	Remove
Add	GetEnumerator	RemoveAll
Clear	GetHashCode	RemoveAt
CopyTo	GetType	ToString
Equals	MemberwiseClone	

Hyperlink Class

Member of System.Web.UI.WebControls.

The Hyperlink class is the ASP.NET server control abstraction of the HTML A element.

Properties

AccessKey	EnabledViewState	Style
Attributes	Events	TabIndex
BackColor	Font	TagKey
BorderColor	ForeColor	TagName
BorderStyle	HasChildViewState	Target
BorderWidth	Height	TemplateSourceDirectory
ChildControlsCreated	ID	Text
ClientID	ImageUrl	ToolTip
Context	IsTrackingViewState	UniqueID
Controls	NamingContainer	ViewState
ControlStyle	NavigateUrl	ViewStateIgnoresCase
ControlStyleCreated	Page	Visible
CssClass	Parent	Width
Enabled	Site	

Methods

AddAttributesToRender	GetHashCode	OnPreRender
AddParsedSubObject	GetType	OnUnload
ApplyStyle	HasControls	RaiseBubbleEvent
ClearChildViewState	IsLiteralContent	Render
CopyBaseAttributes	LoadViewState	RenderBeginTag
CreateChildControls	MapPathSecure	RenderChildren
CreateControlCollection	MemberwiseClone	RenderContents
CreateControlStyle	MergeStyle	RenderControl
DataBind	OnBubbleEvent	RenderEndTag
Dispose	OnDataBinding	ResolveUrl
EnsureChildControls	OnInit	SaveViewState
Equal	OnLoad	ToString
Finalize	OnPreRender	TrackViewState
FindControl	OnUnload	

Use the Text property of the Hyperlink control to specify the text the control should display. Use the NavigateUrl property to determine which page to navigate to. As with the HTML target attribute, you can specify the target window to navigate to by assigning a value to the control's Target property; special values such as "_self" and "_new" are recognized by the control.

Image Class

Member of System.Web.UI.WebControls.

The Image class is the ASP.NET server control abstraction of the HTML IMG element.

Properties

Flags	PhysicalDimension	Size
FrameDimensionsList	PixelFormat	VerticalResolution
Height	PropertyIdList	Width
HorizontalResolution	PropertyItems	
Palette	RawFormat	

Methods

Dispose	GetLifetimeServices	RemovePropertyItem
Equals	GetPixelFormatSize	RotateFlip
Finalize	GetPropertyItem	Save
FromFile	GetThumbnailImage	SaveAdd
FromHbitmap	GetType	SelectActiveFrame
FromStream	InitializeLifetimeService	SetPropertyItem
GetBounds	IsAlphaPixelFormat	ToString
GetEncoderParameterList	IsCanonicalPixelFormat	

Use the ImageUrl property to specify which image to display. To create an image that works like a button, use the ImageButton control instead.

ImageButton Class

Member of System.Web.UI.WebControls.

The ImageButton class is another ASP.NET server control abstraction of the HTML IMG element, with the addition of a behavior that makes the control act like a button.

Properties

AccessKey	ControlStyleCreated	Parent
AlternateText	CssClass	Site
Attributes	Enabled	Style
BackColor	EnableViewState	TabIndex
BorderColor	Events	TagKey
BorderStyle	Font	TagName

Properties

BorderWidth	ForeColor	TemplateSourceDirectory
CausesValidation	HasChildViewState	ToolTip
ChildControlsCreated	Height	UniqueID
ClientID	ID	ViewState
CommandArgument	ImageAlign	ViewStateIgnoresCase
CommandName	ImageUrl	Visible
Context	IsTrackingViewState	Width
Controls	NamingContainer	
ControlStyle	Page	

Methods

AddAttributesToRender	GetHashCode	OnPreRender
AddParsedSubObject	GetType	OnUnload
ApplyStyle	HasControls	RaiseBubbleEvent
CopyBaseAttributes	IsLiteralConent	Render
ClearChildViewState	LoadViewState	RenderBeginTag
CreateChildControls	MapPathSecure	RenderChildren
CreateControlCollection	MemberwiseClone	RenderContents
CreateControlStyle	MergeStyle	RenderEndTag
DataBind	OnBubbleEvent	ResolveUrl
Dispose	OnClick	SaveViewState
Equals	OnCommand	ToString
EnsureChildControls	OnDataBinding	TrackViewState
Finalize	OnInit	
FindControl	OnLoad	

Events

Click	Disposed	PreRender
Command	Init	Unload
DataBinding	Load	

Assign a value to the ImageUrl property to specify which graphic to display (just as you would with the Image control). To execute code in response to a user clicking the image, use the control's Click event, the same as you would for a Button control.

Label Class

Member of System.Web.UI.WebControls.

The Label class provides a way to programmatically create a read-only text region on the page. This region is typically rendered in HTML as a SPAN tag.

Properties

AccessKey	Enabled	Style
Attributes	EnableViewState	TabIndex
BackColor	Events	TagKey
BorderColor	Font	TagName
BorderStyle	ForeColor	Text
BorderWidth	HasChildViewState	TemplateSourceDirectory
ChildControlsCreated	Height	ToolTip
ClientID	ID	UniqueID
Context	IsTrackingViewState	ViewState
Controls	NamingContainer	ViewStateIgnoresCase
ControlStyle	Page	Visible
ControlStyleCreated	Parent	Width
CssClass	Site	

Methods

AddAttributesToRender	FindControl	OnUnload
AddParsedSubObject	Finalize	RaiseBubbleEvent
ApplyStyle	GetHashCode	Render
ClearChildViewState	GetType	RenderBeginTag
CopyBaseAttributes	HasControls	RenderChildren
ClearChildViewState	IsLiteralContent	RenderContents
CreateChildControls	MapPathSecure	RenderControl
CreateControlCollection	MemberwiseClone	RenderEndTag
CreateControlStyle	MergeStyle	ResolveUrl
DataBind	OnDataBinding	SaveViewState
Dispose	OnInit	ToString
Equals	OnLoad	TrackViewState
EnsureChildControls	OnPreRender	

A number of code examples involving the Label class are provided throughout this book. In nearly every case, the only member you'll typically need to access is the control's Text property.

LinkButton Class

Member of System.Web.UI.WebControls.

The LinkButton class merges the functionality of a hyperlink with the functionality of the Button control.

Properties

AccessKey	ControlStyleCreated	Site
Attributes	CssClass	Style
BackColor	Enabled	TabIndex
BorderColor	EnableViewState	TagKey
BorderStyle	Events	TagName
BorderWidth	Font	TemplateSourceDirectory
CausesValidation	ForeColor	Text
ChildControlsCreated	HasChildViewState	ToolTip
ClientID	Height	UniqueID
CommandArgument	ID	ViewState
CommandName	IsTrackingViewState	ViewStateIgnoresCase
Context	NamingContainer	Visible
Controls	Page	Width
ControlStyle	Parent	

Methods

AddAttributesToRender	Finalize	OnLoad
AddParsedSubObject	GetHashCode	OnPreRender
ApplyStyle	GetType	OnUnload
ClearChildViewState	HasControls	RaiseBubbleEvent
CopyBaseAttributes	IsLiteralContent	Render
ClearChildViewState	LoadViewState	RenderBeginTag
CreateChildControls	MapPathSecure	RenderChildren
CreateControlCollection	MemberwiseClone	RenderContents
CreateControlStyle	MergeStyle	RenderControl

Methods

DataBind	OnBubbleEvent	RenderEndTag
Dispose	OnClick	ResolveUrl
Equals	OnCommand	SaveViewState
EnsureChildControls	OnDataBinding	ToString
FindControl	OnInit	TrackViewState

Events

Click	Disposed	PreRender
Command	Init	Unload
DataBinding	Load	

Handle the control's Click event to execute code when the user clicks the control. To navigate to another Web page, use the Hyperlink control instead.

ListBox Class

Member of System.Web.UI.WebControls.

The ListBox class represents the ASP.NET server control abstraction of the HTML SELECT element.

Properties

AccessKey	DataTextField	SelectedIndex
Attributes	DataTextFormatString	SelectedItem
AutoPostBack	DataValueField	SelectionMode
BackColor	Enabled	Site
BorderColor	EnableViewState	Style
BorderStyle	Events	TabIndex
BorderWidth	Font	TagKey
ChildControlsCreated	ForeColor	TagName
ClientID	HasChildViewState	TemplateSourceDirectory
Context	Height	Text
Controls	ID	ToolTip
ControlStyle	IsTrackingViewState	UniqueID
ControlStyleCreated	NamingContainer	ViewState
CssClass	Page	ViewStateIgnoresCase
DataMember	Parent	Visible
DataSource	Rows	Width

Methods

AddAttributesToRender	Finalize	OnSelectedIndexChanged
AddParsedSubObject	GetHashCode	OnUnload
ApplyStyle	GetType	RaiseBubbleEvent
ClearChildViewState	HasControls	Render
CopyBaseAttributes	IsLiteralContent	RenderBeginTag
ClearChildViewState	LoadViewState	RenderChildren
CreateChildControls	MapPathSecure	RenderContents
CreateControlCollection	MemberwiseClone	RenderControl
CreateControlStyle	MergeStyle	RenderEndTag
DataBind	OnBubbleEvent	ResolveUrl
Dispose	OnDataBinding	SaveViewState
Equals	OnInit	ToString
EnsureChildControls	OnLoad	TrackViewState
FindControl	OnPreRender	

Page Class

The Page class represents a page request. All controls on a page, as well as utility objects such as Request, Response, Server, and Application (familiar to ASP.old developers), are members of the Page object in ASP.NET.

The page class is the base class from which all ASP.NET pages derive. If you create a code-behind class, it must inherit from this object.

Properties

Application	Cache	ClientID
ClientTarget	Controls	EnableViewState
ErrorPage	ID	IsPostBack
IsValid	NamingContainer	Page
Parent	Request	Response
Server	Session	Site
SmartNavigation	TemplateSourceDirectory	Trace
UniqueID	User	Validators
Visible		

Methods

DataBind	DesignerInitialize
Dispose	Equals
FindControl	GetHashCode
GetPostBackClientEvent	GetPostBackClientHyperlink
GetPostBackEventReference	GetType
GetTypeHashCode	HasControls
InstantiateIn	IsClientScriptBlockRegistered
IsStartupScriptRegistered	LoadControl
LoadTemplate	MapPath
ParseControl	RegisterArrayDeclaration
RegisterClientScriptBlock	RegisterHiddenField
RegisterOnSubmitStatement	RegisterRequiresPostBack
RegisterRequiresRaiseEvent	RegisterStartupScript
RegisterViewStateHandler	RenderControl
ResolveUrl	SetRenderMethodDelegate
ToString	Validate

Events

AbortTransaction	CommitTransaction	DataBinding
Disposed	Error	Init
Load	PreRender	Unload

It's common for ASP.NET pages to handle the Load event of the Page object as a way to perform initialization when the page loads.

Panel Class

Member of System.Web.UI.WebControls.

The Panel class enables developers to group Web form controls. You may do this for cosmetic purposes (for example, to group the controls on a complicated form into subcategories) or to manipulate controls on a form as a unit.

Properties

AccessKey	Enabled	Style
Attributes	EnableViewState	TabIndex
BackColor	Events	TagKey
BackImageUrl	Font	TagName
BorderColor	ForeColor	TemplateSourceDirectory

Properties

BorderStyle	HasChildViewState	ToolTip
BorderWidth	Height	UniqueID
ChildControlsCreated	HorizontalAlign	ViewState
ClientID	ID	ViewStateIgnoresCase
Context	IsTrackingViewState	Visible
Controls	NamingContainer	Width
ControlStyle	Page	Wrap
ControlStyleCreated	Parent	
CssClass	Site	

Methods

AddAttributesToRender	Finalize	OnSelectedIndexChanged
AddParsedSubObject	GetHashCode	OnUnload
ApplyStyle	GetType	RaiseBubbleEvent
ClearChildViewState	HasControls	Render
CopyBaseAttributes	IsLiteralContent	RenderBeginTag
ClearChildViewState	LoadViewState	RenderChildren
CreateChildControls	MapPathSecure	RenderContents
CreateControlCollection	MemberwiseClone	RenderControl
CreateControlStyle	MergeStyle	RenderEndTag
DataBind	OnBubbleEvent	ResolveUrl
Dispose	OnDataBinding	SaveViewState
Equals	OnInit	ToString
EnsureChildControls	OnLoad	TrackViewState
FindControl	OnPreRender	

RadioButton Class

Member of System.Web.UI.WebControls.

The RadioButton class represents the ASP.NET server control abstraction of the INPUT-type radio. Radio buttons are grouped together; only one button in a group may be selected at a time.

Properties

AccessKey	Enabled	Style
Attributes	EnableViewState	TabIndex
AutoPostBack	Events	TagKey

Properties

BackColor	Font	TagName
BorderColor	ForeColor	TemplateSourceDirectory
BorderStyle	GroupName	Text
BorderWidth		TextAlign
Checked	HasChildViewState	ToolTip
ChildControlsCreated	Height	UniqueID
ClientID	ID	ViewState
Context	IsTrackingViewState	ViewStateIgnoresCase
Controls	NamingContainer	Visible
ControlStyle	Page	Width
ControlStyleCreated	Parent	Wrap
CssClass	Site	

Methods

AddAttributesToRender	Finalize	OnPreRender
AddParsedSubObject	GetHashCode	OnUnload
ApplyStyle	GetType	RaiseBubbleEvent
ClearChildViewState	HasControls	Render
CopyBaseAttributes	IsLiteralContent	RenderBeginTag
ClearChildViewState	LoadViewState	RenderChildren
CreateChildControls	MapPathSecure	RenderContents
CreateControlCollection	MemberwiseClone	RenderControl
CreateControlStyle	MergeStyle	RenderEndTag
DataBind	OnBubbleEvent	ResolveUrl
Dispose	OnCheckedChanged	SaveViewState
Equals	OnDataBinding	ToString
EnsureChildControls	OnInit	TrackViewState
FindControl	OnLoad	

Repeater Class

Member of System.Web.UI.WebControls.

You can use the Repeater control to display bound data in a totally customized way. You do this by creating HTML templates (in a manner similar to the DataList control described earlier in this section).

3

Properties

AlternatingItemTemplate	FooterTemplate	Parent
ChildControlsCreated	HasChildViewState	SeparatorTemplate
ClientID	HeaderTemplate	Site
Context	ID	TemplateSourceDirectory
Controls	IsTrackingViewState	UniqueID
DataMember	Items	ViewState
DataSource	ItemTemplate	ViewStateIgnoresCase
EnableViewState	NamingContainer	Visible
Events	Page	

Methods

AddAttributesToRender	FindControl	OnItemCreated
AddParsedSubObject	Finalize	OnItemDataBound
ApplyStyle	GetHashCode	OnLoad
ClearChildViewState	GetType	OnPreRender
CopyBaseAttributes	HasControls	OnUnload
ClearChildViewState	IsLiteralContent	RaiseBubbleEvent
AddParsedSubObject	LoadViewState	Render
ClearChildViewState	MapPathSecure	RenderChildren
CreateChildControls	MemberwiseClone	RenderControl
CreateControlCollection	MergeStyle	ResolveUrl
DataBind	OnBubbleEvent	SaveViewState
Dispose	OnDataBinding	ToString
Equals	OnInit	TrackViewState
EnsureChildControls	OnItemCommand	

Listing 3.35 shows an example of a Repeater control used to display the contents of the ever-popular Hashtable object. Although you could have used another list control such as the DataGrid or DataList to perform the same work, you can see from the code that the Repeater gives you the capability to embed HTML formatting to have more granular control over the formatting of each row.

LISTING 3.35   Using the Repeater Control to Build Customized Output of a Hashtable

```vb
<%@ Page Language="VB" debug="true" %>
<html>
 <head>
    <script runat="server">

    Sub Page_Load(Sender As Object, e As EventArgs)
      If Not IsPostBack Then
        Dim h As Hashtable = new Hashtable()
        h.Add ("SF", "San Francisco")
        h.Add ("AZ", "Arizona")
        h.Add ("CO", "Colorado")
        h.Add ("SD", "San Diego")
        h.Add ("LA", "Los Angeles")

        Repeater1.DataSource = h
        Repeater1.DataBind
      End If
    End Sub

    </script>

</head>
<body>

    <form runat=server>

       <asp:Repeater id=Repeater1 runat="server">
          <HeaderTemplate>
             <table border="0" cellpadding="5" cellspacing="1"
                bgcolor="#000000">
                <tr>
                   <td bgcolor="#FFFF99"><b>Team</b></td>
                   <td bgcolor="#FFFF99"><b>Abbreviation</b></td>
                </tr>
          </HeaderTemplate>

          <ItemTemplate>
             <tr>
                <td bgcolor="#FFFFFF">
                   <%# DataBinder.Eval(Container.DataItem, "Value") %> </td>
                <td bgcolor="#FFFFFF">
                   <%# DataBinder.Eval(Container.DataItem, "Key") %> </td>
```

LISTING 3.35   Continued

```
        </tr>
      </ItemTemplate>

      <FooterTemplate>
        </table>
      </FooterTemplate>
    </asp:Repeater>
  </form>
</body>
</html>
```

Remember that the Repeater, like all bound controls, can be bound to any list element, not just the Hashtable.

Note, too, that nothing about the Repeater control necessitates outputting data in an HTML table; you can use the Repeater to render data as a comma-delimited list or as a single-column list with line break (BR) elements, for example.

Table Class

Member of System.Web.UI.WebControls.

The Table class is the ASP.NET server control abstraction of the HTML TABLE element.

Properties

AccessKey	CssClass	Rows
Attributes	Enabled	Site
BackColor	EnableViewState	Style
BackImageUrl	Events	TabIndex
BackColor	Font	TagKey
BorderStyle	ForeColor	TagName
BorderWidth	GridLines	TemplateSourceDirectory
CellPadding	HasChildViewState	ToolTip
CellSpacing	Height	UniqueID
ChildControlsCreated	HorizontalAlign	ViewState
ClientID	ID	ViewStateIgnoresCase
Context	IsTrackingViewState	Visible
Controls	NamingContainer	Width
ControlStyle	Page	
ControlStyleCreated	Parent	

Methods

AddAttributesToRender	FindControl	OnItemCreated
AddParsedSubObject	Finalize	OnItemDataBound
ApplyStyle	GetHashCode	OnLoad
ClearChildViewState	GetType	OnPreRender
CopyBaseAttributes	HasControls	OnUnload
ClearChildViewState	IsLiteralContent	RaiseBubbleEvent
AddParsedSubObject	LoadViewState	Render
ClearChildViewState	MapPathSecure	RenderChildren
CreateChildControls	MemberwiseClone	RenderControl
CreateControlCollection	MergeStyle	ResolveUrl
DataBind	OnBubbleEvent	SaveViewState
Dispose	OnDataBinding	ToString
Equals	OnInit	TrackViewState
EnsureChildControls	OnItemCommand	

TableCell Class

Member of System.Web.UI.WebControls.

The TableCell class is the ASP.NET server control abstraction of the HTML TD element.

Properties

AccessKey	Enabled	Site
Attributes	EnableViewState	Style
BackColor	Events	TabIndex
BackColor	Font	TagKey
BorderStyle	ForeColor	TagName
BorderWidth	HasChildViewState	TemplateSourceDirectory
ChildControlsCreated	Height	Text
ClientID	HorizontalAlign	ToolTip
ColumnSpan	ID	UniqueID
Context	IsTrackingViewState	VerticalAlign
Controls	NamingContainer	ViewState
ControlStyle	Page	ViewStateIgnoresCase
ControlStyleCreated	Parent	Visible
CssClass	RowSpan	Width

Methods

AddAttributesToRender	FindControl	OnItemCreated
AddParsedSubObject	Finalize	OnItemDataBound
ApplyStyle	GetHashCode	OnLoad
ClearChildViewState	GetType	OnPreRender
CopyBaseAttributes	HasControls	OnUnload
ClearChildViewState	IsLiteralContent	RaiseBubbleEvent
AddParsedSubObject	LoadViewState	Render
ClearChildViewState	MapPathSecure	RenderBeginTag
CreateChildControls	MemberwiseClone	RenderChildren
CreateControlCollection	MergeStyle	RenderControl
DataBind	OnBubbleEvent	ResolveUrl
Dispose	OnDataBinding	SaveViewState
Equals	OnInit	ToString
EnsureChildControls	OnItemCommand	TrackViewState

TableRow Class

Member of System.Web.UI.WebControls.

The TableRow class is the ASP.NET server control abstraction of the HTML TR element.

Properties

AccessKey	Enabled	Site
Attributes	EnableViewState	Style
BackColor	Events	TabIndex
BackColor	Font	TagKey
BorderStyle	ForeColor	TagName
BorderWidth	HasChildViewState	TemplateSourceDirectory
ChildControlsCreated	Height	Text
ClientID	HorizontalAlign	ToolTip
ColumnSpan	ID	UniqueID
Context	IsTrackingViewState	VerticalAlign
Controls	NamingContainer	ViewState
ControlStyle	Page	ViewStateIgnoresCase
ControlStyleCreated	Parent	Visible
CssClass	RowSpan	Width

Methods

AddAttributesToRender	FindControl	OnItemCreated
AddParsedSubObject	Finalize	OnItemDataBound
ApplyStyle	GetHashCode	OnLoad
ClearChildViewState	GetType	OnPreRender
CopyBaseAttributes	HasControls	OnUnload
ClearChildViewState	IsLiteralContent	RaiseBubbleEvent
AddParsedSubObject	LoadViewState	Render
ClearChildViewState	MapPathSecure	RenderBeginTag
CreateChildControls	MemberwiseClone	RenderChildren
CreateControlCollection	MergeStyle	RenderControl
DataBind	OnBubbleEvent	ResolveUrl
Dispose	OnDataBinding	SaveViewState
Equals	OnInit	ToString
EnsureChildControls	OnItemCommand	TrackViewState

TextBox Class

Member of System.Web.UI.WebControls.

The TextBox class is the ASP.NET server control abstraction of both the HTML INPUT-type textbox as well as the TEXTAREA element.

Properties

AccessKey	EnableViewState	Style
Attributes	Events	TabIndex
AutoPostBack	Font	TagKey
BackColor	ForeColor	TagName
BackColor	HasChildViewState	TemplateSourceDirectory
BorderStyle	Height	Text
BorderWidth	HorizontalAlign	TextMode
ChildControlsCreated	ID	ToolTip
ClientID	IsTrackingViewState	UniqueID
ColumnSpan	MaxLength	VerticalAlign
Context	NamingContainer	ViewState
Controls	Page	ViewStateIgnoresCase
ControlStyle	Parent	Visible

Properties

ControlStyleCreated	ReadOnly	Width
CssClass	RowSpan	Wrap
Enabled	Site	

Methods

AddAttributesToRender	FindControl	OnItemCreated
AddParsedSubObject	Finalize	OnItemDataBound
ApplyStyle	GetHashCode	OnLoad
ClearChildViewState	GetType	OnPreRender
CopyBaseAttributes	HasControls	OnUnload
ClearChildViewState	IsLiteralContent	RaiseBubbleEvent
AddParsedSubObject	LoadViewState	Render
ClearChildViewState	MapPathSecure	RenderBeginTag
CreateChildControls	MemberwiseClone	RenderChildren
CreateControlCollection	MergeStyle	RenderControl
DataBind	OnBubbleEvent	ResolveUrl
Dispose	OnDataBinding	SaveViewState
Equals	OnInit	ToString
EnsureChildControls	OnItemCommand	TrackViewState

WebControl Class

Member of System.Web.UI.Webcontrol. Abstract class.

The WebControl class serves as the base class for Web controls.

Properties

AccessKey	Enabled	Style
Attributes	EnableViewState	TabIndex
BackColor	Events	TagKey
BorderColor	Font	TagName
BorderStyle	ForeColor	TemplateSourceDirectory
BorderWidth	HasChildViewState	ToolTip
ChildControlsCreated	Height	UniqueID
ClientID	ID	ViewState
Context	IsTrackingViewState	ViewStateIgnoresCase

Properties

Controls	NamingContainer	Visible
ControlStyle	Page	Width
ControlStyleCreated	Parent	
CssClass	Site	

Methods

AddAttributesToRender	FindControl	OnUnload
AddParsedSubObject	FindControl	RaiseBubbleEvent
ApplyStyle	GetHashCode	Render
BuildProfileTree	GetType	RenderBeginTag
ClearChildViewState	HasControls	RenderChildren
CopyBaseAttributes	IsLiteralContent	RenderContents
CreateChildControls	LoadViewState	RenderControl
CreateControlCollection	MemberwiseClone	RenderEndTag
CreateControlStyle	MergeStyle	ResolveUrl
DataBind	OnBubbleEvent	SaveViewState
Dispose	OnDataBinding	SetRenderMethodDelegate
EnsureChildControls	OnInit	ToString
Equals	OnLoad	TrackViewState
Finalize	OnPreRender	

Events

DataBinding	Init	PreRender
Disposed	Load	Unload

3

PAGE FRAMEWORK

Debugging ASP.NET Applications

IN THIS CHAPTER

Debugging ASP.old applications was generally only slightly less painful than a trip to the dentist. There was a way to debug ASP.old applications, but it was poorly documented and essentially required Visual InterDev and a team of crack technicians, as well as favorable weather conditions and a whole lot of luck to work correctly.

Many ASP.old developers got into the habit of using code like the following as a way of creating breakpoints in their code:

```
Response.Write "DEBUG: Maybe this will work now."
Response.End
```

This is about the least-efficient kind of debugging code you can possibly write. It's the coding equivalent of driving a car off a cliff just to lift up the hood. At the very least, you should have a way of figuring out what's going on in your application without having to stop its execution.

It should come as no surprise, then, that ASP.NET recognized the severe shortcomings in debugging Web applications and came up with a number of compelling solutions. In ASP.NET, you can perform various useful and detailed inspections into the inner workings of your running applications.

Debugging and tracing in ASP.NET applications doesn't require Visual Studio .NET. (This book doesn't assume you have Visual Studio, either.)

We'll begin our exploration of debugging ASP.NET applications with a discussion of tracing and then move on to debugging and other diagnostic services provided by ASP.NET and the .NET framework.

Tracing Your Web Application's Activity

Tracing is a new feature of ASP.NET that enables you to monitor the activity of your application as it runs. Tracing requires three steps:

1. Equipping a page for tracing
2. Turning tracing on
3. Executing your Web application in Trace mode

When you have gone through these three steps, you'll be able to see the results of the execution of each line of code on each page of your ASP.NET application.

Equipping a Page for Tracing

Any ASP.NET page can run in Trace mode. In fact, you technically don't have to explicitly equip a page for tracing to benefit from Trace mode. But equipping a page for tracing enables you to insert custom markers in the trace output, so it's common to include them in all but the most trivial ASP.NET pages. Even better, Trace mode can be turned on and off on at the page level or the application level, so you never need to remove the code that equips a page for tracing. Trace code won't affect performance of your application when tracing is turned off, and you'll never have to worry about your embarrassing ad hoc test output making its way to users because you forgot to comment something out.

> **NOTE**
>
> The Trace object used in ASP.NET is an instance of the TraceContext class, found in the System.Web namespace. (This class is different from the Trace class found in the System.Diagnostics namespace; TraceContext is specific to ASP.NET.)
>
> The properties, methods, and events of the TraceContext class are summarized in the reference section at the end of this chapter.

To equip a page for Trace mode, you make calls to the Write method of the Trace object anyplace in your code you want to receive trace notification. For example, you may be debugging a function that does not appear to be called during the lifetime of the page. By placing a call to Trace.Write somewhere in the body of the function, you can easily determine whether the function is being called.

> **NOTE**
>
> Because the Trace object is created implicitly by the ASP.NET Page object, you don't need to instantiate it yourself.

Listing 4.1 shows an example of a simple page that is equipped for tracing.

LISTING 4.1   A Simple Page Equipped for Tracing with Calls to Trace.Write

```
<% @Page language="VB" debug="true" trace="true" %>
<html>
<HEAD>
<TITLE>ASP.NET DataList Control</TITLE>

<SCRIPT runat="server">

    Sub Page_Load(sender As Object, e As EventArgs)
      Trace.Write("Page_Load starting.")
      If Not IsPostBack Then
        Trace.Write("IsPostBack is false; creating data source.")
        Dim h As Hashtable = new Hashtable()
```

Listing 4.1 Continued

```
      h.Add ("SF", "San Francisco")
      h.Add ("AZ", "Arizona")
      h.Add ("CO", "Colorado")
      h.Add ("SD", "San Diego")
      h.Add ("LA", "Los Angeles")

      Trace.Write("Data binding.")
      DataList1.DataSource = h
      DataList1.DataBind
    End If
    Trace.Write("Page_Load ending.")
  End Sub

</script>

<body>

  <form runat=server>

    <asp:DataList id="DataList1" runat="server"
        BorderColor="black"
        BorderWidth="1"
        CellPadding="3"
        Font-Name="Verdana"
        Font-Size="8pt">

      <HeaderStyle BackColor="#000000" ForeColor="#FFFF99">
      </HeaderStyle>

      <AlternatingItemStyle BackColor="#FFFF99">
      </AlternatingItemStyle>

      <HeaderTemplate>

        National League West

      </HeaderTemplate>

      <ItemTemplate>

        <%# DataBinder.Eval(Container.DataItem, "Value") %>
        [<%# DataBinder.Eval(Container.DataItem, "Key") %>]

      </ItemTemplate>
```

LISTING 4.1   Continued

```
   </asp:DataList>

  </form>
</body>
</html>
```

You may recognize this page as the DataList example from Chapter 3, "Page Framework." (Book authors enjoy recycling their own code as much as any programmers do.) This version of the code includes calls to Trace.Write to indicate the status of the Page_Load event procedure.

You can see the output of this trace simply by navigating to this page in a browser. The normal page code executes and a voluminous amount of trace information is disgorged to the bottom of the page. Under the heading Trace Information you should be able to see a number of page-generated trace items (such as Begin Init and End Init) as well as the page's own custom trace messages (such as Page_Load starting).

Categorizing Trace Output

You can assign a category to the trace output generated by your code. Categorizing trace output can make it easier to sort out trace messages; it's particularly useful when you view output in SortByCategory mode (described in the next section).

You assign a category to a trace message by using an overloaded version of the Trace.Write method. Listing 4.2 shows an example of this.

LISTING 4.2   Creating Categorized Trace.Write Output

```
Sub Page_Load(sender As Object, e As EventArgs)
  Trace.Write("My Application", "Page_Load starting.")
  If Not IsPostBack Then
    Trace.Write("My Application", "IsPostBack is false;" & _
                " creating data source.")
    Dim h As Hashtable = new Hashtable()
    h.Add ("SF", "San Francisco")
    h.Add ("AZ", "Arizona")
    h.Add ("CO", "Colorado")
    h.Add ("SD", "San Diego")
    h.Add ("LA", "Los Angeles")

    Trace.Write("Data binding.")
    DataList1.DataSource = h
    DataList1.DataBind
```

4

DEBUGGING
ASP.NET
APPLICATIONS

LISTING 4.2 Continued

```
    End If
    Trace.Write("My Application", "Page_Load ending.")
End Sub
```

This is a slightly altered version of the Page_Load event procedure from the previous code example. The only difference is in the pair of strings passed to Trace.Write. When using this form of the method, the first string becomes the category and the second string is the trace message. You can view the trace category alongside the other trace information by viewing the page in Trace mode, as described in the next section.

Enabling Tracing for a Page

You can turn tracing on for a particular page by using an @Page directive. To do this, set the Trace attribute in the @Page directive to truc.

```
<@ Page language='VB' trace="true" %>
```

Two Trace modes specify how trace output is sorted—by time or by category.

You control the Trace mode by using the TraceMode attribute in the @Page directive. To sort Trace mode information by category, set the TraceMode attribute to SortByCategory. The default setting, SortByTime, sorts the trace output by time, oldest to newest.

When tracing is activated at the page level, a wealth of information is displayed at the bottom of the normal page output. (Depending on what's normally supposed to be displayed on the page, you may have to scroll down to see the trace information.)

Trace information is divided into the following categories:

- Request details—This includes the session ID assigned to the user's session by ASP.NET, the time the request was made, the encoding used in the request and response, the HTTP type, and the HTTP status code.
- Trace information—This includes trace information automatically generated by ASP.NET, as well as custom trace items generated by calls to Trace.Write from your code. Included in this information is a measurement of how long each operation took to complete. You can use this information to determine where performance bottlenecks exist in the execution of your page.
- A control tree—This is a hierarchical display of all the controls on the page.
- A list of cookies transferred by the request—Unless you have cookie-based sessions turned off in your application, typically at least one cookie will be transferred per request (the cookie used to identify the user's session).

- HTTP headers—These are sent by the server to the browser.
- Query string values—Values requested by the browser.
- HTTP server variables—A list of all HTTP server variables sent by the server to the browser.

Page-based tracing is useful for performance and debugging purposes. But if you're interested in seeing aggregated tracing information—perhaps to determine how multiple users are accessing elements of an entire Web application—you must use application-level tracing, as described in the next section.

Enabling Tracing in an Application

You can turn tracing on for all the pages in a Web application. To do this, you must make a change in Web.config. Listing 4.3 shows an example of a Web.config settings file that activates tracing.

LISTING 4.3   Using the Web.config File to Activate Tracing for an Entire Web Directory

```
<configuration>
   <system.web>
      <trace enabled="true"
         requestLimit="15"
         pageOutput="true"
         localOnly="true" />
   <system.web>
</configuration>
```

In addition to the enabled and pageOutput settings, you can see that the trace configuration settings in Web.config contain a few options that aren't available in the debug settings found in the @Page directive. Specifically, the requestLimit attribute enables you to limit the number of trace requests stored on the server. This option is meaningful when you view aggregate trace information from a remote browser window, as described in the next section.

The localOnly attribute ensures that trace information can be viewed only by users logged on to the Web server machine directly. This prevents remote users from seeing trace output.

For more information on how Web.config works, see Chapter 6, "Configuration and Deployment."

Using Application Tracing from a Remote Browser Window

When application-level tracing is activated, you can view aggregate trace data from a separate browser window. This gives you an aggregate view of all trace information generated by your Web application.

4

To do this, first equip the application for tracing by adjusting the appropriate settings in Web.config (as described in the previous section).

Next, open two browser windows: one to view a page equipped for tracing in the application; the second to display trace output. (We'll call this second window the trace window.)

In the trace window, navigate to the HTTP handler trace.axd located in the application directory. For example, if your application is located at `http://localhost/myapp/`, the Trace mode URL would be `http://localhost/myapp/trace.axd`. You should be able to see a list of application requests. The list may or may not have any data in it, depending on whether you've refreshed the browser that displays the application page since you started the trace.

After refreshing the application browser a few times, refresh the trace window. You should be able to see a list of trace information. If you navigate to another page in the application and then refresh the trace window, you'll be able to see trace information for that page, too.

You can see that the trace window displays only aggregate information. Further, the number of requests displayed in the window is limited to the number you specified in the Web.config trace setting for the application. You can drill down each row of information by clicking the View Details link; this displays the same detailed information you see when viewing a single page in Trace mode.

> **NOTE**
>
> Trace.axd isn't a file; instead, it's a link to an ASP.NET feature known as an HTTP handler. You can use the .NET framework to create your own HTTP handlers; this is discussed in Chapter 9, "HttpHandlers and HttpModules."

Debugging ASP.NET Applications

The large number of ASP.old programmers migrating their code to ASP.NET ensures that error messages are one of the first things an ASP.NET programmer will typically see. Fortunately, not only is the debugging information provided by ASP.NET much better than ASP.old, but you have much more granular control over how debugging information is displayed in ASP.NET.

An ASP.NET debug page is displayed when an unhandled error is encountered, as long as the appropriate @Page or Web.config settings exist. The output of the page is composed of:

- The application (or Web directory) where the error took place
- The type of error and a description of the error
- Details of the error from the compiler

- Source code displaying where the error took place in your code
- The file in which the error took place
- Links to detailed compiler output and complete source code
- Version information for the .NET runtime and ASP.NET

This rich debugging information isn't turned on by default, however. To access rich debugging information, you must turn debugging on, either at the page level (using an attribute of the @Page directive) or for the entire application (using a setting in Web.config).

Enabling Debugging at the Page Level

You can enable debugging at the page level by using an @Page directive.

```
<@ Page language="VB" debug="True" %>
```

Don't try testing this by creating an incorrectly coded ASP.NET page and loading it on local-host. Errors on the local machine always create debug information. The debug settings control what users on remote machines see. To test debug settings, you'll need to access your error page on a machine other than the Web server machine.

In case you haven't created one of your own already, Listing 4.4 contains an ASP.NET page that contains a bona fide error. You can use this page to test the way ASP.NET generates debug output code.

LISTING 4.4   The First Mistake That Most ASP.NET Programmers Generally Make

```
<% @Page language="VB" debug="false" %>
<HTML>
<HEAD>
<TITLE>ASP.NET Error Page</TITLE>

<SCRIPT runat='server'>
  Sub Page_Load(Sender As Object, e As EventArgs)
    Response.Write "This code will not work."
  End Sub
</SCRIPT>

</HEAD>

<BODY>

  This is my page. There are many others like it, but this one is mine.

</BODY>
</HTML>
```

4

Note that this page has its Debug mode set to `false`. When you first load it (from a remote machine, remember), you'll get a message indicating that something is wrong with the code on the page. But the output won't display any additional information about the error; in particular, the source code display is suppressed. This is an extremely helpful security feature that ensures your source code won't be displayed in an error condition unless you specifically permit it through an @Page attribute setting or a debug setting in Web.config.

Enabling Debugging at the Application Level

Turning debugging on and off at the page level is easy enough when you're making changes to only a few pages. But early in the development process, when nothing works, you may want to be able to turn Debug mode on for every page in your application.

You can turn debugging on for all the pages in a given folder by changing a setting in the Web.config file in that folder. You can activate Debug mode at the application level by setting the Debug attribute of the compilation section in Web.config.

Listing 4.5 shows an example of a Web.config file that activates debugging for an entire application.

LISTING 4.5   A Web.config File That Activates Debugging at the Application Level

```
<configuration>
   <system.web>
      <customErrors mode="Off" />
      <compilation defaultLanguage="VB"
         debug="true"
         numRecompilesBeforeAppRestart="15">
      </compilation>
   </system.web>
</configuration>
```

That's it. Remember that when you test this option, it's meaningful only when you're debugging the application from a remote machine. Debug mode is always on when you're logging in to the Web application from localhost.

Using the Debug Object

The .NET framework provides a Debug object that you can use to assist with debugging your application. The Debug object is a member of System.Diagnostics.Debug. An instance of this object is created for you automatically, so you shouldn't ever need to instantiate it yourself. If you used the Debug object in Visual Basic, the .NET framework Debug object should be familiar to you.

> **NOTE**
>
> A complete reference to the properties and methods of the Debug object appears at the reference section at the end of this chapter.

The Write method is the most common member of Debug you'll use in your day-to-day programming. By using Debug.Write, you can send information to the development environment you run your ASP.NET application in. If you're using Visual Studio, the strings you send to Debug.Write are displayed in the Output window. (You can view them by running your Web application and then selecting View, Other Windows, Output, or by using the keyboard shortcut Ctrl+Alt+O.)

Listing 4.6 shows a typical call to Debug.Write, used to indicate that an ASP.NET page has loaded and its Page_Load event procedure has been entered.

LISTING 4.6   Placing a Call to Debug.Write to Display Debug Information in the Development Environment

```
Private Sub Page_Load(Sender As Object, e As EventArgs)
  Debug.Write("Application initializing. Poot.")
End Sub
```

If you're not using Visual Studio or another integrated development environment to run and debug your ASP.NET application, calls to Debug.Write will go nowhere. A development environment must be present for the output generated by Debug.Write to be meaningful; if you need to send real-time debug information while your application is running, consider using Trace.Write (described earlier in this chapter) or a custom performance monitor (described in the next section).

Creating Custom Performance Monitors

A *performance monitor* is a feature of the Windows NT/2000 operating system used to determine operating system resource consumption in real-time. In Windows, performance monitors track such statistics as the amount of processing time being consumed on the system, how much memory is free, and how many times the hard disk is accessed. Software subsystems that run on the server can have their own performance monitors, as well: ASP.NET and SQL Server have their own set of performance monitors that broadcast meaningful information to the operating system about resources consumed by these services.

Any .NET application can be equipped with performance monitors that you create yourself, called *custom performance monitors*. To expose performance information to the operating system, an application must be equipped to do so.

Running the Windows Performance Monitor Utility

You may have used the Perfmon tool to view the status of various performance monitors on a Windows NT or 2000 server. This tool is found in Windows 2000 under Programs, Administrative Tools, Performance. If you've never used Perfmon before, you can see how it works by running it and then right-clicking its main window and selecting Add Counters from the pop-up menu.

After you do this, a Counters dialog box appears, containing lists of every performance-monitor-equipped application installed on your machine. We'll assume you have ASP.NET installed on your computer, so select the ASP.NET Applications category from the list labeled Performance Object. Then select the Anonymous Requests/Sec counter from the list of counters. Finally, click Add to add this counter to your view.

You should notice that the chart begins ticking off the number of requests, which should hover close to zero unless you happen to be performing these experiments on a production Web server (if so—shame, shame). To generate some activity for this performance monitor, simply launch a browser and navigate to an ASPX page (*not* an ASP page) on localhost. Reload the page in the browser a few times by pressing Ctrl+F5, and then flip back to the Performance window. You should be able to see a modest spike in the number of requests per second.

Creating Performance Monitor Categories

The first step in creating a custom performance monitor is to create your own performance monitor category. Performance monitor categories appear in Perfmon's Performance Object drop-down list; they exist as a way to organize the many performance monitors that can exist on a server.

> **NOTE**
>
> The system provides a number of performance monitor categories, such as Memory, Processor, and so forth. You're not allowed to create performance monitors in these categories. To create a custom performance monitor, you must create your own performance monitor category first.

To create a new performance monitor category, call the Create method of the PerformanceCounterCategory object. This object is a member of System.Diagnostics, so you may want to import that namespace into your application to work with it.

PerformanceCounterCategory.Create is an overloaded method. One particularly useful form of the method call enables you to create a performance category and a performance object at the same time. This initializes everything you need to begin performance monitoring with only a few lines of code.

Listing 4.7 shows a procedure that creates a performance category called My Category and an associated performance monitor in that category called My Counter.

LISTING 4.7   Initializing a New Performance Monitor Category and Performance Monitor Object

```
Sub btnCreateCategory_Click(Sender As Object, e As EventArgs)
   Dim pfc As New PerformanceCounterCategory()
   pfc.Create("My Category", "A category just for me", "My Counter", & _
             "A counter just for me")
   Label1.Text = "Performance category created."
End Sub
```

This form of the PerformanceCounterCategory.Create method takes the following four strings as parameters:

- The name of the new category you want to create
- A text string that describes the category
- The name of the new performance monitor you want to create
- A text string that describes the new performance monitor object

After you run this code, your new performance monitor category and performance monitor object are created. Note that if you attempt to run this code twice, you'll get an exception. Also, if you're running Perfmon in the background when this code is executed, you'll need to shut down and restart Perfmon to get it to recognize the new category and performance monitor.

Sending Information to a Performance Monitor from Your Application

To provide information about your application to performance monitors, you first create an instance of the PerformanceCounter object.

4

DEBUGGING
ASP.NET
APPLICATIONS

> **NOTE**
>
> The properties, methods, and events of the PerformanceCounter class are summarized in the reference section at the end of this chapter.

Performance counters always represent some kind of integer count related to the performance of the operation being monitored. After you've created a PerformanceCounter object, you have a choice about how you want to send information to it. You can increment and decrement the integer count using the Increment and Decrement methods of the PerformanceCounter object.

Listing 4.8 shows an example of incrementing the performance counter in response to a button click.

LISTING 4.8   Incrementing a Performance Monitor Using a PerformanceCounter Object

```
Sub Increment_Click(Sender As System.Object, ByVal e As System.EventArgs)
Handles Increment.Click
  Dim pc As New PerformanceCounter()
  With pc
    .CategoryName = "My Category"
    .CounterName = "My Counter"
    .ReadOnly = False
  End With

  pc.Increment()

End Sub
```

Remember that you must create the performance monitor and its category (described in the previous section) before you can run this code. You can see how this code works by running it while Perfmon is running in the background. If you have set up a counter for this performance monitor, you should be able to see the graph increase each time you click the button.

In addition to incrementing and decrementing the performance counter object, you can also increase or decrease the value of the counter using the IncrementBy or DecrementBy methods. You can also get or set the raw value of the performance counter by using the RawValue property of the PerformanceCounter object.

Deleting Performance Monitor Categories

You can delete a performance monitor category by executing the Delete method of the PerformanceCounterCategory object. Listing 4.9 shows an example.

LISTING 4.9   Deleting a Performance Category

```
Sub btnDeleteCategory_Click(Sender As Object, ByVal e As EventArgs)
  Dim pfc As New PerformanceCounterCategory()
  pfc.Delete("My Category")
End Sub
```

Deleting a performance category deletes all performance monitors associated with that category. If Perfmon is running when you delete a performance category, it will continue monitoring that category; you must shut down and restart Perfmon to see the change.

Writing to the Windows Event Log

It's common for server software to persistently record information about what it's doing. This activity is called *logging*. It's common for programmers to spend time creating logging features in the applications they write—both as a debugging tool and as a way for users and system administrators to see what's going on with the software. However, Windows programmers typically don't create their own logging facilities in the applications they create, because the operating system provides one for them: the Windows event log.

The Windows event log is a central, system-managed place where any application, service, or device can log information. It is available on Windows NT and Windows 2000. Logged events usually contain status information or failure messages. You are free to use the event log from any of your applications, including ASP.NET applications, as a way of persistently storing information pertaining to your application's behavior in a way that's easy for system administrators to access.

> **NOTE**
>
> Logging serves a similar function to performance monitoring (discussed earlier in this chapter). But it differs in the area of how the data is stored. Monitoring is a real-time view of what your application is doing at any given moment. Monitoring information is stored in memory and does not normally survive a system reboot. Logging, on the other hand, is persisted to disk and provides a historical record of your server application's behavior over a long period of time.

4

DEBUGGING
ASP.NET
APPLICATIONS

In Windows 2000 Server, you can access the event log through the Event Viewer application found in the Administrative Tools group under the Start menu. Events are divided into three categories: application, security, and system. Your application can read from any log and write information to the application log, as described in the next section.

Using the EventLog Class

Any application, including ASP.NET applications, can access the event log. Your applications will write information to the application log (rather than to the security or system logs).

The .NET framework provides a class for handling the event log. This is the EventLog class, found in System.Diagnostics.

> **NOTE**
>
> The properties, methods, and events of the EventLog class are summarized in the reference section at the end of this chapter.

To send information to the application log, you use the EventLog class. This class is created for you automatically in Visual Basic, so you do not need to instantiate it (although you can if you need to).

To perform logging, you first use the EventLog object to create an *event source*. An event source is a way of identifying where a log entry came from. Many data sources can write to the same log; for example, many applications typically write error messages to the application log, and a variety of server processes create entries in the system log.

Event sources must be registered before you write information to the log. You do this by calling the CreateEventSource method of the EventLog object.

> **NOTE**
>
> For applications you create, unless you have a really good reason to create your own log, it's probably best to toss your own logs into the application log with everything else. That's where system administrators will look for it.
>
> Only the first eight characters of a log name are significant. This means you can't create a log named, for instance, Application Data, because Application is a built-in log created by Windows.

Listing 4.10 shows an example of how to write information to the Windows event log. This code first checks to see if an event source called MyApp exists; if not, the code creates it. The code then sends information to the event log by calling the WriteEntry method of the EventLog object.

LISTING 4.10   Writing an Event to the Windows Event Log

```
Sub Button1_Click(Sender As Object, e As EventArgs)
  If Not EventLog.SourceExists("MyApp") Then
    EventLog.CreateEventSource("MyApp", "Application")
  End If

  EventLog.WriteEntry("MyApp", "This is just a test.", _
                      EventLogEntryType.Information)
End Sub
```

The WriteEntry method is overloaded; the code example shows the most commonly used form.
The first parameter is a string representing the event source. The second parameter is the message to insert in the log. The third parameter is an event type; this is a member of the enumeration System.Diagnostics.EventLogEntryType.

You can view the output of this code by launching the Event Viewer (found in Programs,
Administrative Tools). After running the code, click Application Log. You should be able to see
an Information entry for the MyApp event source. Double-clicking the event displays a property sheet that shows you the detail for the event (the description "This is just a test").

Reference

This section provides a quick reference to the key objects described in this chapter. Space constraints prevent us from documenting every object in the .NET framework in this book. For the
sake of brevity and conciseness, we include only the most important objects here. For more
information on the other objects in the .NET framework, consult the .NET Framework
Reference online help file.

This chapter covers the debugging, performance-monitoring, and event-logging classes in
ASP.NET. The following sections provide a brief reference to the properties, methods, and
events provided by those classes.

Debug Class

Member of System.Diagnostics.

The Debug object gives developers access to a number of useful tools to manage the debugging process.

It is not necessary to instantiate a Debug object in Visual Basic; an instance of the object is
always available.

Properties

AutoFlush	IndentSize
IndentLevel	Listeners

Methods

Assert	Indent	WriteLine
Close	Unindent	WriteLineIf
Fail	Write	
Flush	WriteIf	

EventLog Class

Member of System.Diagnostics.

The EventLog class is used to read and write information from the Windows event log. This is used primarily to record diagnostic information pertaining to an application, particularly failure information.

Properties

Container	Events	Site
DesignMode	Log	Source
EnableRaisingEvents	LogDisplayName	SynchronizingObject
Entries	MachineName	

Methods

BeginInit	EndInit	InitializeLifetimeService
Clear	Equals	LogNameFromSourceName
Close	Exists	MemberwiseClone
CreateEventSource	Finalize	SourceExists
CreateObjRef	GetEventLogs	ToString
Delete	GetHashCode	WriteEntry
DeleteEventSource	GetLifetimeService	WriteEntry
Dispose	GetService	
Dispose	GetType	

Events

Disposed	EntryWritten

PerformanceCounter Class

Member of System.Diagnostics.

You create an instance of this class to expose your application's performance information to performance monitors.

Properties

CategoryName	CounterType	MachineName
Container	DesignMode	RawValue
CounterHelp	Events	ReadOnly
CounterName	InstanceName	Site

Methods

BeginInit	Equals	InitializeLifetimeService
Close	Finalize	MemberwiseClone
CloseSharedResource	GetHashCode	NextSample
CreateObjRef	GetLifetimeService	NextValue
Decrement	GetService	RemoveInstance
Dispose	GetType	ToString
Dispose	Increment	
EndInit	IncrementBy	

Events

Disposed

TraceContext Class

Member of System.Web.

TraceContext provides Trace mode functionality in ASP.NET Web application development. It is typically accessed as the Trace object contained by the ASP.NET Page object.

Properties

IsEnabled	TraceMode

Methods

Equals	GetType	Warn
Finalize	MemberwiseClone	Write
GetHashCode	ToString	

State Management and Caching

IN THIS CHAPTER

State Management: What's the Big Deal?

HTTP by its very nature is a stateless protocol. This doesn't mean it disregards geographic boundaries; it means that it is not connection oriented. No request of the Web server can rely on data supplied by some other request. To understand this concept, let's look at an example of how a browser requests a Web page.

When a user types in the address of a Web site, www.vergentsoftware.com/default.aspx, for example, the Web browser performs a number of steps prior to displaying the page. First, the Web browser converts the hostname, in this case www, to an IP address. It does this by querying a DNS server and asking for the IP address. In our sample this brings back 192.168.1.200. Next, the Web browser opens a TCP socket to the Web server using port 80. After the connection is made, the Web browser sends a GET /default.asp command. The Web server streams the HTML contents of the page back to the browser. The Web server then closes the TCP socket connection to the Web browser.

> **NOTE**
>
> HTTP 1.1 allows more than one command to be sent without closing the socket connection. This is called Keep-Alive. However, each command stands on its own and should not rely on any state from previous commands.

This series of events is visibly demonstrated by using Telnet instead of a Web browser to communicate with a Web server. Listing 5.1 shows what this would look like.

Listing 5.1   A Sample HTTP Request Using Telnet

```
GET /DEFAULT.ASPX
HTTP/1.1 200 OK
Server: Microsoft-IIS/5.0
Date: Wed, 28 Mar 2001 00:38:29 GMT
Set-Cookie: ASP.NET_SessionId=sfdaa145jb0mdv55nnhgic55; path=/
Cache-Control: private
Content-Type: text/html; charset=iso-8859-1
Content-Length: 130


<html>
<head>
<title>Welcome to ASP.NET</title>
<body>
Welcome to ASP.NET!
```

LISTING 5.1   Continued

```
<img src="/image1.jpg"><img src="/image2.jpg">
</body>
</html>
```

```
Connection to host lost.
```

To replicate this example in Windows 2000, open up a command prompt and type the following:

TELNET localhost 80

This will open up the Telnet connection to your Web server. Now you need to request a page. If you have the default Internet Information Server installation, you can do a GET /localstart.asp to retrieve the Start page. You must type the command exactly; while in Telnet, the backspace key doesn't work to correct mistakes.

The Web browser receives the HTML, parses it, and is then ready to receive additional requests. In this example, two more requests would need to be made: one for image1.jpg and another for image2.jpg. Each request causes another TCP socket connection to be made over port 80 and then a GET /image1.jpg command to be sent. The Web server streams back the image and then closes the port. A diagram of this process is shown in Figure 5.1.

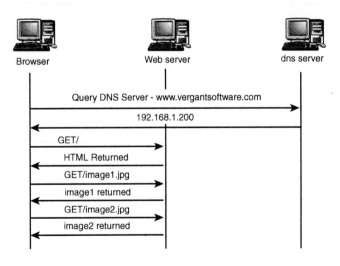

FIGURE 5.1

Steps in a standard browser request.

5

STATE
MANAGEMENT
AND CACHING

Note that after each request, the Web server terminates the socket connection. The connection does not exist across multiple requests—it is not connection oriented. Also note that each request must pass to the Web server all information required to satisfy that request. This is fine if all that the ASP code does is take the values from a single form and save them to a database. If the application needs to do something more difficult, such as maintaining a shopping cart, matters are more complicated.

What Are Cookies?

Early in the genesis of the Web, folks working on the HTTP spec realized that there had to be some way to persist state information across Web requests. Cookies were designed for this purpose. If you look again at the code in Listing 5.1, you will notice that a number of headers appear before the HTML. These headers are terminated by a double CRLF before the HTML starts. One of the headers is Set-Cookie:. When an HTTP 1.0-compliant browser sees this header, it assumes responsibility for storing that cookie in whatever fashion it sees fit. Furthermore, the browser is expected to include that cookie value with all future requests it makes of the Web server.

> **NOTE**
>
> This is important. The browser returns the cookie value only to the server that set it, not to other servers. Therefore, a lot of the hype about cookies tracking users across multiple Web sites is nonsense.

User agents (that is, browsers) are expected to accept at least 300 cookies in total with a minimum size of 4KB, but some browsers implement higher limits. Even though the minimum size of 4KB is quite large, cookies were never intended to be a place to cache large amounts of information. Instead, they are intended to be used as a key into state information that is maintained on the server.

For more information on cookies, read RFC 2109 at
http://www.w3.org/Protocols/rfc2109/rfc2109.

Cookie-Based Session Identity

ASP.NET provides a way to maintain state using cookies that is very much in line with the recommendations in RFC 2109. On a user agent's first visit to a page that uses cookies, a cookie is sent to the user agent by the Set-Cookie header in the HTTP page. See Listing 5.2 for an example.

LISTING 5.2   A Typical Set-Cookie Header

```
Set-Cookie: ASP.NET_SessionId=sfdaa145jb0mdv55nnhgic55; path=/
```

This cookie persists for as long as the Web browser is open. This is called a session cookie. If the Web browser is closed, the cookie is lost. The `SessionId` is a 120-bit string containing URL-legal ASCII characters.

It is generated in such a way that it is unique and random. Uniqueness is obviously important. If an application is storing credit card numbers for a shopping cart in session state, it shouldn't accidentally connect a different user to that session! Randomness is a little harder to understand. The `SessionID` should be random so that someone can't calculate the session of someone else who is currently on the server and hijack that person's session. This situation would be just as bad as giving out nonunique `SessionIDs`.

Cookieless Session Identity

Cookie-based session identity is a great idea and uses a feature of HTTP—cookies—that is intended for maintaining state information. Some people got it into their tiny minds that cookies were invented by the same people who track you through the streets using silent black helicopters. An alarmist cry went out and users insisted that cookies are an invasion of their privacy—a way for their viewing habits to be tracked across the Web. They were a way for aliens to read their thoughts. You and I both know better after reading RFC 2109, but people who believe in little green men don't always think rationally.

At about this time, the folks who write Web browsers (such as Internet Explorer 5.5) needed some new features to add to their feature checklists, so they added a feature to disable cookies! This seemed like a great idea, but the problem is that no great way exists for an application to check to see whether cookies are disabled. It can look at the user-agent string to see if the user agent is Internet Explorer 5.5, for example, and then make the assumption that cookies are enabled...but you know what they say about assumptions. If the user has disabled cookies and the application still thinks they are enabled, it is just going to end up re-creating a new session for the user each time he or she visits. Mighty inconvenient.

Because Microsoft writes one of the more popular Web browsers, Internet Explorer, and because the company added features to it to disable cookies, it only seems fitting that several years later Microsoft would upgrade ASP so that there is a way to maintain state without relying on cookies. Hence, cookieless session state was born.

Cookieless session state works by "munging," or modifying, the URL so that the `SessionID` is included as part of the URL. When a user accesses the first page of a site that uses cookieless session state, ASP.NET performs a 302 Redirect back to the same page with the `SessionID`

included in the URL. If, for example, a user types in
http://localhost/simplecounter.aspx, the user is redirected back to
http://localhost/(adu2o155emcqlbme5gofcu45)/simplecounter.aspx. The goofy looking
string between the () is the SessionID and varies for each session. The conversation is shown
in Figure 5.2.

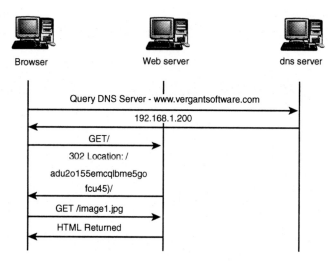

FIGURE 5.2
HTTP conversation establishing SessionID.

To maintain the session state, this SessionID must be included in all future requests to the
Web server. ASP.NET does not alter the application's HTML code and add the SessionID to
the anchor tags. Take a look at the sample page in Listing 5.3.

LISTING 5.3   Sample Page with Relative and Absolute References—RelAbsolute.aspx

```
<% Session("Count") = Session("Count") + 1 %>

<html>
<body>
    <b>Count=</b><% = Session("Count") %>

    <br><a href="http://localhost/simplecounter.aspx">Absolute</a>
    <br><a href="simplecounter.aspx">Relative</a>
    <br><a href="/simplecounter.aspx">Mixed</a>
    <Br><A href="~/simplecounter.aspx">Tilde</a>
</body>
</html>
```

This code shows a page with two anchor tags. When clicked, the first absolute reference loses the `SessionID`. When the absolute reference is requested from ASP.NET, a new session initiation conversation takes place and all session state is lost. In the second anchor tag, the relative reference maintains session state. The Web browser takes the root of the URL from the currently accessed page, `http://localhost/(4ldjqh55tnnq124545dg50ix)/`, and automatically prefixes the URL with it. The request then becomes `http://localhost/(4ldjqh55tnnq124545dg50ix)/simplecounter.aspx`. Because the `SessionID` is passed to the next request, session state is maintained. The third anchor tag in Listing 5.3 is relative to the site but not to the directory structure. In this case the browser takes `http://localhost/` as the prefix and requests `http://localhost/simplecounter.aspx`. This has the same effect as the absolute reference, causing the session initiation conversation to take place again and losing the session state. The fourth tag uses an undocumented feature in ASP.NET. For any server side control that uses an HREF, you can start the HREF with a ~ character. At runtime the tilde will be replaced with the application root and the current directory. This works well for path-independent code that may be reused in multiple pages in your application.

If an application needs to programmatically determine whether cookieless sessions are in use, it can use the `Session.IsCookieless()` method on the `HttpSessionState` object.

Using the Session

When a page starts executing, an event is fired that the Session HTTP Module listens for. The Session module sinks this event and automatically populates the `Session` property if session state is required. Using the session object to store data is very simple. Listing 5.3 shows a simple page that increments a counter each time it is accessed. Listing 5.4 shows how to store a value in the session collection. The key `"Counter"` can be any arbitrary value that the application specifies. The namespace is global within the ASP.NET application.

LISTING 5.4   Setting a Session Value

```
Session("Counter") = 0
```

If the application saved a value, it is probably because the application will need to use it later. Specifying the same key allows the application to retrieve the value, as shown in Listing 5.5.

LISTING 5.5   Getting a Session Value

```
Response.Write(Session("Counter"))
```

That's it. That is the minimum work required to use session state.

Initializing a User's State

When a new session is set up, it might be nice to preload some information about the user into session state. This is easily done by handling the `Session_Start` event. Listing 5.6 shows how to place an event handler in global.asax and store a value into the Session object itself. The example grabs the date and time that the user started up the session and saves it into a Session value called LogonTime.

Listing 5.6 When a Session Starts Up, *Session_Start* Fires

```
<script language="VB" runat=server>
    Sub Session_Start(ByVal Sender As Object, ByVal e As EventArgs)
        Session("LogonTime") = Now
    End Sub

    Sub Session_End(ByVal Sender As Object, ByVal e As EventArgs)

    End Sub

</script>
```

The application can handle the Session_End event, which fires when the session has timed out. It can use this event to clean up things outside session state.

> **Note**
>
> In times of high load, Session_End might not fire.

Cleaning Up After Using Session State

So now you know how to create session state. However, if you are a programmer who obsesses over perfect indenting, you probably wonder what needs to be done to clean up after yourself when using session state. You just saved a bunch of data into process memory, thereby using a valuable resource. What needs to be done to clean this up? As it turns out, the session object already has the concept of a finite lifetime. If you don't clean up after yourself, it takes on the role of your mother and cleans up after you after a specified interval. This interval is controlled using the TimeOut property of HttpSessionState. If a client doesn't access a page in the application for 20 minutes, by default, the session data associated with that SessionID is deleted.

If you still feel the need to clean up after yourself, the Remove methods are for you. Remove() enables you to remove a single item from the Session(). RemoveAll() allows you to remove all items from the session.

Adding Session Values

Now that you understand the basics, let's create a little more interesting example: a page that allows you to add arbitrary sets of information to the session. Listing 5.7 shows a form that allows the user to type in a key and a value and then saves the pair in session state. It then loops through the Session collection to return all the keys in the collection and display all the values.

LISTING 5.7 Adding and Displaying Session Values—AddDisplay.aspx

```vb
<%@ Page Language="VB" %>
<script language="VB" runat=server>
    Sub btnAdd_Click(Sender As Object, e As EventArgs)
        ' Add the Key:Value pair
        Session(txtKey.Text) = txtValue.Text
    End Sub

    Sub btnClear_Click(Sender As Object, e As EventArgs)
        Session.RemoveAll()
    End Sub
</script>

<html>
<body>
    <b>Manipulating Session</b><br>
    <form action="AddRemoveSession.aspx" METHOD="POST" runat=server>
        <asp:label id="lblKey" text="Key:" runat=server />
        <asp:textbox id="txtKey" runat=server />
        <asp:label id="lblValue" text="Value:" runat=server />
        <asp:textbox id="txtValue" runat=server />
        <asp:button id="btnAdd" Text="Add" OnClick="btnAdd_Click"
            runat=server />
        <BR>
        <HR>
            <table border="1">
                <tr>
                    <th>Key</th>
                    <th>Value</th>
                </tr>
<%
            Dim szItem as String

            ' Loop through the session keys
            For Each szItem in Session
                Response.Write("<tr>")
                ' Output the key
```

Listing 5.7 Continued

```
                Response.Write("<td>" + szItem + "</td>")
                ' Output the value
                ' Use ToString() to co-erce possible objects in session to
                ' a string
                Response.Write("<td>" + Session(szItem).ToString() + "</td>")
                Response.Write("</tr>")
            Next
%>

            </table>
            <asp:button id="btnClear" Text="Clear All"
                OnClick="btnClear_Click" runat=server />
        </form>
    </body>
```

Beyond the Default Session Configuration

All the work we have done with session state so far uses the default configuration: in process session state. This is the only option that was available in ASP 3.0. Now three options exist for storing session state in ASP.NET: in process, out of process, and SQL Server.

In Process Session State

In process session state works just as the name implies. The data structure that holds the session information is allocated from memory that belongs to the aspnet_wp.exe process. The advantage to this approach is that access to the data is very quick. It is only slightly different from looking up an item in a collection or array that might be in the program itself. When an object is stored using In Process session state, a reference to the object is actually what is stored.

The disadvantage to this approach is that the life of the session data mirrors the life of its host process. When aspnet_wp.exe shuts down, it behaves like any well-mannered program and cleans up all its data structures, releasing the memory back to the system. At this point the session data ceases to exist.

> **Note**
>
> Editing the global.asax file or Web.Config file and saving it will also clear all the in process session states.

The session data is also trapped inside this process. If an application needs to take advantage of a Web farm approach in order to scale, it could run into trouble. Figure 5.3 illustrates what happens in this case. As Web servers are added to the Web farm, each is going to be running its own copy of aspnet_wp.exe, so each will have its own copy of the current session state.

This means that a user, on first requesting a page, will have that session set up on a particular server, such as Web1. A subsequent request for a page from the same user is not guaranteed to return to Web1; in a Web farm, the request can be routed to a different server. If the subsequent request is directed to a new Web server, Web2, the session state that the first request set up will not be there.

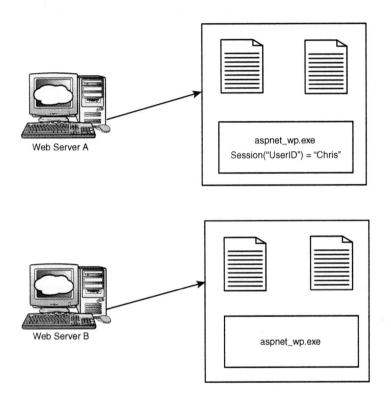

FIGURE 5.3
Web farm using in process session state.

In the figure, a user logs on to Web Server A. The login process saves the UserID in session state for later use. Everything works fine until the user gets transferred over to Web Server B. The UserID is no longer saved as part of session state. The developer must anticipate and solve this problem when using a Web farm.

Session State Using a State Server

To avoid the problems shown in Figure 5.3, the developer needs to come up with a way to move the session state data structures outside the aspnet_wp.exe process. In fact, to solve the Web farm scenario, the session state data structures must be moved entirely outside the Web server. The ASP.NET State Server provides a solution.

The ASP.NET State Server is a Windows service that runs on any machine where ASP.NET is installed. This service hosts the data structures that were in the `aspnet_wp.exe` process before. The advantage of this configuration is that now when `aspnet_wp.exe` shuts down, the process data is no longer in its process space but is on the state server instead, so the data survives the shutdown of the process. This configuration also solves the issue of state that arises as the application is scaled using a Web farm. Figure 5.4 illustrates how moving the session state out of the `aspnet_wp.exe` process allows multiple Web servers to connect to the state server, thereby maintaining a consistent session state across all servers in the farm. One downside of this approach is that storing an object requires you to serialize, or "freeze dry," the object for transfer to the state server. When you later access it, this process must be reversed. This adds some overhead to persisting objects into out of process session state.

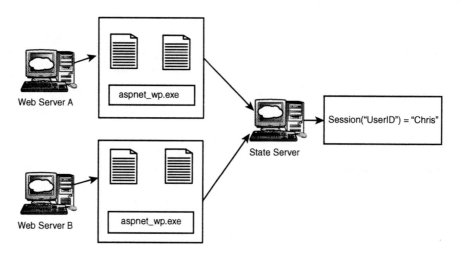

FIGURE 5.4
ASP.NET State Server allows multiple servers to share state.

If one of the Web servers in the Web farm gets rebooted, it comes up and immediately starts sharing in the current session state maintained by the ASP.NET State Server. This is so cool that you might wonder why this isn't the default setting for ASP.NET. Well, moving the data structures out of process comes with a cost. By moving the data to another server, accessing it requires a little more work. Instead of just accessing process memory directly, the `SessionState` class must now connect to a remote server over TCP/IP to access the data. This connection is clearly slower than accessing a memory location.

So how do you change the default for ASP.NET? Like many of the other settings, this one is stored in the Web.Config file in the application root.

> **NOTE**
>
> See Chapter 6, "Configuration and Deployment," for more information on Web.Config.

If you don't have a Web.Config yet, create it using the XML in Listing 5.8.

LISTING 5.8   Sample Web.Config That Enables Out of Process Session State

```
<configuration>
    <system.web>
        <sessionState
            mode="stateserver"
            stateConnectionString="tcpip=127.0.0.1:42424"
            sqlConnectionString="data source=127.0.0.1;user id=sa;password="
            cookieless="false"
            timeout="20"
        />
    </system.web>
</configuration>
```

The mode attribute, by default, is set to inproc. Changing it to state server and saving Web.Config causes all new requests to be directed at the local instance of the state server. This won't work until you fire up the state server. Listing 5.9 shows the command you can use to start this server.

LISTING 5.9   Command to Start State Server

```
Net start "ASP.NET State"
```

If you want to move the state server off the local Web server, you need to change the stateConnectionString attribute in the Web.Config. It is of the form IP Address:Port. Change the IP address from the loopback address of 127.0.0.1 to the IP address of your state server. Finally, fire up or restart the state server.

> IMPORTANT: The ASP.NET State Server performs no authentication. For security purposes you should make sure that you block the port it uses in a firewall in front of your server.

5

STATE
MANAGEMENT
AND CACHING

Storing Session State in SQL Server

By moving the session state out of process, the application is able to work effectively in a Web farm as well as protect itself against restarts of the process or the Web server. In this environment, however, there is now a single point of failure—the state server. In the case of a restart of the box where the state server resides, all the Web servers that rely on it get an instant lobotomy and lose their state information. For some design patterns this might be unacceptable, so a third option exists in ASP.NET: storing the state information in SQL Server.

> **NOTE**
>
> This option is called SQL Server for a reason. It works only with SQL Server and will not work with Oracle, Sybase, or any other database server.

By storing the information in SQL Server, a durable session store is achieved that will survive restarts of every machine in your Web farm, except the database server. With some manual changes to the setup you can even configure it to survive a restart of the SQL Server. Setting up ASP.NET to store session state in SQL Server requires more steps than the other two options. The hardest part really relates to the configuration of the SQL Server.

A script, `InstallSqlState.sql`, is installed with ASP.NET to do all the hard work. This script can be found in the Framework SDK directory on your machine. Under Windows 2000 this would be `c:\winnt\Microsoft.NET\Framework\v1.0.2914` (where the last number is the build number that you have installed). The script creates a database called ASPState that contains only stored procedures. It also creates two tables inside tempdb, called `ASPStateTempApplications` and `ASPStateTempSessions`, that store the session state. See Figure 5.5 for the database schema.

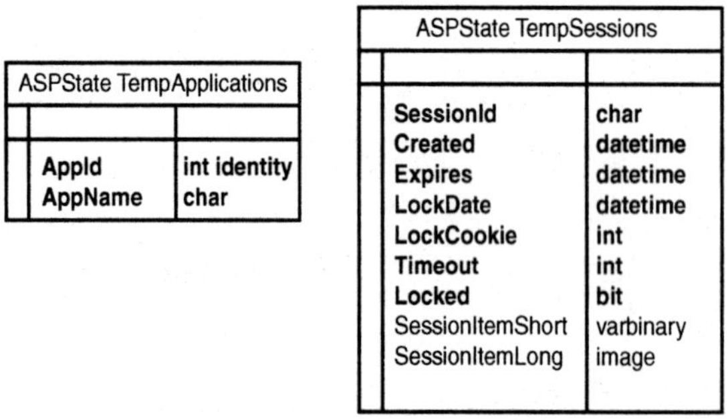

ASPState TempApplications	
AppId	int identity
AppName	char

ASPState TempSessions	
SessionId	char
Created	datetime
Expires	datetime
LockDate	datetime
LockCookie	int
Timeout	int
Locked	bit
SessionItemShort	varbinary
SessionItemLong	image

FIGURE 5.5

Schema for SQL Server State.

All the tables are placed into tempdb for a reason. Tempdb is the only database in SQL Server that allows a query to return before data is fully committed to the hard drive. This is good for performance. During a restart of SQL Server tempdb is cleared, which is not good for durability. You can move the tables out of tempdb into the ASPState database, but realize you are going to be trading durability for performance. If you do move the tables you need to modify most of the stored procedures in the ASPState database to point to the new location of the tables.

`ASPStateTempApplications` contains a row for each application root that is using the state service. The AppName field contains the ADSI path to the root. For the default Web root, this would be /LM/W3SVC/1/ROOT. The `ASPStateTempSessions` table is where all the work is done. One row is inserted for each `SessionID` that is associated with session state. This last point is important. Until the application attempts to save an item into the session state, no row is inserted. This delay is a small performance optimization so that pages that are not using session state don't take the hit of creating a row in the database. Also note that a row is not inserted for each session state value that is saved. Instead, a single row is inserted and a blob dropped into one of two columns. If the blob is smaller than 7,000 bytes, it is put into SessionItemShort, avoiding the need to allocate additional pages for an image field. If it is greater than 7,000 bytes, the extra work is done to allocate additional pages for storing the image data.

> **NOTE**
>
> This means that storing items of fewer than 7000 bytes is more efficient from a performance perspective.

The last item `InstallSqlState.sql` creates is a Job that is scheduled to run a stored procedure once a minute. This stored procedure, `DeleteExpiredSessions`, looks at the Expired field of `ASPStateTempSessions` and is responsible for removing expired session records. If the current timestamp is past the timestamp in the Expired field, the row is deleted. Each time the row is updated, the Expired field is updated to be the current timestamp plus the `Session.TimeOut` value.

Which One to Use?

ASP.NET gives you three choices for session state. Which should you use? The answer is...it depends on what you need. Each option offers unique advantages. You might think at first that significant performance differences exist among each of the options. However, running the code in Listing 5.10 shows that the performance differences among the three options are relatively minor.

LISTING 5.10   Code to Time Read and Write Operations on Session State—Timing.aspx

```
<html>
<head>
<title>Session Usage Timing</title>
<meta http-equiv="Content-Type" content="text/html; charset=iso-8859-1">
<script language="VB" runat=server>
    Sub Page_Load(Sender As Object, e As EventArgs)
        Dim iCount As Integer, iTemp as Integer
        Dim dStart As DateTime, dEnd As DateTime
        Dim szTemp As String
        Dim rnd as New Random(Now.Millisecond)

        dStart = Now
        For iCount = 1 to 1000000
            szTemp = rnd.Next(Now.Millisecond).ToString()
            Session(iCount.ToString()) = szTemp
        Next
        dEnd = Now

        lblWriteStart.Text = dStart.ToString("T")
        lblWriteEnd.Text = dEnd.ToString("T")
        lblWriteElapsed.Text = dEnd.Subtract(dStart).ToString()

        dStart = Now
        For iCount = 1 to 1000000
            szTemp = rnd.Next(Now.Millisecond).ToString()
            szTemp = Session(iCount.ToString())
        Next
        dEnd = Now

        lblReadStart.Text = dStart.ToString("T")
        lblReadEnd.Text = dEnd.ToString("T")
        lblReadElapsed.Text = dEnd.Subtract(dStart).ToString()

    End Sub
</script>

</head>

<body bgcolor="#FFFFFF" text="#000000">
    <table border=1>
        <tr>
            <th>Operation</th>
            <th>Start</th>
            <th>End</th>
            <th>Elapsed</th>
```

LISTING 5.10   Continued

```
        </tr>
        <tr>
            <td>Write</td>
            <td><asp:label id="lblWriteStart" runat=server /></td>
            <td><asp:label id="lblWriteEnd" runat=server /></td>
            <td><asp:label id="lblWriteElapsed" runat=server /></td>
        </tr>
        <tr>
            <td>Read</td>
            <td><asp:label id="lblReadStart" runat=server /></td>
            <td><asp:label id="lblReadEnd" runat=server /></td>
            <td><asp:label id="lblReadElapsed" runat=server /></td>
        </tr>
    </table>
</body>
</html>
```

Running this code for 1,000,000 iterations for each configuration with the state server and SQL Server residing on the same machine as the Web server, you will find that there are only slight differences in performance between the methods for simple object types. This admittedly unscientific test shows that you can worry more about the problem you are trying to solve instead of worrying about the performance of the session state mode. Each of the three options has its advantages and disadvantages.

Mode	Advantages	Disadvantages
In Process	Default. No extra work to configure. Can store complex objects by reference.	Process restart kills session state. Web farms don't share session state.
Out of Process	Works in Web farms.	Single point of failure. Must serialize complex objects.
SQL Server	Survives restart of any Web server. With modifications, will survive restart of SQL Server.	Must administer SQL Server. Must serialize complex objects.

Most developers will likely start development using in process session state because it is the default. As they start to attempt to scale things up, they are likely to choose either out of process or SQL Server session state to help their applications scale in a Web farm.

5

STATE
MANAGEMENT
AND CACHING

Caching

Do you have a page on your Web site that is built from the database, but the data changes only once a day? Perhaps you have a busy order page that must populate a list of states and countries out of the database several thousand times a day. How often do you need to add a new state? Clearly, these sorts of updates happen very infrequently. Are you hitting the limits of how far you can scale your database server? Are you looking for ways to reduce the load instead of spending $100,000 to upgrade the server? These are the types of scenarios where it makes sense to take a hard look at caching.

Output Caching: Caching an Entire Page

The simplest type of caching in ASP.NET is called output caching. Output caching takes the results from an ASP.NET page request and stores it in memory. Future requests for the same page are then served out of memory instead of served by re-creating the page from scratch. This can yield enormous savings in processor utilization on both the Web server and the database server, depending on the work the page performs. Page load times are decreased because after the first request, the page behaves as though it is a static HTML page. See Figure 5.6.

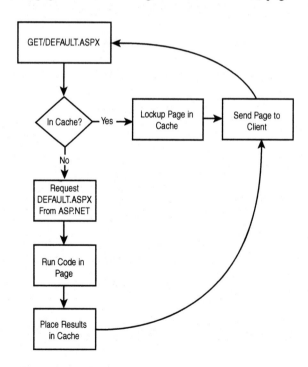

FIGURE 5.6

Page requests are intercepted and served from cache.

Solutions are out there that compile ASP pages into static HTML. These solutions are great for producing CD-ROMs to send with salespeople, but they become a management nightmare when used for caching. The ideal cache solution will dynamically build the cached page when the first request is made and then refresh it in the cache when it gets too old to be useful. Output caching behaves in this fashion.

Turning on output caching requires a single directive to the top of any page that will be cached. See Listing 5.11 for an example of a very simple page that utilizes output caching. This page defines the OutputCache directive at the top to indicate that the page should be cached.

LISTING 5.11   Page with Cache Directive to Cache for 5 Minutes—Cache5.aspx

```
<%@ OutputCache Duration="300" VaryByParam="None" %><html>
<head>
<title>Cached Time</title>
</head>
<body bgcolor="#FFFFFF" text="#000000">
    Time = <% = Now %>
</body>
</html>
```

Loading a page into cache and never refreshing it runs counter to one of the criteria for a good caching solution. The Duration attribute of the OutputCache directive is the solution. The Duration attribute indicates the number of seconds this page should remain in cache. In Listing 5.11, the 300 indicates that the page should stay in the cache for 300 seconds (that is, 5 minutes). This value does not appear to have an upper limit, so 31536000 seconds is a valid value, even though it represents a cache duration of a year!

The cache cooperates with the downstream client, such as proxy servers, browsers, or other caching devices located in the network, to manage the content that exists in the cache. By setting the Location attribute on the output cache header, you indicate where the cached copy of the page is allowed to exist. This attribute works by cooperating with the downstream clients. The first time ASP.NET returns a cached page to the client, it includes two new headers in the response: Cache-Control and Last-Modified. The Cache-Control directive is related to the Location attribute. If the Location attribute is left off the OutputCache directive, the Cache-Control is set to public. This flag marks the output as cacheable by any downstream client. If the Location attribute is set to Client, the Cache-Control directive is set to private. This setting indicates that the page in cache should not be stored in any public caching device such as a proxy server but can be stored in a cache private to the user—for example, the browser cache. With the Location directive set to Server, the Cache-Control header is set to no-cache, and an additional Pragma: no-cache header is added. This setting should prevent any downstream device that is following the HTTP 1.1 specification from caching the page. Instead, the page is cached on the server.

Location	Cache-Control	Description
Omitted or Any Downstream	public	Any downstream client can cache.
Client	private	Cannot be stored in public caches, only private.
Server	no-cache	Caches content on the server.
None	no-cache	Cached nowhere.

After a page gets into the cache, how is it expired? This is where the Last-Modified header comes into play. If the Location attribute was set to Client, Any, or Downstream, the client checks to see if the cached content is still valid with the server. It does this by sending another GET request that includes the header If-Modified-Since. The date after the header is the date that was sent to the client with the Last-Modified header in the previous response. ASP.NET then takes a look at the page in cache. If the cached page is still valid, it returns an HTTP/1.1 304 Not Modified response. This response indicates to the client that it should use the version of the page that it has in its local cache. If the page has expired, the entire contents of the page are returned as part of an HTTP/1.1 200 OK response. However, if the Location is set to server, this conversation doesn't take place because the client doesn't have a cached copy of the page; only the server does. From the client's perspective, the server is running the page each and every time. In Internet Explorer, the user can manually bypass this conversation by pressing Ctrl+F5 to refresh the page. The conversation is bypassed and the page is loaded directly from the server.

What type of a performance gain is expected with caching? On the first page request, no performance gain occurs; the page must always execute the first time around before caching. On subsequent page requests, however, response can be almost instantaneous versus the time required to execute. If the first page request takes 8 seconds and the subsequent requests take approximately 2 seconds, the application has realized a 25% performance gain. Extrapolating beyond the initial two requests, that percentage rapidly rises. As you can see, this technique can yield large performance gains. Figure 5.7 shows a chart of cumulative request times for a cached versus a noncached page. The performance gain is quite evident.

Dealing with Browser Differences

Although caching yields huge performance gains, it can cause problems. Take, for example, an ASP page that detects browser types using the HttpBrowserCapabilities class. It is pretty common for applications to detect whether the page is going to be sent to Internet Explorer or Netscape and then send slightly different content to the client. Listing 5.12 shows a sample page that is cached and outputs the browser string. This page is cached for 5 minutes. If the first page hit comes from Internet Explorer, the page is customized for Internet Explorer. If subsequent hits to the page occur within 5 minutes, the cached page is served, still customized for Internet Explorer no matter what browser is used for those subsequent hits. Clearly wrong! ASP.NET has cached the page and even though the page contains browser-specific code, the same page is rendered to all clients.

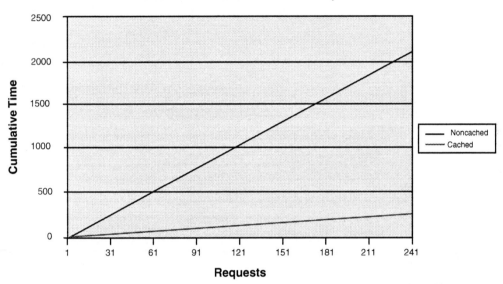

FIGURE 5.7
Cached versus noncached cumulative request time.

LISTING 5.12   Cached Page That Uses Browser Capabilities—CachedBrowser.aspx

```
<%@ OutputCache Duration="300" VaryByParam="None" %><html>
<head>
<title>Cached Browser Problem</title>
</head>
<body bgcolor="#FFFFFF" text="#000000">
<%
    Response.Write("Browser: " + Request.Browser.Browser)
%>
</body>
</html>
```

The ASP.NET Validation controls rely on this browser-sniffing capability to determine how to render the controls. If an application includes them in a page using output caching, it can display some unexpected behavior. Listing 5.13 shows a simple form that includes a `RequiredFieldValidation` control. This control relies on downloading some JavaScript on Internet Explorer but reverts to a server-side validation under Netscape. When this page is first hit from Internet Explorer, it displays correctly. However, subsequent hits to the cached page from Netscape yield a JavaScript error, which is not the intended result.

LISTING 5.13   Cached Form That Uses `RequiredFieldValidator`—
`VaryBrowserBroken.aspx`

```
<%@ OutputCache Duration="300" VaryByParam="None" %><html>
<head>
<title>Validate a Name - Broken</title>
</head>
<body bgcolor="#FFFFFF" text="#000000">
    <form id="frmName" runat=server>
        <asp:RequiredFieldValidator ControlToValidate="txtName"
            ErrorMessage="You must enter a name." runat=server /><br>
        Enter a name:<asp:textbox id="txtName" runat=server />
        <br><asp:button id="btnSubmit" Text="Validate" runat=server />
    </form>
</body>
</html>
```

The OutputCache directive has an additional parameter, `VaryByCustom`, to correct this problem. If you specify `VaryByCustom="browser"`, ASP.NET creates a different cached copy of the page for each browser it detects. Modifying the example as shown in Listing 5.14 causes ASP.NET to create a different version of the page for Internet Explorer and Netscape, correcting the problem with the `RequiredFieldValidator` control.

LISTING 5.14   Cached Form That Creates a Copy for Each Browser—
`VaryBrowserFixed.aspx`

```
<%@ OutputCache Duration="300" VaryByParam="None" VaryByCustom="browser"
%><html>
<head>
<title>Validate a Name - Fixed</title>
</head>

<body bgcolor="#FFFFFF" text="#000000">
    <form id="frmName" runat=server>
```

LISTING 5.14   Continued

```
        <asp:RequiredFieldValidator ControlToValidate="txtName"
            ErrorMessage="You must enter a name." runat=server /><br>
        Enter a name:<asp:textbox id="txtName" runat=server />
        <br><asp:button id="btnSubmit" Text="Validate" runat=server />
    </form>
</body>
</html>
```

Dealing with Other Differences

VaryByCustom can behave like a specialized form of another attribute available as part of the OutputCache directive, VaryByHeader. VaryByHeader enables you to specify that a new page should be created in cache for each new value of an HTTP header that is included in the request. VaryByHeader="User-Agent" performs a similar function as VaryByCustom="browser". One difference is how many cached pages they will create. VaryByHeader creates one for each unique User-Agent. Because the User-Agent header includes a number of items such as operating system, you could end up with multiple cached pages just for Internet Explorer 5.0. VaryByCustom, however, looks at Request.Browser.Type and the major version number only. VaryByCustom also allows you to override the GetVaryByCustomString() to allow you to customize the behavior of GetVaryByCustom to follow rules you define. In GetVaryByCustom() you essentially create the key that is used to uniquely identify each cached page. VaryByHeader allows the application to do additional things, such as create a cached copy of the page for each host header. Listing 5.15 shows a page that creates a cached copy of the page for each request that uses a different host header.

LISTING 5.15   Creates a Cached Page for Each Page Header—CachedHost.aspx

```
<%@ OutputCache Duration="300" VaryByParam="None" VaryByHeader="Host" %><html>
<head>
<title>Cached Host</title>
</head>
<body bgcolor="#FFFFFF" text="#000000">
    TimeStamp = <% = Now %>
</body>
</html>
```

Caching the Result of a Form

What happens when the output on a cached page changes based on arguments in the command line or input from a form? In this case, nothing is in the headers to differentiate the requests, so VaryByHeader will detect no differences in the page requests. The VaryByCustom attribute

5

might help if the application implements a custom algorithm. Listing 5.16 shows a page that exhibits this problem. This page queries the Northwind database and looks up employees by last name. When output caching is added to this page, anything typed into the last name box always gets the cached page!

LISTING 5.16 Page That Caches Form Output Incorrectly—CachedSearchBroken.aspx

```
<%@ OutputCache Duration="300" VaryByParam="None" %>
<%@ Import Namespace="System.Data" %>
<%@ Import Namespace="System.Data.SqlClient" %>
<html>
<head>
<title>Cached Search - Broken</title>
<script language="VB" runat=server>
    Public Sub Page_Load(Sender As Object, e As EventArgs)
        If Trim(Request("txtLastName")) <> "" Then
            Dim cn as SqlConnection
            Dim cmd as SqlCommand
            Dim dr As SqlDataReader
            Dim sb As StringBuilder

            ' Open the database
            cn = New SqlConnection("server=localhost;uid=sa;pwd=;" & _
                "database=Northwind;")
            cn.Open()

            ' Search the database
            cmd = New SqlCommand("SELECT * FROM Employees " & _
                "WHERE LastName Like '" + Trim(Request("txtLastName")) + _
                "%'", cn)
            dr = cmd.ExecuteReader()

            ' Start building the output table
            sb = New StringBuilder("<table><tr><th>LastName</th><th>" & _
                "Phone</th></tr>")
            ' Build the body of the table
            Do While dr.Read()
                sb.Append("<tr><td>" + dr("LastName").ToString() + _
                "</td><td>" + dr("HomePhone").ToString() + "</td></tr>")
            Loop
            ' finish the table
            sb.Append("</table>")
            ' Output the table
            output.InnerHTML = sb.ToString()

            dr.Close()
            cn.Close()
```

LISTING 5.16   Continued

```
          End If
     End Sub
</script>
</head>

<body bgcolor="#FFFFFF" text="#000000">
     <form method="post" id="Search">
          Last Name:
          <input type=text name="txtLastName">
          <input type="submit">
     </form>
<hr>
<span id="output" runat=server></span>
</body>
</html>
```

Wanting to cache the output of a form is such a common thing that another attribute is on the `OutputCache` directive, called `VaryByParam`. `VaryByParam` allows the application to specify a parameter in a `GET` request so that a separate copy of the cached page will be kept for each combination of the parameters specified.

Modifying the previous example to include the new attribute yields the code in Listing 5.17. When you specify the `VaryByParam` attribute and indicate `txtLastName`, ASP.NET creates a cached copy of the page for each `txtLastName` typed in.

LISTING 5.17   Page That Correctly Caches Results from a Form GET—
CachedSearchFixed.aspx

```
<%@ OutputCache Duration="300" VaryByParam="txtLastName" %>
<%@ Import Namespace="System.Data" %>
<%@ Import Namespace="System.Data.SqlClient" %>
<html>
<head>
<title>Cached Search - Fixed</title>
<meta http-equiv="Content-Type" content="text/html; charset=iso-8859-1">
<script language="VB" runat=server>
     Public Sub Page_Load(Sender As Object, e As EventArgs)
          If Trim(Request("txtLastName")) <> "" Then
               Dim cn as SqlConnection
               Dim cmd as SqlCommand
               Dim dr As SqlDataReader
               Dim sb As StringBuilder
```

Listing 5.17   Continued

```
              ' Open the database
              cn = New SqlConnection("server=localhost;uid=sa;pwd=;" & _
                  "database=Northwind;")
              cn.Open()

              ' Search the database
              cmd = New SqlCommand("SELECT * FROM Employees " + _
                  "WHERE LastName Like '" + Trim(Request("txtLastName")) + _
                  "%'", cn)
              dr = cmd.ExecuteReader()

              ' Start building the output table
              sb = New StringBuilder("<table><tr><th>LastName</th><th>Phone" & _
                  "</th></tr>")
              ' Build the body of the table
              Do While dr.Read()
                  sb.Append("<tr><td>" + dr("LastName").ToString() + _
                      "</td><td>" + dr("HomePhone").ToString() + "</td></tr>")
              Loop
              ' finish the table
              sb.Append("</table>")
              ' Output the table
              output.InnerHTML = sb.ToString()

              dr.Close()
              cn.Close()
          End If
      End Sub
  </script>
  </head>
  <body bgcolor="#FFFFFF" text="#000000">
      <form method="GET" id="Search">
          Last Name:
          <input type=text name="txtLastName">
          <input type="submit">
      </form>
  <hr>
  <span id="output" runat=server></span>
  </body>
  </html>
```

Caching Part of a Page

What happens when you have mixed types of content on the same page? The OutputCache directive affects the entire page and doesn't allow the application to specify regions on the page to cache or to exclude from the cache. Figure 5.8 shows a diagram of a page containing two sections, which are outlined. The first section contains data that changes constantly. The second section contains data that changes very infrequently. You can probably think of many examples of pages like this.

FIGURE 5.8
A page with two regions that need to be cached differently. The sales data is updated in real-time, whereas the phone list needs to be updated only once a day.

The solution to this issue is to take the data that needs to be cached and place it in a user control. A user control is allowed to define its own OutputCache directive and thereby affect its cache lifetime independent of the page as a whole.

When talking about caching user controls, we are speaking only about Location="Server" style caching. Because the user control ultimately becomes part of the page, it cannot cache itself in any downstream devices. Instead, when the server inserts the user control into the page at runtime, it grabs a copy of the output from the page cache and inserts it into the page. Listing 5.18 shows a user control using the OutputCache directive, and Listing 5.19 shows a page that consumes the user control.

LISTING 5.18   A User Control That Generates a Phone List—SalesPeople.ascx

```
<%@ OutputCache duration="300" VaryByParam="None" %>
<%@ Import Namespace="System.Data" %>
<%@ Import Namespace="System.Data.SqlClient" %>
<B>Sales Phone List</B>
<BR>
<%
            Dim cn as SqlConnection
            Dim cmd as SqlCommand
            Dim dr As SqlDataReader

            ' Open the database
            cn = New SqlConnection("server=localhost;uid=sa;pwd=;" & _
                "database=Northwind;")
            cn.Open()

            ' Search the database
            cmd = New SqlCommand("SELECT * FROM Employees", cn)
            dr = cmd.ExecuteReader()

            ' Start building the output table
            Response.Write("<table border=1><tr><th>LastName</th>" & _
                "<th>Phone</th></tr>")
            ' Build the body of the table
            Do While dr.Read()
               Response.Write("<tr><td>" + dr("LastName").ToString() + _
                    "</td><td>" + dr("HomePhone").ToString() + "</td></tr>")
            Loop
            ' finish the table
            Response.Write("</table>")

            dr.Close()
            cn.Close()
%>
<br>
<i>Updated:<%=Now%></i>
```

LISTING 5.19   A Page That Utilizes the SalesPeople.ascx User Control—
SalesByEmployee.aspx

```
<%@ Register TagPrefix="ASPBOOK" TagName="SalesPhoneList"
    Src="SalesPeople.ascx" %>
<%@ Import Namespace="System.Data" %>
<%@ Import Namespace="System.Data.SqlClient" %>
<html>
<head>
<title>Sales By Employee</title>
```

LISTING 5.19   Continued

```vb
<script language="VB" runat=server>
    Public Sub Page_Load(Sender As Object, e As EventArgs)
        Dim cn as SqlConnection
        Dim cmd as SqlCommand
        Dim dr As SqlDataReader
        Dim sb As StringBuilder
        Dim iRow as integer


        ' Open the database
        cn = New SqlConnection("server=localhost;uid=sa;pwd=;" & _
            "database=Northwind;")
        cn.Open()

        ' Get the list of total sales
        cmd = New SqlCommand("select LastName, " & _
            "sum(UnitPrice * Quantity) Total FROM Employees e, Orders o, " & _
            "[Order Details] d WHERE e.EmployeeID = o.EmployeeID AND " & _
            "o.OrderID = d.OrderID GROUP BY    LastName ORDER BY Total " & _
            "DESC", cn)
        dr = cmd.ExecuteReader()

        ' Start building the output table
        sb = New StringBuilder("<table><tr><th> </th><th>LastName" & _
            "</th><th>Phone</th></tr>")
        ' Build the body of the table
        Do While dr.Read()
            iRow = iRow + 1
            sb.Append("<tr><td>" + iRow.toString() + ".</td><td>" + _
                dr("LastName").ToString() + "</td><td>" + _
                Format(dr("Total"),"C") + "</td></tr>")
        Loop
        ' finish the table
        sb.Append("</table>")
        SalesPeople.InnerHtml = sb.ToString()

        dr.Close()
        cn.Close()
    End Sub
</script>
</head>
<body bgcolor="#FFFFFF" text="#000000">
<h1>Sales By Employee</h1>
<table width="75%" border="0">
  <tr>
    <td><span id="SalesPeople" runat=server></span></td>
```

LISTING 5.18   Continued

```
   <td valign="top"><aspbook:SalesPhoneList runat=server/></td>
  </tr>
</table>
</body>
</html>
```

All the attributes for the OutputCache directive, with the exception of Location, will work inside a user control. VaryByParam can be very useful if the user control relies on form or request parameters to create its content. ASP.NET will create a cached copy of the user control for each combination of parameters in the VaryByParam attribute. Listing 5.20 shows a user control that takes the value of a request parameter and saves it into an ArrayList to create a crumb trail of previous search terms. This user control has the OutputCache directive set to VaryByParam="txtLastName". This is the search term on the parent page, which is shown in Listing 5.21.

LISTING 5.20   User Control That Creates a Breadcrumb Trail of Previous Search Terms—
LastFiveSearchTerms.ascx

```
<%@ OutputCache duration="60" VaryByParam="txtLastName" %>
<%
    Dim al as ArrayList
    Dim iRow as Integer

    ' Get the list from the Session
    al = Session("alSearchTerms")

    ' Did we get it?
    If al Is Nothing Then
        ' Create new array list if not
        al = New ArrayList()
    End If

    ' Add the item to the array
    al.Add(Request("txtLastName"))
    ' Store the array
    Session("alSearchTerms") = al

    Response.Write("<b>Past Terms:</b><br><table border=1>")
    ' Output the array
    For iRow = 0 to al.Count - 1
        Response.Write("<tr><td>" + al(iRow) + "</td></tr>")
    Next
    Response.Write("</table>")
%>
```

LISTING 5.21   Search Page That Includes Breadcrumb Control—BreadCrumbSearch.aspx

```vb
<%@ OutputCache Duration="300" VaryByParam="txtLastName" %>
<%@ Register TagPrefix="ASPBOOK" TagName="LastFiveSearchItems"
    Src="LastFiveSearch.ascx" %>
<%@ Import Namespace="System.Data" %>
<%@ Import Namespace="System.Data.SqlClient" %>
<html>
<head>
<title>Cache Search - Fixed</title>
<meta http-equiv="Content-Type" content="text/html; charset=iso-8859-1">
<script language="VB" runat=server>
    Public Sub Page_Load(Sender As Object, e As EventArgs)
        If Trim(Request("txtLastName")) <> "" Then
            Dim cn as SqlConnection
            Dim cmd as SqlCommand
            Dim dr As SqlDataReader
            Dim sb As StringBuilder

            ' Open the database
            cn = New SqlConnection("server=localhost;uid=sa;pwd=;" & _
                "database=Northwind;")
            cn.Open()

            ' Search the database
            cmd = New SqlCommand("SELECT * FROM Employees WHERE " & _
                "LastName Like '" + Trim(Request("txtLastName")) + "%'", cn)
            dr = cmd.ExecuteReader()

            ' Start building the output table
            sb = New StringBuilder("<table><tr><th>LastName" & _
                "</th><th>Phone</th></tr>")
            ' Build the body of the table
            Do While dr.Read()
                sb.Append("<tr><td>" + dr("LastName").ToString() + _
                    "</td><td>" + dr("HomePhone").ToString() + "</td></tr>")
            Loop
            ' finish the table
            sb.Append("</table>")
            ' Output the table
            output.InnerHTML = sb.ToString()

            dr.Close()
            cn.Close()
        End If
    End Sub
```

Listing 5.21   Continued

```
</script>
</head>

<body bgcolor="#FFFFFF" text="#000000">
    <form method="post" id="Search">
        Last Name:
        <input type=text name="txtLastName">
        <input type="submit">
    </form>
<hr>
<span id="output" runat=server></span>
<hr>
<aspbook:lastfivesearchitems runat=server />
</body>
</html>
```

Some combinations of user control and page caching can yield unexpected results. We have shown examples where the containing page does not have a cache directive but the user control does, and examples where both have cache directives. What about the case where the containing page has a cache directive but the user control does not? In this case, the entire page is cached, including the user control, and delivered to the client. A user control cannot override the caching behavior of its container. Figure 5.9 shows the valid and invalid combinations.

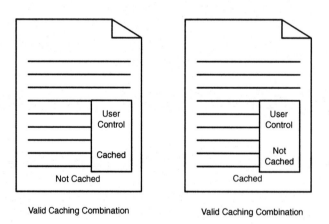

Figure 5.9

This figure shows the allowed combinations for user control and output caching.

If the container is cached, the control will also be cached. Listings 5.22 and 5.23 show examples of this behavior. The containing page in Listing 5.22 defines a cache directive. The user control in Listing 5.23 does not; therefore, the entire page is cached.

LISTING 5.22   Containing Page Uses `OutputCache`—`ContainerPage.aspx`

```
<%@ OutputCache Duration="300" VaryByParam="None" %>
<%@ Register TagPrefix="ASPBOOK" TagName="Inside" Src="Inside.ascx" %>
<html>
<head>
<title>Untitled Document</title>
</head>
<body bgcolor="#FFFFFF" text="#000000">
Page TimeStamp = <% = Now %>
<hr>
<aspbook:inside runat=server />
<hr>
</body>
</html>
```

LISTING 5.23   User Control Does Not Use `OutputCache`—`Inside.ascx`

```
User Control TimeStamp = <% = Now %>
```

If you need more control over caching behavior than the `OutputCache` directive provides, it is time to take a look at the `HttpCachePolicy` class. This class allows you to dynamically set any of the properties contained in the OutputCache directive.

Caching a Database Query

Caching entire pages is simple—just add the `OutputCache` directive. Let's take a look at a different caching technique that is a little more complicated. Unlike the previous technique, this one is likely to require changes to your source code.

Output caching eliminates two factors that contribute to the amount of time it takes to load a page: code execution and query execution. What if you still want the code on the page to execute, but you want to maintain the advantage of eliminating query execution? ASP.NET provides a group of caching classes that can be used to cache frequently used resources such as the results from a query on a server.

You might wonder why this new `Cache` object? Why not just use the `Application` or `Session` objects? The `Application` or `Session` objects make good sense for settings that must persist for the life of the application or for the life of the currently connected user. They make much less sense to cache the output of a commonly run query. If the output of a query goes into the application object, it remains there until the application shuts down. With a large number of queries, what happens as memory gets low?

The cache class deals with each of these issues and more. The visibility of items in the cache is very similar to the visibility of items in the application object. The cache is private to each application root but is shared among all users. The cache can be treated like a dictionary using keys paired with values, just like the application object. The similarities end there.

If an object is placed in the cache and isn't used for a while, the cache is smart enough to drop it out of memory to conserve valuable server resources. This process, called scavenging, takes into account when the object was last accessed as well as the priority assigned to the object when determining which objects to drop from the cache.

Let's take a look at a simple example. Listing 5.24 shows a page that queries the Northwind database for a list of territories and places them into a drop-down list box.

Listing 5.24   Page That Queries Northwind for a List of Territories—
`CacheTerritories.aspx`

```
<%@ Import Namespace="System.Data" %>
<%@ Import Namespace="System.Data.SqlClient" %>
<html>
<head>
<title>Territories</title>
<script language="VB" runat=server>
    Sub Page_Load(Sender As Object, E As EventArgs)
        ' Dim variables
        Dim cn As SqlConnection
        Dim cmd As SqlDataAdapter
        Dim ds As New DataSet

        ' Open a connection
        cn = New SQLConnection("server=localhost;uid=sa;pwd=;" & _
            "database=Northwind")
        ' Create an adapter
        cmd = New SqlDataAdapter("select * from territories", cn)

        ' Fill the dataset
        cmd.Fill(ds, "Territories")

        ' Bind the data
        lstTerritory.DataSource = ds.Tables(0).DefaultView
        lstTerritory.DataBind()
    End Sub
</script>
</head>

<body bgcolor="#FFFFFF" text="#000000">
    <form id="Territory" runat=server>
```

LISTING 5.24   Continued

```
        Territory:
        <asp:dropdownlist DataValueField="TerritoryID"
            DataTextField="TerritoryDescription"
            id="lstTerritory" runat=server />
    </form>
</body>
</html>
```

The list of territories rarely changes, so it is an ideal candidate to place into the cache. When using cached objects, a familiar design pattern emerges—check the cache before creating an object. Instead of immediately building the object of interest, in this case a DataSet, the application first attempts to retrieve it from the cache. Next, it checks the reference to see if anything was successfully retrieved from the cache. If the reference is Nothing, it does the work required to create the object from scratch and saves the newly created object into the cache. Finally the application does the work to create the page.

Listing 5.25 takes the previous example and modifies it to store the list of territories in cache. It first attempts to retrieve the DataSet containing the territories from cache. If this fails, it will then connect to the database, rebuild the dataset from scratch, and save it into the cache. Finally, the drop-down list box is bound to the dataset.

LISTING 5.25   Modification to Store DataSet Containing Territories in Cache—
CacheExpiration.aspx

```
<%@ Import Namespace="System.Data" %>
<%@ Import Namespace="System.Data.SqlClient" %>
<html>
<head>
<title>Cached Territories</title>
<script language="VB" runat=server>
    Sub Page_Load(Sender As Object, E As EventArgs)
        Dim ds As DataSet

        ' Attempt to retrieve the dataset from cache
        ds = Cache("Territories")

        ' Did we get it?
        If ds Is Nothing Then
            ' Dim variables
```

Listing 5.25   Continued

```
            Dim cn As SqlConnection
            Dim cmd As SqlDataAdapter


            ' Open a connection
            cn = New SQLConnection("server=localhost;uid=sa;pwd=;" & _
                "database=Northwind")
            ' Create an adapter
            cmd = New SqlDataAdapter("select * from territories", cn)

            ' Fill the dataset
            ds = New DataSet()
            cmd.Fill(ds, "Territories")

            ' Cache the dataset
            Cache("Territories") = ds
        End If

        ' Bind the data
        lstTerritory.DataSource = ds.Tables(0).DefaultView
        lstTerritory.DataBind()
    End Sub
</script>
</head>
<body bgcolor="#FFFFFF" text="#000000">
    <form id="Territory" runat=server>
        Territory:
        <asp:dropdownlist DataValueField="TerritoryID"
            DataTextField="TerritoryDescription"
            id="lstTerritory" runat=server />
    </form>
</body>
</html>
```

This technique is not limited to ADO.NET objects. Any object can be placed into the cache and utilized in the same fashion. The cache does consume resources, however, so carefully consider what is placed into it. Candidates for caching are items that can be re-created when needed but whose creation extracts a performance penalty.

Expiring Items from the Cache

The cache is not intended to be a shared memory space for communication between pages. Using the cache as a shared memory space, an application can run into the same types of problems as attempting to use the Application object as a communication mechanism. Objects placed in the cache should be treated as read-only and updated only when they expire.

So how does expiration work? To use expiration, items must be placed into the cache using `Cache.Insert` or `Cache.Add` instead of treating the cache like a dictionary. `Insert` and `Add` differ only in that `Add` returns a reference to the cached item.

Expiring Cached Items Based on Time

Two options are available for expiring an item from the cache: `AbsoluteExpiration` and `SlidingExpiration`. `AbsoluteExpiration` specifies the date and time when an item should expire from the cache. When that date and time are reached, the item is dropped. This might not always be the appropriate action. In most instances it would be better to drop an item from cache if it has not been used for a certain amount of time. With this method, frequently used items would remain in cache while less frequently used items would eventually drop out of the cache. The `SlidingExpiration` argument of `Insert` provides this type of functionality. `SlidingExpiration` also takes a time span, but in this case, the time is measured from the last time the item was accessed, not from the time that the item was placed in the cache. Behind the scenes, this method sets the `AbsoluteExpiration` value equal to `Now +` `SlidingExpiration`. Each time the item is accessed, this "sliding" process is repeated, moving the `AbsoluteExpiration` further into the future. So on initial load, a page can put a dataset into cache with an expiration of 10 minutes. As long as that page is accessed at least once every 10 minutes, the object will remain in cache indefinitely. If no more requests for the page are made, the dataset will drop out of cache 10 minutes after the last request.

When both a `SlidingExpiration` and an `AbsoluteExpiration` are specified, the `SlidingExpiration` will overwrite the `AbsoluteExpiration` with `Now + SlidingExpiration`. To specify only one or the other, special constants are made available to provide a default setting for the unspecified method. `Cache.NoAbsoluteExpiration` is used for the `AbsoluteExpiration` parameter only when specifying `SlidingExpiration`. `Cache.NoSlidingExpiration` is used for the `SlidingExpiration` parameter only when specifying the `AbsoluteExpiration` parameter. The `SlidingExpiration` parameter of the `Cache` object is very similar in behavior to the `Duration` attribute of the `OutputCache` directive.

Taking the earlier example from Listing 5.25 and updating it to use a `SlidingExpiration` of 60 seconds, we get the code shown in Listing 5.26. A message will be printed at the bottom of the screen whenever the DataSet is refreshed from the database. If this page is refreshed at least once every 60 seconds, the results will always be returned from cache. Wait 61 seconds and then refresh it, and the results will be reloaded from the database.

Listing 5.26 Example Updated to Use a SlidingExpiration of 60 Seconds—
SlidingExpiration.aspx

```
<%@ Import Namespace="System.Data" %>
<%@ Import Namespace="System.Data.SqlClient" %>
<html>
<head>
<title>Territories Sliding Expiration</title>
<script language="VB" runat=server>
    Sub Page_Load(Sender As Object, E As EventArgs)
        Dim ds As DataSet

        ' Attempt to retrieve the dataset from cache
        ds = Cache("Territories")

        ' Did we get it?
        If ds Is Nothing Then
            ' Dim variables
            Dim cn As SqlConnection
            Dim cmd As SqlDataAdapter


            ' Open a connection
            cn = New SQLConnection("server=localhost;uid=sa;pwd=;" & _
                "database=Northwind")
            ' Create an adapter
            cmd = New SqlDataAdapter("select * from territories", cn)

            ' Fill the dataset
            ds = New DataSet()
            cmd.Fill(ds, "Territories")

            ' Cache the dataset
            Cache.Insert("Territories", ds, Nothing, _
                Cache.NoAbsoluteExpiration, TimeSpan.FromSeconds(60))

            ' Indicate we did not use cache
            Message.InnerHTML = "Territories loaded from database. " + Now
        End If

        ' Bind the data
        lstTerritory.DataSource = ds.Tables(0).DefaultView
        lstTerritory.DataBind()
    End Sub
```

LISTING 5.26   Continued

```
</script>
</head>

<body bgcolor="#FFFFFF" text="#000000">
    <form id="Territory" runat=server>
        Territory:
        <asp:dropdownlist DataValueField="TerritoryID"
        DataTextField="TerritoryDescription" id="lstTerritory" runat=server />
    </form>
    <span id="Message" runat=server></span>
</body>
</html>
```

Notifying the Next of Kin

When an item is dropped out of cache, a notification can be fired to let your program know that the item has been removed from cache. The callback routine can then preemptively re-add the item back into the cache before the page is requested again. This prevents the first page that attempts to use the item after it has been dropped out of cache from experiencing a delay. Listing 5.27 shows how to use another variant of the Insert() method to specify a callback that should be invoked when the items is removed from cache.

LISTING 5.27   Page That Caches a List of Territories; When the List Is Dropped Out of Cache, It Is Replaced Proactively—CacheCallback.aspx

```
<%@ Import Namespace="System.Data" %>
<%@ Import Namespace="System.Data.SqlClient" %>
<html>
<head>
<title>Territories Sliding Expiration</title>
<script language="VB" runat=server>
    Sub Page_Load(Sender As Object, E As EventArgs)
        Dim ds As DataSet

        ' Attempt to retrieve the dataset from cache
        ds = Cache("Territories")

        ' Did we get it?
        If ds Is Nothing Then
            ' Cache the territories
            ds = CacheTerritories()
            ' Indicate we did not use cache
```

Listing 5.27   Continued

```vb
            Message.InnerHTML = "Territories loaded from database. " + Now
        End If


        ' Check for the callback message
        If Not Cache("Callback") Is Nothing Then
            Message.InnerHTML = Cache("Callback")
        End If


        ' Bind the data
        lstTerritory.DataSource = ds.Tables(0).DefaultView
        lstTerritory.DataBind()
End Sub

Public Sub CacheItemRemoved(strKey as string, oValue as object, _
    reason as CacheItemRemovedReason)
        Cache("Callback") = "Recached at " + Now

        ' Recache the territories
        CacheTerritories()
End Sub

Public Function CacheTerritories() as DataSet
    ' Dim variables
    Dim cn As SqlConnection
    Dim cmd As SqlDataAdapter
    Dim ds as DataSet


    ' Open a connection
    cn = New SQLConnection("server=localhost;uid=sa;pwd=;" & _
        "database=Northwind")
    ' Create an adapter
    cmd = New SqlDataAdapter("select * from territories", cn)

    ' Fill the dataset
    ds = New DataSet()
    cmd.Fill(ds, "Territories")

    ' Cache the dataset
    Cache.Insert("Territories", ds, Nothing, _
        Cache.NoAbsoluteExpiration, TimeSpan.FromSeconds(60), _
        CacheItemPriority.Normal, CacheItemPriorityDecay.Medium, _
        new CacheItemRemovedCallback(AddressOf Me.CacheItemRemoved))
```

LISTING 5.27 Continued

```
      return ds
   End Function
</script>
</head>

<body bgcolor="#FFFFFF" text="#000000">
    <form id="Territory" runat=server>
        Territory:
        <asp:dropdownlist DataValueField="TerritoryID"
        DataTextField="TerritoryDescription" id="lstTerritory" runat=server />
    </form>
    <span id="Message" runat=server></span>
</body>
</html>
```

Cache Dependencies

Sometimes items that you place into the cache might need to be refreshed because of an external event other than the passage of time. Cache dependencies allow a cache item to be based on a file, a directory, or the key of another item in the cache. Listing 5.28 shows a new version of the Territory example in which the list of territories is placed in the cache until the page is changed, at which time the results are recached.

LISTING 5.28 Page That Caches a List of Territories Until the Page Is Changed— CacheDependency.aspx

```
<%@ Import Namespace="System.Data" %>
<%@ Import Namespace="System.Data.SqlClient" %>
<html>
<head>
<title>Territories</title>
<script language="VB" runat=server>
    Sub Page_Load(Sender As Object, E As EventArgs)
        Dim ds As DataSet

        '  Attempt to retrieve the dataset from cache
        ds = Cache("Territories")

        ' Did we get it?
        If ds Is Nothing Then
            ' Dim variables
```

LISTING 5.28   Continued

```
            Dim cn As SqlConnection
            Dim cmd As SqlDataAdapter


            ' Open a connection
            cn = New SQLConnection("server=localhost;uid=sa;pwd=;" & _
                "database=Northwind")
            ' Create an adapter
            cmd = New SqlDataAdapter("select * from territories", cn)

            ' Fill the dataset
            ds = New DataSet()
            cmd.Fill(ds, "Territories")

            ' Cache the dataset
            Cache.Insert("Territories", ds, new CacheDependency( _
                Server.MapPath("CacheDependency.aspx")))

            ' Indicate we did not use cache
            Message.InnerHTML = "Territories loaded from database. " + Now
        End If

        ' Bind the data
        lstTerritory.DataSource = ds.Tables(0).DefaultView
        lstTerritory.DataBind()
    End Sub
</script>
</head>

<body bgcolor="#FFFFFF" text="#000000">
    <form id="Territory" runat=server>
        Territory:
        <asp:dropdownlist DataValueField="TerritoryID"
        DataTextField="TerritoryDescription" id="lstTerritory" runat=server />
    </form>
    <span id="Message" runat=server></span>
</body>
</html>
```

Listing 5.29 shows an example that pulls together all these cache concepts. This code adds items to the cache, specifying an `AbsoluteExpiration`, `SlidingExpiration`, `Priority`,

PriorityDecay, and a Cache Dependency. Items can also be removed from the cache. All items currently in the cache are displayed. Iterating the items in the cache to display their data type resets their sliding expiration. If you would like to see the results of the sliding expiration, you must wait the requisite amount of time before refreshing the page. When running this sample, you will notice that quite a few items in the cache start with System.Web. ASP.NET uses the cache to store a number of items during execution. Be aware that this raises the possibility of namespace collisions, so name your cache items accordingly.

LISTING 5.29 An Example of Removing and Inserting Items from Cache with Expirations—WorkingWithCache.aspx

```
<html>
<head>
<title>Working with the Cache</title>
<script language="VB" runat=server>
    Sub ListCache()
        Dim sbOutput As StringBuilder
        Dim oItem As Object
        Dim szType As String

        ' Show the number of items in the cache
        sbOutput = New StringBuilder("Items in Cache = " _
        + Cache.Count.ToString() + "<Br>")

        ' Start the table
        sbOutput.Append("<table border=1><tr><th>Key</th>" & _
        "<th>Data Type</th></tr>")

        ' Clear the list
        lstCache.Items.Clear()

        ' Loop through the cache
        For Each oItem In Cache
            ' Add To List
            lstCache.Items.Add(oItem.Key)
            ' Have to watch for a null object during expiration
            If Cache(oItem.Key) Is Nothing Then
                szType = "Nothing"
            Else
                szType = Cache(oItem.Key).GetType().ToString()
            End If

            ' Add to table
            sbOutput.Append("<tr><td>" + oItem.Key + "</td><td>" _
```

LISTING 5.29 Continued

```
                + szType + "</td></tr>")
        Next

        ' Close the table
        sbOutput.Append("</table>")

        ' Place in page
        tblCache.InnerHtml = sbOutput.ToString()
    End Sub

    Sub Page_Load(Sender As Object, E As EventArgs)
        ' Only run it if no other event is happening
        If Not IsPostBack Then
            ListCache()
        End If
    End Sub

    Sub btnRemove_Click(Sender As Object, E As EventArgs)
        ' Remove theitem
        Cache.Remove(lstCache.SelectedItem.Text)
        ' List out the cache
        ListCache()
    End Sub

    Sub btnAdd_Click(Sender As Object, E As EventArgs)
        Dim p As CacheItemPriority

        ' Get the cache item priority
        Select Case ddPriority.SelectedItem.Text
            Case "High"
                p = CacheItemPriority.High
            Case "Above Normal"
                p = CacheItemPriority.AboveNormal
            Case "Normal"
                p = CacheItemPriority.Normal
            Case "Below Normal"
                p = CacheItemPriority.BelowNormal
            Case "Low"
                p = CacheItemPriority.Low
            Case "Not Removable"
```

LISTING 5.29   Continued

```
                    p = CacheItemPriority.NotRemovable
        End Select

        If txtSliding.Text <> "" Then
            ' Save the value with a sliding expiration
            Cache.Insert(txtKey.Text, txtValue.Text, Nothing, _
                Cache.NoAbsoluteExpiration, _
                TimeSpan.FromSeconds(txtSliding.Text), p, Nothing)
        ElseIf txtAbsolute.Text <> "" Then
            ' Save the value with an absolute expiration
            Cache.Insert(txtKey.Text, txtValue.Text, Nothing, _
                DateTime.Now.AddSeconds(txtAbsolute.Text), _
                Cache.NoSlidingExpiration, p, Nothing)
        Else
            ' Save the value
            Cache.Insert(txtKey.Text, txtValue.Text, Nothing, _
                Nothing, Nothing, p, Nothing)
        End If
        ' List out the cache
        ListCache()
    End Sub

</script>
</head>

<body bgcolor="#FFFFFF" text="#000000">
    <form id="CacheWork" runat=server>
        <table>
            <tr>
                <td>Key:</td>
                <td><asp:textbox id="txtKey" runat=server /></td>
                <td>Value: </td>
                <td><asp:textbox id="txtValue" runat=server /></td>
                <td><asp:button id="btnAdd" Text="Add" runat=server
                    OnClick="btnAdd_Click" /></td>
            </tr>
            <tr>
                <td>Absolute:</td>
                <td><asp:textbox id="txtAbsolute" runat=server /></td>
                <td>Sliding:</td>
                <td><asp:textbox id="txtSliding" runat=server /></td>
```

5

LISTING 5.29   Continued

```
                    <td> </td>
                </tr>
                <tr>
                    <td>Priority:</td>
                    <td colspan=3><asp:dropdownlist id="ddPriority" runat=server>
                            <asp:listitem>High</asp:listitem>
                            <asp:listitem>Above Normal</asp:listitem>
                            <asp:listitem Selected="true">Normal</asp:listitem>
                            <asp:listitem>Below Normal</asp:listitem>
                            <asp:listitem>Low</asp:listitem>
                            <asp:listitem>Not Removable</asp:listitem>
                        </asp:dropdownlist></td>
                    <td> </td>
                </tr>
            </table>
            <hr>
                <asp:listbox id="lstCache" runat=server />
                <asp:button id="btnRemove" Text="Remove" runat=server
                    OnClick="btnRemove_Click" />
        </form>
        <hr>
        <span id="tblCache" runat=server></span>
</body>
</html>
```

Class Reference

This section provides a quick interface reference to the key objects described in this chapter. Space constraints prevent us from documenting every object in the .NET framework in this book, so for the sake of brevity and conciseness, we include only the most important objects here. For more information on the other objects in the .NET framework, consult the .NET Framework Reference online help file.

HttpSessionState Class

Member of System.Web.SessionState

Assembly: System.Web.dll

The HttpSessionState class is instantiated and placed inside the Session property of the Page object.

Properties

CodePage	Contents	Count
IsCookieless	IsNewSession	IsReadOnly
IsSynchronized	Item	Keys
LCID	Mode	SessionID
StaticObjects	SyncRoot	TimeOut

Methods

Abandon	Add	Clear
CopyTo	GetEnumerator	Remove
RemoveAll	RemoveAt	

HttpCachePolicy

Member of System.Web

Assembly: System.Web.dll

The HttpCachePolicy class allows you to control many of the parameters that the <%@
OutputCache %> directive controls. It also adds several more methods to give additional control over caching.

Properties

VaryByHeaders	VaryByParams

Methods

AddValidationCallback	AppendCacheExtension	Equals
GetHashCode	GetType	SetCacheability
SetETag	SetETagFromFile Dependencies	SetExpires
SetLastModified	SetLastModifiedFrom FileDependencies	SetMaxAge
SetNoServerCaching	SetNoStore	SetNoTransforms
SetProxyMagAge	SetRevalidation	SetSliding Expiration
SetValidUntilExpires	SetVaryByCustom	ToString

HttpCacheVaryByHeaders

Member of System.Web

Assembly: **System.Web.dll**

The `HttpCacheVaryByHeaders` class provides a type-safe way to set the `VaryByHeaders` property of the `HttpCachePolicy` class for a number of well-known headers.

Properties

AcceptTypes	Item	UserAgent
UserCharSet	UserLanguage	

Methods

VaryByUnspecifiedParameters

HttpCacheVaryByParams

Member of `System.Web`

Assembly: **System.Web.dll**

The `HttpCacheVaryByParams` class provides a type safe way to set the `VaryByParams` property of the `HttpCachePolicy` class.

Properties

IgnoreParams	Item

Cache

Member of **System.Web.Caching**

Assembly: **System.Web.dll**

The cache class is a store for caching frequently used resources on the server.

Fields

NoAbsoluteExpiration	NoSlidingExpiration

Properties

Count	Item

Methods

Add	Get	GetEnumerator
Insert	Remove	

CacheDependency

Member of `System.Web.Caching`

Assembly: **System.Web.dll**

Keeps track of dependencies for items in the cache. This class cannot be inherited from.

Constructors
```
Overloads Public Sub New(String)
Overloads Public Sub New(String())
Overloads Public Sub New(String(), String())
```

Configuration and Deployment

IN THIS CHAPTER

Deploying applications under ASP.old was fairly simple—most of the time. You designated a folder as scriptable under Internet Services Manager, copied your script files into that folder, and requested the ASP pages through a Web browser. If something went wrong, you got a 404 Not Found error, which sent you back either to Windows Explorer to locate the missing file or into Internet Services Manager to change an incorrect setting. On paper, it all looked pretty simple.

Under this old model, the trouble came when your ASP application depended on external resources to run. For example, if your application needed to periodically retrieve or store information from the system registry, or (even worse) if your application depended on one or more COM components, you found yourself in a situation in which you could not easily and automatically replicate your Web application on another server. This meant that for all but the most trivial ASP.old applications, it was a pain to move your application from a development server to a production server. The problems involved in replicating external dependencies got much worse in situations in which you were required to deploy your application to a series of identical servers (such as a Web farm).

ASP.NET promises to make the process of deploying your Web applications much easier, no matter what kind of application architecture or server you're working with. It does this by doing away with certain dependencies (such as the system registry and the IIS metabase) and minimizing the impact of others—most notably, it got rid of the requirement that a precompiled component be registered, as is the case with COM components.

In addition to making deployment simpler, ASP.NET makes the process of configuration much easier, as well. In the past, IIS and ASP configuration files were stored in the registry and were accessible only through the registry editor or (more commonly) Internet Services Manager. But in many cases, important configuration information would get lost in the GUI of the management console, which changed from one version of Windows to the next.

Storing IIS and ASP configuration data in the registry also meant that configuration itself became a new kind of deployment problem, too, because you couldn't easily provide registry settings for your Web applications to suit multiple machines or multiple customers.

In ASP.NET, many application-level settings are available through XML configuration files that you can view and change using any text editor. This has advantages and disadvantages, as we'll discuss later in this chapter. But by and large, the capability to easily distribute your configuration file along with the application itself is a huge boon to application developers.

Understanding Configuration Files

Most software applications need to maintain bits of information about how the software is supposed to run. Web applications are no different.

In ASP.old, you had a limited number of ways to manage application configuration data. You could

- Embed configuration data in the registry and hope that the person who deploys your application could insert the necessary registry settings properly.
- Use script files such as global.asa or constants located in your own script files.
- Use custom text files that could be read and written to as needed.

All three of these techniques have significant drawbacks. Registry-based configuration is difficult to manage. Changing a script file often requires a programmer, and errors inserted into script files can sabotage an entire application. Custom text files alleviate this problem, but in many cases using an external file means that a reference to that file must be explicitly included in every script file that accesses it.

The designers of ASP.NET recognized that application configuration was never as straightforward as it could be. In .NET, Web applications have a number of new configuration options and features (which we'll discuss in this chapter and elsewhere in this book). But more importantly, the manner in which you configure your Web application is now totally standard and fairly simple to manage. In ASP.NET, applications are configured with just two XML files—Machine.Config and Web.Config. You can easily make changes to and redistribute these to enforce settings in your applications, as you'll see in the next section.

Global and Local Configuration Files

Servers that run .NET Web applications will typically have multiple ASP.NET configuration files. One such file, known as the machinewide or global configuration file, is named Machine.Config; this file is created for you when you install the .NET framework. The exact location of this file depends on your machine configuration and the version of the .NET framework you're running, but it should be located in \Windows\Microsoft.NET\Framework\ *[version]*\CONFIG. (Replace [version] with whichever version you're actually running.)

Additionally, any Web-accessible folder can optionally contain a Web.Config file that stores settings that are relevant to the ASP.NET scripts in that folder. These settings override the machinewide settings found in Machine.Config.

ASP.NET Web applications can actually have multiple Web.Config files. This can occur when the application contains subfolders. Each subfolder can have its own Web.Config; the configuration settings found in folders that are located deeper in the hierarchy override the settings found at higher levels.

It's not necessary for any of your ASP.NET Web applications to have Web.Config files. If your application has no configuration file, it inherits the settings found in the global configuration file (Machine.Config). When you make a change to a configuration file, ASP.NET automatically picks up the change and applies it. You do not have to restart the server or reboot the machine to get ASP.NET to recognize the changes you made. Also, although the Web.Config file is by definition located in a Web-accessible directory, client browsers are prohibited from downloading Web-configuration files (through an IIS security setting that is set at the time the .NET framework is installed on your system).

Structure of Configuration Files

As mentioned earlier, ASP.NET configuration files are XML documents. The root node of the document is always called *configuration*. Within the configuration node are a variety of nodes and subnodes that contain additional settings; these are grouped into *section handlers*.

The next few sections describe the default section handlers in the System.Web section of a Web configuration file. Because each Web.Config file ultimately inherits its settings from Machine.Config, the descriptions apply to both files.

Authentication Settings

Authentication refers to the process whereby a user is granted or denied access to the page based on security credentials.

ASP.NET supports three authentication modes:

- Windows authentication
- Cookie-based authentication
- Microsoft Passport authentication

In *Windows authentication*, the user has an account on the Windows NT/Windows 2000 server on which the Web application is located; if the user is not located on the same subnet as an authenticating server, the user must supply a username and password when the browser initially accesses a Web application.

In *cookie-based authentication*, an encrypted chunk of data is deposited on the user's computer and read by the server each time the user accesses the site.

Passport authentication is similar to cookie-based authentication. It enables users to use the same security credentials to access any one of a number of sites. This is accomplished by storing and authenticating user information in a central location (managed by Microsoft).

NOTE

It is possible to use Passport authentication whether or not your site uses ASP.NET. You can get more information about implementing Passport authentication on your site at http://www.passport.com/business.

To specify one of these authentication schemes, you make a change to the authentication section of the Web.Config or Machine.Config files.

Figure 6.1 shows a typical authentication section and describes some of its settings.

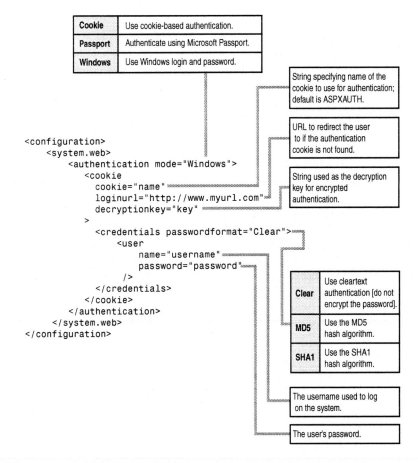

Cookie	Use cookie-based authentication.
Passport	Authenticate using Microsoft Passport.
Windows	Use Windows login and password.

String specifying name of the cookie to use for authentication; default is ASPXAUTH.

URL to redirect the user to if the authentication cookie is not found.

String used as the decryption key for encrypted authentication.

```
<configuration>
    <system.web>
        <authentication mode="Windows">
            <cookie
                cookie="name"
                loginurl="http://www.myurl.com"
                decryptionkey="key"
            >
                <credentials passwordformat="Clear">
                    <user
                        name="username"
                        password="password"
                    />
                </credentials>
            </cookie>
        </authentication>
    </system.web>
</configuration>
```

Clear	Use cleartext authentication [do not encrypt the password].
MD5	Use the MD5 hash algorithm.
SHA1	Use the SHA1 hash algorithm.

The username used to log on the system.

The user's password.

FIGURE 6.1

Description of the authentication section of the Web configuration file.

The details of implementing various authentication methods are discussed in Chapter 8, "Security."

Authorization Settings

An authorization is a permission that belongs to a user. This is different from authentication. Authentication determines who the user *is*, whereas authorization determines what that user is *allowed to do*.

Authorization settings are based on the user's identity as determined by the operating system. This identity is typically established through the user logging in to a Windows NT/2000 domain. Users who access your Web application anonymously (as is often the case with public Internet applications) have a login identity; the username is IUSR_MACHINE where MACHINE is the name of the server.

To specify one of these authorization modes, you create entries in the authorization section of the Web.Config or Machine.Config files. To permit a user or group to access the application, you create an entry in the allow subsection of the authorization section. To explicitly deny users or groups access to the application, create an entry in the deny subsection.

You can denote "all users" in an allow or deny section by using an asterisk (*). To denote anonymous users, use a question mark (?). You can denote multiple users by creating a comma-delimited list of users and/or groups. In this case, *groups* are collections of users as defined in Windows NT/2000 security settings on the server.

Browser Capabilities Settings

Browser capabilities refer to the way that ASP.NET detects whether clients' Web browsers have the capability to process special features such as cookies, JavaScript, and so on. Certain features of ASP.NET have the capability to tailor themselves to different browser types. An example of this is a validation control, which can emit client-side JavaScript for browsers that support it or fall back to server-side validation for non-JavaScript browsers. (For more on how this works, see Chapter 10, "Building User Controls and Server Controls.")

To add browser capabilities information, you insert a section in the browserCaps section of the Web.Config or Machine.Config files.

Compilation Settings

Compilation settings cover a range of attributes that pertain to how the ASP.NET application uses the compiler. These settings are crucial because of the way that ASP.NET provides seamless integration with the .NET compilers. The compilation section also contains debugging settings.

To change a compilation setting, you make a change to the compilation section of the Web.Config or Machine.Config files.

Figure 6.2 shows a typical compilation settings section and describes some of its settings.

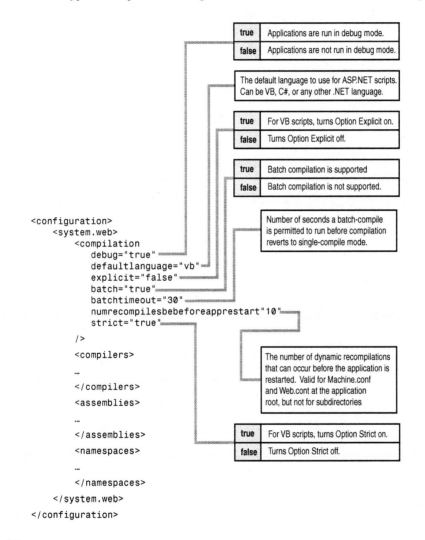

| true | Applications are run in debug mode. |
| false | Applications are not run in debug mode. |

| | The default language to use for ASP.NET scripts. Can be VB, C#, or any other .NET language. |

| true | For VB scripts, turns Option Explicit on. |
| false | Turns Option Explicit off. |

| true | Batch compilation is supported |
| false | Batch compilation is not supported. |

| | Number of seconds a batch-compile is permitted to run before compilation reverts to single-compile mode. |

```
<configuration>
    <system.web>
        <compilation
            debug="true"
            defaultlanguage="vb"
            explicit="false"
            batch="true"
            batchtimeout="30"
            numrecompilesbebeforeapprestart"10"
            strict="true"
        />
        <compilers>
        ...
        </compilers>
        <assemblies>
        ...
        </assemblies>
        <namespaces>
        ...
        </namespaces>
    </system.web>
</configuration>
```

| | The number of dynamic recompilations that can occur before the application is restarted. Valid for Machine.conf and Web.cont at the application root, but not for subdirectories |

| true | For VB scripts, turns Option Strict on. |
| false | Turns Option Strict off. |

FIGURE 6.2
Description of the compilation settings section of the Web configuration file.

NOTE

For VB .NET developers, a number of settings are of special interest in the compilation section—the `explicit` and `strict` attributes enable you to turn on Option Strict and Option Explicit on an applicationwide or serverwide basis, without forcing your developers to include the `Option Strict` or `Option Explicit` directives on every page.

Custom Error Settings

You can change the way that ASP.NET deals with errors by adjusting settings in the `customErrors` section of the Web.Config or Machine.Config files. By making changes in this section, you can specify a page to redirect to when various errors occur.

Figure 6.3 shows a typical `customErrors` section and describes some of its settings.

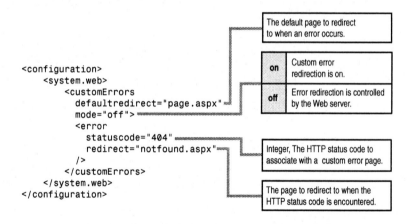

FIGURE 6.3
Description of the `customErrors` section of the Web configuration file.

The `error` subsection of the `customErrors` section can appear multiple times in a single Web configuration document; each section can have a different HTTP result code mapping, thereby causing the browser to redirect to a different page when an error occurs.

Execution Timeout Settings

The execution timeout section provides a serverwide or applicationwide setting that controls how long a script is permitted to run before it times out. This can be overridden by using a page-level directive.

To change the execution timeout, you make a change to the value attribute of the `executionTimeout` section of the Web.Config or Machine.Config files. This integer value represents the number of seconds that scripts are permitted to run before ASP.NET will generate an error.

Globalization Settings

The globalization section determines the international language settings for a Web application. This information includes the encoding types both for requests and responses. It also controls culture-specific settings.

To specify a globalization setting, you make a change to the globalization section of the Web.Config or Machine.Config files.

Figure 6.4 shows a typical globalization section and describes some of its settings.

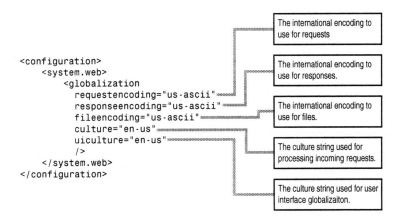

FIGURE 6.4
Description of the globalization section of the Web configuration file.

HTTP Handler Settings

An HTTP handler is a component that intercepts and handles HTTP requests at a lower level than ASP.NET is capable of handling.

To add an HTTP handler to your server, you make a change to the `httpHandlers` section of the Machine.Config file.

The order of entries in the `httpHandlers` section is significant. Handlers that are entered lower in the list take precedence over like-named entries that appear higher in the list.

See Chapter 9, "HttpHandlers and HttpModules," for more information on custom HTTP handlers in ASP.NET.

HTTP Module Settings

To add an HTTP module to your system, you make a change to the httpModules section of the Web.Config or Machine.Config files.

The order of entries in the httpModules section is significant. Modules that are entered lower in the list take precedence over like-named entries that appear higher in the list.

Page Settings

<pages> settings control how individual ASP.NET pages are rendered in the browser. This section controls such settings as enableSessionState, enableViewState, buffer, and autoEventWireup.

To change page settings, you make a change to the pages section of the Web.Config or Machine.Config files.

Figure 6.5 shows a typical pages section and describes some of its settings.

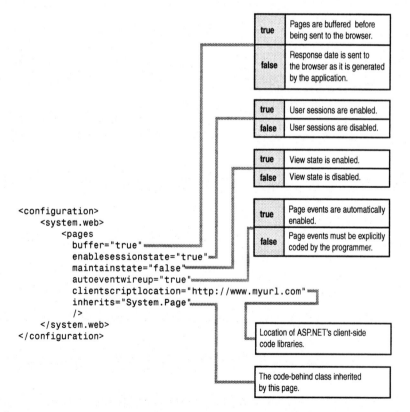

FIGURE 6.5

Description of the <pages> section of the Web configuration file.

Page settings such as buffer, autoEventWireup, and enableViewState are covered in Chapter 3, "Page Framework."

Process Model Settings

Process model settings control how your Web application uses certain system resources, such as CPUs on a multiple-processor machine. It also gives you control over how IIS assigns processes to ASP.NET requests. You can change these settings to tune performance.

To change `processModel` settings, you make a change to the `processModel` section of the Web.Config or Machine.Config files.

Figure 6.6 shows a typical `processModel` section and describes some of its settings.

Session State Settings

Session state settings determine how user session information is stored by ASP.NET. In ASP.NET you can store user session information either in process (in memory on the same machine as the Web server), out of process (on a separate machine), or in Microsoft SQL Server.

To change session state settings, you make a change to the `sessionState` section of the Web.Config or Machine.Config files.

Figure 6.7 shows a typical `sessionState` section and describes some of its settings.

The various session state options available in ASP.NET are discussed in more detail in Chapter 3.

Trace Settings

Trace settings are typically used for debugging purposes. You activate Trace mode in ASP.NET when you want to show the output of trace code (calls to the `Trace` method of the `System.Web.TraceContext` object).

To turn tracing on, you set the enabled attribute to `true` in the trace section of the Web.Config or Machine.Config file.

Figure 6.8 shows a typical trace section and describes some of the trace section's other settings.

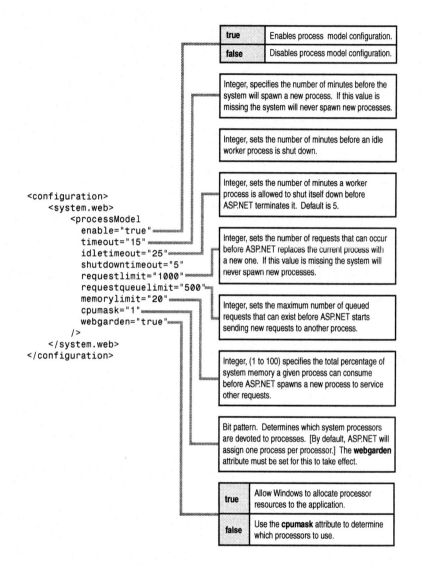

FIGURE 6.6

Description of the processModel *section of the Web configuration file.*

Tracing arean ASP.NET application is discussed in more detail in Chapter 4, "Debugging ASP.NET Applications."

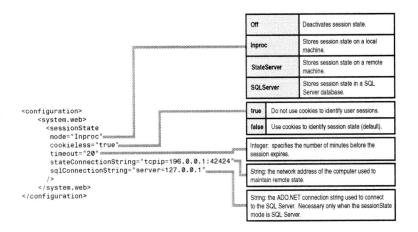

FIGURE 6.7
Description of the sessionState *section of the Web configuration file.*

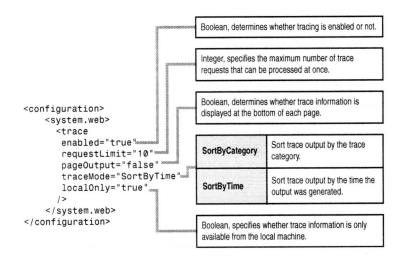

FIGURE 6.8
Description of the trace section of the Web configuration file.

Web Services Settings

XML Web services settings enable you to control settings pertaining to the exposure of Web services functionality on the Web server. Remember that in .NET, XML Web services are a superset that comprises a number of Web protocols, including SOAP, HTTP POST, and HTTP

GET. All XML Web services protocols are configured in the same section of the Web configuration file.

To specify an XML Web services setting, you make a change to the `webServices` section of the Web.Config or Machine.Config files.

XML Web services are discussed in more detail in Chapter 7, "Web Services."

Configuring Multiple Locations in Web.Config

The Web.Config file supplies settings for scripts found in that directory. If no Web.Config file exists in a given directory, configuration settings are inherited from the parent directory; if no Web.Config file exists there, the settings from Machine.Config are used.

This situation can lead to problems in managing the configuration of a complex Web application with many subdirectories. If you have three levels of subdirectories, each with its own set of permissions, you could easily have a half-dozen Web.Config files in various locations in your application directory hierarchy.

You can get around this problem by placing a *location section* in Web.Config. A location section enables you to manage special permissions for subdirectories in one Web.Config file, located in a parent directory.

For example, suppose your Web application contains a root directory and two subdirectories, as illustrated in Figure 6.9.

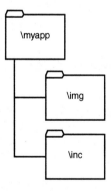

FIGURE 6.9
Hierarchical Web application directories example.

To specify different settings for scripts contained in the three directories that compose this application, you could include three separate Web.Config files, one in each subdirectory; or you could create a single Web.Config file in the \myapp directory and include location sections that apply to the subdirectories \img and \inc.

Listing 6.1 shows an example of a Web.Config file that has separate settings for files located in subdirectories.

LISTING 6.1   Web.Config file Example with Location Section to Handle Subdirectory Settings

```
<configuration>
   <!-- Configuration for the current directory -->
   <system.web>
      <compilation debug="false">
   </system.web>

   <!-- Configuration for \img -->
   <location path="img">
      <system.web>
        <compilation debug="false">
      </system.web>
   </location>

   <!-- Configuration for \inc -->
   <location path="inc">
      <system.web>
        <compilation debug="true">
      </system.web>
   </location>

</configuration>
```

You can see that this file contains two sections that correspond to the two subdirectories (\img and \inc) underneath the application directory. Each location section in the configuration file contains settings that are normally found under the system.web section.

You can test this by putting ASP.NET scripts that contain syntax errors into each of the three directories and then navigating to them in the browser. You should be able to see that scripts in the \inc directory will provide debugging information when they fail, whereas scripts in the \img and \myapp directories will not.

Locking Down Web Configuration Settings

Although Web configuration files can inherit their settings from other configuration files, you may want to prevent subordinate configuration files from changing certain settings.

For example, for security reasons you may want to turn off debugging at the level of Machine.Config, thereby preventing any ASP.NET application on that server from going into debug mode when an error occurs. Shutting down debugging is important because turning on the debug attribute can expose your source code to the user.

To lock down a configuration setting, you use the `allowOverride` attribute, found in the `<location>` element. This attribute is a Boolean; when set to `false`, Web configuration files that inherit from the current file cannot change the settings in the section.

Accessing Configuration Files Programmatically

Because the Web configuration files are XML documents, you could use the XML-handling objects (discussed in Chapter 11, "Using XML") to store and retrieve information in Web.Config and Machine.Config. This might be useful when you want to store application-specific information in Web.Config, such as a database connection string, for example.

However, you don't need to go to the trouble of parsing Web.Config to store and retrieve custom values from the file—there is an easier way. To store application-specific settings in Web.Config, simply create a section called appSettings and add the settings you want as key/value pairs in that section.

```
<configuration>
    <system.web>
        <customErrors mode="Off" />
    </system.web>
    <appSettings>
      <add key="pubsdata"
➥value="SERVER=localhost;DATABASE=pubs;UID=sa;PWD=mypass;" />
    </appSettings>
</configuration>
```

In this example, the connection string is given the key "pubsdata"; the value of the setting is the familiar ADO connection string. Note that you aren't limited to storing database connection strings in appSettings, but appSettings is a reasonable solution to the common problem of where to store connection string data without sticking it into a constant in your code or using a conventional include file.

To retrieve the custom application setting, you use the AppSettings collection contained in the ConfigurationSettings object. This object, a member of the System.Configuration namespace in the .NET framework, enables you to access the values stored in Web.Config by their key. So, for example, to retrieve the `pubsdata` value specified in the previous example, you'd use the expression

```
Response.Write ConfigurationSettings.AppSettings("eqguild")
```

Note that it's not necessary to create an instance of the ConfigurationSettings object. As with other objects such as Page and Response, a single instance of ConfigurationSettings is always available to code that executes in your ASP.NET page.

Editing Web Configuration Files in Visual Studio .NET

Like any other XML file, you can edit Web configuration files in Visual Studio .NET. In fact, when you create a Web application project in Visual Studio .NET, the system adds a default Web.Config file to your project automatically.

Several advantages exist to editing Web configuration files in Visual Studio .NET. Among these are color-coded syntax and the capability to navigate quickly through the configuration file using the outline mode common to all XML files in the Visual Studio development environment.

Initializing Web Applications Using Global.asax

ASP.old provided a file, global.asa, that provided functionality specific to the ASP application and session. You would typically put initialization code in global.asa, which provided a set of event-handling procedures for this purpose.

ASP.NET provides a similar functionality in the file Global.asax. Four categories of entries can appear in a Global.asax file:

- Application directives
- Code declaration blocks
- Server-side object tags
- Server-side includes

Each of these four categories of entries is discussed in more detail in the next few sections.

Note that when you make a change to Global.asax, as with all ASP.NET files, the binary representation of the script will be automatically recompiled. This isn't a big deal in the case of most scripts, but in the case of Global.asax, making a change and recompiling has the potentially troublesome side effect of wiping out all existing sessions (including any data stored in session variables). Be aware of this when making changes to Global.asax on a production system; as with any major change to a production site, you may want to use Windows Scheduler to upload the updated version of the file to the production server at a time when traffic on your site is at its lowest, such as the middle of the night or on a weekend.

Note, too, that the code in Global.asax can't be run directly; nothing happens when a user navigates to Global.asax using a browser, for example. This prevents users from viewing or running the code contained in this file.

Application Directives in Global.asax

An application directive is a line of code that instructs ASP.NET to take some special action regarding the execution of the page.

Three application directives are supported in Global.asax:

- `@Application`, which allows you to specify an inheritance relationship between the application object and another object
- `@Assembly`, which links an assembly to the application
- `@Import`, which imports a namespace

You've seen example of `@Import` directives in virtually every code example in this book so far, so we won't go into them again here.

Using the `@Application` Directive in Global.aspx

The `@Application` directive supports two attributes: a class name and a description string.

```
<%@ Application inherits="MyComp.MyApp"
            description="My Custom Application %>
```

You use the `@Application` directive in situations where you want to create a custom Application object that inherits from another object.

Note that the options available in the `@Application` directive in Global.aspx are different from the attributes of the `@Application` directive that are legal in normal ASPX pages.

Using the `@Assembly` Directive in Global.aspx

The `@Assembly` directive represents a reference to an external assembly (a component) that is not contained in the application's \bin directory. The advantage of referencing an assembly is that you get the performance and type-safety benefits of early binding, as well as IntelliSense when working with the assembly's objects in the Visual Studio development environment.

```
<%@ Assembly Name="PrattleFreeApp.Customer" %>
```

ASP.NET assemblies are typically contained in a \bin subdirectory under the application directory. Such assemblies are automatically referenced by all pages in an ASP.NET application. The `@Assembly` directive is used in situations where, for some reason, the assembly is stored in an unexpected place.

The syntax for referencing an external assembly in Global.aspx is the same as referencing an external assembly in a normal ASP.NET page.

Code Declaration Blocks in Global.asax

Code declaration blocks are events associated with Page objects such as Server and Application. You can write code in event handlers for these objects in Global.asax. The advantage of this is centralized management of initialization code. Because code in Global.asax is guaranteed to execute no matter which page initially uses to access the application, you don't have to worry about including it (or copying it) into every file of your application.

The event procedures that can be included in Global.asax (in the order in which the events fire) are

- Application_OnStart
- Session_OnStart
- Session_OnEnd
- Application_OnEnd

Listing 6.2 shows an example of an event handler for the Session object.

LISTING 6.2   Example of an OnStart Event Handler in Global.asax

```
<SCRIPT runat='server'>

  Sub Session_OnStart()
    Response.Write("Starting a new session!<BR>")
    Session("StartTime") = Now()
    Session.Timeout = 45
  End Sub

</SCRIPT>
```

You can test this script by dropping it into a Web-accessible directory and then navigating to an ASPX script file located in that directory. Don't try to navigate directly to Global.asax; it won't work. Also, the code in Global.asax isn't accessible from ASP.old scripts, so don't try testing it with an .ASP file.

.NET Developer's Guide to ASP.NET, XML, and ADO.NET

This code is very straightforward; it sends a message to the browser for debugging purposes, stores the date and time the session began in a `Session` variable, and then sets the session timeout to 45 minutes. The code in this event procedure executes only the first time a user navigates to one of the pages in the Web application; a Web application is defined as any ASP.NET Web script in a given directory.

Server-Side Object Tags in Global.asax

In many cases, it's useful for a Web application to have access to an object globally. This enables you to share objects across multiple pages. You can also specify whether the object has application or sessionwide scope. You use server-side object tags in Global.asax to do this, as shown in Listing 6.3.

LISTING 6.3   Declaring an `Application-Scoped` Object in Global.asax

```
<object id="users"
        scope="application"
        class="System.Collections.ArrayList"
        runat="server">

<SCRIPT runat='server'>

    Public Sub Session_OnStart()
        Dim usr As String
        usr = Request.UserHostAddress

        users.Add(usr)

        Response.Write("Global.asax: New session created.")

    End Sub

</SCRIPT>
```

In addition to the definition of the application-level object called users, the code includes a `Session_OnStart` event handler that adds the user's IP address to the user's `ArrayList` at the time the session is initiated. (In a real application, you would need a corresponding `Session_OnEnd` code to remove the user's IP address from the array when the session timed out.)

To display the contents of the array, use code similar to that shown in Listing 6.4.

LISTING 6.4   Displaying Results of the Active-User Array

```
<HTML>

<SCRIPT runat='server'>

  Sub Page_Load(Sender As Object, e As EventArgs)
    ' NB the variable 'users' is defined in global.asax
    Dim usr As String

    Response.Write(users.Count & " users have active sessions.<BR>")

    For Each usr In users
      Response.Write(usr & "<BR>" )
    Next

  End Sub
</SCRIPT>
```

This code will work in any script that is contained in the application directory. To test it, you will either have to access the same page from two computers or launch two separate sessions on the same machine by using a different Web browser (such as Netscape or Opera) for your second session.

When you access the Web server from your local machine, the IP address will always be 127.0.0.1.

Note that you don't have to use this technique to use an object globally; instead, you can place objects in the Session object or (better yet) place the object in the ASP.NET cache. For information on this, see Chapter 5, "State Management and Caching."

Server-Side Includes in Global.asax

Server-side includes (SSIs) are the same in Global.asax as they are in any other server-side script. The SSI directive tells the Web server to include an external file in the script; it works the same as if you had copied and pasted it into the script yourself.

The syntax for a server-side include in Global.asax is the same as in any other server-side script in ASP or ASP.NET:

```
<!-- #include File = "MyFile.inc" -->
```

It's typical to see server-side includes used as a code-sharing tactic. Unfortunately, maintaining server-side includes can be unwieldy, particularly in situations where the includes are numerous or contain large amounts of code. Other disadvantages exist to using includes, notably that you don't have access to IntelliSense in the Visual Studio development for procedures contained in SSIs.

Rather than using SSIs, you may want to consider defining your global procedures as objects and referencing them as components instead.

Using XCOPY for Deployment

Microsoft uses a shorthand term for the ease-of-deployment features in ASP.NET—it's called *XCOPY deployment*. This refers to a command that was brought into Windows from the DOS world. An evolved version of the DOS COPY command, XCOPY adds more powerful features, including the capability to create entire folders and subfolder structures where necessary. In situations in which you use the command to copy a folder and child subfolders, XCOPY can create identical folder structures on the destination disk.

Additionally, XCOPY has the capability to copy only those files that are newer than files on the destination drive. This is a big benefit for large sites that don't want to copy all 10,000 files each time they make a few changes, but it's an even more important feature for developers who frequently make little changes to several files and then forget which files are newer—the ones on the development machine or the ones on the server. You can painstakingly compare the dates and times that each file in your application was last modified, but that's grunt work the computer should take care of for you. XCOPY deployment performs that grunt work for you.

The ultimate goal of XCOPY deployment is to have an automated way to send changes from your development machine to your test server and on to your production machine when everything is all ready. With that in mind, we'll run through a few scenarios that demonstrate how to use XCOPY in real life. (At the end of this section, you'll find a quick reference to all XCOPY's options in case you ever need to do something more exotic.)

In our scenarios, we'll set up two folders on the same machine, C:\SOURCE and C:\TARGET. The objective in each case will be to copy some files (and, optionally, a directory structure) from one place to another. Figure 6.10 illustrates the state of the file system when we begin.

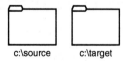

c:\source   c:\target

FIGURE 6.10
Initial state of file system before using XCOPY.

Deploying a Single Directory

To begin, we'll copy all the files from C:\SOURCE to C:\TARGET. To do this, use the command

```
XCOPY c:\source c:\target
```

When you execute this command, you'll get the following message:

```
C:\source\file1.aspx
C:\source\file2.aspx
C:\source\web.config
C:\source\deploy.bat
4 File(s) copied
```

This means that all four files in C:\SOURCE were copied. So far, so good.

Deploying a Directory Tree

Now let's use a somewhat more realistic example. Suppose your Web site has a few subdirectories that contain binary components and images, as illustrated in Figure 6.11.

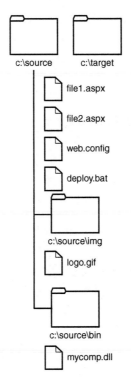

FIGURE 6.11

Folder with subfolders.

In this case, using XCOPY by itself won't do the trick, because you need to tell XCOPY to copy subdirectories (and files within them) as well. To copy this structure, use the command

```
XCOPY c:\source c:\target /S
```

The /S switch tells XCOPY to copy over all the files, including subdirectories and files within those subdirectories. The /S switch will work no matter how many files and how many directories (including subdirectories within those subdirectories) you have.

> **NOTE**
>
> When you're developing a site, you may want to consider using the /E switch in place of the /S switch. The /E switch creates subdirectories on the destination even if the subdirectories on the source are empty. The /S switch won't create empty subdirectories on the destination drive.
>
> Creating empty subdirectories on the destination drive for a site in development can be useful for a number of reasons. For example, you might do it as a placeholder, to tell other developers working on the site that a subdirectory containing files is going to be created here eventually, but you haven't gotten around to creating files to go in it yet.

Excluding Files from Deployment

But wait; the file deploy.bat is your deployment script. It's not appropriate for that file to be deployed to the test Web server. We need to be able to tell XCOPY not to copy certain files. To do this, we need to create an *exclude file*, a text file that contains names of files we don't want XCOPY to touch.

You can create an exclude file using a text editor such as Notepad (or our favorite Notepad replacement, TextPad, available for download at www.textpad.com). In our example, the exclude file is called exclude.txt. It contains two entries: one for itself; the other for the deployment batch file, deploy.bat. Listing 6.5 contains the complete contents of exclude.txt.

LISTING 6.5   Contents of a Sample XCOPY Exclude File

```
exclude.txt
deploy.bat
```

You use the /EXCLUDE: switch with XCOPY to denote the existence of an exclude file. Therefore, to use the exclude file in our directory structure example, you would use the command

```
XCOPY c:\source c:\target /EXCLUDE:exclude.txt /S
```

The resulting structure would appear as illustrated in Figure 6.12.

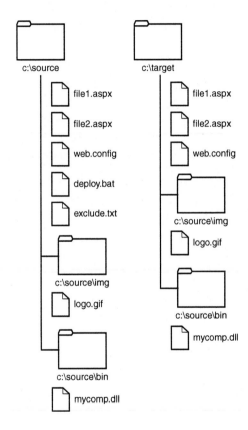

FIGURE 6.12
File and directory structure after being copied with an exclude file.

Confirmations and Overwriting

If you've been experimenting with XCOPY without deleting all the files in the destination directory each time, you may have noticed that XCOPY gives you a warning when it's about to overwrite an existing file. You have two choices here: You can either lean on the Y key on your keyboard, or you can shut these warnings off altogether by using the /Y switch (also known as Yes mode).

For example, this command does the same thing as the previous example, but without the yes/no/always confirmation prompts:

```
XCOPY c:\source c:\target /EXCLUDE:exclude.txt /S /Y
```

You definitely want to use Yes mode in unattended (batch) XCOPY operations. Otherwise, there's a chance that XCOPY will sit there, possibly eternally, waiting for you to confirm a file overwrite.

> **NOTE**
>
> Microsoft changed the behavior of XCOPY (as well as the related commands MOVE and COPY) in Windows 2000 to make the commands work the same way they did in DOS and Windows 95. Specifically, when copying files in Windows 2000, you'll get warning messages when attempting to overwrite existing files on the target drive. Use the /Y switch to avoid these messages. This means that if you wrote batch files that used XCOPY, MOVE, or COPY in Windows NT, you may need to change those batch files for Windows 2000.
>
> For more information on this change, see Microsoft Knowledge Base article Q240268 located at http://support.microsoft.com/support/kb/articles/Q240/2/68.ASP.

Deploying Only Files with Changes

Now suppose you've made changes to a few files on your development machine (the source) and you want to copy to the destination only those files that have changed. This isn't a problem for small sites (just recopy the whole thing whether or not the files changed), but for larger sites (or slower network connections) it may take a long time to refresh the whole site.

You can use XCOPY to copy only those files that have changed by using the /D switch. The /D switch compares the date stamp on each file and copies those files that are newer than those on the target. The complete command looks like this:

```
XCOPY c:\source c:\target /EXCLUDE:exclude.txt /S /Y /D
```

If you're testing this on your machine, you can examine what happens by making a change to the file file1.aspx in your source directory and then executing this XCOPY command. XCOPY should copy the file you changed (and only the file you changed), returning the message:

```
C:\source\file1.aspx
```

```
1 File(s) copied
```

XCOPY Switches

Now that we've covered some common scenarios, Table 6.1 shows a list of all the switches available with XCOPY in Windows 2000.

TABLE 6.1 XCOPY Switches

Switch	Description
/A	Copies only files whose archive attribute has been set. (The archive attribute is a property of the file that tells backup utilities that the file has been backed up; if you use the archive attribute, you can use XCOPY as a sort of rudimentary backup system.)
/M	Copies only files whose archive attribute has been set; turns off the archive attribute after copying.
/D	Copies files that have been modified on or after a specified date. If you don't specify a date, XCOPY will copy only files that are newer than those on the target. An example is XCOPY /D:11-18-01.
/EXCLUDE:filename	Excludes one or more files. To use this option, you should create an exclude file (described earlier in this section). Wildcard characters are not supported in an exclude file.
/S	Copies entire subdirectories that contain files.
/E	Copies subdirectories whether or not they contain files.
/V	Verifies while copying. This causes the copy to take a little longer and is not normally needed for script files.
/P	Provides a prompt before copying each file.
/W	Prompts you to press a key before copying.
/C	Continues copying even if errors occur.
/I	Specifies the Destination of the copy.
/Q	Quiet mode (suppresses display of filenames while copying).
/F	Displays both source and destination filenames while copying. (By default, XCOPY displays only source filenames while copying.)
/L	Lists files that would be copied (without actually copying them).
/H	Copies hidden and system files. (By default, XCOPY does not copy these files.)
/R	Overwrites read-only files in the target.
/T	Creates the target directory structure that would result from a copy operation, but does not actually copy files.

TABLE 6.1   Continued

Switch	Description
/U	Copies only files that already exist on the destination drive.
/K	Retains the read-only attribute on copied files. (By default, XCOPY removes the read-only attribute from the files it copies. This can be useful in some situations—most notably when copying files from a CD-ROM to your hard disk.)
/N	Copies using short filenames. This is used for compatibility with 16-bit File Allocation Table (FAT) file systems (such as DOS and Windows 3.1).
/O	Copies file ownership and Access Control List (ACL) information.
/X	Copies file audit settings. This setting copies file ownership and ACL information as well.
/Y	Answers "yes" to prompts that ask you whether you want to overwrite destination files.
/-Y	Defines prompting before overwriting existing files on the target computer.
/Z	Copies network files in restartable mode.

Managing the Global Assembly Cache

One of the advantages to working with ASP.NET is that code you write is compiled for you seamlessly and transparently. This is a useful feature; however, you may find yourself in a situation where you want to reuse the functionality found in one application in another. You may even want to share software functionality across two radically different types of applications. A Web application and a thick-client application on the Windows desktop, for example, might share a common set of code that performs a set of operations specific to your business. You can accomplish this through the use of components. (Because corporate application developers often use components to share standard business-specific code functionality across multiple applications, components are sometimes also referred to as *business logic* components.)

A component is a piece of software designed to be used by another piece of software. Windows has had components throughout its history. Initially, components were packaged in the form of procedural dynamic link libraries (DLLs), but for ease of programming and interoperability, application developers eventually came to package their DLLs in the form of Component Object Model (COM) libraries. Although these libraries do provide the capability to reuse code, they also suffer from limitations that .NET attempts to overcome.

As we've mentioned earlier in this book, one of the major problems with COM DLLs is that COM requires you to register a DLL on a machine before you can use it. This means that with a COM component, you can have only one version of a component installed on a machine at a time. This is a problem because there's no guarantee that future versions of a given component will provide the same functionality as the version you deploy your application with. (This is one aspect of the problem known as "DLL Hell.")

> **NOTE**
>
> Components and assemblies aren't technically the same thing. However, for the purposes of this (and most) discussions of components in Microsoft.NET, they are pretty close to the same thing. So we'll refer to components and assemblies more or less interchangeably in this section.

Microsoft.NET attempts to get around DLL Hell problems by encouraging developers to deploy dependent components in a subdirectory under their application directories. For ASP.NET applications, this means that components will be installed in a subdirectory called \bin under the application directory. But a problem occurs here. Component code that is accessible based on its physical location in the file system can't be shared across multiple applications. You could deploy multiple copies of the component to each application that required it (in fact, in the .NET world this may be preferable for compatibility reasons), but you may find yourself in a situation where you develop a tool or library whose functionality is so generically useful that you may want to provide access to that library in a global fashion.

Microsoft.NET provides a way do to this, called the Global Assembly Cache (GAC). Components that are installed into the GAC are available from any .NET application running on that computer. (Note that this includes other types of .NET applications, including Windows Forms applications, not just ASP.NET applications.)

You can install a component into the GAC using a command-line tool called gacutil. To install a component into the Global Assembly Cache, use the command

```
gacutil -i mycomp.dll
```

in which `mycomp.dll` is the name of your component.

> **NOTE**
>
> You can create .NET components in Visual Studio. To do this, create a project using the "Class Library" project type.

To uninstall a component from the GAC, use the command

```
gacutil /u mycomp.dll
```

Be careful when using this command, because applications that rely on the component will break when it is removed from the GAC.

To see a list of the components in the GAC, use the command

```
gacutil /l
```

You'll see a list of all the components that have been installed on the system. Initially, this list will just be composed of Microsoft.NET assemblies (which you typically don't want to mess with).

Numerous configuration files and attributes can be configured quite easily and in a prompt manner. The Web.Config and Machine.Config files are the two most commonly used configuration files, and any changes to these files can be easily distributed by using the XCOPY functionality.

Web Services

IN THIS CHAPTER

There is no way you could have existed on the planet Earth in the year 2001 and not heard about the latest solution to all of mankind's problems—XML Web services. Depending on who you listen to, XML Web services will enable frictionless e-commerce or eliminate world hunger. So what are XML Web services, really?

Let's take a look back at the genesis of the Web. How did it start? It was the combination of a document format, HTML, and a protocol, HTTP, that enabled scientists to share documents in a standard fashion and to link those documents together. This was nothing new. We had a myriad of document formats: WordPerfect, Word, or even LATEX. The problem was that none of these document formats was interoperable. The guy who used WordPerfect couldn't read the LATEX documents, and vice versa. An interoperable document format alone, however, wouldn't solve the problem. A way also had to exist for scientists to discover papers published by other colleagues. This was done initially by placing hyperlinks into the document to enable navigation to other documents. Theoretically, given a starting point, a scientist could read a document and (by utilizing the hyperlinks) navigate to information related to the subject at hand. This navigation scheme assumed that there was a known starting point. This problem gave rise to the directory, such as Yahoo, as a starting point. It was up to the directory to catalog the Web and indicate the appropriate starting point.

This clearly was a successful paradigm for finding, navigating to, and reading information. As the Internet grew, it became clear that a need existed for businesses to exchange information and transact business online. Although the Web was successful for humans to exchange information, it had far too little organization to make it an effective way for very literal-minded computers to take advantage of it.

What was appropriate (if not ideal) for a human being was far from ideal for a computer. First, computers need a fairly rigid structure to be applied to the information that they are exchanging. This structure must go beyond the document format to also encompass the structure and organization of the actual information itself. Second, if computers are going to trade information, there needs to be a way to agree on the format of information that is being exchanged. Finally, a need still exists to find partners to trade with. Given a partner, a business can negotiate with them to determine what services they might expose, but how does it find new partners? It still has a need for a directory service, but in this case it's one that the computer can query to find appropriate partners.

One answer to this problem is the concept of a Web service. This is in contrast to the ubiquitous Web page that we all know and love. A Web service is just what it sounds like: a facility that provides a way to do work. That being said, a Web service is not a Web page. It is not intended to be consumed by human eyes; it is intended to be consumed by a computer and is optimized for this type of access. If you want to make an analogy to the existing computer world, you could think of a Web service as a new form of Remote Procedure Call (RPC). Historically, the problem with RPC has been the lack of an open and widely accepted standard that defines how to represent data on the network, how to identity endpoint locations, and how to advertise the endpoints. Wait! This sounds very much like the problems just mentioned that the Web was created to solve! So let's take each of those three problems and think about how to translate the lessons of the Web to services.

Network Data Representation

One of the two big breakthroughs that enabled the Web was HTML. HTML was an open and standards-based data-formatting language that could be used to represent the data in a document. It was not a binary format but a text-based format based on the concept of markup "tags" that were inserted into the content to provide formatting. This had been done before. The Word file format is a binary form of formatting that holds both the content and the information required to format it. It, however, is not open nor standards based. Microsoft created it and controls it.

Perhaps more important is that it is binary. The barrier to entry for a binary format is that the user typically must create a program just to read or write the format. But with a text-based format such as HTML, anything that can create an ASCII text file can create and/or read the source of the format. The agreed upon format is to use ASCII, which is a common standard, and to build on that by including inline markup tags.

How can this extend to the services model? HTML isn't a good fit because its primary mission is to control the formatting of content. Machines rarely care that a particular word is displayed in pink or blue. They are more concerned that the word itself is "pink" and what that might mean in a certain context. The idea, however, of using ASCII as a standard representation and then adding markup to create structure is a concept that can be generalized—and indeed has been—for something called eXtensible Markup Language (XML). XML is about the *meaning* of the document's content, as opposed to how the content is displayed.

Let's take a look at an example. I am going to express the same thing, an invoice, two ways. First, let's look at a screenshot of the invoice. Figure 7.1 shows what the invoice would look like in the browser.

This is what I would see as a human being browsing this Web page. What would I see if I were a computer browsing this page? I would see the underlying HTML markup. The same page in this format is shown in Listing 7.1.

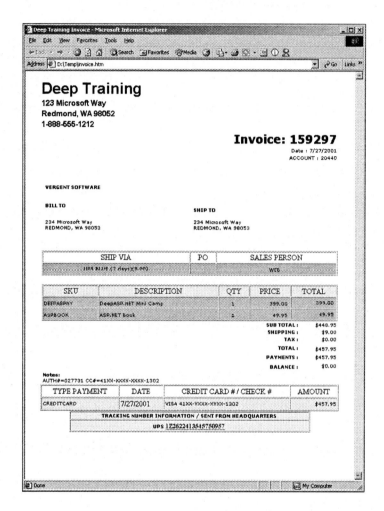

FIGURE 7.1

An invoice page in Internet Explorer.

LISTING 7.1   The Same Invoice from Figure 7.1 Seen from a Computer's Perspective

```
<html>
<head>
<title>Deep Training Invoice</title>
<meta http-equiv="Content-Type" content="text/html; charset=iso-8859-1">
</head>
<body bgcolor="#FFFFFF" text="#000000">
<table cellSpacing="0" cellPadding="0" width="640" border="0" align="center">
```

LISTING 7.1   Continued

```html
<tr>
  <td ALIGN="RIGHT">
    <table cellSpacing="1" cellPadding="1" width=640 border="0"
        align="center">
      <tr>
        <td><font face=Arial size=6><b>Deep Training</b></font></td>
      </tr>
      <tr>
        <td><font face=Arial size=3><b>123 Microsoft Way</b></font></td>
      </tr>
      <tr>
        <td><font face=Arial size=3><b>Redmond, WA 98052</b></font></td>
      </tr>
      <tr>
        <td><font face=Arial size=3><b>1-888-555-1212</b></font></td>
      </tr>
      <tr>
        <td></td>
      </tr>
    </table>
  </td>
</tr>
<tr>
  <td ALIGN="center">
    <table cellSpacing="1" cellPadding="1" width="99%" border="0"
        align="center">
      <tr>
        <td ALIGN="RIGHT"> <font face="Verdana" size="5">
            <b>Invoice: 159297</b></font>
        </td>
      </tr>
      <tr>
        <td align="right">
            <font face="Verdana" size="1">Date : 7/27/2001 </font>
        </td>
      </tr>
      <tr>
        <td align="right">
            <font face="Verdana" size="1">ACCOUNT : 20440 </font>
        </td>
      </tr>
    </table>
    <table cellSpacing="1" cellPadding="1" width="99%" border="0"
        align="center">
```

LISTING 7.1   Continued

```
        <tr>
          <td> <BR>
          </td>
        </tr>
        <tr>
          <td>
            <table cellSpacing="1" cellPadding="1" width="99%" border="0"
                align="center">
            <tr>
              <td align="left"> <font face="Verdana" size="-2">
                  <b>VERGENT SOFTWARE  
                </b></font></td>
              <td>
                  <BR><BR>
<BR>
              </td>
            </tr>
            <tr>
              <td align="left"> <font face="Verdana" size="-2"> <b> BILL TO
                </b></font><BR>
                <BR>
              </td>
              <td>
                  <font face="Verdana" size="-2"> <b> SHIP TO </b></font>
                   <BR>
              </td>
            </tr>
            <tr>
              <td><font face="Verdana" size="-2">234 Microsoft Way<BR>
                REDMOND, WA 98053 <br>
                </font></td>
              <td><font face="Verdana" size="-2">234 Microsoft Way<BR>
                REDMOND, WA 98053 <br>
                </font></td>
            </tr>
            </table>
          </td>
        </tr>
        </table>
        <BR>
        <BR>
        <table cellSpacing="1" cellPadding="1" width="99%" border="1"
            align="center">
          <tr align="center">
```

LISTING 7.1 Continued

```
      <td>SHIP VIA</td>
      <td>PO</td>
      <td>SALES PERSON</td>
   </tr>
   <tr align="center" BGCOLOR="#c5c5c5">
      <td>
          <font face="Verdana" size="-2"> UPS BLUE (2 days)(23.51) </font>
      </td>
      <td><font face="Verdana" size="-2">   </font></td>
      <td><font face="Verdana" size="-2"> WEB  </font> </td>
   </tr>
</table>
<BR>
<table cellSpacing="1" cellPadding="1" width="99%" align="center"
    border="1" bgcolor="#eeeeee">
   <tr>
     <td align="center">COURSE</td>
     <td align="center">DESCRIPTION</td>
     <td align="center">QTY</td>
     <td align="center">PRICE</td>
     <td align="center">TOTAL</td>
   </tr>
   <tr BGCOLOR="#c5c5c5">
     <td align="left">
         <font face="Verdana" size="-2">DEEPASPNY</font>
    </td>
     <td align="left">
         <font face="Verdana" size="-2">DeepASP.NET Mini Camp</font>
     </td>
     <td align="middle">
         <font face="Verdana" size="-2">1 </font>
     </td>
     <td align="right">
         <font face="Verdana" size="-2">399.00 </font>
     </td>
     <td align="right">
         <font face="Verdana" size="-2">399.00  </font>
     </td>
   </tr>
</table>
<table cellSpacing="1" cellPadding="1" width="99%" align="center"
      border="0">
   <tr>
     <td align="LEFT"> </td>
```

Listing 7.1 Continued

```html
      <td align="right"> <font face="Verdana" size="-2"><b>SUB TOTAL :</b>
        </font> </td>
      <td align="right">
          <font face="Verdana" size="-2">$399.00 </font>
      </td>
    </tr>
    <tr>
      <td align="LEFT"> </td>
      <td align="right">
          <font face="Verdana" size="-2"><b>(Non Taxable)OTHER
          CHARGES :</b> </font>
      </td>
      <td align="right"> <font face="Verdana" size="-2">$0.00 </font></td>
    </tr>
    <tr>
      <td align="LEFT"> </td>
      <td align="right"> <font face="Verdana" size="-2"><b>DISCOUNT :</b>
        </font> </td>
      <td align="right"> <font face="Verdana" size="-2">$0.00</font> </td>
    </tr>
    <tr>
      <td align="LEFT"> </td>
      <td align="right"> <font face="Verdana" size="-2">
          <b>FREIGHT :</b> </font>
      </td>
      <td align="right"> <font face="Verdana" size="-2">$0.00 </font></td>
    </tr>
    <tr>
      <td align="LEFT"> </td>
      <td align="right">
          <font face="Verdana" size="-2"><b>TAX :</b> </font>
      </td>
      <td align="right"> <font face="Verdana" size="-2">$0.00 </font></td>
    </tr>
    <tr>
      <td align="LEFT"> </td>
      <td align="right">
          <font face="Verdana" size="-2"><b>TOTAL :</b> </font>
      </td>
      <td align="right">
          <font face="Verdana" size="-2">$399.00</font>
      </td>
    </tr>
    <tr>
```

LISTING 7.1 Continued

```html
        <td align="LEFT"> </td>
        <td align="right"> <font face="Verdana" size="-2"><b>PAYMENTS :</b>
          </font> </td>
        <td align="right">
            <font face="Verdana" size="-2">$399.00 </font>
        </td>
      </tr>
      <tr>
        <td align="LEFT"> </td>
        <td align="right">
            <font face="Verdana" size="-2"><b>BALANCE :</b></font>
        </td>
        <td align="right">
            <font face="Verdana" size="-2">$0.00 </font>
        </td>
      </tr>
      <tr>
        <td align="LEFT">
            <font face="Verdana" size="-2"><B>Notes:</B><BR>
            AUTH#=027731 CC#=41XX-XXXX-XXXX-1302 </font>
        </td>
      </tr>
    </table>
    <TABLE cellSpacing=1 cellPadding=2 border=1 width="80%"
        align="left">
      <TR>
        <TD ALIGN=MIDDLE>TYPE PAYMENT</TD>
        <TD align=middle>DATE</TD>
        <TD ALIGN=MIDDLE>CREDIT CARD # / CHECK #</TD>
        <TD ALIGN=MIDDLE>AMOUNT</TD>
      </TR>
      <tr bgcolor="#eeeecc">
        <td><font face="Verdana" size="-2"> CREDITCARD </font></td>
        <td> 7/27/2001 </td>
        <td>
            <font face="Verdana" size="-2"> VISA 41XX-XXXX-XXXX-1302</font>
        </td>
        <td align=right><font face="Verdana" size="-2"> $399.00 </Font></td>
      </tr>
    </TABLE>
      </td>
      </tr>
</TABLE>
```

LISTING 7.1   Continued

```
<TABLE cellSpacing=1 cellPadding=1 width="75%" align=center border=1
    bgcolor="#eeeeee">
  <TR>
    <TD ALIGN="CENTER">
        <font face="Verdana" size="-2"><B>TRACKING NUMBER INFORMATION
        / SENT FROM HEADQUARTERS</B></font>
    </TD>
  </TR>
  <TR>
    <TD ALIGN="CENTER"> <font face="Verdana" size="-2"> <b>UPS</b> </font><A
HREF=http://wwwapps.ups.com/tracking/tracking.cgi?tracknum=1Z2622413545750957
      target=new>
      <B><FONT size=2>1Z2622413545750957</FONT></b></A>
    </TD>
  </TR>
</TABLE>
</body>
</html>
```

Look at this HTML. Without the visual formatting, it is no longer nearly as easy to pick out the various pieces. How would you find the total or the authorization code? From a machine's perspective, this is mainly gobbledygook. I could say that the total is always going to come after a text string `"TOTAL :</b> </font></td><td align="right"> <font face="Verdana" size="-2">"`. But what happens when the developer of the page decides that the total should be shown in Helvetica? The string I am matching no longer works and my code breaks.

How can this be extended to a services model? To create a system whereby computers communicate without human intervention, HTML isn't going to cut it. It requires something that is more concerned with representing the data in a meaningful manner instead of making it look pretty. This is where XML comes in. Let's look at a representation of the same invoice in XML. Listing 7.2 shows one way to do it. XML is explained more thoroughly in Chapter 11, "Using XML."

LISTING 7.2   A Representation of the Invoice in Listing 7.1 in XML

```
<?xml version="1.0" encoding="utf-8" ?>
<invoice number="159297" date="7272001">
    <account>20440</account>
    <company>Vergent Software</company>
    <billto>
        <address>234 Microsoft Way</address>
        <city>Redmond</city>
```

LISTING 7.2   Continued

```xml
        <state>WA</state>
        <zip>98053</zip>
    </billto>
    <shipto>
        <address>234 Microsoft Way</address>
        <city>Redmond</city>
        <state>WA</state>
        <zip>98053</zip>
    </shipto>
    <shipvia>
        <transport>UPS Blue</transport>
        <days>2</days>
        <cost>9.00</cost>
        <tracking>1Z2622413545750957</tracking>
    </shipvia>
    <salesperson>web</salesperson>
    <items>
        <item sku="DEEPASPNY">
            <description>DeepASP.NET Mini Camp</description>
            <qty>1</qty>
            <price>399.00</price>
        </item>
        <item sku="ASPBOOK">
            <description>ASP.NET Book</description>
            <qty>1</qty>
            <price>49.95</price>
        </item>
    </items>
    <subtotal>448.95</subtotal>
    <shipping>9.00</shipping>
    <tax>0.00</tax>
    <total>457.95</total>
    <payments>457.95</payments>
    <balance>0.00</balance>
    <paymenttype>CREDITCARD</paymenttype>
    <creditcard>
        <type>VISA</type>
        <number>43XX-XXXX-XXXX-1302</number>
        <auth>027731</auth>
        <date>07-27-2001</date>
        <amount>457.95</amount>
    </creditcard>
</invoice>
```

Now is it clear where the total for this invoice is? It is enclosed by the `<total>` and `</total>` tags. These are tags totally unrelated to the display of the information. Their only purpose is to define where to look in the document to find the total. This makes them great candidates for string matching to pick apart the document in a standard way.

Location

How do I define the location or endpoint of a page on the World Wide Web? The Web popularized the concept of a URL, or uniform resource locator. You have seen these. They are strings such as `http://www.deeptraining.com/default.aspx`. The URL in the preceding example is made up of several parts. A syntax-style definition of a URL is as follows:

```
<protocol> "://" <host> [":" <port>] [<path> ["?" <query>]]
```

The first part identifies the protocol. The HTTP at the beginning of the earlier example means that when accessing this URL, you should use the Hypertext Transfer Protocol. Another valid protocol identifier for most browsers is FTP, or File Transfer Protocol. Internet Explorer accepts either

```
file://c:\temp\invoice.htm
```

or

```
ftp://localhost/temp/invoice.htm
```

The second part identifies the host that contains the resource. This is permitted to contain an IP address, but in most cases, it will contain a `hostname.domain.network` combo such as `www.deeptraining.com`. The third part is an optional port designation. If not specified, the default convention is to use port 80 for all HTTP traffic. By specifying a port, you can potentially host more than one Web server on a single IP address. This is frequently used by natural address translation (NAT)-based firewalls to direct incoming traffic to Web servers behind the firewall. The fourth part is one of the more important parts. It indicates the path to the resource. This is a standard path of the form `/temp/invoice.htm`. Note the forward slashes used in the path. The HTTP protocol was invented in the Unix world in which path delimiters are forward-slash characters, in contrast to the backslash characters used in the DOS/Windows world. The last part is optional information that varies for a particular path. You have seen this when you go to a search page. You type in what you are interested in and a page is displayed with a URL like

```
http://www.deeptraining.com/searchresults.aspx?Query=ASP.
```

The ?Query=ASP part on the end is a query parameter used to pass additional information to the search results page.

The combination of all these parts represents a unique endpoint in the scheme of the universe. In addition, it is an endpoint that even my 8-year-old daughter can attribute some meaning to, given the ubiquity of Web usage in today's Internet-savvy world.

In a world where I want to make services available, URLs are useful to uniquely identify the location of my service. I can also potentially use the query parameters portion of the URL to optionally pass information to my service.

Advertisement

How do you find information on the wildly popular Ichiro Suzuki bobblehead doll? If you are like most people today, you fire up a Web browser and look it up. But how do you find the information? Your first try is probably to go to www.ichirosuzuki.com or perhaps even www.seattlemariners.com. If that didn't have the information you were looking for, what is the next step? You can head to a search engine such as www.google.com and type in "Ichiro Bobblehead." In no time at all, Google will spit back dozens of matches for Web sites that have information on the latest craze to hit Safeco field.

Let's translate this to the idea of services. I have a great Web site that I built recently to sell some of those Ichiro bobblehead dolls. When billing the customers an exorbitant amount, I want to make sure that I also charge a sufficient amount for shipping. It would make sense that given the shipping address I need to send the doll to, I want to calculate how much it is going to cost to ship it. I want to utilize a Web service to do this in real-time. I know I am going to be shipping the dolls to eagerly waiting customers using United Parcel Services (UPS) and need to find a service that calculates UPS 2-day rates.

My first guess is to go to www.ups.com, but I quickly determine that they don't yet offer UPS ground rate calculation as a Web service. How can I find out who else might? This is where a search engine analogous to Google would be valuable. As it turns out, several vendors are building directories of services that allow a developer to query them and discover trading partners that offer the services they are interested in. These directories provide a standard interface—universal description, discovery, and integration (UDDI)—for the categorization of services, companies, and the schemas they use. They are accessible via a Web-based interface for you to initially find the services that will fulfill your needs. The UDDI directories also expose themselves using XML Web services so that your applications can dynamically use them also.

After I have a reference to a server, I also need to be able to determine what services that particular server exposes to the outside world. This browsing of services is facilitated by placing an XML file, called a DISCO file, in the root of the Web server. DISCO stands for Discovery, and this XML file provides links to all the XML Web services exposed on that server.

What Is a Web Service?

So what is a Web service? You probably have some ideas based on the parallels I have drawn with the genesis of the World Wide Web. XML Web services are an open way to perform standards-based remote-procedure calls over standard Internet protocols. Wow—that's quite a mouthful. I am sure more than one person might argue with that definition because it is difficult to encapsulate the idea of something as large as XML Web services into a single sentence.

So let's examine this. What does that really mean? XML Web services are not Web pages. They are intended to be created and consumed by applications, not users. Instead of designing the look, you define the schema. The schema is what is important in a Web service.

They are standards based. Several standards apply to XML Web services today. XML Web services communicate over HTTP/1.1, a standard protocol defined in RFC 2616 and RFC 2068. The data that is passed back and forth between XML Web services is encapsulated in XML, which is a W3C recommendation at the present time. Simple Object Access Protocol (SOAP) is an XML grammar that defines the layout of the requests sent to XML Web services and the response received back. As of this writing, SOAP is at W3C NOTE status and more information can be found at `http://www.w3.org/TR/SOAP/`. Web Services Description Language (WSDL) is another XML grammar for defining the application-specific content of SOAP requests and responses. Universal Description, Discovery, and Integration (UDDI) is a standard protocol for quickly and easily finding XML Web services run by trading and business partners.

Whew! Those are quite a few standards. I also said that XML Web services were open. At their very simplest, XML Web services are a way to take SOAP (XML text) and send it over HTTP. This means that any language that is capable of performing TCP socket operations and string manipulation can play in this space. Granted, if TCP sockets and string manipulation were all you had at your fingertips, it would be like deciding to dig a swimming pool in your backyard with a teaspoon. It would not be trivial, but it would definitely be possible. Fortunately, a number of development platforms, including .NET, are building a significant amount of the infrastructure to make creating and consuming XML Web services trivial.

Why Web Services?

The concept of RPC is nothing new. In the preceding years we have been proselytized to use DCOM, CORBA, and a number of other RPC protocols. However, none of these protocols has received enough support to make them ubiquitous and thus enable any trading between partners. DCOM and CORBA both used their own data representations that, while similar in many respects, are different enough to prevent any interoperation. They each define their own protocols that don't work very well in a high-latency WAN such as the Internet. DCOM in particular is very "chatty," requiring numerous round trips just to negotiate a simple remote procedure call with no arguments. In addition, with the paranoid mentality of corporations connecting to the Internet through firewalls and the like, the chances are slim of either an IIOP or DCOM request making it through a firewall. Finally, DCOM is a connection-oriented protocol. The downside of this is that after a connection has been set up, DCOM expects to have a long-running conversation with the remote object, making load balancing and load farming a difficult proposition at best.

On the other hand, the underlying protocol of XML Web services, HTTP, has had untold millions of dollars spent on it in the last few years to solve the problems of scalability and fault tolerance in support of the boom in the Web space during the mid 1990s. Well-known best practices exist for scaling HTTP by creating farms of Web servers, using dynamic location-based DNS, and even performing switching in layers 2–7 of TCP/IP to support quite intelligent load balancing. All this work can now be applied to XML Web services.

With the creation of SOAP came a standard for an XML grammar that can be used to overcome the differences that plagued the various RPC implementations in the past. SOAP defines how any data type, for example an int, should be encoded, regardless of platform.

ASP.NET Web Services

All this is great, but as a Web developer, I don't want to have to go out and learn HTTP, XML, SOAP, WSDL, and DISCO just so that I can trade with my partners. I don't have the time. ASP.NET to the rescue.

The model for creating XML Web services in ASP.NET is very similar to the model for creating programmable pages. Let's create a very simple Web service and look at what it is composed of. In its simplest form, a Web service is a file with an extension, ASMX, that is new to ASP.NET. As you would expect, no HTML is in this page, only code. Listing 7.3 shows the canonical HelloWorld that in some shape or another tends to be every programmer's first application.

LISTING 7.3   A Simple Web Service Saying Hello to the World

```
<%@ WebService Language="vb" Class="HelloWorld" %>
Imports System.Web.Services

Public Class HelloWorld
    Inherits System.Web.Services.WebService

    <WebMethod()> Public Function HelloWorld() As String
        HelloWorld = "Hello World"
    End Function
End Class
```

That's it! After all the talk of SOAP, XML, and so on, this looks just like a standard class. The .NET framework hides the ugly part of creating XML Web services from you, the developer, allowing you to concentrate on what you need the Web service to do instead of how it does it. Well, the code is cool but we want to see it do something. Remember that what we just wrote is intended to be called by a program, not by a user. Having to immediately write a test harness just to test a simple Web service is kind of a pain. Consequently the .NET framework provides a default test harness that will appear if you enter the URL for a Web service endpoint into the browser. If a particular method in a Web service is not specified, it is assumed that the end user needs some more information about the Web service. If I enter `http://localhost/book/ webservices/helloworld/HelloWorld.asmx`, the address for the Web service in Listing 7.3, I get the browser display shown in Figure 7.2.

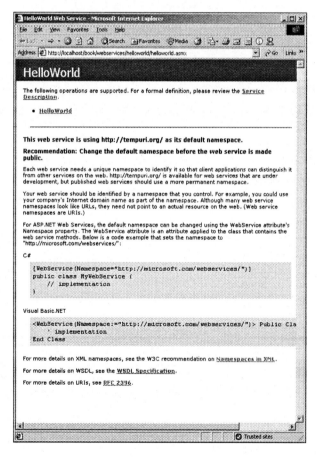

FIGURE 7.2

The automatically created documentation page.

This page gives some general information about the Web service, including the methods in my Web service. If I click the method name, I get the page shown in Figure 7.3.

7

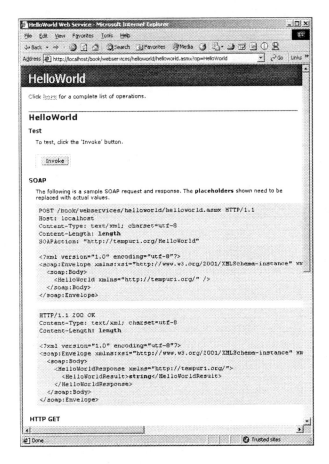

FIGURE 7.3

The automatically created test harness.

This page gives me a way to invoke the method, and it documents the appropriate ways to call my method using SOAP, HTTP GET, and HTTP POST. If I click the Invoke button, my Web service is called using HTTP GET, and I receive a response back that is shown in Figure 7.4.

Figure 7.4
The XML returned by calling the Web method via HTTP GET.

WebMethod

One thing shown in Listing 7.3 does look a little unusual, though. The keyword that looks like <WebMethod()> is called an attribute in .NET. Attributes are a way for the programmer to declaratively affect the operation of an application without having to write code. This particular attribute does a considerable amount of work. The WebMethod() attribute is somewhat similar to the standard access modifier public. By placing the WebMethod() attribute on my method, I have indicated that I want to make it publicly callable from the outside world. Only functions with WebMethod() are accessible by clients of the Web service. This restriction allows me to continue to have internal methods that I rely on within the class, without having to worry about them being accidentally called by clients. Specifying WebMethod() also tells .NET that it should include this method in the WSDL that it generates for clients. WSDL is the way that clients are going to figure out the proper way to call my methods. To see the WSDL that is automatically generated by .NET, I can call my Web service (shown in Listing 7.3) with this URL: http://localhost/book/webservices/helloworld/helloworld.asmx?WSDL. The output of this is shown in Figure 7.5.

> **Note**
>
> This URL points to where I placed the sample code on my system and can vary on your system, depending on where you save the source code.

You can see the HelloWorld method clearly delineated in the WSDL. We will take a look at what the WSDL is good for when we show how to consume XML Web services. The WebMethod attribute also provides a way to configure several optional attributes on a Web service.

FIGURE 7.5
The Web Services Description Language (WSDL) output from the Web service.

WebMethodAttribute

The WebMethodAttribute class is used to set the options for a Web method.

The BufferResponse property controls how data is sent back to the client from the Web service. The most efficient method for returning data over TCP is to batch it all up and send it in large blocks to the client. This is what is considered buffered mode and is the default both for

Web pages and XML Web services. In the case of a large database query, however, it might be nice to start streaming the contents back to the client before the query has finished retrieving all the rows. To do this, set buffer response to `false`. When buffering is turned off, the results are sent back to the client in 16KB chunks.

The `EnableSession` property enables session state for a Web service. By default, this attribute is set to `false`. Think hard about whether you need to enable session state on a Web service, because storing state on the server is going to affect the scalability of your service. However, session state can be utilized with all the attendant options, as discussed in Chapter 5, "State Management and Caching." This includes the State Server and SQL Server modes that are new to ASP.NET.

Listings 7.4 and 7.5 include a sample Web service that provides a Web service-based state service. The service provides two methods, `SetValue` and `GetValue`. `SetValue` allows the user to store some data with a keyname and a value. `GetValue` allows the user to retrieve data with a keyname. This example also uses the code-behind model (discussed in Chapter 3, "Page Framework") for creating XML Web services. As you can see, the activator for the Web service, the `.asmx` file, is minimal. In all future examples, I won't even include the `.asmx` as part of the listing.

LISTING 7.4   The Activator `.asmx` File

```
<%@ WebService Language="vb" Codebehind="State.asmx.vb"
Class="HelloWorld.State" %>
```

LISTING 7.5   The Code-Behind File for the Simple State Service

```
Imports System.Web.Services

Public Class State
    Inherits System.Web.Services.WebService

    Public Sub New()
        MyBase.New()
    End Sub

    <WebMethod(True)> Public Function SetValue(ByVal Name As String, _
        ByVal Value As String)
        Session(Name) = Value
    End Function

    <WebMethod(True)> Public Function GetValue(ByVal Name As String) As String
        Return Session(Name)
    End Function
End Class
```

The `Description` property supplies a description, which is shown in the Web service help page that is created as an automatic test harness. Listing 7.6 shows the code-behind class for the War Games Web service.

LISTING 7.6 A Web Service That Utilizes the `Description` Property.

```
Imports System.Web.Services

Public Class WarGames
    Inherits System.Web.Services.WebService

    Public Sub New()
        MyBase.New()
    End Sub


    <WebMethod(Description:="List of games")> Public Function Games() As String
        Return "Tic Tac Toe, Chess, Thermonuclear War"
    End Function
End Class
```

The `WebMethodAttribute` uses the `Description` property to indicate what each Web method does. The `Description` property is set using the syntax for named properties in an attribute. Figure 7.6 shows how the `Description` property conveniently identifies the Games Web method so we know that it returns a list of games we can play with the WOPR.

The `CacheDuration` property controls how a Web service is cached. The default for cache duration is 0, meaning that no caching is performed. As mentioned in Chapter 5, "State Management and Caching," huge performance increases can be realized by utilizing caching. The `Cache[]` object discussed in Chapter 5 is also available in XML Web services. The `CacheDuration` property is analogous to `OutputCaching` in a Web page. When this is set to some number of seconds, all output from the Web service is cached for this period of time. Listing 7.7 shows an example of a time service that only updates its output every 60 seconds.

LISTING 7.7 The Code Behind Web Service Class That Implements a Cached Time Service

```
Imports System.Web.Services

Public Class Time
    Inherits System.Web.Services.WebService

    Public Sub New()
        MyBase.New()
    End Sub
```

7

WEB SERVICES

Listing 7.7 Continued

```
<WebMethod(False, System.EnterpriseServices.TransactionOption.Disabled, _
    60)> Public Function GetTime() As String
    GetTime = System.DateTime.Now()
End Function

End Class
```

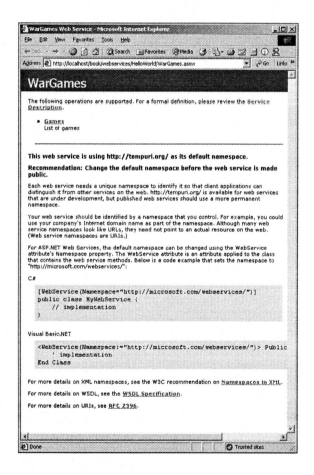

Figure 7.6
The test harness page when we hack into War Games.

> **NOTE**
>
> If this doesn't appear to work, make sure you are using the test harness outside Visual Studio .NET. Visual Studio .NET performs cache busting that penetrates the cache. The correct behavior will be displayed in Internet Explorer.

The `TransactionOption` property controls how the Web service interacts with the transaction-processing support found in the common language runtime. By altering the attribute of the Web method, you can control how the method participates in transactions. The default setting for the transaction option is `Disabled`. This means that by default, a Web method does not participate in any transactions. A Web service is limited to acting as the root in a transaction in version 1.0 of .NET. This limitation means that several of the transaction options provide the same functionality. `Required` and `RequiresNew` do the same thing because the Web method must be the root. This possibly could change in future versions.

Serialization

All our samples so far have utilized relatively simple data types. As it turns out, almost any object in .NET can be serialized to XML. This includes Collections, Arrays, and even DataSets. The exception to this rule is any object that is based on `System.Collections.Hashtable` internally. This includes many of the dictionary-based collections in the base class library with the exception of `ListDictionary`. Serialization is the process whereby a running object provides a static representation of itself that can be used to later reconstitute this object and create a new running object.

Listing 7.8 shows a Web service that returns an array list of shipping methods.

LISTING 7.8 A Web Service That Returns an `ArrayList`

```
Imports System.Web.Services

Public Class Collections
    Inherits System.Web.Services.WebService

    Public Sub New()
        MyBase.New()
    End Sub
```

LISTING 7.8   Continued

```
<WebMethod()> Public Function GetShippingMethods() As ArrayList
    Dim al As New ArrayList()

    al.Add("UPS Ground")
    al.Add("UPS Blue")
    al.Add("UPS Red")
    al.Add("FedEx Ground")
    al.Add("FedEx 2 Day")

    GetShippingMethods = al
End Function
End Class
```

Figure 7.7 shows what the returned XML looks like.

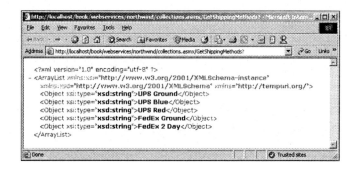

FIGURE 7.7
The output XML from the Web service that serializes the ArrayList.

The most interesting data type in my mind, however, is the DataSet. The DataSet is a new feature of ADO.NET that appears to be a perfect data structure for transporting data between XML Web services and client code. A DataSet has schema, which is just like a database. This schema defines the tables, their columns, and the relationship between tables within the DataSet. In this chapter, we aren't going to discuss all the features of DataSets. For more in-depth information on DataSets, see Chapter 12, "Creating Database Applications with ADO.NET."

We are going to look at the ways in which data sets can be used to move data between a Web service and a client. Let's look at a simple case first. The SimpleDataSet example has a single WebMethod Simple() showing in Listing 7.9. This method returns a list of orders in a DataSet.

It first builds up the orders by creating a DataSet from scratch. It then creates a DataTable and adds columns to it. Each of these columns is strongly typed. System.Type.GetType() is used to get a type structure to pass to the constructor for the DataColumn. Types are classes, too, and need to be specified using full namespace syntax, so the data types are System.String and System.DateTime. After the DataTable has been created, we add rows to it. Calling NewRow() gives us a new row template whose strong typing is based on the DataTable it came from. Finally, the DataTable is added to the DataSet, and the DataSet is returned to the client. The complete WebMethod can be seen in Listing 7.9.

LISTING 7.9   The Simple() WebMethod of SimpleDataSet. It Returns a DataSet Containing a Strongly Typed DataTable.

```
Imports System.Web.Services
Imports System.Data

Public Class DataSetSample
    Inherits System.Web.Services.WebService

    Public Sub New()
        MyBase.New()
    End Sub

    <WebMethod()> Public Function Simple() As DataSet
        Dim dsOrders As New System.Data.DataSet()
        Dim dt As DataTable

        ' Build a data set with four columns
        dt = New DataTable("Orders")
        Dim dc As New DataColumn("OrderID", _
            System.Type.GetType("System.String"))
        dt.Columns.Add(dc)
        dc = New DataColumn("Date", System.Type.GetType("System.DateTime"))
        dt.Columns.Add(dc)
        dc = New DataColumn("Name", System.Type.GetType("System.String"))
        dt.Columns.Add(dc)
        dc = New DataColumn("Amount", System.Type.GetType("System.Currency"))
        dt.Columns.Add(dc)
```

LISTING 7.9   Continued

```
            ' Populate the dataset
            Dim dr As DataRow
            dr = dt.NewRow()

            dr("OrderID") = System.Guid.NewGuid()
            dr("Date") = DateTime.Now
            dr("Name") = "Chris Kinsman"
            dr("Amount") = 123.45
            dt.Rows.Add(dr)

            dr = dt.NewRow()
            dr("OrderID") = System.Guid.NewGuid()
            dr("Date") = DateTime.Now.AddDays(1)
            dr("Name") - "Jeffrey McManus"
            dr("Amount") = "234.45"
            dt.Rows.Add(dr)

            ' Add the datatable to the dataset
            dsOrders.Tables.Add(dt)

            Return dsOrders
        End Function
    End Class
```

Figure 7.8 shows the output from this Web service. It starts with the Schema information for the dataset that we are returning. It defines each of the columns along with the data types. After this section, it uses the predefined schema to represent the data. You can pick out each of the Order rows along with each of the columns data quite easily. It should be quite evident that it would be simple to consume this data in a rigorous fashion.

Let's do a little bit more complex example now. A common data construct is the idea of a Master-Detail relationship. You saw one of these when we were looking at the XML for the invoice. For an order (the master) I had multiple items (the detail). This type of relationship is common in databases, and any method of transferring data must take relationships into account. The example in Listing 7.10 will also return order data; however, this time we will utilize the Northwind database that ships with SQL Server as the source for our data. Listing 7.10 shows the new Web method.

FIGURE 7.8
The XML output from SimpleDataSet.

LISTING 7.10   A Web Method That Returns a Dataset with a Master Detail Relationship

```
Imports System.Web.Services

Public Class Orders
    Inherits System.Web.Services.WebService
```

Listing 7.10 Continued

```
Public Sub New()
    MyBase.New()
End Sub

<WebMethod()> Public Function GetOrders(ByVal OrderDate As DateTime) _
    As DataSet
    ' Setup the connection
    Dim cn As New SqlClient.SqlConnection(Application("DSN"))

    ' Open the connection
    cn.Open()

    ' Create the orders data adapter
    Dim daOrders As New SqlClient.SqlDataAdapter(_
        "SELECT * FROM ORDERS WHERE OrderDate = '" + _
        OrderDate.ToShortDateString() + "'", cn)

    ' Create the order item data adapter
    Dim daOrderDetails As New SqlClient.SqlDataAdapter(_
        "SELECT * FROM [Order Details] od, Orders o WHERE o.OrderID " + _
        "= od.OrderID AND o.OrderDate = '" + _
        OrderDate.ToShortDateString() + "'", cn)

    ' Create a data set
    Dim ds As New DataSet()

    ' Get the orders
    daOrders.Fill(ds, "Orders")
    ' Get the order details
    daOrderDetails.Fill(ds, "OrderDetails")

    ' Relate the two on the order id
    ds.Relations.Add("OrderID", ds.Tables("Orders").Columns("OrderID"), _
        ds.Tables("OrderDetails").Columns("OrderID"))

    ' Return the dataset
    Return ds
End Function
End Class
```

This code is somewhat similar to the previous example, but a few differences exist. First, we are using the ADO.NET SqlClient to retrieve the data (for more information on this, see Chapter 12). Second, we are not returning just a single table containing data. We are retrieving all the order and order details for all orders that were placed on OrderDate. The database defines a relationship between these two DataTables on the OrderID column that is present in each of the tables. This yields a DataSet that not only contains the data that matches the criteria from both tables, but that also knows about the relationship between the data. Listing 7.11 shows the output when we call the GetOrders WebMethod with a date of 7/8/1996.

Listing 7.11 The XML Output from Calling the GetOrders WebMethod with a Date of 7/8/1996

```
<?xml version="1.0" encoding="utf-8" ?>
- <DataSet xmlns="http://tempuri.org/">
- <xsd:schema id="NewDataSet" targetNamespace="" xmlns=""
xmlns:xsd="http://www.w3.org/2001/XMLSchema" xmlns:msdata="urn:schemas-
➥microsoft-com:xml-msdata">
- <xsd:element name="NewDataSet" msdata:IsDataSet="true">
- <xsd:complexType>
- <xsd:choice maxOccurs="unbounded">
- <xsd:element name="Orders">
- <xsd:complexType>
- <xsd:sequence>
  <xsd:element name="OrderID" type="xsd:int" minOccurs="0" />
  <xsd:element name="CustomerID" type="xsd:string" minOccurs="0" />
  <xsd:element name="EmployeeID" type="xsd:int" minOccurs="0" />
  <xsd:element name="OrderDate" type="xsd:dateTime" minOccurs="0" />
  <xsd:element name="RequiredDate" type="xsd:dateTime" minOccurs="0" />
  <xsd:element name="ShippedDate" type="xsd:dateTime" minOccurs="0" />
  <xsd:element name="ShipVia" type="xsd:int" minOccurs="0" />
  <xsd:element name="Freight" type="xsd:decimal" minOccurs="0" />
  <xsd:element name="ShipName" type="xsd:string" minOccurs="0" />
  <xsd:element name="ShipAddress" type="xsd:string" minOccurs="0" />
  <xsd:element name="ShipCity" type="xsd:string" minOccurs="0" />
  <xsd:element name="ShipRegion" type="xsd:string" minOccurs="0" />
  <xsd:element name="ShipPostalCode" type="xsd:string" minOccurs="0" />
  <xsd:element name="ShipCountry" type="xsd:string" minOccurs="0" />
  </xsd:sequence>
  </xsd:complexType>
  </xsd:element>
- <xsd:element name="OrderDetails">
- <xsd:complexType>
- <xsd:sequence>
  <xsd:element name="OrderID" type="xsd:int" minOccurs="0" />
  <xsd:element name="ProductID" type="xsd:int" minOccurs="0" />
  <xsd:element name="UnitPrice" type="xsd:decimal" minOccurs="0" />
  <xsd:element name="Quantity" type="xsd:short" minOccurs="0" />
  <xsd:element name="Discount" type="xsd:float" minOccurs="0" />
```

Listing 7.11   Continued

```xml
<xsd:element name="OrderID1" type="xsd:int" minOccurs="0" />
<xsd:element name="CustomerID" type="xsd:string" minOccurs="0" />
<xsd:element name="EmployeeID" type="xsd:int" minOccurs="0" />
<xsd:element name="OrderDate" type="xsd:dateTime" minOccurs="0" />
<xsd:element name="RequiredDate" type="xsd:dateTime" minOccurs="0" />
<xsd:element name="ShippedDate" type="xsd:dateTime" minOccurs="0" />
<xsd:element name="ShipVia" type="xsd:int" minOccurs="0" />
<xsd:element name="Freight" type="xsd:decimal" minOccurs="0" />
<xsd:element name="ShipName" type="xsd:string" minOccurs="0" />
<xsd:element name="ShipAddress" type="xsd:string" minOccurs="0" />
<xsd:element name="ShipCity" type="xsd:string" minOccurs="0" />
<xsd:element name="ShipRegion" type="xsd:string" minOccurs="0" />
<xsd:element name="ShipPostalCode" type="xsd:string" minOccurs="0" />
<xsd:element name="ShipCountry" type="xsd:string" minOccurs="0" />
</xsd:sequence>
</xsd:complexType>
</xsd:element>
</xsd:choice>
</xsd:complexType>
- <xsd:unique name="Constraint1">
<xsd:selector xpath=".//Orders" />
<xsd:field xpath="OrderID" />
</xsd:unique>
- <xsd:keyref name="OrderID" refer="Constraint1">
<xsd:selector xpath=".//OrderDetails" />
<xsd:field xpath="OrderID" />
</xsd:keyref>
</xsd:element>
</xsd:schema>
- <diffgr:diffgram xmlns:msdata="urn:schemas-microsoft-com:xml-msdata"
➥xmlns:diffgr="urn:schemas-microsoft-com:xml-diffgram-v1">
- <NewDataSet xmlns="">
- <Orders diffgr:id="Orders1" msdata:rowOrder="0">
<OrderID>10250</OrderID>
<CustomerID>HANAR</CustomerID>
<EmployeeID>4</EmployeeID>
<OrderDate>1996-07-08T00:00:00.0000000-07:00</OrderDate>
<RequiredDate>1996-08-05T00:00:00.0000000-07:00</RequiredDate>
<ShippedDate>1996-07-12T00:00:00.0000000-07:00</ShippedDate>
<ShipVia>2</ShipVia>
<Freight>65.83</Freight>
<ShipName>Hanari Carnes</ShipName>
<ShipAddress>Rua do Paço, 67</ShipAddress>
<ShipCity>Rio de Janeiro</ShipCity>
```

LISTING 7.11   Continued

```xml
<ShipRegion>RJ</ShipRegion>
<ShipPostalCode>05454-876</ShipPostalCode>
<ShipCountry>Brazil</ShipCountry>
</Orders>
<Orders diffgr:id="Orders2" msdata:rowOrder="1">
<OrderID>10251</OrderID>
<CustomerID>VICTE</CustomerID>
<EmployeeID>3</EmployeeID>
<OrderDate>1996-07-08T00:00:00.0000000-07:00</OrderDate>
<RequiredDate>1996-08-22T00:00:00.0000000-07:00</RequiredDate>
<ShippedDate>1996-07-15T00:00:00.0000000-07:00</ShippedDate>
<ShipVia>1</ShipVia>
<Freight>41.5</Freight>
<ShipName>Victuailles en stock</ShipName>
<ShipAddress>2, rue du Commerce</ShipAddress>
<ShipCity>Lyon</ShipCity>
<ShipPostalCode>69004</ShipPostalCode>
<ShipCountry>France</ShipCountry>
</Orders>
<OrderDetails diffgr:id="OrderDetails1" msdata:rowOrder="0">
<OrderID>10250</OrderID>
<ProductID>41</ProductID>
<UnitPrice>7.7</UnitPrice>
<Quantity>10</Quantity>
<Discount>0</Discount>
<OrderID1>10250</OrderID1>
<CustomerID>HANAR</CustomerID>
<EmployeeID>4</EmployeeID>
<OrderDate>1996-07-08T00:00:00.0000000-07:00</OrderDate>
<RequiredDate>1996-08-05T00:00:00.0000000-07:00</RequiredDate>
<ShippedDate>1996-07-12T00:00:00.0000000-07:00</ShippedDate>
<ShipVia>2</ShipVia>
<Freight>65.83</Freight>
<ShipName>Hanari Carnes</ShipName>
<ShipAddress>Rua do Paço, 67</ShipAddress>
<ShipCity>Rio de Janeiro</ShipCity>
<ShipRegion>RJ</ShipRegion>
<ShipPostalCode>05454-876</ShipPostalCode>
<ShipCountry>Brazil</ShipCountry>
</OrderDetails>
<OrderDetails diffgr:id="OrderDetails2" msdata:rowOrder="1">
<OrderID>10250</OrderID>
<ProductID>51</ProductID>
<UnitPrice>42.4</UnitPrice>
```

Listing 7.11   Continued

```
<Quantity>35</Quantity>
<Discount>0.15</Discount>
<OrderID1>10250</OrderID1>
<CustomerID>HANAR</CustomerID>
<EmployeeID>4</EmployeeID>
<OrderDate>1996-07-08T00:00:00.0000000-07:00</OrderDate>
<RequiredDate>1996-08-05T00:00:00.0000000-07:00</RequiredDate>
<ShippedDate>1996-07-12T00:00:00.0000000-07:00</ShippedDate>
<ShipVia>2</ShipVia>
<Freight>65.83</Freight>
<ShipName>Hanari Carnes</ShipName>
<ShipAddress>Rua do Paço, 67</ShipAddress>
<ShipCity>Rio de Janeiro</ShipCity>
<ShipRegion>RJ</ShipRegion>
<ShipPostalCode>05454-876</ShipPostalCode>
<ShipCountry>Brazil</ShipCountry>
</OrderDetails>
- <OrderDetails diffgr:id="OrderDetails3" msdata:rowOrder="2">
<OrderID>10250</OrderID>
<ProductID>65</ProductID>
<UnitPrice>16.8</UnitPrice>
<Quantity>15</Quantity>
<Discount>0.15</Discount>
<OrderID1>10250</OrderID1>
<CustomerID>HANAR</CustomerID>
<EmployeeID>4</EmployeeID>
<OrderDate>1996-07-08T00:00:00.0000000-07:00</OrderDate>
<RequiredDate>1996-08-05T00:00:00.0000000-07:00</RequiredDate>
<ShippedDate>1996-07-12T00:00:00.0000000-07:00</ShippedDate>
<ShipVia>2</ShipVia>
<Freight>65.83</Freight>
<ShipName>Hanari Carnes</ShipName>
<ShipAddress>Rua do Paço, 67</ShipAddress>
<ShipCity>Rio de Janeiro</ShipCity>
<ShipRegion>RJ</ShipRegion>
<ShipPostalCode>05454-876</ShipPostalCode>
<ShipCountry>Brazil</ShipCountry>
</OrderDetails>
- <OrderDetails diffgr:id="OrderDetails4" msdata:rowOrder="3">
<OrderID>10251</OrderID>
<ProductID>22</ProductID>
<UnitPrice>16.8</UnitPrice>
<Quantity>6</Quantity>
<Discount>0.05</Discount>
```

LISTING 7.11   Continued

```xml
<OrderID1>10251</OrderID1>
<CustomerID>VICTE</CustomerID>
<EmployeeID>3</EmployeeID>
<OrderDate>1996-07-08T00:00:00.0000000-07:00</OrderDate>
<RequiredDate>1996-08-22T00:00:00.0000000-07:00</RequiredDate>
<ShippedDate>1996-07-15T00:00:00.0000000-07:00</ShippedDate>
<ShipVia>1</ShipVia>
<Freight>41.5</Freight>
<ShipName>Victuailles en stock</ShipName>
<ShipAddress>2, rue du Commerce</ShipAddress>
<ShipCity>Lyon</ShipCity>
<ShipPostalCode>69004</ShipPostalCode>
<ShipCountry>France</ShipCountry>
</OrderDetails>
<OrderDetails diffgr:id="OrderDetails5" msdata:rowOrder="4">
<OrderID>10251</OrderID>
<ProductID>57</ProductID>
<UnitPrice>15.6</UnitPrice>
<Quantity>15</Quantity>
<Discount>0.05</Discount>
<OrderID1>10251</OrderID1>
<CustomerID>VICTE</CustomerID>
<EmployeeID>3</EmployeeID>
<OrderDate>1996-07-08T00:00:00.0000000-07:00</OrderDate>
<RequiredDate>1996-08-22T00:00:00.0000000-07:00</RequiredDate>
<ShippedDate>1996-07-15T00:00:00.0000000-07:00</ShippedDate>
<ShipVia>1</ShipVia>
<Freight>41.5</Freight>
<ShipName>Victuailles en stock</ShipName>
<ShipAddress>2, rue du Commerce</ShipAddress>
<ShipCity>Lyon</ShipCity>
<ShipPostalCode>69004</ShipPostalCode>
<ShipCountry>France</ShipCountry>
</OrderDetails>
<OrderDetails diffgr:id="OrderDetails6" msdata:rowOrder="5">
<OrderID>10251</OrderID>
<ProductID>65</ProductID>
<UnitPrice>16.8</UnitPrice>
<Quantity>20</Quantity>
<Discount>0</Discount>
<OrderID1>10251</OrderID1>
<CustomerID>VICTE</CustomerID>
<EmployeeID>3</EmployeeID>
<OrderDate>1996-07-08T00:00:00.0000000-07:00</OrderDate>
```

LISTING 7.11 Continued

```
<RequiredDate>1996-08-22T00:00:00.0000000-07:00</RequiredDate>
<ShippedDate>1996-07-15T00:00:00.0000000-07:00</ShippedDate>
<ShipVia>1</ShipVia>
<Freight>41.5</Freight>
<ShipName>Victuailles en stock</ShipName>
<ShipAddress>2, rue du Commerce</ShipAddress>
<ShipCity>Lyon</ShipCity>
<ShipPostalCode>69004</ShipPostalCode>
<ShipCountry>France</ShipCountry>
</OrderDetails>
</NewDataSet>
</diffgr:diffgram>
</DataSet>
```

Dig into the XML and look for the tag "- <xsd:unique name="Constraint1">". This starts the section that defines the relationship between the tables. It says that a constraint named Constraint1 defines the relationship between the DataTable named Orders and the DataTable named OrderDetails. The relationship is on a field named OrderID in each DataTable.

Consuming Web Services

Now that we have created several XML Web services, let's take a look at how to consume them. As mentioned earlier, XML Web services can be consumed by any client that is capable of making a request over HTTP and parsing out the returned XML. The .NET framework is capable of working in this fashion, but it also has tools for creating something called a Web service proxy that greatly simplifies access to a Web service. You can create a Web service proxy in two ways. If you are using Visual Studio .NET, you can add what is called a Web Reference by pointing Visual Studio .NET to the URL of the Web service. If you are not using Visual Studio .NET, you can use a tool called Web Service Description Language Tool (wsdl.exe) to create the Web service proxy.

Let's take a look at wsdl.exe first. At a minimum, the utility requires a path to a Web service or to the WSDL that describes the Web service—hence the name of the utility. Given this, it will generate the proxy class. This class has the same method signatures as the Web service and hides the implementation details so that calling the Web service is transparent. If we run wsdl.exe against the SimpleDataSet example with the following command line:

```
Wsdl http://localhost/book/webservices/simpledataset/dataset.asmx /language:vb
```

We get back a new file named after the class contained within the dataset.asmx file, datasetsample.vb. This file is shown in Listing 7.12.

LISTING 7.12 A Proxy Class (datasetsample.vb) for `SimpleDataSet` Generated with the WSDL Tool

```vb
'..............................................................................
' <autogenerated>
'     This code was generated by a tool.
'     Runtime Version: 1.0.2914.16
'
'     Changes to this file may cause incorrect behavior and will be lost if
'     the code is regenerated.
' </autogenerated>
'..............................................................................

Option Strict Off
Option Explicit On

Imports System
Imports System.Diagnostics
Imports System.Web.Services
Imports System.Web.Services.Protocols
Imports System.Xml.Serialization

'
'This source code was auto-generated by wsdl, Version=1.0.2914.16.
'

<System.Web.Services.WebServiceBindingAttribute(Name:="DataSetSampleSoap", _
[Namespace]:="http://tempuri.org/")> _
Public Class DataSetSample
    Inherits System.Web.Services.Protocols.SoapHttpClientProtocol

    <System.Diagnostics.DebuggerStepThroughAttribute()> _
    Public Sub New()
        MyBase.New
        Me.Url = "http://localhost/book/webservices/SimpleDataSet/DataSet.asmx"
    End Sub

    <System.Diagnostics.DebuggerStepThroughAttribute(), _
     System.Web.Services.Protocols.SoapDocumentMethodAttribute(_
         "http://tempuri.org/Simple", _
         Use:=System.Web.Services.Description.SoapBindingUse.Literal, _
ParameterStyle:=System.Web.Services.Protocols.SoapParameterStyle.Wrapped)> _
    Public Function Simple() As System.Data.DataSet
        Dim results() As Object = Me.Invoke("Simple", New Object(-1) {})
```

LISTING 7.12   Continued

```
        Return CType(results(0),System.Data.DataSet)
    End Function

    <System.Diagnostics.DebuggerStepThroughAttribute()> _
    Public Function BeginSimple(ByVal callback As System.AsyncCallback, _
        ByVal asyncState As Object) As System.IAsyncResult
        Return Me.BeginInvoke("Simple", New Object(-1) {}, callback, _
            asyncState)
    End Function

    <System.Diagnostics.DebuggerStepThroughAttribute()> _
    Public Function EndSimple(ByVal asyncResult As System.IAsyncResult) _
        As System.Data.DataSet
        Dim results() As Object = Me.EndInvoke(asyncResult)
        Return CType(results(0),System.Data.DataSet)
    End Function
End Class
```

This new proxy class can then be included in a project to encapsulate access to the Web service. If we want to use it in a Windows Forms project, we can include it in our project. We then use it by creating a new instance of the Web service object as though it is a local object instead of a remote one. Listing 7.13 shows a Windows form with a data grid on it, which retrieves the DataSet from `SimpleDataSet` and binds it to a form.

LISTING 7.13   A Form That Is Bound to the `SimpleDataSet` Web Service

```
Public Class Form1
    Inherits System.Windows.Forms.Form

#Region " Windows Form Designer generated code "

    Public Sub New()
        MyBase.New()

        'This call is required by the Windows Form Designer.
        InitializeComponent()
    End Sub

    'Form overrides dispose to clean up the component list.
    Protected Overloads Overrides Sub Dispose(ByVal disposing As Boolean)
        If Disposing Then
            If Not (components Is Nothing) Then
                components.Dispose()
```

LISTING 7.13 Continued

```
            End If
        End If
        MyBase.Dispose(Disposing)
    End Sub
    Friend WithEvents DataGrid1 As System.Windows.Forms.DataGrid

    'Required by the Windows Form Designer
    Private components As System.ComponentModel.Container

  <System.Diagnostics.DebuggerStepThrough()> Private Sub InitializeComponent()
        Me.DataGrid1 = New System.Windows.Forms.DataGrid()
        CType(Me.DataGrid1, _
            System.ComponentModel.ISupportInitialize).BeginInit()
        Me.SuspendLayout()
        '
        'DataGrid1
        '
        Me.DataGrid1.DataMember = ""
        Me.DataGrid1.Location = New System.Drawing.Point(8, 8)
        Me.DataGrid1.Name = "DataGrid1"
        Me.DataGrid1.Size = New System.Drawing.Size(320, 280)
        Me.DataGrid1.TabIndex = 0
        '
        'Form1
        '
        Me.AutoScaleBaseSize = New System.Drawing.Size(5, 13)
        Me.ClientSize = New System.Drawing.Size(336, 301)
        Me.Controls.AddRange(New System.Windows.Forms.Control() {Me.DataGrid1})
        Me.Name = "Form1"
        Me.Text = "Form1"
        CType(Me.DataGrid1, System.ComponentModel.ISupportInitialize).EndInit()
        Me.ResumeLayout(False)

    End Sub

#End Region

    Private Sub Form1_Load(ByVal sender As System.Object, _
        ByVal e As System.EventArgs) Handles MyBase.Load
        Dim dss As New DataSetSample()

        DataGrid1.DataMember = "Orders"
        DataGrid1.DataSource = dss.Simple()
    End Sub
End Class
```

The important stuff is in the last few lines. I have added three lines of code which do all the work to the form load. The first lines get a new instance of the Web service proxy class. Then calling the `WebMethod` on the new class is as simple as the last line: `dss.Simple()`. That's it. The .NET framework hides all the hard stuff, making calling remote Web methods on a Web service as easy as calling methods on local classes. Figure 7.9 shows the resulting form.

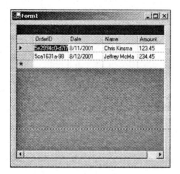

FIGURE 7.9
A Windows form showing the result of calling the SimpleDataSet Web service.

SoapHttpClientProtocol

This is the class from which the Web proxies generated by WSDL and Visual Studio .NET derive.

Of course, you aren't limited to calling XML Web services from Windows forms. It is just as easy to call a Web service from a Web form. This time around, I am going to include a Web reference in a Visual Studio .NET Web form project. I do this by pointing the Add Web Reference dialog box to the URL where the XML Web services resides. The dialog box will automatically find the WSDL and allow me to add the reference. Visual Studio .NET will then create the proxy class for me, eliminating the need for `wsdl.exe`. Visual Studio .NET names the proxy slightly differently than when you create it with `wsdl.exe`. The biggest difference is that it creates a namespace that is set to the hostname.domainname combination of the Web service that you created it from. Listing 7.14 shows the proxy that was created by Visual Studio .NET.

LISTING 7.14   The Proxy Created for SimpleDataSet by Visual Studio .NET

```
' - - - - - - - - - - - - - - - - - - - - - - - - - - - - - - - - - - - - - - - - - - - - - - - - - -
' <autogenerated>
'     This code was generated by a tool.
'     Runtime Version: 1.0.2914.16
'
```

LISTING 7.14   Continued

```vb
'      Changes to this file may cause incorrect behavior and will be lost if
'      the code is regenerated.
' </autogenerated>
'.................................................................

Option Strict Off
Option Explicit On

Imports System
Imports System.Diagnostics
Imports System.Web.Services
Imports System.Web.Services.Protocols
Imports System.Xml.Serialization

Namespace localhost

    <System.Web.Services.WebServiceBindingAttribute(Name:="DataSetSampleSoap", _
[Namespace]:="http://tempuri.org/")>  _
    Public Class DataSetSample
        Inherits System.Web.Services.Protocols.SoapHttpClientProtocol

        <System.Diagnostics.DebuggerStepThroughAttribute()>  _
        Public Sub New()
            MyBase.New
            Me.Url = _
              "http://localhost/book/webservices/SimpleDataSet/DataSet.asmx"
        End Sub

        <System.Diagnostics.DebuggerStepThroughAttribute(),  _
         System.Web.Services.Protocols.SoapDocumentMethodAttribute(_
         "http://tempuri.org/Simple", _
         Use:=System.Web.Services.Description.SoapBindingUse.Literal, _
  ParameterStyle:=System.Web.Services.Protocols.SoapParameterStyle.Wrapped)>
        Public Function Simple() As System.Data.DataSet
            Dim results() As Object = Me.Invoke("Simple", New Object(-1) {})
            Return CType(results(0),System.Data.DataSet)
        End Function

        <System.Diagnostics.DebuggerStepThroughAttribute()>  _
        Public Function BeginSimple(ByVal callback As System.AsyncCallback, _
            ByVal asyncState As Object) As System.IAsyncResult
            Return Me.BeginInvoke("Simple", New Object(-1) {}, callback, _
                asyncState)
        End Function
```

LISTING 7.14 Continued

```
        <System.Diagnostics.DebuggerStepThroughAttribute()>  _
        Public Function EndSimple(ByVal asyncResult As System.IAsyncResult) _
            As System.Data.DataSet
            Dim results() As Object = Me.EndInvoke(asyncResult)
            Return CType(results(0),System.Data.DataSet)
        End Function
    End Class
End Namespace
```

When using a Web form to create this object, we have to use slightly different syntax, which in this case is `localhost.DataSetSample`. The namespace is fixed, even if you change the location that you use to access the Web service. If you right-click the localhost reference in Visual Studio .NET, you can rename the localhost, which will change the namespace. If you want to change the location that is used to access the Web service, you can use the URL property of the Proxy class. This property expects a fully qualified reference to the .ASMX file that matches the proxy class. The web form client for `SimpleDataSet` shown in Listing 7.15 uses the URL property to change the location.

LISTING 7.15 A Web Form Client for SimpleDataSet

```
Public Class WebForm1
    Inherits System.Web.UI.Page
    Protected WithEvents DataGrid1 As System.Web.UI.WebControls.DataGrid

#Region " Web Form Designer Generated Code "

    'This call is required by the Web Form Designer.
    <System.Diagnostics.DebuggerStepThrough()> _
        Private Sub InitializeComponent()

    End Sub

    Private Sub Page_Init(ByVal sender As System.Object, _
        ByVal e As System.EventArgs) Handles MyBase.Init
        'CODEGEN: This method call is required by the Web Form Designer
        'Do not modify it using the code editor.
        InitializeComponent()
    End Sub

#End Region
```

LISTING 7.15   Continued

```
    Private Sub Page_Load(ByVal sender As System.Object, _
        ByVal e As System.EventArgs) Handles MyBase.Load
        Dim dss As New localhost.DataSetSample()

        ' Change the location of the web service we connect to
        dss.Url = _
        "http://steptoe.kinsman.net/book/webservices/SimpleDataSet/DataSet.asmx"

        ' Indicate which table in the dataset should be bound to
        DataGrid1.DataMember = "Orders"
        ' Get the dataset and set it to the source
        DataGrid1.DataSource = dss.Simple()
        ' Force the binding to happen
        DataGrid1.DataBind()
    End Sub
End Class
```

Again, the interesting lines are the ones in Page_Load. The first line creates a new instance of the proxy class using the localhost namespace. The next line changes the URL from the initial one used to create the proxy to the one that will be used in the "production" environment. Then the datagrid binding syntax binds the returned dataset directly to the grid. The last line calls DataBind() to tell the framework that it is now time to perform the binding.

Asynchronous Clients

XML Web services are a convenient way to access services over the Internet. The Internet itself can introduce some uncertainties in calling your XML Web services, however. The latencies involved in transiting data from point A to point B on the Internet change on an hourly basis, if not second to second. You don't want to have your application block or appear to be sluggish because you are retrieving information from a Web service over the Internet. The solution is to call the Web service in an asynchronous fashion. This enables you to fire off the request to a Web service and then continue doing other work. When the Web service request returns, you can retrieve the data and display it to the user.

Asynchronous access is more useful in a Windows Form type of application where you can go ahead and make the form available to the user immediately. When the data becomes available, just update it in the already displayed form. The Web service proxy again does the majority of the heavy lifting. In addition to creating mirrors of all the Web methods for the Web service, it creates a Begin<methodname> and End<methodname> method for each Web method.

In the proxy for the SimpleDataSet Web service shown in Listing 7.13, you will see, in addition to the Simple() method, a BeginSimple and EndSimple method. These are already set up to work with the AsyncResult interface. When the `Begin` method is called, it expects to be passed, in addition to any arguments the Web method requires, the address of a callback method. A callback method is just a method that is called when the operation completes. Optionally, you can stick any object into the `AsyncState` parameter and retrieve it later in the callback. This is useful to get a handle to the Web service so that you don't have to store a reference to it in a global variable. You will need this reference to call the `End` method so that you can retrieve the results from the Web service. Listing 7.16 shows a Web form that utilizes this methodology.

LISTING 7.16   A Web Form That Calls the NorthwindOrder Web Service Asynchronously

```
Public Class Form1
    Inherits System.Windows.Forms.Form

#Region " Windows Form Designer generated code "

    Public Sub New()
        MyBase.New()

        'This call is required by the Windows Form Designer.
        InitializeComponent()

        'Add any initialization after the InitializeComponent() call

    End Sub

    'Form overrides dispose to clean up the component list.
    Protected Overloads Overrides Sub Dispose(ByVal disposing As Boolean)
        If disposing Then
            If Not (components Is Nothing) Then
                components.Dispose()
            End If
        End If
        MyBase.Dispose(disposing)
    End Sub
    Friend WithEvents DataGrid1 As System.Windows.Forms.DataGrid

    'Required by the Windows Form Designer
    Private components As System.ComponentModel.Container

    'NOTE: The following procedure is required by the Windows Form Designer
    'It can be modified using the Windows Form Designer.
    'Do not modify it using the code editor.
    <System.Diagnostics.DebuggerStepThrough()> Private Sub
➥InitializeComponent()
```

LISTING 7.16   Continued

```
        Me.DataGrid1 = New System.Windows.Forms.DataGrid()
        CType(Me.DataGrid1,
➡System.ComponentModel.ISupportInitialize).BeginInit()
        Me.SuspendLayout()
        '
        'DataGrid1
        '
        Me.DataGrid1.DataMember = ""
        Me.DataGrid1.Dock = System.Windows.Forms.DockStyle.Fill
        Me.DataGrid1.Name = "DataGrid1"
        Me.DataGrid1.Size = New System.Drawing.Size(584, 389)
        Me.DataGrid1.TabIndex = 0
        '
        'Form1
        '
        Me.AutoScaleBaseSize = New System.Drawing.Size(5, 13)
        Me.ClientSize = New System.Drawing.Size(584, 389)
        Me.Controls.AddRange(New System.Windows.Forms.Control() {Me.DataGrid1})
        Me.Name = "Form1"
        Me.Text = "Form1"
        CType(Me.DataGrid1, System.ComponentModel.ISupportInitialize).EndInit()
        Me.ResumeLayout(False)

    End Sub

#End Region

    Public Delegate Sub SetData(ByVal ar As IAsyncResult)

    Private Sub Form1_Load(ByVal sender As System.Object, ByVal e As
➡System.EventArgs) Handles MyBase.Load
        Dim oOrders As New localhost.Orders()

        ' Create the callback to pass to the asynchronous invocation
        Dim wscb As New AsyncCallback(AddressOf WebServiceCallback)
        ' Call the web method asynchronously passing in the callback and the
➡service itself
        oOrders.BeginGetAllOrders(wscb, oOrders)
    End Sub

    Public Sub SetDataInGrid(ByVal ar As IAsyncResult)
        Dim oOrders As localhost.Orders
```

LISTING 7.16   Continued

```
      ' Grab the web service out of the async result object AsyncState
➥property
      oOrders = ar.AsyncState
      ' Get the data out of the finished web service
      Dim ds As DataSet = oOrders.EndGetAllOrders(ar)

      ' Put the data into the grid
      DataGrid1.DataMember = "Orders"
      DataGrid1.DataSource = ds
   End Sub

   Public Sub WebServiceCallback(ByVal ar As IAsyncResult)
      ' When this callback executes we are on a different thread than the
➥grid
      ' Windows Forms is single threaded so we need to call invoke to cross
➥threads
      Dim dlg As New SetData(AddressOf SetDataInGrid)
      DataGrid1.Invoke(dlg, New Object() {ar})
   End Sub
End Class
```

Don't get confused by the invoke in `WebServiceCallback`. Windows forms are single threaded by nature. When the callback from the Web service fires, you are not on the thread that created the control. If you attempt to set the DataSource property while on the wrong thread, you can cause undesirable results, including your program hanging. The invoke is used to transfer control to the thread that created the datagrid and then load the data on that thread.

Asynchronous calls are harder in a Web page than in a Windows form. After a Web page has been sent back to the browser, there is no way to update information in it further. Asynchronous calls are still of limited use in a Web page, however. If you have several Web service calls to make to create a page, fire them all off in an asynchronous fashion at the start of page processing and then continue doing other work in the page—perhaps retrieving information from a database, performing calculations, or doing anything else required to build the page.

This brings us to the other ways of calling a Web service asynchronously. It is possible to call the Web method using Begin, but without specifying a callback method. You can then continue with other processing. When you need the data from the Web service, you have two options:

1. Loop while looking at the `IsCompleted` property of the `AsyncResult` object. If all you are doing in the loop is checking the `IsCompleted` property, this is not the most efficient technique. It has the disadvantage of chewing up CPU cycles that other processes could be using. It has the advantage, however, of letting you do other work while waiting for the Web service to finish its work.

2. Utilize the `AsyncWaitHandle` of the `AsyncResult` object to cause the thread to wait until the Web service signals completion. This doesn't spin the CPU, wasting needless processing cycles. You can specify a timeout for the wait and then check the `IsCompleted` property to see if a timeout has occurred. The disadvantage of this, however, is that your code can't be off doing other processing while waiting for the call to return.

Listing 7.17 shows an example of a Web form calling the NorthwindOrders Web service asynchronously.

LISTING 7.17   A Web Form That Calls the NorthwindOrders Service Asynchronously and Loads the Orders into a Grid

```
Public Class WebForm1
    Inherits System.Web.UI.Page
    Protected WithEvents DataGrid1 As System.Web.UI.WebControls.DataGrid

    Private Sub Page_Load(ByVal sender As System.Object, _
        ByVal e As System.EventArgs) Handles MyBase.Load
        Dim ar As IAsyncResult
        Dim oOrders As New localhost.Orders()
        Dim bTimeout As Boolean

        ' Start the web service call
        ar = oOrders.BeginGetAllOrders(Nothing, Nothing)

        ' Do other work....

        ' All done so wait for the web service to come back
        ' This waitone waits for 5 seconds and then continues
        ar.AsyncWaitHandle.WaitOne(5000, False)

        ' Check to see if the async call completed.
        ' If not write a timeout message
        If Not ar.IsCompleted Then
            Response.Write("Timed out")
        Else
            ' Data is ready so put it into the grid
            DataGrid1.DataMember = "Orders"
            DataGrid1.DataSource = oOrders.EndGetAllOrders(ar)
            DataGrid1.DataBind()
        End If
    End Sub
End Class
```

This code fires off the asynchronous Web method right at the beginning of page load. It then continues to do other processing. Just before rendering the page back to the user, it waits for the results from the WebMethod for 5 seconds. If the Web method completes sooner, WaitOne exits as soon as the method completes. This means that WaitOne will wait at most 5 seconds, but might wait for as few as 0 seconds.

Cookies and Proxies

By default, the proxies created by WSDL or Visual Studio .NET do not interact with cookies. This means that even though you might turn on Session state in the Web service, unless you take a few extra steps on the client, you will never get persistent session state.

SoapHttpClientProtocol has a CookieContainer property, which is intended to hold a reference to the cookie container class that can be used to maintain cookie information across invocations of Web methods. By default, this property is empty. It is quite easy, however, to create a new cookie container and put a reference to it into the property. Either the Web service reference or the cookie container must persist across invocations, most likely as a member of your top-level class for this to work. Listing 7.18 shows an example of a Windows form that creates a cookie container and puts it into the Web proxy. It utilizes the state Web service that we created back in Listing 7.5.

LISTING 7.18   A Windows Form That Creates a Cookie Container and Utilizes the State Web Service

```
Public Class Form1
    Inherits System.Windows.Forms.Form

#Region " Windows Form Designer generated code "

    Public Sub New()
        MyBase.New()

        'This call is required by the Windows Form Designer.
        InitializeComponent()

        'Add any initialization after the InitializeComponent() call

    End Sub

    'Form overrides dispose to clean up the component list.
    Protected Overloads Overrides Sub Dispose(ByVal disposing As Boolean)
        If disposing Then
            If Not (components Is Nothing) Then
                components.Dispose()
```

LISTING 7.18 Continued

```
        End If
    End If
    MyBase.Dispose(disposing)
End Sub
Friend WithEvents lblSetKey As System.Windows.Forms.Label
Friend WithEvents lblSetValue As System.Windows.Forms.Label
Friend WithEvents txtSetKey As System.Windows.Forms.TextBox
Friend WithEvents txtSetValue As System.Windows.Forms.TextBox
Friend WithEvents btnSet As System.Windows.Forms.Button
Friend WithEvents txtGetKey As System.Windows.Forms.TextBox
Friend WithEvents lblGetKey As System.Windows.Forms.Label
Friend WithEvents lblGetValue As System.Windows.Forms.Label
Friend WithEvents lblGetValueText As System.Windows.Forms.Label
Friend WithEvents btnGet As System.Windows.Forms.Button


'Required by the Windows Form Designer
Private components As System.ComponentModel.Container

'NOTE: The following procedure is required by the Windows Form Designer
'It can be modified using the Windows Form Designer.
'Do not modify it using the code editor.
<System.Diagnostics.DebuggerStepThrough()> _
    Private Sub InitializeComponent()
    Me.lblSetValue = New System.Windows.Forms.Label()
    Me.lblSetKey = New System.Windows.Forms.Label()
    Me.btnGet = New System.Windows.Forms.Button()
    Me.lblGetValueText = New System.Windows.Forms.Label()
    Me.btnSet = New System.Windows.Forms.Button()
    Me.lblGetValue = New System.Windows.Forms.Label()
    Me.lblGetKey = New System.Windows.Forms.Label()
    Me.txtSetKey = New System.Windows.Forms.TextBox()
    Me.txtSetValue = New System.Windows.Forms.TextBox()
    Me.txtGetKey = New System.Windows.Forms.TextBox()
    Me.SuspendLayout()
    '
    'lblSetValue
    '
    Me.lblSetValue.Location = New System.Drawing.Point(8, 48)
    Me.lblSetValue.Name = "lblSetValue"
    Me.lblSetValue.Size = New System.Drawing.Size(88, 16)
    Me.lblSetValue.TabIndex = 2
    Me.lblSetValue.Text = "Value:"
    '
```

LISTING 7.18 Continued

```
'lblSetKey
'
Me.lblSetKey.Location = New System.Drawing.Point(8, 8)
Me.lblSetKey.Name = "lblSetKey"
Me.lblSetKey.Size = New System.Drawing.Size(72, 16)
Me.lblSetKey.TabIndex = 0
Me.lblSetKey.Text = "Key:"
'
'btnGet
'
Me.btnGet.Location = New System.Drawing.Point(120, 104)
Me.btnGet.Name = "btnGet"
Me.btnGet.TabIndex = 9
Me.btnGet.Text = "Get"
'
'lblGetValueText
'
Me.lblGetValueText.Location = New System.Drawing.Point(8, 160)
Me.lblGetValueText.Name = "lblGetValueText"
Me.lblGetValueText.Size = New System.Drawing.Size(100, 16)
Me.lblGetValueText.TabIndex = 8
'
'btnSet
'
Me.btnSet.Location = New System.Drawing.Point(120, 8)
Me.btnSet.Name = "btnSet"
Me.btnSet.TabIndex = 4
Me.btnSet.Text = "Set"
'
'lblGetValue
'
Me.lblGetValue.Location = New System.Drawing.Point(8, 144)
Me.lblGetValue.Name = "lblGetValue"
Me.lblGetValue.Size = New System.Drawing.Size(88, 16)
Me.lblGetValue.TabIndex = 7
Me.lblGetValue.Text = "Value:"
'
'lblGetKey
'
Me.lblGetKey.Location = New System.Drawing.Point(8, 104)
Me.lblGetKey.Name = "lblGetKey"
Me.lblGetKey.Size = New System.Drawing.Size(72, 16)
Me.lblGetKey.TabIndex = 5
Me.lblGetKey.Text = "Key:"
'
```

LISTING 7.18   Continued

```
'txtSetKey
'
Me.txtSetKey.Location = New System.Drawing.Point(8, 24)
Me.txtSetKey.Name = "txtSetKey"
Me.txtSetKey.TabIndex = 1
Me.txtSetKey.Text = "Key"
'
'txtSetValue
'
Me.txtSetValue.Location = New System.Drawing.Point(8, 64)
Me.txtSetValue.Name = "txtSetValue"
Me.txtSetValue.TabIndex = 3
Me.txtSetValue.Text = "Value"
'
'txtGetKey
'
Me.txtGetKey.Location = New System.Drawing.Point(8, 120)
Me.txtGetKey.Name = "txtGetKey"
Me.txtGetKey.TabIndex = 6
Me.txtGetKey.Text = "Key"
'
'Form1
'
Me.AutoScaleBaseSize = New System.Drawing.Size(5, 13)
Me.ClientSize = New System.Drawing.Size(208, 181)
Me.Controls.AddRange(New System.Windows.Forms.Control() {_
    Me.btnGet, Me.lblGetValueText, Me.lblGetValue, Me.txtGetKey, _
    Me.lblGetKey, Me.btnSet, Me.txtSetValue, Me.txtSetKey, _
    Me.lblSetValue, Me.lblSetKey})
Me.Name = "Form1"
Me.Text = "Form1"
Me.ResumeLayout(False)

End Sub

#End Region

' Create a new instance of the web services
Dim ss As New localhost.State()


Private Sub btnSet_Click(ByVal sender As System.Object, _
    ByVal e As System.EventArgs) Handles btnSet.Click
    ' Set the value
```

7

WEB SERVICES

LISTING 7.18   Continued

```
        ss.SetValue(Me.txtSetKey.Text, Me.txtSetValue.Text)
    End Sub

    Private Sub Form1_Load(ByVal sender As System.Object, _
        ByVal e As System.EventArgs) Handles MyBase.Load
        ' Initialize the cookie container and set it so we can
        ' maintain state
        ss.CookieContainer = New System.Net.CookieContainer()
    End Sub

    Private Sub btnGet_Click(ByVal sender As System.Object, _
        ByVal e As System.EventArgs) Handles btnGet.Click
        ' Get the value
        Me.lblGetValueText.Text = ss.GetValue(Me.txtGetKey.Text)
    End Sub
End Class
```

In this form, the Web service is a member variable of Form1. It persists for the life of the form. On form load, a cookie container is created and associated with the instance of the Web service. This enables session state to work across each of the Web service method calls.

Class Reference

This section provides a quick interface reference to the key objects described in this chapter. Space constraints prevent us from documenting every object in the .NET framework in this book, so for the sake of brevity and conciseness, we include only the most important objects here. For more information on the other objects in the .NET framework, consult the .NET Framework Reference online help file.

WebService

Member of System.Web.Services

Assembly: System.Web.Services.dll

The WebService class is what all XML Web services derive from.

Properties		
Application	Context	Server
Session	User	

WebMethodAttribute

Member of System.Web.Services

Assembly: System.Web.Services.dll

The `WebMethodAttribute` class is used to set the options for a Web method.

Properties

BufferResponse	CacheDuration	Description
EnableSession	MessageName	TransactionOption
TypeID		

SoapHttpClientProtocol

Member of System.Web.Services.Protocols.HttpWebClientProtocol

Assembly: System.Web.Services.dll

This is the class from which the Web proxies generated by WSDL and Visual Studio .NET derive.

Properties

AllowAutoRedirect	ClientCertificates	ConnectionGroupName
CookieContainer	Credentials	PreAuthenticate
Proxy	RequestEncoding	Timeout
Url	UserAgent	

Methods

Abort	Discover

Security

IN THIS CHAPTER

Overview

ASP.NET offers a number of ways to secure your Web application. Securing a Web application usually breaks down to two tasks: authentication and authorization.

Authentication is the process of determining who the user is. This is frequently done by requiring users to first indicate who they are by providing a name or e-mail address. Second, users are frequently required to provide some shared secret, which, theoretically, only they know. The most common example of a shared secret is a password. The combination of the name and shared secret is then compared against some store containing user information. This combination of a username and password is frequently referred to as a set of credentials. If the provided credentials match the information in the store, the user is deemed authentic and is allowed access to the application. If the information does not match, the user is typically given another chance to provide valid credentials. ASP.NET includes three implementations of authentication schemes: Windows, Forms, and Passport.

The other task, authorization, is the process of determining what resources users should have access to after they have been authenticated. This process is typically performed by comparing a list of roles applicable to the authenticated user against a list of roles that are required for access to a particular resource. These resources could be Web pages, graphics, or pieces of information from a database. ASP.NET includes two implementations of authorization schemes: file and URL.

Identity and Principal

Two key objects closely associated with security in .NET are identities and principal objects. An *identity* represents a user's identity and the method used to authenticate the user. Two identity classes are provided by default in .NET. The GenericIdentity is a generic implementation of the IIdentity interface that is not specific to any particular type of authentication. It implements the required interface and no more. The WindowsIdentity is an implementation of IIdentity that adds more methods and properties particular to Windows-based authentication.

Windows Authentication

ASP.NET still requires Internet Information Server (IIS) to handle Web requests. ASP.NET is layered on top of IIS using an ISAPI filter just like ASP.old. What this means is that ASP.NET participates in the IIS security model.

Before ASP.NET is even called on to execute a page, IIS must be satisfied that the user has permission to request the page. This permission check is done using any of the standard mechanisms built in to IIS, including Basic Authentication, Digest Authentication, or Integrated Windows Authentication.

When the user first requests a page that requires authentication, IIS initially returns an HTTP 1.1 401 Access Denied error to the browser. Included in the response is the WWW-Authenticate header, which indicates that the browser should collect user credentials and include them with the next request. After Internet Information Server receives the credentials, they are authenticated against the account database and, if they match, the page is executed.

ASP.NET allows the developer to further interact with these built-in Windows-based authentication mechanisms through the use of the WindowsPrincipal and WindowsIdentity classes mentioned earlier.

By default, when you create a Web Application using Visual Studio .NET, or even using the Internet Services Manager, anonymous access is enabled by default for the Web site. To force IIS to authenticate all requests aimed at a directory, you must disable anonymous authentication. This will cause IIS to authenticate the user against the Windows account database.

To force ASP.NET to do its part, you must change an entry in the application's web.config file. Specifically, the authentication section must be set to Windows as follows:

```
<authentication mode="Windows" />
```

With this setting in place, ASP.NET will create a WindowsPrincipal object for each authenticated request that it receives and will populate it with a WindowsIdentity. The groups that the user belongs to will also be loaded into the principal allowing IsInRole() to test for role membership. The username that is placed into the WindowsIdentity will be of the form *DOMAIN\UserName*. The groups that IsInRole() checks for are of the form *DOMAIN\Group*, with the exception of built-in groups such as Administrator. Built-in groups are of the form *BUILTIN\Administrator*, or alternatively, you can use the WindowsBuiltInRole enumeration.

WindowsBuiltInRole Enumeration

Listings 8.1 and 8.2 show a page that is executed after the user is authenticated. It uses the WindowsPrincipal object to

- Check whether the user is authenticated
- Get the username
- Get the authentication method
- Check whether the user is an administrator

8

SECURITY

LISTING 8.1   ASP.NET Page That Utilizes the WindowsPrincipal Object to Obtain Information About the User

```
<%@ Page Language="vb" AutoEventWireup="false" Codebehind="default.aspx.vb"
Inherits="Windows.CAdministratordefault"%>
<!DOCTYPE HTML PUBLIC "-//W3C//DTD HTML 4.0 Transitional//EN">
<HTML>
    <HEAD>
        <title></title>
        <meta name="GENERATOR" content="Microsoft Visual Studio.NET 7.0">
        <meta name="CODE_LANGUAGE" content="Visual Basic 7.0">
        <meta name="vs_defaultClientScript" content="JavaScript">
        <meta name="vs_targetSchema"
            content="http://schemas.microsoft.com/intellisense/ie5">
    </HEAD>
    <body>
        <form id="Form1" method="post" runat="server">
            <P>
                I am an Administrator
            </P>
            <P>
                IsAuthenticated:
                <asp:Label id="lblIsAuthenticated" runat="server"></asp:Label>
            </P>
            <P>
                Authentication Type:
                <asp:Label id="lblAuthenticationType" runat="server" />
➥</P>
            <P>
                User Name:
                <asp:Label id="lblUserName" runat="server"></asp:Label>
            </P>
            <P>
                Administrator?
                <asp:Label id="lblAdministrator" runat="server"></asp:Label>
            </P>
        </form>
    </body>
</HTML>
```

LISTING 8.2   Class File for ASP.NET Page in Listing 8.1

```
Imports System.Web.UI.WebControls

Public Class CAdministratordefault
    Inherits System.Web.UI.Page
```

LISTING 8.2   Continued

```vb
        Protected WithEvents lblAuthenticationType As Label
        Protected WithEvents lblIsAuthenticated As Label
        Protected WithEvents Label1 As Label
        Protected WithEvents lblAdministrator As Label
        Protected WithEvents lblUserName As Label

#Region " Web Form Designer Generated Code "

        'This call is required by the Web Form Designer.
        <System.Diagnostics.DebuggerStepThrough()> _
            Private Sub InitializeComponent()

        End Sub

        Private Sub Page_Init(ByVal sender As System.Object, _
            ByVal e As System.EventArgs) Handles MyBase.Init
            'CODEGEN: This method call is required by the Web Form Designer
            'Do not modify it using the code editor.
            InitializeComponent()
        End Sub

#End Region

        Private Sub Page_Load(ByVal sender As System.Object, _
            ByVal e As System.EventArgs) Handles MyBase.Load
            ' Check if the user is authenticated
            lblIsAuthenticated.Text = _
                HttpContext.Current.User.Identity.IsAuthenticated.ToString()
            ' Output the authentication type
            lblAuthenticationType.Text = _
                HttpContext.Current.User.Identity.AuthenticationType.ToString()
            ' Output the user name
            lblUserName.Text = HttpContext.Current.User.Identity.Name
            ' Is the user an administrator?
            lblAdministrator.Text = _
                HttpContext.Current.User.IsInRole(_
                System.Security.Principal.WindowsBuiltInRole.Administrator)
                ).ToString()
        End Sub

End Class
```

8

SECURITY

Forms Authentication

The previous section showed how easy it is to use Windows authentication in ASP.NET. ASP.NET provides another security mechanism as well: forms authentication. Why would you want to use it? Windows authentication, although easy to use, makes several assumptions:

1. It assumes you have a scalable Windows domain implementation already in place.

   This is not always a given. Many Web site administrators prefer not to go to the trouble of designing, implementing, and maintaining the Active Directory implementation on which domain-based security rests. Others might not have the expertise or budget to figure out how to get Active Directory to scale into the millions of users. Without an Active Directory implementation, you can authenticate against the account database that every Windows 2000 server maintains. However, this approach means that this account database must be replicated in some fashion among servers in a cluster or you are limited to a single server. Ultimately, what all of this comes down to is that you might want to authenticate users against a credential store other than a Windows 2000 domain. Forms authentication provides one way to do this.

2. Windows authentication assumes you want only minimal control over the user interface presented to the user.

   By default, Windows-based authentication uses a standard browser dialog box to collect the user's credentials. If you want to integrate the form to collect credentials into an existing Web page or provide your own login form, you are out of luck. Forms authentication provides a way for you, the developer, to determine what interface the user receives.

   All the advantages of forms authentication are not free, however. First, forms authentication requires that the user has cookies enabled. Although ASP.NET has provided a way to track session state without cookies, it has not provided a way to track forms authentication without cookies. Hopefully, this will come in a future version of ASP.NET. Second, you, the developer, need to create a login page and write some code to make this all work. ASP.NET provides the infrastructure, but you need to provide the specific implementation.

What's the Big Deal?

Maybe you already do this type of authentication. So what's the big deal with forms authentication? Perhaps the most common security mechanism in place today among ASP developers provides many of the same advantages. I provide a customized login page for my users and authenticate them against my credential store. After they are authenticated, I either write a cookie or save their authentication into a session variable. In every page, I have an include file that looks for the Session() value or cookie. If it isn't there, I redirect the user back to the login page. This can be very effective, but it has two big problems:

1. What if I forget the include file?
2. How do I protect PDF, ZIP, or JPG files? There is no place to put the code!

Forms authentication enables me to do all this without having to include code in every page to check whether the user was properly authenticated.

> **NOTE**
>
> ASP.NET authentication and authorization is applied only to files that are mapped to the ASP.NET ISAPI filter. This means that, by default, it will not be applied to any file that is loaded, other than the built-in ASP.NET file types listed in Chapter 3—for example, a JPG or a ZIP file. If you add these file types to the ISAPI filter, they can participate in the security model.

Process

When forms authentication is enabled and a request is made for a page, ASP.NET first determines whether authentication is needed. If it is, ASP.NET then checks for an authentication cookie in the request. If it is not present, ASP.NET redirects the user to the login page and passes the URL of the original page as a query string parameter, named ReturnURL, to the login page.

> **NOTE**
>
> The user is sent to the login page using a 302 location-moved redirection. This means that any form data that might have been included with the request is lost.

The login page collects users' credentials and is responsible for validating them against a credential store. This is where you as the developer get control. The credential store could consist of an LDAP directory, a database, or even something as simple as an XML file. When the credentials have been verified, RedirectFromLoginPage() is called to write an authentication ticket into a cookie and redirect the user to the original content that the user requested. A diagram of this process is shown in Figure 8.1.

8

SECURITY

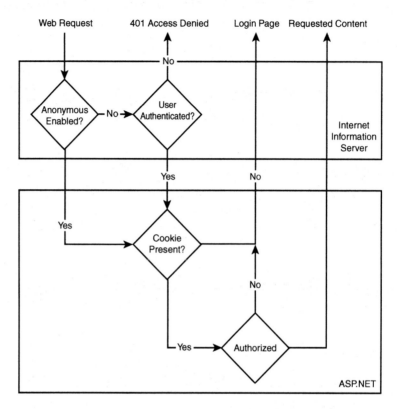

FIGURE 8.1

A process flow for the forms authentication process.

Settings

Forms authentication is enabled in the web.config file by setting the mode attribute of the authentication element to Forms. When the authentication mode is set to Forms, the authentication element might contain a forms element with additional information specific to forms authentication.

```
<authentication mode="Forms">
    <forms name="FORMURL" loginUrl="login.aspx" protection="All"
        timeout="30" path="/" />
</authentication>
```

The path attribute specifies the path that should be used to set the cookie. The default value is a slash (/). It is best to stick with the default here because many browsers use case-sensitive paths. Depending on the URL requested, the cookie might not be available, preventing you from ever authenticating successfully.

The name attribute specifies the name of the cookie that should be used to store the authentication ticket. Varying the name is useful if you have more than one authenticated area in your Web site, but you still want to leave the path set to / to avoid the case-sensitivity issue. The default value for the name is .ASPXAUTH.

The loginurl attribute specifies the URL of the login page used to authenticate the user. The default value is default.aspx, which in most cases doesn't make much sense. You will probably want to set this to login.aspx or something similar.

The protection attribute determines what type of protection is applied to the authentication ticket. Two options are available for protecting the authentication ticket: encryption and validation. Encryption encrypts the authentication ticket using Triple DES or DES, depending on the length of the encryption key. If the key is more than 48 bytes in length, Triple DES is used. Validation verifies that an encrypted ticket has not been altered in transit between the client and the server. This is done by concatenating a validation key onto the cookie data, computing a Message Authentication Code, and appending the Message Authentication Code to the cookie. The method used for creating the Message Authentication Code is set in the machine.config file as part of the <machineKey> element and includes options for SHA1, MD5, or Triple DES. Both the encryption key and validation key are also set in this config file. By default, both are autogenerated. This is fine for a site that consists of a single Web server, but if you have load-balanced Web servers, it is important to set this to a manual value to ensure that all Web servers can properly encrypt and validate keys.

The timeout attribute determines the amount of time (in minutes) that the authentication ticket is good. This is a sliding expiration value; that is, the timeout clock is reset each time the user requests a page successfully. If the time between page requests exceeds this value, the user is automatically logged out. This is sometimes confusing, so let's look at an example. Assume that the timeout value is set to 5 minutes. You make a page request and authenticate yourself via the login page. You then request a new page once every two minutes for the next twenty minutes. You will not be asked to log in again 5 minutes after the first page you requested. In fact, in this scenario you will not be requested to log in again until after 26 minutes have passed. However, if you make a page request and authenticate yourself via the login page and then wait 6 minutes to request the next page, you will be asked to log in again. The interval between the page requests has exceeded the timeout value.

The timeout is implemented by specifying an expiration date for the cookie that is written to the browser. When the cookie is initially written it is given an absolute expiration date *timeout* minutes in the future. If I don't make a request within *timeout* minutes of when the cookie was set, it expires and the browser gets rid of it, thus logging me out.

There is one small wrinkle. For performance reasons, ASP.NET doesn't write the cookie to the browser on every request. Instead, it writes the cookie only when more than half the timeout value has elapsed. Revisiting the earlier example, this means that if I log in, wait 2 minutes, request a page, and then wait 4 minutes and request another page, I will be asked to log in again. At no point did the interval between my requests exceed 5 minutes, but when I made my initial request at 0:00 the cookie was written out with an expiration of 5:00. When I made my second request at 2:00, because I was not halfway to the timeout, the cookie was not rewritten and its expiration remained 5:00 from the first page request (not the most recent one). When I then made my third request at 6:00, although it was only 4 minutes from my second request, the cookie had expired because its expiration was set to 5:00. The real takeaway here is to realize that the sliding timeout value means that the interval between requests could be anywhere from *timeout*/2 to *timeout* because of the algorithm for rewriting cookies.

Now that you know how it works, let's take a look at an example. First, you need to ensure that anonymous authentication is on in the IIS.

Second, you need to change the authentication element's mode attribute in your application's web.config to Forms and add the Forms element. To force authentication, you also need to change the `<authorization>` element to contain a `<deny users="?">`. More about this last setting is in the section on authorization. The web.config should look like Listing 8.3.

LISTING 8.3   web.config for Simple Forms Authentication

```
<?xml version="1.0" encoding="utf-8" ?>
<configuration>
    <system.web>
        <!-- AUTHENTICATION
          This section sets the authentication policies of the application.
          Possible modes are "Windows","Forms", "Passport" and "None"
    -->
        <authentication mode="Forms">
            <forms loginUrl="login.aspx" timeout="5" protection="All" />
        </authentication>
        <!-- AUTHORIZATION
          This section sets the authorization policies of the application.
```

LISTING 8.3 Continued

```
            You can allow or deny access
            to application resources by user or role. Wildcards:
            "*" mean everyone, "?" means anonymous
            (unauthenticated) users.
    -->
        <authorization>
            <deny users="?" /> <!-- Allow all users -->
            <!-- <allow      users="[comma separated list of users]"
                             roles="[comma separated list of roles]"/>
                  <deny      users="[comma separated list of users]"
                             roles="[comma separated list of roles]"/>
            -->
        </authorization>
    </system.web>
</configuration>
```

Next, you need to create a login form. Listings 8.4 and 8.5 contain a sample login page that collects a username and password. If the username equals "Chris" and the password equals "Kinsman", the authentication ticket is written. The user is directed to the page she initially requested by calling `RedirectFromLoginPage()` and passing it the username.

LISTING 8.4 Simple Login Page

```
<%@ Page Language="vb" AutoEventWireup="false" Codebehind="login.aspx.vb"
Inherits="SimpleForm.WebForm1"%>
<!DOCTYPE HTML PUBLIC "-//W3C//DTD HTML 4.0 Transitional//EN">
<HTML>
    <HEAD>
        <title></title>
        <meta name="GENERATOR" content="Microsoft Visual Studio.NET 7.0">
        <meta name="CODE_LANGUAGE" content="Visual Basic 7.0">
        <meta name="vs_defaultClientScript" content="JavaScript">
        <meta name="vs_targetSchema"
            content="http://schemas.microsoft.com/intellisense/ie5">
    </HEAD>
    <body MS_POSITIONING="GridLayout">
        <form id="Form1" method="post" runat="server">
            <asp:Label id="Label1"
                style="Z-INDEX: 101; LEFT: 8px; POSITION: absolute; TOP: 8px"
                runat="server">User Name:</asp:Label>
            <asp:Button id="btnLogin"
                style="Z-INDEX: 105; LEFT: 254px; POSITION: absolute; TOP: 7px"
                runat="server" Text="Login"></asp:Button>
```

8

SECURITY

Listing 8.4   Continued

```
                <asp:TextBox id="txtPassword"
                    style="Z-INDEX: 104; LEFT: 89px; POSITION: absolute; TOP: 38px"
                  runat="server"></asp:TextBox>
                <asp:Label id="Label2"
                    style="Z-INDEX: 103; LEFT: 8px; POSITION: absolute; TOP: 41px"
                  runat="server">Password:</asp:Label>
                <asp:TextBox id="txtUserName"
                    style="Z-INDEX: 102; LEFT: 89px; POSITION: absolute; TOP: 5px"
                  runat="server"></asp:TextBox>
                <asp:Label id="lblMessage"
                    style="Z-INDEX: 106; LEFT: 15px; POSITION: absolute; TOP: 81px"
                    runat="server" Width="281px" Height="19px" ForeColor="Red"
                    Visible="False">Invalid Login!</asp:Label>
            </form>
        </body>
</HTML>
```

Listing 8.5   Class File for ASP.NET Page in Listing 8.4

```
Imports System.Web.Security

Public Class WebForm1
    Inherits System.Web.UI.Page
    Protected WithEvents Label1 As System.Web.UI.WebControls.Label
    Protected WithEvents txtUserName As System.Web.UI.WebControls.TextBox
    Protected WithEvents Label2 As System.Web.UI.WebControls.Label
    Protected WithEvents txtPassword As System.Web.UI.WebControls.TextBox
    Protected WithEvents lblMessage As System.Web.UI.WebControls.Label
        Protected WithEvents btnLogin As System.Web.UI.WebControls.Button

#Region " Web Form Designer Generated Code "

    'This call is required by the Web Form Designer.
    <System.Diagnostics.DebuggerStepThrough()> _
    Private Sub InitializeComponent()

    End Sub

    Private Sub Page_Init(ByVal sender As System.Object, _
        ByVal e As System.EventArgs) Handles MyBase.Init
        'CODEGEN: This method call is required by the Web Form Designer
        'Do not modify it using the code editor.
```

LISTING 8.5 Continued

```
        InitializeComponent()
    End Sub

#End Region

    Private Sub Page_Load(ByVal sender As System.Object, _
        ByVal e As System.EventArgs) Handles MyBase.Load
        'Put user code to initialize the page here
    End Sub

    Private Sub btnLogin_Click(ByVal sender As System.Object, _
        ByVal e As System.EventArgs) Handles btnLogin.Click
        If txtUserName.Text = "Chris" And txtPassword.Text = "Kinsman" Then
            ' Authenticate the user
            FormsAuthentication.RedirectFromLoginPage(txtUserName.Text, False)
        Else
            ' Show the invalid login message
            lblMessage.Visible = True
        End If
    End Sub
End Class
```

Now, if you hit the URL for this application, you should be redirected to the login page. When you enter Username: Chris and Password: Kinsman, you will be redirected to the default page for the application.

Passport Authentication

Forms authentication is cool, but it has one potential failing. It requires users to create and maintain a set of credentials for every Web site that they visit. Wouldn't it be nice to have just one username and password that you could use at any site? That is the idea behind Microsoft Passport.

The first step to using Microsoft Passport is to request a Site ID. The Site ID identifies your site as a valid Passport partner and is used as a key by Passport to identify settings related to your site. When you have acquired a Site ID, you can configure your site to use Passport. Change the mode attribute of <authentication> element to Passport. A second optional element <passport> enables you to specify the location of the Passport login page via the redirectUrl attribute. A sample web.config for Passport authentication is shown in Listing 8.6.

Listing 8.6   A web.config Setup for Passport Authentication

```
<?xml version="1.0" encoding="utf-8" ?>
<configuration>
    <system.web>
        <compilation defaultLanguage="vb" debug="true" />
        <authentication mode="Passport">
            <passport redirectUrl="login.aspx" />
        </authentication>
        <authorization>
            <allow users="*" /> <!-- Allow all users -->
        </authorization>
    </system.web>
    <location path="attendees">
        <system.web>
            <authorization>
            <deny users="?" />
            </authorization>
        </system.web>
    </location>
</configuration>
```

The rest of the web.config is very similar to what you used before with forms authentication. Now you need to provide a way for the user to log in. This is typically done with most participating Passport sites using a Passport logo that indicates whether the user is logged in or out. The PassportIdentity object provides a method LogoTag2() that returns the HTML necessary to display this logo.

PassportIdentity

This class contains functionality for interacting with the Passport authentication service.

If the user is not logged in, however, no PassportIdentity object is available. If User.Identity.IsAuthenticated returns false, you need to create a new instance of PassportIdentity and use it to output the login logo. This logo is frequently placed in a number of locations around a site, so it is a good idea to wrap it up in a Web user control. Listing 8.7 shows an example of this control.

Listing 8.7   A Web User Control That Wraps the Display of the Passport Logo

```
Public MustInherit Class passportlogo
    Inherits System.Web.UI.UserControl

#Region " Web Form Designer Generated Code "
```

LISTING 8.7 Continued

```
    'This call is required by the Web Form Designer.
    <System.Diagnostics.DebuggerStepThrough()> Private Sub
➡InitializeComponent()

    End Sub

    Private Sub Page_Init(ByVal sender As System.Object, ByVal e As
➡System.EventArgs) Handles MyBase.Init
        'CODEGEN: This method call is required by the Web Form Designer
        'Do not modify it using the code editor.
        InitializeComponent()
    End Sub

#End Region

    Private Sub Page_Load(ByVal sender As System.Object, ByVal e As
➡System.EventArgs) Handles MyBase.Load
        Dim pi As System.Web.Security.PassportIdentity

        If (HttpContext.Current.User.Identity.IsAuthenticated) Then
            pi = CType(HttpContext.Current.User.Identity,
➡System.Web.Security.PassportIdentity)
        Else
            pi = New System.Web.Security.PassportIdentity()
        End If
        If Request("ReturnURL") Is Nothing Then
            Response.Write(pi.LogoTag2("http://" +
➡Request.ServerVariables("SERVER_NAME").ToString() +
➡HttpContext.Current.Request.Path, 600, False, "", 1033, False, "", 0, False))
        Else
            Response.Write(pi.LogoTag2(Request("ReturnURL"), 600, False, "",
➡1033, False, "", 0, False))
        End If
    End Sub

End Class
```

The user control first looks to see whether the user has been authenticated. If he is authenticated, the user control then grabs the PassportIdentity of the user. If he is not authenticated, a new PassportIdentity is created. The LogoTag2 method of the PassportIdentity object is then used to output the appropriate login or logout logo for Passport.

This user control can now be placed on the home page to provide a way to log in. When a user attempts to access a page for which he has insufficient permissions, he is redirected to the

URL indicated in the `redirectUrl` attribute of the `<passport>` element. This page should show a message indicating to the user that he attempted to access authenticated content and provide a way to log in. The easiest way to do this is to include the passportlogo user control that you created in Listing 8.7. A sample login.aspx page is shown in Listing 8.8.

LISTING 8.8   The login.aspx Page That Is Shown When Users Attempt to Access Content When They Are Not Authenticated

```
<%@ Page Language="vb" AutoEventWireup="false" Codebehind="login.aspx.vb"
Inherits="Passport.login"%>
<%@ Register TagPrefix="uc1" TagName="passportlogo" Src="passportlogo.ascx" %>
<!DOCTYPE HTML PUBLIC "-//W3C//DTD HTML 4.0 Transitional//EN">
<HTML>
    <HEAD>
        <title></title>
        <meta name="GENERATOR" content="Microsoft Visual Studio.NET 7.0">
        <meta name="CODE_LANGUAGE" content="Visual Basic 7.0">
        <meta name="vs_defaultClientScript" content="JavaScript">
        <meta name="vs_targetSchema"
➥content="http://schemas.microsoft.com/intellisense/ie5">
    </HEAD>
    <body>
        <form id="Form1" method="post" runat="server">
            <P>
                You must login to access that content... Click on the passport
➥logo to log
                in...
            </P>
            <P>
                 
                <uc1:passportlogo id="Passportlogo1" runat="server">
                </uc1:passportlogo>
            </P>
        </form>
    </body>
</HTML>
```

If you want to use the personalization features of Microsoft Passport, you will also be interested in the Profile collection. The `GetProfileObject` method of the `PassportIdentity` allows you to retrieve attributes from the users Passport profile. The valid attributes are listed in Table 8.1.

TABLE 8.1 Valid Passport Attributes

Attribute name	Description	Validation rules
Accessibility	Indicates whether accessibility features should be enabled on participant sites for this user. 0=no; 1=yes.	Must be 0 or 1.
BDay_precision	Defines the precision of the Birthdate attribute.	0, 1, 2, 3, or Null.
Birthdate	Contains the user's birth year or birth date.	Only dates since 12/30/1899 are valid.
City	GeoID that maps to the user's city.	Must be a valid GeoID.
Country	ISO 3166 country code for the user's country.	
Gender	Gender of user.	Must be Null, M, F, or U.
Lang_Preference	LCID of the user's preferred language.	
MemberName	A legacy attribute that no longer contains a sign-in name, but can be used to determine a user's domain. Use `DomainFromMemberName()`.	
Nickname	Friendly name the user would like to be greeted by.	
PreferredEmail	The user's e-mail address.	
PostalCode	Stores the postal code for the United States and other countries, where appropriate.	
ProfileVersion	Represents the version of the user's core profile.	N/A
Region	GeoID that maps to the region within the user's country.	Must be a valid GeoID.
Wallet	Indicates whether the user has established a Passport wallet.	0=no; 1=yes.

8

SECURITY

To use the profile data, just pass the name of the core attribute you are interested in to the `GetProfileAttribute()` method. Listing 8.9 shows a page that retrieves the e-mail address and member name of a user.

Listing 8.9 A Page That Displays the PUID, E-mail Address, and Member Name of a Logged-in Passport User

```
Public Class Cdefault
    Inherits System.Web.UI.Page

#Region " Web Form Designer Generated Code "

    'This call is required by the Web Form Designer.
    <System.Diagnostics.DebuggerStepThrough()> Private Sub
➥InitializeComponent()

    End Sub

    Private Sub Page_Init(ByVal sender As System.Object, ByVal e As
➥System.EventArgs) Handles MyBase.Init
        'CODEGEN: This method call is required by the Web Form Designer
        'Do not modify it using the code editor.
        InitializeComponent()
    End Sub

#End Region

    Private Sub Page_Load(ByVal sender As System.Object, ByVal e As
➥System.EventArgs) Handles MyBase.Load
        'Put user code to initialize the page here

        If (User.Identity.IsAuthenticated) Then
            Dim pi As System.Web.Security.PassportIdentity = User.Identity
            Response.Write("<BR>")
            Response.Write("User.Identity.Name: " + User.Identity.Name)
            Response.Write("<BR>")
            Response.Write("Preferred Email: " +
pi.Item("preferredemail").ToString())
            Response.Write("<BR>")
            Response.Write("Member name: " + pi.Item("membername").ToString())
            Response.Write("<BR>")
        End If
    End Sub

End Class
```

When using Passport Authentication, User.Identity.Name does not return the login name of the user; instead, it returns a Passport User ID (PUID). You should use this as a key to any user-specific data you are storing, rather than using the member name or e-mail address (which can change) from the profile.

File Authorization

Now that you know how users are authenticated, you need to control what resources they have access to. File authorization is the method of authorization that existed in ASP.old and migrates forward in ASP.NET.

> **NOTE**
>
> File authorization is the only method of authorization that IIS supports. If Allow Anonymous is off in IIS, authorization is handled by IIS. If Allow Anonymous is on, ASP.NET applies File Authorization.

File Authorization utilizes Access Control Lists (ACLs) to specify the roles that a user must be in to access a file. After the user has been authenticated, the File Authorization module will take each group in the ACL for a file and call `IsInRole()` on the passing the name of the group as a parameter to `IsInRole()`. If `IsInRole()` returns true, the user is permitted to access the resource. If the File Authorization module iterates across each group in the ACL and never receives a true response from `IsInRole()`, the user is asked to authenticate again.

File Authorization will work with any type of authentication as long as the principal is populated with the applicable roles as part of the authentication process.

URL Authorization

One of the downsides of File Authorization is the maintenance of the ACLs on the resources that you want to protect. ACLs are frequently lost when using FTP to transfer files to a Web site. ACLs also have a sometimes confusing inheritance model that for a large site can cause maintenance headaches. ASP.NET provides URL Authorization as a way to authorize users by attaching role information to URLs within a Web site. This URL to Role mapping is done in the web.config file. The URL Authorization module uses the <authorization> element to store this mapping. You saw this earlier in the web.config file used in Listing 8.3. The authorization element can contain both allow and deny elements. Both allow and deny elements have a users attribute, a roles attribute, and a verb attribute. Each attribute will accept a comma-separated list of items. The users attribute is used to match identities. There are two special identities. The "*" identity is used to represent all users. The "?" is used to represent anonymous users.

Before evaluating the authorization element, a merged authorization list is created by taking the authorization list from all of the applicable .config files, including the machine.config file. This merged list is then evaluated from the top to the bottom. Let's look at some examples.

8

```
<authorization>
    <deny users="?"/>
</authorization>
```

This is a fragment from the web.config in Listing 8.3. What this says is that I want to deny all anonymous users—"?" means anonymous users. But if I am denying all anonymous users, don't I have to allow authenticated users? As it turns out, no. Remember that the preceding list is merged with machine.config at the very least. Machine.config by default contains the following fragment:

```
<authorization>
    <allow users="*"/>
</authorization>
Which means that the merged list during evaluation will look like:
<authorization>
    <deny users="?" />
    <allow users="*" />
</authorization>
```

The first deny users makes sure that no anonymous users are allowed in. The second allow users says that everyone is allowed in which means everything other than anonymous users in this case, meaning only authenticated users. Let's take a look at another fragment.

```
<authorization>
    <allow roles="BUILTIN\Administrators" />
    <deny users="*" />
</authorization>
```

What does this do? Can you guess? Remember top to bottom evaluation. The first element says that if the Principal is a member of the built-in Windows NT group Administrators, I should be allowed access. If I am not a member of this group, the next element takes effect, denying anyone else. You might wonder why the <allow users="*"/> in machine.config doesn't still let everyone in. When the list is merged, conflicting rules are ordered based on which one is contained within a .config file that is "closer" to the page being requested. Because the web.config is "closer" to the page than the machine.config, the <deny users="*"/> element overrides the <allow users="*"/>. Let's try one more:

```
<authorization>
    <allow users="sa" roles="BUILTIN\Administrators, KINSMAN\Publishers" />
    <deny users="*" />
</authorization>
```

In this case, the one allow element is doing a lot of work. It says that if I am logging in with an account called "sa" *or* a Principal with the "BUILTIN\Administrators" role *or* a Principal with the "KINSMAN\Publishers" role, I am granted access. Anyone else is denied access.

<Location>

The authorization element that we have looked at so far applies to the Web site as a whole. In many cases I might want to apply different authorization elements to different parts of the URI namespace. The location element provides a way to do this. The location element allows the developer to specify a different set of settings for a subset of the URI namespace. The location element has two attributes. The first, path, indicates what part of the namespace the settings apply to. The second, allowOverride, can be set to false to prevent another web.config lower in the hierarchy from overriding the settings contained within the location element.

Let's take a Web site that has a need to secure three paths. The http://www. deeptraining.com/attendees path should be available only to people in the attendee, publisher, or administrator roles. The http://www.deeptraining.com/publish path should be available only to people in the publisher or administrator roles. Finally the path http://www.deeptraining.com/admin should be available only to users in the administrator role. The web.config in Listing 8.10 shows a way to do this using the location element.

LISTING 8.10 A web.config That Uses the Location Element to Specify Different Authorization Requirements for Different Directories

```xml
<?xml version="1.0" encoding="utf-8" ?>
<configuration>
    <system.web>
        <authentication mode="Forms">
            <forms name="FORMURL" loginUrl="login.aspx" protection="All"
timeout="30" />
        </authentication>
        <authorization>
            <allow users="*" />
        </authorization>
    </system.web>
    <location path="admin">
        <system.web>
            <authorization>
                <allow roles="Administrator" />
                <deny users="*" />
            </authorization>
        </system.web>
    </location>
    <location path="publish">
        <system.web>
            <authorization>
                <allow roles="Administrator" />
                <allow roles="Publisher" />
```

8

SECURITY

Listing 8.10   Continued

```
                    <deny users="*" />
                </authorization>
            </system.web>
        </location>
        <location path="attendees">
            <system.web>
                <authorization>
                    <allow roles="Administrator" />
                    <allow roles="Publisher" />
                    <allow roles="Attendees" />
                    <deny users="*" />
                </authorization>
            </system.web>
        </location>
</configuration>
```

Note that I allow all users to access the root of the application. At the very least, I must allow all users to access the login.aspx form, which happens to reside in the root. If you don't want users to be able to access the root in an unauthenticated fashion, create a location element specifically to allow access to login.aspx, like this:

```
<location path="login.aspx">
    <system.web>
        <authorization>
            <allow users="*" />
        </authorization>
    </system.web>
</location>
```

Custom Roles with Forms Authentication

We have discussed so far how to authenticate a user with forms authentication. This process gives you an identity to authorize against. With Windows authentication, you have both an identity and a list of roles to authorize against. How do you use role mappings with forms authentication to authorize against?

With a little work, you can add roles to the forms authentication model. You will use the web.config in Listing 8.11, which defines the roles that are required for access to various URLs in the application.

LISTING 8.11   web.config That Uses Location Mapping and URL Authorization to Map
Roles to Application Locations

```
<?xml version="1.0" encoding="utf-8" ?>
<configuration>
    <system.web>
        <authentication mode="Forms">
            <forms name="FORMURL" loginUrl="login.aspx" protection="All"
➥timeout="30" />
        </authentication>
        <!-- AUTHORIZATION
            This section sets the authorization policies of the application. You
➥can allow or deny access
            to application resources by user or role. Wildcards: "*" mean
➥everyone, "?" means anonymous
            (unauthenticated) users.
        -->
        <authorization>
            <allow users="*" /> <!-- Allow all users -->
            <!-- <allow     users="[comma separated list of users]"
                            roles="[comma separated list of roles]"/>
                 <deny      users="[comma separated list of users]"
                            roles="[comma separated list of roles]"/>
            -->
        </authorization>
    </system.web>
    <location path="Administrator">
        <system.web>
            <authorization>
                <allow roles="Administrator" />
                <deny users="*" />
            </authorization>
        </system.web>
    </location>
    <location path="Publisher">
        <system.web>
            <authorization>
                <allow roles="Administrator" />
                <allow roles="Publisher" />
                <deny users="*" />
            </authorization>
        </system.web>
    </location>
    <location path="User">
        <system.web>
            <authorization>
```

8

LISTING 8.11   Continued

```
            <allow roles="Administrator" />
            <allow roles="User" />
            <deny users="*" />
        </authorization>
      </system.web>
    </location>
</configuration>
```

Next, create another simple login form. It will collect a set of credentials and allow a user with a username of either "Administrator" or "Chris" into the application. Listings 8.12 and 8.13 show the login page.

LISTING 8.12   A Login Page for Gathering Credentials That Will Authenticate Only Two Users: Chris and Administrator

```
<%@ Page Language="vb" AutoEventWireup="false" Codebehind="login.aspx.vb"
Inherits="FormAuthorizationURL.login" %>
<!DOCTYPE HTML PUBLIC "-//W3C//DTD HTML 4.0 Transitional//EN">
<HTML>
    <HEAD>
        <title></title>
        <meta name="GENERATOR" content="Microsoft Visual Studio.NET 7.0">
        <meta name="CODE_LANGUAGE" content="Visual Basic 7.0">
        <meta name="vs_defaultClientScript" content="JavaScript">
        <meta name="vs_targetSchema"
➥content="http://schemas.microsoft.com/intellisense/ie5">
    </HEAD>
    <body MS_POSITIONING="GridLayout">
        <form id="Form1" method="post" runat="server">
            <asp:Label id="lblUserName" style="Z-INDEX: 101; LEFT: 36px;
➥POSITION: absolute; TOP: 43px" runat="server">User Name:</asp:Label>
            <asp:Button id="btnLogin" style="Z-INDEX: 105; LEFT: 290px;
➥POSITION: absolute; TOP: 40px" runat="server" Text="Login"
➥tabIndex="4"></asp:Button>
            <asp:TextBox id="txtPassword" style="Z-INDEX: 104; LEFT: 119px;
➥POSITION: absolute; TOP: 74px" runat="server" tabIndex="3"
➥TextMode="Password"></asp:TextBox>
            <asp:TextBox id="txtUserName" style="Z-INDEX: 102; LEFT: 119px;
➥POSITION: absolute; TOP: 41px" runat="server" tabIndex="1"></asp:TextBox>
            <asp:Label id="lblPassword" style="Z-INDEX: 103; LEFT: 36px;
➥POSITION: absolute; TOP: 77px" runat="server"
➥tabIndex="2">Password:</asp:Label>
```

LISTING 8.12 Continued

```
            <asp:RequiredFieldValidator id="RequiredFieldValidator1" style="Z-
➥INDEX: 106; LEFT: 44px; POSITION: absolute; TOP: 131px" runat="server"
➥ErrorMessage="User Name is required."
ControlToValidate="txtUserName"></asp:RequiredFieldValidator>
            <asp:RequiredFieldValidator id="RequiredFieldValidator2" style="Z-
➥INDEX: 107; LEFT: 46px; POSITION: absolute; TOP: 165px" runat="server"
➥ErrorMessage="Password is required."
ControlToValidate="txtPassword"></asp:RequiredFieldValidator>
            <asp:Label id="lblMessage" style="Z-INDEX: 108; LEFT: 44px;
➥POSITION: absolute; TOP: 8px" runat="server" Width="285px" Height="19px"
➥ForeColor="Red"></asp:Label>
        </form>
    </body>
</HTML>
```

LISTING 8.13 The Class File for the Page in Listing 8.12

```
Public Class login
    Inherits System.Web.UI.Page
    Protected WithEvents lblUserName As System.Web.UI.WebControls.Label
    Protected WithEvents txtUserName As System.Web.UI.WebControls.TextBox
    Protected WithEvents lblPassword As System.Web.UI.WebControls.Label
    Protected WithEvents txtPassword As System.Web.UI.WebControls.TextBox
    Protected WithEvents RequiredFieldValidator1 As
➥System.Web.UI.WebControls.RequiredFieldValidator
    Protected WithEvents RequiredFieldValidator2 As
➥System.Web.UI.WebControls.RequiredFieldValidator
    Protected WithEvents lblMessage As System.Web.UI.WebControls.Label
    Protected WithEvents btnLogin As System.Web.UI.WebControls.Button

#Region " Web Form Designer Generated Code "

    'This call is required by the Web Form Designer.
    <System.Diagnostics.DebuggerStepThrough()> Private Sub
➥InitializeComponent()

    End Sub

    Private Sub Page_Init(ByVal sender As System.Object, ByVal e As
➥System.EventArgs) Handles MyBase.Init
        'CODEGEN: This method call is required by the Web Form Designer
        'Do not modify it using the code editor.
```

LISTING 8.13   Continued

```
        InitializeComponent()
    End Sub

#End Region

    Private Sub Page_Load(ByVal sender As System.Object, ByVal e As
➥System.EventArgs) Handles MyBase.Load
        'Put user code to initialize the page here
    End Sub

    Private Sub btnLogin_Click(ByVal sender As System.Object, ByVal e As
➥System.EventArgs) Handles btnLogin.Click
        Select Case txtUserName.Text
            ' Allow a user name Chris or Administrator
            Case "Chris", "Administrator"
                System.Web.Security.FormsAuthentication.
➥RedirectFromLoginPage(txtUserName.Text, False)
            Case Else
                lblMessage.Text = "Invalid User"
        End Select
    End Sub
End Class
```

This so far is similar to past examples. Now you need to add one more thing to the mix. Before the authorization process begins, an application event is raised, AuthorizeRequest. By handling this event, you can do some extra work before any page is authorized. In this case, you are going to replace the default principal with a new instance of GenericPrincipal, with one important difference. You are going to fill in the role information. This will allow you to then perform authorization against the roles. The constructor for GenericPrincipal allows you to pass a list of roles into it. After creating the new GenericPrincipal, you will replace the default one with the one you have created.

> **NOTE**
>
> The AuthorizeRequest event is fired for every request, including the initial one when the user isn't authenticated, the one that returns in the login form, and so on. It is a good idea to check whether the user is authenticated prior to attempting to perform the role mapping. This is easily done using the IsAuthenticated property of the identity.

Application events are typically handled in the global.asax. Listing 8.14 shows a global.asax that handles the AuthorizeRequest event. The code first checks to make sure the user is authenticated. If she is, it then maps her into roles based on her identity. A new GenericPrincipal is created with the appropriate role information, and that is it!

LISTING 8.14 The global.asax Class That Handles the AuthorizeRequest Application Event

```
Imports System.Web
Imports System.Web.SessionState

Public Class Global
    Inherits System.Web.HttpApplication

#Region " Component Designer Generated Code "

    Public Sub New()
        MyBase.New()

        'This call is required by the Component Designer.
        InitializeComponent()

        'Add any initialization after the InitializeComponent() call

    End Sub

    'Required by the Component Designer
    Private components As System.ComponentModel.Container

    'NOTE: The following procedure is required by the Component Designer
    'It can be modified using the Component Designer.
    'Do not modify it using the code editor.
    <System.Diagnostics.DebuggerStepThrough()> Private Sub
➥InitializeComponent()
        components = New System.ComponentModel.Container()
    End Sub

#End Region

    Sub Application_BeginRequest(ByVal sender As Object, ByVal e As EventArgs)
        ' Fires at the beginning of each request
    End Sub

    Sub Application_AuthenticateRequest(ByVal sender As Object, ByVal e As
➥EventArgs)
```

Listing 8.14   Continued

```
        ' Fires upon attempting to authenticate the use
    End Sub

    Sub Application_Error(ByVal sender As Object, ByVal e As EventArgs)
        ' Fires when an error occurs
    End Sub

    Private Sub Global_AuthenticateRequest(ByVal sender As Object, ByVal e As
➥System.EventArgs) Handles MyBase.AuthenticateRequest
    End Sub

    Private Sub Global_AuthorizeRequest(ByVal sender As Object, ByVal e As
➥System.EventArgs) Handles MyBase.AuthorizeRequest
        ' Make sure the user is authenticated
        If (HttpContext.Current.User.Identity.IsAuthenticated) Then
            ' Map the user to a role based on their identity
            Select Case HttpContext.Current.User.Identity.Name
                Case "Chris"
                    HttpContext.Current.User = New
System.Security.Principal.GenericPrincipal(HttpContext.Current.User.Identity,
➥New String() {"Publisher"})
                Case "Administrator"
                    HttpContext.Current.User = New
System.Security.Principal.GenericPrincipal(HttpContext.Current.User.Identity,
➥New String() {"Administrator", "Publisher"})
                Case Else
                    HttpContext.Current.User = New
System.Security.Principal.GenericPrincipal(HttpContext.Current.User.Identity,
➥New String() {"User"})
            End Select
        End If
    End Sub
End Class
```

Pulling It All Together

So far we have looked at each feature in isolation. Let's try to pull together a realistic example that you might be able to use in your work that combines all these concepts. You are going to create a Web, as mentioned earlier, that contains three authenticated and authorized subdirectories: attendees, publish, and admin. Forms authentication will be used to authenticate the users against a Microsoft SQL Server–based credential store. URL authorization will be used to protect the subdirectories based on role information stored in Microsoft SQL Server. First, you need to create a web.config file that turns on forms authentication and defines the authorization elements for the appropriate subdirectories. Listing 8.15 shows the web.config.

LISTING 8.15 web.config File Sets Authentication to Forms and Defines the URL Authorization Settings for the Three Subdirectories

```
<?xml version="1.0" encoding="utf-8" ?>
<configuration>
    <system.web>
        <authentication mode="Forms">
            <forms loginUrl="login.aspx" />
        </authentication>
        <authorization>
            <allow users="*" /> <!-- Allow all users -->
        </authorization>
    </system.web>
    <location path="admin">
        <system.web>
            <authorization>
                <allow roles="Administrator" />
                <deny users="*" />
            </authorization>
        </system.web>
    </location>
    <location path="publish">
        <system.web>
            <authorization>
                <allow roles="Administrator,Publisher" />
                <deny users="*" />
            </authorization>
        </system.web>
    </location>
    <location path="attendee">
        <system.web>
            <authorization>
                <allow roles="Administrator,Publisher,Attendee" />
                <deny users="*" />
            </authorization>
        </system.web>
    </location>
</configuration>
```

This sets up the following restrictions:

- The admin directory requires the Administrator role
- The publish directory accepts either the Administrator or Publisher roles
- The attendee directory accepts the Administrator, Publisher, or Attendee roles

After this structure is in place, you need to create a login page as in the previous examples. The HTML for this login page is similar to the ones we have shown before; however, the code behind it is very different.

In this example, you are storing the roles associated with a user in Microsoft SQL Server. Each time the user comes back to the site after the initial authentication, you need to add the role information to the Principal as shown in earlier examples. Hitting the database on every request just to retrieve the role information is clearly inefficient. You could potentially cache the role information in Session(), but if you are operating in a Web farm, you would have to make sure you are using some form of shared session state. Remember, however, that each time you authenticate a user, a cookie is sent down and used for future authentications. It appears to be an ideal location to store the role information. As it turns out, the ticket that is stored in the cookie is represented by the FormsAuthenticationTicket class.

FormsAuthenticationTicket

Member of **System.Web.Security**

Assembly: System.Web.dll

The FormsAuthenticationTicket class represents the data that is encrypted and stored in a cookie for use in forms authentication.

Properties

CookiePath	Expiration	Expired
IsPersistent	IssueDate	Name
UserData	Version	

This class provides a member, UserData, that can be used to store the role information. This member is a string, not a name/value collection as you might expect. During the initial request on retrieving the role information from the database, you will place it into a comma-separated value string and place this string into the UserData member.

> **NOTE**
>
> Remember that the UserData is passed back and forth from the client to the server on potentially every request. You don't want to store a large amount of data in UserData, because it will slow down performance.

During future requests, you will retrieve the role information from the UserData and use the Split() function to break it up into a string array suitable for passing to the GenericPrincipal constructor. One downside of doing this is that you can no longer use the simple RedirectFromLoginPage() function in the Login page. It instead must do all the work to create the ticket, encrypt it, add it to the Response.Cookies collection, and finally redirect the user to the initial page that he requested. Listings 8.16 and 8.17 show login.aspx, which implements all this functionality.

LISTING 8.16   The HTML for login.aspx

```
<%@ Page Language="vb" AutoEventWireup="false" Codebehind="login.aspx.vb"
➥Inherits="DBFormURL.login"%>
<!DOCTYPE HTML PUBLIC "-//W3C//DTD HTML 4.0 Transitional//EN">
<HTML>
    <HEAD>
        <title>Login</title>
    </HEAD>
    <body MS_POSITIONING="GridLayout">
        <form id="Form1" method="post" runat="server">
            <asp:Label id="lblEmail" style="Z-INDEX: 101; LEFT: 8px; POSITION:
➥absolute; TOP: 8px" runat="server">Email:</asp:Label>
            <asp:TextBox id="txtEmail" style="Z-INDEX: 102; LEFT: 78px;
➥POSITION: absolute; TOP: 5px" runat="server"></asp:TextBox>
            <asp:Label id="lblPassword" style="Z-INDEX: 103; LEFT: 8px;
➥POSITION: absolute; TOP: 44px" runat="server">Password:</asp:Label>
            <asp:TextBox id="txtPassword" style="Z-INDEX: 104; LEFT: 78px;
➥POSITION: absolute; TOP: 39px" runat="server"
➥TextMode="Password"></asp:TextBox>
            <asp:Button id="btnLogin" style="Z-INDEX: 105; LEFT: 249px;
➥POSITION: absolute; TOP: 6px" runat="server" Text="Login"></asp:Button>
            <asp:RequiredFieldValidator id="rfvEmail" style="Z-INDEX: 106;
➥LEFT: 13px; POSITION: absolute; TOP: 78px" runat="server" ErrorMessage="You
➥must enter an email address."
ControlToValidate="txtEmail"></asp:RequiredFieldValidator>
            <asp:RequiredFieldValidator id="rfvPassword" style="Z-INDEX: 107;
➥LEFT: 13px; POSITION: absolute; TOP: 105px" runat="server" ErrorMessage="You
➥must enter a password."
ControlToValidate="txtPassword"></asp:RequiredFieldValidator>
            <asp:Label id="lblInvalidPassword" style="Z-INDEX: 108; LEFT: 13px;
➥POSITION: absolute; TOP: 135px" runat="server" ForeColor="Red"
➥Visible="False">Invalid
password.</asp:Label>
        </form>
    </body>
</HTML>
```

LISTING 8.17   The Class for the login.aspx Page in Listing 8.16

```vb
Public Class login
    Inherits System.Web.UI.Page
    Protected WithEvents lblEmail As System.Web.UI.WebControls.Label
    Protected WithEvents txtEmail As System.Web.UI.WebControls.TextBox
    Protected WithEvents lblPassword As System.Web.UI.WebControls.Label
    Protected WithEvents txtPassword As System.Web.UI.WebControls.TextBox
    Protected WithEvents rfvEmail As
➥System.Web.UI.WebControls.RequiredFieldValidator
    Protected WithEvents rfvPassword As
➥System.Web.UI.WebControls.RequiredFieldValidator
    Protected WithEvents lblInvalidPassword As System.Web.UI.WebControls.Label
        Protected WithEvents btnLogin As System.Web.UI.WebControls.Button


#Region " Web Form Designer Generated Code "

    'This call is required by the Web Form Designer.
    <System.Diagnostics.DebuggerStepThrough()> Private Sub
InitializeComponent()

    End Sub


    Private Sub Page_Init(ByVal sender As System.Object, ByVal e As
➥System.EventArgs) Handles MyBase.Init
        'CODEGEN: This method call is required by the Web Form Designer
        'Do not modify it using the code editor.
        InitializeComponent()
    End Sub

#End Region

    Private Sub Page_Load(ByVal sender As System.Object, ByVal e As
➥System.EventArgs) Handles MyBase.Load
        'Put user code to initialize the page here
    End Sub

    Private Sub btnLogin_Click(ByVal sender As System.Object, ByVal e As
➥System.EventArgs) Handles btnLogin.Click
        Dim sdr As SqlClient.SqlDataReader
        ' Create a connection
        Dim sc As New SqlClient.SqlConnection(Application("DSN"))

        ' Open the database connection
        sc.Open()
```

LISTING 8.17 Continued

```
        ' Create a command to get the user
        Dim cmd As New SqlClient.SqlCommand("GetUser '" + txtEmail.Text + "',
➥'" + txtPassword.Text + "'", sc)

        ' Execute the command
        sdr = cmd.ExecuteReader()

        ' Attempt to read the first record
        If (sdr.Read()) Then
            ' close the datareader
            sdr.Close()
            ' Get the list of roles the user is in
            Dim drRoles As SqlClient.SqlDataReader
            Dim cmdRoles As New SqlClient.SqlCommand("GetRoles '" +
➥txtEmail.Text + "'", sc)

            Dim arRoles As New ArrayList()

            ' Execute the command
            drRoles = cmdRoles.ExecuteReader()

            ' Get a string builder to store the roles in a csv list
            Dim bldr As New System.Text.StringBuilder()

            ' Loop through the list of roles and get them
            While (drRoles.Read())
                bldr.Append(drRoles("Role"))
                bldr.Append(",")
            End While

            ' Strip the last comma
            bldr.Remove(bldr.Length - 1, 1)

            ' Create an authentication ticket
            ' Place a serialized representation of the roles into the
➥authentication ticket
            Dim ticket As New System.Web.Security.FormsAuthenticationTicket(1,
➥txtEmail.Text, DateTime.Now, DateTime.Now.AddMinutes(20), False,
➥bldr.ToString())

            ' Get the encrypted version of the ticket
            Dim strEncrypted As String =
➥System.Web.Security.FormsAuthentication.Encrypt(ticket)

            ' Put it into a cookie
            Dim hc As New
```

LISTING 8.17   Continued

```
➥HttpCookie(System.Web.Security.FormsAuthentication.FormsCookieName(),
➥strEncrypted)
            hc.Expires = DateTime.Now.AddMinutes(20)


            ' Add it to the cookies collection
            Response.Cookies.Add(hc)

            ' Redirect the user to the page they requested
            Dim strReturnURL As String = Request.Params("ReturnUrl").ToString()
            If (strReturnURL <> "") Then
                Response.Redirect(strReturnURL)
            End If
        Else
            ' Show a message that the credentials are invalid
            lblInvalidPassword.Visible = False
        End If
    End Sub
End Class
```

This code relies on three tables in Microsoft SQL Server to store the credentials: Users, Roles, and UserRoleMappings. Figure 8.2 shows the relationships between these tables. Listing 8.18 is a script that can be used to create the tables and stored procedures that are used by the login.aspx page.

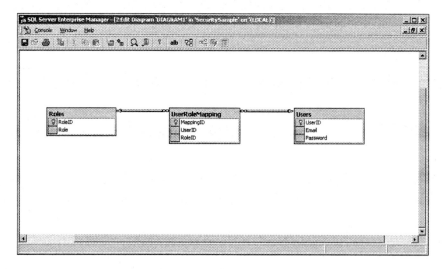

FIGURE 8.2

The relationships between the Users, Roles, and UserRoleMappings tables.

LISTING 8.18   The Transact SQL to Create the Tables and Stored Procedures Used by login.aspx

```
IF EXISTS (SELECT name FROM master.dbo.sysdatabases WHERE name =
➡N'SecuritySample')
    DROP DATABASE [SecuritySample]
GO

CREATE DATABASE [SecuritySample]  ON (NAME = N'SecuritySample_Data', FILENAME =
➡N'c:\Program Files\Microsoft SQL Server\MSSQL\data\SecuritySample_Data.MDF' ,
➡SIZE = 1, FILEGROWTH = 10%) LOG ON (NAME = N'SecuritySample_Log', FILENAME =
➡N'C:\Program Files\Microsoft SQL Server\MSSQL\data\SecuritySample_Log.LDF' ,
➡SIZE = 1, FILEGROWTH = 10%)
 COLLATE SQL_Latin1_General_CP1_CI_AS
GO

exec sp_dboption N'SecuritySample', N'autoclose', N'false'
GO

exec sp_dboption N'SecuritySample', N'bulkcopy', N'false'
GO

exec sp_dboption N'SecuritySample', N'trunc. log', N'false'
GO

exec sp_dboption N'SecuritySample', N'torn page detection', N'true'
GO

exec sp_dboption N'SecuritySample', N'read only', N'false'
GO

exec sp_dboption N'SecuritySample', N'dbo use', N'false'
GO

exec sp_dboption N'SecuritySample', N'single', N'false'
GO

exec sp_dboption N'SecuritySample', N'autoshrink', N'false'
GO

exec sp_dboption N'SecuritySample', N'ANSI null default', N'false'
GO

exec sp_dboption N'SecuritySample', N'recursive triggers', N'false'
GO
```

8

SECURITY

Listing 8.18   Continued

```
exec sp_dboption N'SecuritySample', N'ANSI nulls', N'false'
GO

exec sp_dboption N'SecuritySample', N'concat null yields null', N'false'
GO

exec sp_dboption N'SecuritySample', N'cursor close on commit', N'false'
GO

exec sp_dboption N'SecuritySample', N'default to local cursor', N'false'
GO

exec sp_dboption N'SecuritySample', N'quoted identifier', N'false'
GO

exec sp_dboption N'SecuritySample', N'ANSI warnings', N'false'
GO

exec sp_dboption N'SecuritySample', N'auto create statistics', N'true'
GO

exec sp_dboption N'SecuritySample', N'auto update statistics', N'true'
GO

use [SecuritySample]
GO

if exists (select * from dbo.sysobjects where id =
➥object_id(N'[dbo].[FK_UserRoleMapping_Roles]') and OBJECTPROPERTY(id,
➥N'IsForeignKey') = 1)
ALTER TABLE [dbo].[UserRoleMapping] DROP CONSTRAINT FK_UserRoleMapping_Roles
GO

if exists (select * from dbo.sysobjects where id =
➥object_id(N'[dbo].[FK_UserRoleMapping_Users]') and OBJECTPROPERTY(id,
➥N'IsForeignKey') = 1)
ALTER TABLE [dbo].[UserRoleMapping] DROP CONSTRAINT FK_UserRoleMapping_Users
GO

if exists (select * from dbo.sysobjects where id =
➥object_id(N'[dbo].[GetRoles]') and OBJECTPROPERTY(id, N'IsProcedure') = 1)
drop procedure [dbo].[GetRoles]
GO
```

LISTING 8.18   Continued

```
if exists (select * from dbo.sysobjects where id =
➥object_id(N'[dbo].[GetUser]') and OBJECTPROPERTY(id, N'IsProcedure') = 1)
drop procedure [dbo].[GetUser]
GO

if exists (select * from dbo.sysobjects where id = object_id(N'[dbo].[Roles]')
➥and OBJECTPROPERTY(id, N'IsUserTable') = 1)
drop table [dbo].[Roles]
GO

if exists (select * from dbo.sysobjects where id =
➥object_id(N'[dbo].[UserRoleMapping]') and OBJECTPROPERTY(id, N'IsUserTable') =
➥1)
drop table [dbo].[UserRoleMapping]
GO

if exists (select * from dbo.sysobjects where id = object_id(N'[dbo].[Users]')
➥and OBJECTPROPERTY(id, N'IsUserTable') = 1)
➥drop table [dbo].[Users]
GO

CREATE TABLE [dbo].[Roles] (
    [RoleID] [int] IDENTITY (1, 1) NOT NULL ,
    [Role] [varchar] (50) COLLATE SQL_Latin1_General_CP1_CI_AS NOT NULL
) ON [PRIMARY]
GO

CREATE TABLE [dbo].[UserRoleMapping] (
    [MappingID] [int] IDENTITY (1, 1) NOT NULL ,
    [UserID] [int] NOT NULL ,
    [RoleID] [int] NOT NULL
) ON [PRIMARY]
GO

CREATE TABLE [dbo].[Users] (
    [UserID] [int] IDENTITY (1, 1) NOT NULL ,
    [Email] [varchar] (100) COLLATE SQL_Latin1_General_CP1_CI_AS NOT NULL ,
    [Password] [varchar] (10) COLLATE SQL_Latin1_General_CP1_CI_AS NULL
) ON [PRIMARY]
GO

ALTER TABLE [dbo].[Roles] WITH NOCHECK ADD
    CONSTRAINT [PK_Roles] PRIMARY KEY  CLUSTERED
    (
```

8

SECURITY

LISTING 8.18   Continued

```
        [RoleID]
    )  ON [PRIMARY]
GO


ALTER TABLE [dbo].[UserRoleMapping] WITH NOCHECK ADD
    CONSTRAINT [PK_UserRoleMapping] PRIMARY KEY  CLUSTERED
    (
        [MappingID]
    )  ON [PRIMARY]
GO


ALTER TABLE [dbo].[Users] WITH NOCHECK ADD
    CONSTRAINT [PK_Users] PRIMARY KEY  CLUSTERED
    (
        [UserID]
    )  ON [PRIMARY]
GO


 CREATE  INDEX [IX_UserRoleMapping] ON [dbo].[UserRoleMapping]([UserID]) ON
➡[PRIMARY]
GO


 CREATE  INDEX [IX_Users] ON [dbo].[Users]([Email]) ON [PRIMARY]
GO


ALTER TABLE [dbo].[UserRoleMapping] ADD
    CONSTRAINT [FK_UserRoleMapping_Roles] FOREIGN KEY
    (
        [RoleID]
    ) REFERENCES [dbo].[Roles] (
        [RoleID]
    ),
    CONSTRAINT [FK_UserRoleMapping_Users] FOREIGN KEY
    (
        [UserID]
    ) REFERENCES [dbo].[Users] (
        [UserID]
    )
GO


SET QUOTED_IDENTIFIER ON
GO
SET ANSI_NULLS OFF
GO
```

LISTING 8.18   Continued

```
CREATE PROCEDURE GetRoles(@email varchar(200)) AS

declare @UserID int

SELECT @UserID = UserID From Users WHERE Email = @Email

SELECT Roles.Role FROM Roles, UserRoleMapping WHERE Roles.RoleID =
➥UserRoleMapping.RoleID and UserRoleMapping.UserID = @UserID

GO
SET QUOTED_IDENTIFIER OFF
GO
SET ANSI_NULLS ON
GO

SET QUOTED_IDENTIFIER ON
GO
SET ANSI_NULLS OFF
GO

CREATE PROCEDURE GetUser(@Email varchar(200), @Password varchar(50)) AS

SELECT * FROM Users WHERE Email = @Email AND Password = @Password
GO
SET QUOTED_IDENTIFIER OFF
GO
SET ANSI_NULLS ON
GO
```

The last piece of code you need to write is the code that is responsible for unpacking the list of roles from the FormsAuthenticationTicket and creating a new GenericPrincipal that contains the roles. You will implement this functionality by handling the Application_ AuthenticateRequest in global.asax. Listing 8.19 shows this code.

LISTING 8.19   The global.asax Containing the Application_AuthenticateRequest Handler

```
Imports System.Web
Imports System.Web.SessionState

Public Class Global
    Inherits System.Web.HttpApplication
```

LISTING 8.19   Continued

```vb
#Region " Component Designer Generated Code "

    Public Sub New()
        MyBase.New()

        'This call is required by the Component Designer.
        InitializeComponent()

        'Add any initialization after the InitializeComponent() call

    End Sub

    'Required by the Component Designer
    Private components As System.ComponentModel.Container

    'NOTE: The following procedure is required by the Component Designer
    'It can be modified using the Component Designer.
    'Do not modify it using the code editor.
    <System.Diagnostics.DebuggerStepThrough()> Private Sub
➥InitializeComponent()
        components = New System.ComponentModel.Container()
    End Sub

#End Region

    Sub Application_BeginRequest(ByVal sender As Object, ByVal e As EventArgs)
        Application("DSN") =
➥"SERVER=localhost;UID=sa;PWD=;DATABASE=SecuritySample"
        ' Fires at the beginning of each request
    End Sub

    Sub Application_AuthenticateRequest(ByVal sender As Object, ByVal e As
➥EventArgs)
        ' Make sure the user has been authenticated
        ' This event fires for unauthenticated users also
        If Request.IsAuthenticated Then
            ' Get the users identity
            Dim fiUser As System.Web.Security.FormsIdentity =
➥CType(User.Identity, System.Web.Security.FormsIdentity)
            ' Get the ticket
            Dim at As System.Web.Security.FormsAuthenticationTicket =
➥fiUser.Ticket
            ' Grab out the roles
            Dim strRoles As String = at.UserData
```

LISTING 8.19   Continued

```
            ' Renew the ticket if need be
            System.Web.Security.FormsAuthentication.RenewTicketIfOld(at)

            ' Create a new principal which includes our role information from
➡the cookie
            HttpContext.Current.User = New
➡System.Security.Principal.GenericPrincipal(fiUser, strRoles.Split(","))
        End If
        ' Fires upon attempting to authenticate the use
    End Sub

    Sub Application_Error(ByVal sender As Object, ByVal e As EventArgs)
        ' Fires when an error occurs
    End Sub
```

```
End Class
```

In the AuthenticateRequest handler, you first check whether the user has been authenticated yet. If the user has not been authenticated yet, the Identity property of the User object will be null and you will not have a ticket from which to retrieve the role information. After the login.aspx form has authenticated the user, subsequent firings of the AuthenticateRequest event will include an identity. After you know there is an Identity to be had, grab the Identity and cast it to a FormIdentity. The FormIdentity implementation of the IIdentity interface provides a property called Ticket for you to use to retrieve the ticket. After you have the ticket, retrieve the user data containing the role information. The final and most important step is to create a new principal object containing the roles. The last line of the handler creates a new GenericPrincipal and passes a string array of roles that that retrieved from the ticket to it.

Impersonation

Impersonation is the capability for the ASP.NET process to run in the context of a particular user identity. It is said to "impersonate" the logged-in user and is capable of using the logged-in user's identity to act on the user's behalf.

By default, Impersonation is not enabled in ASP.NET. You might initially doubt this because if you look at the User.Identity.Name property with Windows authentication enabled, it will be set to the logged-in user. This, however, is not the identity that the ASP.NET application is using to access resources. The identity that is shown here is used during URL authorization and file authorization, but will not be used as the identity when calling other base class functionality. To determine the identity under which the ASP.NET process is running, you can use a static method, GetCurrent, of the WindowsIdentity to return the identity under which the current process is executing. When you examine the name returned by GetCurrent, you will see that you are really running under the SYSTEM account. Listings 8.20 and 8.21 show a page that compares the results from User.Identity and WindowsIdentity.GetCurrent().

LISTING 8.20   Webform1.aspx

```
<%@ Page Language="vb" AutoEventWireup="false" Codebehind="WebForm1.aspx.vb"
Inherits="DefaultImpersonation.WebForm1" smartNavigation="True"%>
<!DOCTYPE HTML PUBLIC "-//W3C//DTD HTML 4.0 Transitional//EN">
<HTML>
    <HEAD>
        <title>Default: Impersonation not Enabled</title>
        <meta name="vs_targetSchema"
➥content="http://schemas.microsoft.com/intellisense/ie5">
    </HEAD>
    <body>
        <form id="Form1" method="post" runat="server">
            <P>
                <STRONG style="FONT-FAMILY: Verdana">Default Impersonation not
➥enabled</STRONG>
            </P>
            <TABLE style="FONT-FAMILY: Verdana" cellSpacing="1" cellPadding="1"
➥width="300" border="1">
                <TR>
                    <TD>
                        <STRONG>User</STRONG>
                    </TD>
                    <TD>
                    </TD>
                </TR>
                <TR>
                    <TD>
                        IsAuthenticated:
                    </TD>
                    <TD>
                        <asp:Label id="lblUserIsAuthenticated"
➥runat="server"></asp:Label>
                    </TD>
                </TR>
                <TR>
                    <TD>
                        Authentication Type:
                    </TD>
                    <TD>
```

LISTING 8.20 Continued

```
                        <asp:Label id="lblUserAuthenticationType"
➥runat="server"></asp:Label>
                    </TD>
                </TR>
                <TR>
                    <TD>
                        Name:
                    </TD>
                    <TD>
                        <asp:Label id="lblUserName" runat="server"></asp:Label>
                    </TD>
                </TR>
                <TR>
                    <TD>
                    </TD>
                    <TD>
                    </TD>
                </TR>
                <TR>
                    <TD>
                        <STRONG>WindowsIdentity</STRONG>
                    </TD>
                    <TD>
                    </TD>
                </TR>
                <TR>
                    <TD>
                        IsAuthenticated
                    </TD>
                    <TD>
                        <asp:Label id="lblWIIsAuthenticated"
➥runat="server"></asp:Label>
                    </TD>
                </TR>
                <TR>
                    <TD>
                        AuthenticationType
                    </TD>
                    <TD>
                        <asp:Label id="lblWIAuthenticationType"
➥runat="server"></asp:Label>
                    </TD>
                </TR>
                <TR>
```

Listing 8.20   Continued

```
                    <TD>
                        Name:
                    </TD>
                    <TD>
                        <asp:Label id="lblWIName" runat="server"></asp:Label>
                    </TD>
                </TR>
                <TR>
                    <TD>
                    </TD>
                    <TD>
                    </TD>
                </TR>
            </TABLE>
        </form>
    </body>
</HTML>
```

Listing 8.21   The Code Behind Class for WebForm1.aspx Showing the Difference Between User.Identity and WindowsIdentity.GetCurrent() with Impersonation Disabled

```
Public Class WebForm1
    Inherits System.Web.UI.Page
    Protected WithEvents lblUserIsAuthenticated As
➡System.Web.UI.WebControls.Label
    Protected WithEvents lblUserAuthenticationType As
➡System.Web.UI.WebControls.Label
    Protected WithEvents lblUserName As System.Web.UI.WebControls.Label
    Protected WithEvents lblWIIsAuthenticated As
➡System.Web.UI.WebControls.Label
    Protected WithEvents lblWIAuthenticationType As
➡System.Web.UI.WebControls.Label
    Protected WithEvents lblWIName As System.Web.UI.WebControls.Label

#Region " Web Form Designer Generated Code "

    'This call is required by the Web Form Designer.
    <System.Diagnostics.DebuggerStepThrough()> Private Sub
➡InitializeComponent()

    End Sub
```

LISTING 8.21   Continued

```
    Private Sub Page_Init(ByVal sender As System.Object, ByVal e As
➥System.EventArgs) Handles MyBase.Init
        'CODEGEN: This method call is required by the Web Form Designer
        'Do not modify it using the code editor.
        InitializeComponent()
    End Sub

#End Region

    Private Sub Page_Load(ByVal sender As System.Object, ByVal e As
➥System.EventArgs) Handles MyBase.Load
        Me.lblUserIsAuthenticated.Text =
➥User.Identity.IsAuthenticated.ToString()
        Me.lblUserAuthenticationType.Text =
➥User.Identity.AuthenticationType.ToString()
        Me.lblUserName.Text = User.Identity.Name

        Dim wi As System.Security.Principal.WindowsIdentity =
➥System.Security.Principal.WindowsIdentity.GetCurrent()
        Me.lblWIAuthenticationType.Text = wi.AuthenticationType.ToString()
        Me.lblWIIsAuthenticated.Text = wi.IsAuthenticated.ToString()
        Me.lblWIName.Text = wi.Name
    End Sub
End Class
```

8

SECURITY

Running this page returns the following:

User

IsAuthenticated:	True
Authentication Type:	NTLM
Name:	KINSMAN\ckinsman

WindowsIdentity

IsAuthenticated	True
AuthenticationType	NTLM
Name:	NT AUTHORITY\SYSTEM

Now, turn impersonation on. This is done by adding the <identity> element to the web.config and setting the impersonate attribute to true. The modified web.config is shown in Listing 8.22.

LISTING 8.22   web.config Set up for Impersonation

```
<?xml version="1.0" encoding="utf-8" ?>
<configuration>
    <system.web>
        <identity impersonate="true" />
        <compilation defaultLanguage="vb" debug="true" />
        <authentication mode="Windows" />
        <authorization>
            <allow users="*" /> <!-- Allow all users -->
        </authorization>
    </system.web>
</configuration>
```

If you run the same page shown in Listing 8.21, you will find that the names returned by `WindowsIdentity.GetCurrent` and by `User.Identity` are the same. The output from the page will look like this:

User	
IsAuthenticated:	True
Authentication Type:	NTLM
Name:	KINSMAN\ckinsman

WindowsIdentity	
IsAuthenticated	True
AuthenticationType	NTLM
Name:	KINSMAN\ckinsman

Now calls to access resources will operate as though you were the logged in user, in my case, KINSMAN\ckinsman. What happens with an unauthenticated or anonymous user when impersonation is enabled? In this case, the ASP.NET behavior closely mirrors ASP.old behavior. The user appears to be unauthenticated and IsAuthenticated returns false. If you check `WindowsIdentity.IsAuthenticated`, however, you will see that it has IsAuthenticated set to true. It has to be, because this is the identity that ASP.NET is running under. It is impossible for the process to be running with no associated identity. So what identity is it using in this case? It is using the IUSR_<machinename> identity that IIS creates during installation. The same page run in a directory with anonymous enabled will look like this:

User	
IsAuthenticated:	False
Authentication Type:	
Name:	

WindowsIdentity	
IsAuthenticated	True
AuthenticationType	NTLM
Name:	KINSMAN\IUSR_STEPTOE

The machine I ran this code on was named STEPTOE, and as you would expect, the identity that the ASP.NET process is running under is shown to be IUSR_STEPTOE.

ASP.NET provides an additional option for impersonation. It is possible within the <identity> element to hard-code the account that you would like ASP.NET to run under. If you hard-code the account into the identity element, this account is used to run the ASP.NET process regardless of whether the user is authenticated or not. Let's take a look at this. Listing 8.23 shows the modified web.config with a hard-coded user account.

LISTING 8.23   web.config with a Hard-Coded Impersonation Account

```
<?xml version="1.0" encoding="utf-8" ?>
<configuration>
    <system.web>
        <identity impersonate="true" userName="KINSMAN\ChrisKinsman"
            password="password" />
        <compilation defaultLanguage="vb" debug="true" />
        <authentication mode="Windows" />
        <authorization>
            <allow users="*" /> <!-- Allow all users -->
        </authorization>
    </system.web>
</configuration>
```

If you modify the web.config as shown in Listing 8.23 and run the same page with anonymous enabled, you will get the following output:

User	
IsAuthenticated:	False
Authentication Type:	
Name:	

WindowsIdentity	
IsAuthenticated	True
AuthenticationType	NTLM
Name:	KINSMAN\ChrisKinsman

Notice that the name is now set to the account that you specified in web.config. If you disable anonymous, you will get this output:

User	
IsAuthenticated:	True
Authentication Type:	NTLM
Name:	KINSMAN\ckinsman

WindowsIdentity	
IsAuthenticated	True
AuthenticationType	NTLM
Name:	KINSMAN\ChrisKinsman

Notice in this case that the name differs. Both are domain accounts. The
`WindowsIdentity.GetCurrent()`.Name is the account that I hard-coded in the web.config. The
`User.Identity.Name` is the account that I used to authenticate the Web request.

Class Reference

This section provides a quick interface reference to the key objects described in this chapter.
Space constraints prevent us from documenting every object in the .NET framework in this
book; for the sake of brevity and conciseness, we include only the most important objects here.
For more information on the other objects in the .NET framework, consult the .NET
Framework Reference online help file.

GenericIdentity Class

Member of **System.Security.Principal**

Assembly: `mscorlib.dll`

The `GenericIdentity` class represents the identity of authenticated users and the method used
to authenticate them. Derive from this class to provide additional information to the Identity
specific to a custom authentication method.

Properties		
AuthenticationType	IsAuthenticated	Name

WindowsIdentity Class

Member of **System.Security.Principal**

Assembly: `mscorlib.dll`

The `WindowsIdentity` class is used when you want to rely on Windows security. This class
implements IIdentity and adds additional properties dealing with Windows security.

Properties

AuthenticationType	IsAnonymous	IsAuthenticated
IsGuest	IsSystem	Name
Token		

Methods

GetAnonymous	GetCurrent	Impersonate

The IPrincipal interface represents the security context of a user. The principal contains an Identity for the user as well as any role-based information about the user. Just as .NET provided two implementations of IIdentity, it also provides two implementations of IPrincipal. The first, GenericPrincipal, is a generic implementation of IPrincipal with a simple array of strings representing the roles. The roles are passed in as part of the constructor. It also provides an implementation of IsInRole() that checks whether a passed-in role is contained within the list of roles.

GenericPrincipal Class

Member of **System.Security.Principal**

Assembly: mscorlib.dll

The GenericPrincipal class is a minimal implementation of the IPrincipal interface.

Properties

Identity

Methods

IsInRole

WindowsPrincipal Class

Member of **System.Security.Principal**

Assembly: mscorlib.dll

The WindowsPrincipal class is an implementation of IPrincipal intended for use with Windows-based groups. The implementation of IsInRole() checks the user's membership in a Windows local or domain group.

Properties

Identity

Methods

IsInRole

8

WindowsBuiltInRole Enumeration

Member of **System.Security.Principal**

Assembly: mscorlib.dll

The WindowsBuiltInRole enumeration provides a language-independent way to check for membership in the built-in Windows groups.

Values

AccountOperator	Administrator	BackupOperator
Guest	PowerUser	PrintOperator
Replicator	SystemOperator	User

PassportIdentity

Member of **System.Web.Security**

Assembly: System.Web.dll

This class contains functionality for interacting with the passport authentication service.

Properties

AuthenticationType	Error	GetFromNetworkServer
HasSavedPassword	HasTicket	IsAuthenticated
Item	Name	TicketAge
TimeSinceSignIn		

Methods

AuthUrl2	GetDomainAttribute	GetDomainFromMemberName
GetIsAuthenticated	GetProfileObject	HasFlag
HasProfile	HaveConsent	LoginUser
LogoTag2		

Static Methods

Compress	CryptIsValid	CryptPutHost
CryptPutSite	Decompress	Decrypt
Encrypt	SignOut	

HttpHandlers and HttpModules

IN THIS CHAPTER

In ASP.old, you just couldn't do certain things using ASP. If you wanted to create something similar to the output caching in ASP.NET, you were forced to step outside ASP.old and use Internet Server API (ISAPI) filters. If you wanted to create a program that handled all files with a certain extension, you had to step outside ASP.old. If you wanted to write something that participated in the processing of each and every page, you had to step outside ASP.old.

One of the goals of ASP.NET was to allow you to do everything you could potentially conceive of related to Web programming directly in the product. It shouldn't limit you. To that end, Microsoft added two new concepts: HttpModules and HttpHandlers. These did not exist inside of ASP.old. To find analogous functionality, you had to step outside into the world of ISAPI programming. HttpModules and HttpHandlers are fairly similar to ISAPI filters, but they implement slightly different functionality.

To understand how HttpModules and HttpHandlers fit into the scheme of things, you have to understand the way that ASP.NET handles a request. When a request is received by Internet Information Server (IIS), it looks at the extension to determine which ISAPI filter should handle the request. For any of the supported file extensions, such as .aspx or .asmx, the answer is `aspnet_isapi.dll`. When ASP.NET fires up, it performs almost the same process again. It looks at the request and compares it to the `<httpHandlers>` section of the .config file. By default, machine.config maps .aspx files to the PageHandlerFactory and .asmx files to the WebServiceHandlerFactory. This mapping determines the HttpHandler (class) that is responsible for handling the request. With the concept of mapping, you can create a new HttpHandler and map it to a new type of request. In fact, this is exactly what Microsoft did with Trace.axd. You will find that it is a new HttpHandler that is registered in machine.config for any request path that ends in trace.axd.

While processing a request received from IIS, ASP.NET raises several events. They are raised in the following order:

1. BeginRequest
2. AuthenticateRequest
3. AuthorizeRequest
4. AcquireRequestState
5. ResolveRequestCache
6. Page Constructor
7. AcquireRequestState
8. PreRequestHandlerExecute
9. Page.Init
10. Page.Load

11. PostRequestHandlerExecute

12. ReleaseRequestState

13. UpdateRequestCache

14. EndRequest

15. PreSendRequestHeaders

16. PreSendRequestContent

The items in bold represent several of the page-level events that are raised during the execution of a page. Each of these events can be sunk, providing opportunities to participate in the processing of each page in an application. In Chapter 8, "Security," in which we talk about security, we looked at sinking the AuthenticateRequest and AuthorizeRequest events.

HttpModules

Many of these events can be sunk in the global.asax of an application. By doing this, however, you limit the functionality to that application. To sink these events in a more reusable fashion, create an HttpModule. By adding a single line to the machine.config, your HttpModule affects all applications on the machine; by adding instead a single line to the web.config file, your HttpModule affects just that one application. The line to load an HttpModule looks like the following:

```
<httpModules>
    <add type="SimpleModules.SimpleHttpModule, SimpleModules"
name="SimpleHttpModule" />
</httpModules>
```

Let's take a look at a couple of sample HttpModules that handle some of the events on this class.

A Simple BeginRequest and EndRequest Module

BeginRequest is the first event to fire when processing a request. EndRequest is almost the last event to fire. Let's write an HttpModule that sinks these events and uses them to time stamp the output HTML with the time that the request began processing and when it finished processing. This information might be useful if you were trying to profile a group of pages.

We will create this as our first HttpModule. First, we need to create a class. This class will implement the IHttpModule interface. To implement this interface, we need to supply two members: Init and Dispose. When ASP.NET loads our HttpModule to participate in processing a request, a reference to the HttpApplication object is passed to the Init method. We will then save a reference to this in a member variable for use later in our module. This reference is

saved into a variable that is dimmed WithEvents so that we can sink events raised by the
HttpApplication in our HttpModule.

After we have implemented IHttpModule, we can get into doing the things that are specific to
our task. In this example, we need to create EventHandlers for BeginRequest and EndRequest.
We do this using the standard Visual Basic Handles syntax.

```
Public Sub BeginRequest(ByVal sender As Object, ByVal e As EventArgs) Handles
mApplication.BeginRequest
```

Inside of BeginRequest and EndRequest, we will utilize the saved reference for
HttpApplication to write into the output stream a comment tag containing the date and time.
The complete HttpModule is shown in Listing 9.1.

LISTING 9.1   Implementation of a Module That Stamps the Begin and End Times into the
Page

```
Public Class BeginEnd
    Implements IHttpModule
    ' Put this in web.config
    '<add type="SimpleModules.BeginEnd, SimpleModules" name="BeginEnd" />
    Private WithEvents mApplication As HttpApplication

    Sub Init(ByVal app As HttpApplication) Implements IHttpModule.Init
        mApplication = app
    End Sub

    Sub Dispose() Implements IHttpModule.Dispose

    End Sub

    Public Sub BeginRequest(ByVal sender As Object, _
        ByVal e As EventArgs) Handles mApplication.BeginRequest
        mApplication.Response.Write("<!-- Begin Request Time: " + _
            DateTime.Now.ToString("HH:mm:ss.fffffff") + " -->")
    End Sub

    Public Sub EndRequest(ByVal sender As Object, _
        ByVal e As EventArgs) Handles mApplication.EndRequest
        mApplication.Response.Write("<!-- End Request Time: " + _
            DateTime.Now.ToString("HH:mm:ss.fffffff") + " -->")
    End Sub

End Class
```

To get this module to execute for a single application, we need to place it into the /bin directory and modify the web.config to include it in the httpModules section. The web.config should look like Listing 9.2.

LISTING 9.2   The web.config to Load the BeginEnd HttpModule

```
<?xml version="1.0" encoding="utf-8" ?>
<configuration>
    <system.web>
        <httpModules>
            <add type="SimpleModules.BeginEnd, SimpleModules" name="BeginEnd"
/>
        </httpModules>
    </system.web>
</configuration>
```

Now if we fire off a page in this application root, we will see the time stamps introduced as comments into the HTML. A sample page output is shown in Listing 9.3.

LISTING 9.3   The View Source of a Page That Has Been Affected by the BeginEnd Module

```
<!-- Begin Request Time: 19:02:04.1024016 -->
<!DOCTYPE HTML PUBLIC "-//W3C//DTD HTML 4.0 Transitional//EN">
<html>
    <head>
        <title>Begin End</title>
    </head>
    <body MS_POSITIONING="GridLayout">
        <form name="Form1" method="post" action="WebForm1.aspx" id="Form1">
<input type="hidden" name="__VIEWSTATE" value="dDwxNDEzNDIyOTIxOzs+" />

            Time:
            8/23/2001 7:02:04 PM
        </form>
    </body>
</html>
<!-- End Request Time: 19:02:04.4729344 -->
```

Right now, the module works with a single application. Move it to machine.config, and every ASP.NET page on the entire server would suddenly get these time stamps! This is clearly an incredibly powerful technique.

Filtering Output

The preceding example showed how to insert content into the output using `Response.Write()`. What if you want to filter the content in the page? Perhaps you are writing an advertising system that needs to be able to find certain tags in a page and replace them with an advertisement. Although this is a common type of task, this task is a bit tougher to do. No property on the response object allows you to retrieve the contents of a page and modify it in situ. If you think about how ASP.NET sends pages to the client, however, you can understand why this is so. Depending on the buffering state and the programmer's use of `Response.Flush()`, the entire page might never exist on the server. Instead, it might be streamed to the client in dribs and drabs. However, ASP.NET by default enables buffering, so it certainly would have been nice to give us access to that buffer. Perhaps in v.Next (the next version) the object model will be updated to allow this access.

So how do you get the page output? As it turns out, you don't get it—you filter it. It is possible to put a filter in place that inserts itself between ASP.NET and the client. As ASP.NET streams data back to the user, your "filter" can alter it. This filtering is done using the base classes in the .NET framework. .NET provides an abstract class called a Stream. The Stream class is used as a pattern for writing to memory, files, and even sockets. It should come as no surprise then that ASP.NET gives you access to the stream that is connected to the client via the `Response.Filter` property.

To filter the page output, create an object that derives from Stream and pass it the `Response.Filter` property. Then set the `Response.Filter` property to this object. Now when ASP.NET sends page output to the client, it is actually sending the page output to your object. You can then modify the content as you see fit, and when you're done, you write it to the client stream that was passed to your constructor.

This is easier to show than describe, so let's take a look at some code. Listing 9.4 shows the complete source for the ad insertion filter `AdInserter.vb`. Like the previous example, we implement IHttpModule. The difference is that in the BeginRequest event handler, we create an instance of the AdStream object, passing it the `Response.Filter`, which contains a stream pointed at the user. We then take the stream object and set the `Response.Filter` property to it.

Now the interesting work is actually done in AdStream. This is our "filter." Everything up to the `Write()` method toward the bottom is just implementing the required stream members. The `Write()` method is where things get interesting. ASP.NET calls `Write()` when it wants to send data to the client. The data is passed into `Write()` as a byte array. Byte arrays are great if we want to inspect things character-by-character, but in this case we are more interested in dealing in strings so that we can do some pattern matching. To convert the byte array to a string, use the UTF8Encoding class. This class converts a byte array to a Unicode string using UTF8 encoding. The result string is placed into a StringBuilder so that we can do simple replacement operations on it.

Strings are immutable, so simple string concatenations behind the scenes are really creating and destroying the underlying strings, causing a performance drain. The StringBuilder is a much more efficient way to do operations on a string. In this case, we are looking for the `<adinsert></adinsert>` tags, but this is a simplified task just for this example. In real life, you should instead search for `<adinsert>` only, do a string scan to find the `</adinsert>`, and then—based on position—replace what is between them. For simplicity, here we are replacing the exact match in this sample with a string that's derived by taking a random entry from the astrAds array. In a real ad insertion engine, this step would also be more complicated, most likely entailing a selection algorithm against a cache of items from a backing database store. Finally, the resulting string is written to the client stream using a StreamWriter, which supports writing a string to a stream without first having to convert it to a byte array.

LISTING 9.4   A Simple Ad Insertion Engine That Replaces `<adinsert>` Tags with an Ad

```
Public Class AdInserter
    Implements IHttpModule

    Private WithEvents mApplication As HttpApplication

    Sub Init(ByVal app As HttpApplication) Implements IHttpModule.Init
        mApplication = app
    End Sub

    Sub Dispose() Implements IHttpModule.Dispose

    End Sub

    Public Sub BeginRequest(ByVal sender As Object, +
        ByVal e As EventArgs) Handles mApplication.BeginRequest
        ' Create a new filter
        Dim mStreamFilter As New AdStream(mApplication.Response.Filter)
        ' Insert it onto the page
        mApplication.Response.Filter = mStreamFilter
    End Sub

    ' My AdStream filter
    Public Class AdStream
        Inherits System.IO.Stream

        ' Random number to use to grab ads
        Dim oRandom As New Random()
```

Listing 9.4   Continued

```vb
' Array of ads
Dim astrAds() As String = { _
    "<adinsert><img src=""deep_468x60a.gif""></adinsert>", _
    "<adinsert><img src=""deepASPNET_color.gif""></adinsert>"}

' The stream to the client
Private moStream As System.IO.Stream
' Used to track properties not supported by the client stream
Private mlLength As Long
Private mlPosition As Long
' An easy way to write a strng to the client stream
Private m_SR As System.IO.StreamWriter

' Constructor
Sub New(ByVal stream As System.IO.Stream)
    ' Save client stream
    moStream = stream
    ' Create a stream write for later use
    m_SR = New System.IO.StreamWriter(moStream)
End Sub

Overrides ReadOnly Property CanRead() As Boolean
    Get
        Return False
    End Get
End Property

Overrides ReadOnly Property CanSeek() As Boolean
    Get
        Return True
    End Get
End Property

Overrides ReadOnly Property CanWrite() As Boolean
    Get
        Return True
    End Get
End Property

Overrides ReadOnly Property Length() As Long
    Get
        Return mlLength
    End Get
End Property
```

LISTING 9.4 Continued

```
      Overrides Property Position() As Long
          Get
              Return mlPosition
          End Get
          Set(ByVal Value As Long)
              mlPosition = Value
          End Set
      End Property

      Public Overrides Function Read(ByVal buffer() As Byte, _
          ByVal offset As Integer, ByVal count As Integer) As Integer
          Throw New NotSupportedException()
      End Function

      Public Overrides Function Seek(ByVal offset As Long, _
          ByVal direction As System.IO.SeekOrigin) As Long
          Return moStream.Seek(offset, direction)
      End Function

      Public Overrides Sub SetLength(ByVal length As Long)
          mlLength = length
      End Sub

      Public Overrides Sub Close()
          moStream.Close()
      End Sub

      Public Overrides Sub Flush()
          moStream.Flush()
      End Sub

      Public Overrides Sub Write(ByVal buffer() As Byte, _
          ByVal offset As Integer, ByVal count As Integer)
          Dim utf8 As New System.Text.UTF8Encoding()
          ' Get the string into a stringbuilder
          Dim strBuff As New
System.Text.StringBuilder(utf8.GetString(buffer))
          ' Go through and find <adinsert></adinsert> tags
          strBuff.Replace("<adinsert></adinsert>", _
              astrAds(oRandom.Next(astrAds.GetLowerBound(0), _
              astrAds.GetUpperBound(0))))
          ' Write to the stream
          m_SR.Write(strBuff.ToString())
      End Sub
  End Class
End Class
```

The end result is a page that contains text from one of the elements in astrAds. Listing 9.5 shows the resulting HTML.

Listing 9.5   The Output from `AdInserter.vb` to a Page with `<adinsert>` Tags

```
<!DOCTYPE HTML PUBLIC "-//W3C//DTD HTML 4.0 Transitional//EN">
<html>
    <head>
        <title></title>
        <meta name="GENERATOR" content="Microsoft Visual Studio.NET 7.0">
        <meta name="CODE_LANGUAGE" content="Visual Basic 7.0">
        <meta name="vs_defaultClientScript" content="JavaScript">
        <meta name="vs_targetSchema"
                    content="http://schemas.microsoft.com/intellisense/ie5">
    </head>
    <body MS_POSITIONING="GridLayout">
        <adinsert><img src="deep_468x60a.gif"></adinsert><br>
        <form name="Form1" method="post" action="WebForm1.aspx" id="Form1">
<input type="hidden" name="__VIEWSTATE" value="dDwtMTI3OTM2NDM4NDs7Pg==" />

        Time:
        8/23/2001 8:27:12 PM</form>
    </body>
</html>
```

Note the `<img>` tag that was inserted by the filter between the `<adinsert>` tags.

Forking the Filter

Filters work great if the task at hand calls for modifying the content as it streams to the client. Some tasks, however, don't fit this model. Suppose that you want to create something similar to the OutputCache in ASP.NET. For this to work, you need to have the entire contents of the page available after it has been written to the client. You might be thinking, "No problem, the stream has a read method." As it turns out, HttpResponseStream, which is the stream that ASP.NET uses to respond to a request, doesn't support the read operation. If you attempt to use it, you will get an UnsupportedException thrown. To make this idea work, your stream implementation must "Fork" the data written to it. One copy will be written to the client stream. The other copy will be written to an in-memory buffer that can then be read from at a later time. This way, when request processing is over, we can still access the content of the page.

The next example implements a very simplistic caching mechanism. It has an internal hash table that it uses to store pages that are keyed on the request URL. This example also uses two new events: ResolveRequestCache and UpdateRequestCache. You might wonder why two new events are needed. ResolveRequestCache is the appropriate event in this case because BeginRequest happens prior to the authentication and authorization stages. If you checked the cache for a page before those events fired, you could potentially return a cached page to an unauthorized user. That clearly would be undesirable. UpdateRequestCache is to place an executed page into the cache when it is done executing. Listing 9.6 contains the implementation of SimpleCache.

LISTING 9.6   Implementation of SimpleCache, an Output-Caching Mechanism

```
Public Class SimpleCache
    Implements IHttpModule
    ' The application object
    Private WithEvents mApplication As HttpApplication
    ' Hash to store cached pages
    Private mHash As New Hashtable()

    Sub Init(ByVal app As HttpApplication) Implements IHttpModule.Init
        mApplication = app
    End Sub


    Sub Dispose() Implements IHttpModule.Dispose

    End Sub


    Public Sub ResolveRequestCache(ByVal sender As Object, _
        ByVal e As EventArgs) Handles mApplication.ResolveRequestCache
        ' Is it in the cache?
        If mHash.Contains(mApplication.Request.Url) Then
            ' Write it back from the cache
            mApplication.Response.Write(mHash(mApplication.Request.Url))
            ' Finish the request
            mApplication.CompleteRequest()
        Else
            ' Create a new filter
            Dim mStreamFilter As New CacheStream(mApplication.Response.Filter)
            ' Insert it onto the page
            mApplication.Response.Filter = mStreamFilter
            ' Save a reference to the filter in the request context so we
            " can grab it in EndRequest
            mApplication.Context.Items.Add("mStreamFilter", mStreamFilter)
        End If
    End Sub
End Sub
```

9

HTTPHANDLERS
AND
HTTPMODULES

LISTING 9.6   Continued

```vb
Public Sub UpdateRequestCache(ByVal sender As Object, _
    ByVal e As EventArgs) Handles mApplication.UpdateRequestCache
    ' Is this something that isn't in the cache yet?
    If Not mHash.Contains(mApplication.Request.Url) Then
        ' Grab the CacheStream out of the context
        Dim mStreamFilter As CacheStream = _
            CType(mApplication.Context.Items.Item("mStreamFilter"), _
            CacheStream)
        ' Remove the reference to the filter
        mApplication.Context.Items.Remove("mStreamFilter")
        ' Create a buffer
        Dim bBuffer(mStreamFilter.Length) As Byte
        ' Rewind the stream
        mStreamFilter.Position = 0
        ' Get the bytes
        mStreamFilter.Read(bBuffer, 0, mStreamFilter.Length)
        ' Convert to a string
        Dim utf8 As New System.Text.UTF8Encoding()
        Dim strBuff As New System.Text.StringBuilder(_
            utf8.GetString(bBuffer))
        ' Insert the cached timestamp
        strBuff.Insert(0, "<!-- Cached: " + DateTime.Now.ToString("r") + _
            " -->")
        ' Save it away
        mHash.Add(mApplication.Request.Url, strBuff.ToString())
    End If
End Sub

Public Class CacheStream
    Inherits System.IO.Stream
    ' My copy
    Private moMemoryStream As New System.IO.MemoryStream()
    ' Client Stream
    Private moStream As System.IO.Stream

    Sub New(ByVal stream As System.IO.Stream)
        moStream = stream
    End Sub

    Overrides ReadOnly Property CanRead() As Boolean
        Get
            Return True
        End Get
    End Property
```

LISTING 9.6   Continued

```vb
Overrides ReadOnly Property CanSeek() As Boolean
    Get
        Return True
    End Get
End Property

Overrides ReadOnly Property CanWrite() As Boolean
    Get
        Return True
    End Get
End Property

Overrides ReadOnly Property Length() As Long
    Get
        Return moMemoryStream.Length
    End Get
End Property

Overrides Property Position() As Long
    Get
        Return moMemoryStream.Position
    End Get
    Set(ByVal Value As Long)
        moMemoryStream.Position = Value
    End Set
End Property

Public Overrides Function Read(ByVal buffer() As Byte, _
    ByVal offset As Integer, ByVal count As Integer) As Integer
    ' Create a buffer
    Dim lBuff(count) As Byte
    ' Position myself at the beginning of the stream
    moMemoryStream.Position = 0
    ' Read the bytes
    Dim iBytesRead As Integer = moMemoryStream.Read(lBuff, offset, _
        count)
    ' Copy the bytes to the output array
    System.Buffer.BlockCopy(lBuff, 0, buffer, 0, count)
    ' Return the bytes read
    Return iBytesRead
End Function

Public Overrides Function Seek(ByVal offset As Long, _
    ByVal direction As System.IO.SeekOrigin) As Long
```

9

HTTPHANDLERS
AND
HTTPMODULES

LISTING 9.6   Continued

```
                Return moMemoryStream.Seek(offset, direction)
        End Function

        Public Overrides Sub SetLength(ByVal length As Long)
            moMemoryStream.SetLength(length)
        End Sub

        Public Overrides Sub Close()
            moStream.Close()
        End Sub

        Public Overrides Sub Flush()
            moStream.Flush()
        End Sub

        Public Overrides Sub Write(ByVal buffer() As Byte, _
            ByVal offset As Integer, ByVal count As Integer)
            ' Write it to the client
            moStream.Write(buffer, offset, count)
            ' Write it to my copy
            moMemoryStream.Write(buffer, offset, count)
        End Sub
    End Class
End Class
```

The pattern should be familiar by now. First, implement IHttpModule and save off a copy of the application. ResolveRequestCache is where things start to diverge from prior examples. In ResolveRequestCache, look in mHash to see if a cached copy of the page already exists. Call the Contains method, passing the URL of the request to determine if it is in the cache. If it is, retrieve the string from mHash, Response.Write it to the client, and then call HttpApplication.CompleteRequest. This call short-circuits execution of the request and causes ASP.NET to bypass the rest of the steps and stream the result back to the client. If the page is not in the cache, place an instance of CacheStream into Response.Filter, and also place a reference to CacheStream into HttpContext.Items. This reference is needed because the Response.Filter property always returns the stream that points to the client, even after it's set to point to a different stream. That way, multiple filters can be inserted and each can act on the stream. In this case, however, we need to get access to CacheStream later during the UpdateRequestCache event.

To facilitate communication between events in HttpModules and/or HttpModules themselves, the HttpContext provides the items collection that allows data to be associated with the request.

In this case, use it to store a reference to CacheStream. CacheStream inherits Stream and acts as the forking filter. Everything that is written to CacheStream is also written to an internal MemoryStream. CacheStream, unlike the previous examples, supports the Read method. When Read is called, information from the internal MemoryStream is returned. When UpdateRequestCache finally fires, it checks again to see if the current request is already in mHash. If it isn't, grab the CacheStream from the HttpContext and retrieve the copy of the page data that it contains. Add a comment to the beginning of the page data that stamps it with the date and time that the page was cached. This page is then placed into mHash, keyed off the URL. That's it! The OutputCacheModule in real life, of course, does considerably more than this, including aging of items from the cache and varying by parameters, but this HttpModule effectively demonstrates how to use the Filter property to get at the content of the page.

An Error Module

One of the coolest new application events in ASP.NET is the Error event. As mentioned before with an HttpModule you can sink this event in an application-specific way in global.asax. You can redirect the user away from the error page to some other part of the site that is more appropriate than just an error message. It might be interesting to sink the error event in a module, however, to provide a non-application-specific piece of functionality. A common idea is to log the error to the event log for later analysis or perhaps even to e-mail it to the Web master. This can be done in an application-independent way, which indicates the need for an HttpModule.

Listing 9.7 shows an HttpModule that logs the error information to an event log and e-mails the Webmaster with the error information. It first attempts to connect to an event log called ASP.NET ErrorModule, which is created if it doesn't already exist. Next, it gathers the error information from the HttpApplication.Context.Error property. This property returns the exception that was thrown during the processing of this request. Several of the Exception properties are bundled into a string, which is then logged to the event log. Finally, the error is sent to the Webmaster using the SmtpMailClass.

LISTING 9.7   An HttpModule That Handles Errors in an Application by Writing Them to the Event Log and E-mailing the Webmaster

```
Public Class ErrorModule
    Implements IHttpModule
    ' The application object
    Private WithEvents mApplication As HttpApplication
    ' Name of the event log
    Private Const strEventLogName As String = "ASP.NET ErrorModule"
```

LISTING 9.7   Continued

```
Sub Init(ByVal app As HttpApplication) Implements IHttpModule.Init
    mApplication = app
End Sub

Sub Dispose() Implements IHttpModule.Dispose

End Sub

' Handle any errors in the site
Public Sub ErrorHandler(ByVal sender As Object, _
    ByVal e As EventArgs) Handles mApplication.Error
    ' Create the event source if it doesn't exist
    If Not System.Diagnostics.EventLog.SourceExists(strEventLogName) Then
        System.Diagnostics.EventLog.CreateEventSource(strEventLogName, _
            strEventLogName + " Log")
    End If

    ' Create an event log instance and point to the source
    Dim el As New System.Diagnostics.EventLog()
    el.Source = strEventLogName

    ' Create the error text
    Dim strErrorMessage As String = _
        "An uncaught exception was thrown in your application" + _
        vbNewLine + "Url: " + mApplication.Request.Url.ToString() + _
        vbNewLine + "Message:" + mApplication.Context.Error.Message + _
        vbNewLine + "Stack Trace:" + mApplication.Context.Error.StackTrace

    ' Write the event log entry
    el.WriteEntry(strErrorMessage, Diagnostics.EventLogEntryType.Error)

    ' Mail the message to the webmaster
    Dim ms As New System.Web.Mail.SmtpMail()
    ms.Send("webserver@vergentsoftware.com", _
        "ckinsman@vergentsoftware.com", "Web Site Error", strErrorMessage)
End Sub
End Class
```

This code results in the Event Log entry shown in Figure 9.1 and the e-mail message shown in Figure 9.2.

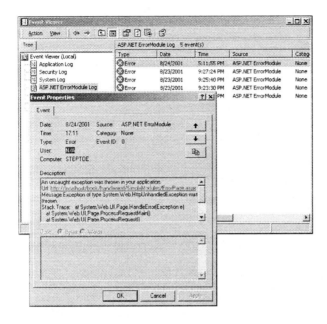

FIGURE 9.1
The resulting event log entry.

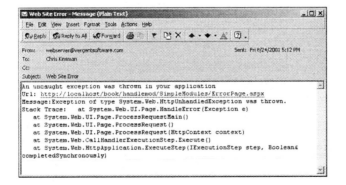

FIGURE 9.2
The resulting e-mail.

9

HTTPHANDLERS
AND
HTTPMODULES

Notice that this HttpModule doesn't actually do any redirection. That is expected to be handled in an application-specific way. The sample shows another event handler defined in global.asax for the Error event. This event handler is responsible for redirecting the user to a friendly error page. Both error event handlers fire during the processing of the request. This fact is important because it points out that multiple HttpModules can each be sinking the same events. Listing 9.8 shows the global.asax.

LISTING 9.8   global.asax Does the Actual Redirection in an Application-Specific Way

```
Imports System.Web
Imports System.Web.SessionState

Public Class Global
    Inherits System.Web.HttpApplication

    Public Sub New()
        MyBase.New()
    End Sub

    Sub Application_Error(ByVal sender As Object, ByVal e As EventArgs)
        Response.Redirect("friendlyerror.htm")
    End Sub
End Class
```

Raising Events from an HttpModule

As mentioned previously, HttpModules are intended to be generic, containing no application logic. In many cases, however, you might want the developer of the application to tie application-specific code to your HttpModule. One way to do this is to raise events as part of your processing that the developer can sink in global.asax to provide application-specific processing. Several of the built-in HttpModules raise events of this nature.

The way this is done is a little odd. No Handles statement is used. Instead, events are raised based on a naming convention. If you have a public event prototype in your code of the form:

```
Public Event OnMyEvent(ByVal sender As Object, ByVal e As EventArgs)
```

You can then put an event handler in the global.asax in the form *friendlymodulename_eventname*. When ASP.NET loads your HttpModule, it will dynamically wire up the event in the module to the event handler in the global.asax for you, based on the matching signatures. Listing 9.9 shows an HttpModule that raises an event in the global.asax of the application. It defines OnMyEvent and then raises it as part of the processing of BeginRequest.

LISTING 9.9   An HttpHandler That Raises an Event in global.asax

```
Public Class EventRaise
    Implements IHttpModule

    Private WithEvents mApplication As HttpApplication
    ' My event
    Public Event OnMyEvent(ByVal sender As Object, ByVal e As EventArgs)
```

LISTING 9.9   Continued

```
    Sub Init(ByVal app As HttpApplication) Implements IHttpModule.Init
        mApplication = app
    End Sub

    Sub Dispose() Implements IHttpModule.Dispose

    End Sub

    Sub BeginRequest(ByVal sender As Object, ByVal e As EventArgs) _
        Handles mApplication.BeginRequest
        ' Raise the event to allow the user to participate
        RaiseEvent OnMyEvent(Me, New EventArgs())
    End Sub
End Class
```

Listing 9.10 shows the global.asax sinking the event, based on the friendly name of the
HttpModule, EventRaise, and the name of the event, OnMyEvent.

LISTING 9.10   The global.asax That Sinks the OnMyEvent Event from the HttpModule

```
Imports System.Web
Imports System.Web.SessionState

Public Class Global
    Inherits System.Web.HttpApplication

    Public Sub New()
        MyBase.New()
    End Sub

    Sub EventRaise_OnMyEvent(ByVal sender As Object, ByVal e As EventArgs)
        Response.Write("MyEventFired!")
    End Sub
End Class
```

9

Authentication Modules

In the previous chapter, we wrote an AuthenticateRequest handler that was used to do role
mapping based on Forms Authentication with a custom ticket. None of the code in
AuthenticateRequest was really application specific. It could easily be abstracted into an
HttpModule that sinks the AuthenticateRequest event and can then be reused in many other
applications. Converting this code to work in an HttpModule is straightforward. Listing 9.11
shows AuthModule, an implementation of the functionality from the DbFormUrl Listing 8.16
in Chapter 8.

LISTING 9.11   AuthenticateRequest in a Web Module for the DbFormUrl Example in Chapter 8

```vb
Public Class AuthModule
    Implements IHttpModule
    Private WithEvents mApplication As HttpApplication

    Sub Init(ByVal app As HttpApplication) Implements IHttpModule.Init
        mApplication = app
    End Sub

    Sub Dispose() Implements IHttpModule.Dispose

    End Sub

    ' Does a generic role mapping.
    ' Based on the DbFormUrl example in Listing 8.16 Chapter 8.
    ' Assumes the roles are in the user ticket attached as UserData
    ' in a CSV string
    Sub AuthenticateRequest(ByVal sender As Object, _
        ByVal e As EventArgs) Handles mApplication.AuthenticateRequest
        ' Make sure the user has been authenticated
        ' This event fires for unauthenticated users also
        If mApplication.Context.Request.IsAuthenticated Then
            ' Get the users identity
            Dim fiUser As System.Web.Security.FormsIdentity = _
                CType(mApplication.Context.User.Identity, _
                System.Web.Security.FormsIdentity)
            ' Get the ticket
            Dim at As System.Web.Security.FormsAuthenticationTicket = _
                fiUser.Ticket
            ' Grab out the roles
            Dim strRoles As String = at.UserData
            ' Renew the ticket if need be
            System.Web.Security.FormsAuthentication.RenewTicketIfOld(at)

            ' Create a new principal which includes our
            ' role information from the cookie
            mApplication.Context.User = _
                New System.Security.Principal.GenericPrincipal(fiUser, _
                strRoles.Split(","))
        End If
    End Sub
End Class
```

Rewriting Paths

Occasionally, a technique that you come up with for conveying information in a URL doesn't fit the standard model for URLs. A great example of this is the cookieless session management that we looked at in Chapter 5, "State Management and Caching." The URLs used in cookie-less session management take on the following form:

```
http://localhost/sessionid/default.aspx
```

Where the `sessionid` part varies on a user-by-user basis. This is an invalid URL in the normal context of ASP.NET, so how is it handled? Behind the scenes, the cookieless session state HttpModule uses a method of the HttpApplication, `RewritePath()`. RewritePath allows you to take an incoming URL and change it to point to a different page. This is not a redirect, which requires a round trip to the client. It is also not a `Server.Transfer`; it happens prior to the `PageHandlerFactory` executing any code in a page.

RewritePath allows the cookieless session state HttpModule to change the preceding URL that ASP.NET looks for to the following:

```
http://localhost/default.aspx
```

The URL in the user's browser remains unchanged—there's no noticeable difference. Let's take a look at an HttpModule that does something of this sort. The `RewritePath` module in Listing 9.12 sinks the `BeginRequest` event. Inside this event, it rewrites any request that is received by ASP.NET to instead point to the Webform1.aspx file that is in the application root.

LISTING 9.12   RewritePath Module That Changes Every Request to Map to Webform1.aspx

```vb
Public Class RewritePath
    Implements IHttpModule
    Private WithEvents mApplication As HttpApplication

    Sub Init(ByVal app As HttpApplication) Implements IHttpModule.Init
        mApplication = app
    End Sub

    Sub Dispose() Implements IHttpModule.Dispose

    End Sub

    Sub RewritePath(ByVal Sender As Object, ByVal e As EventArgs) _
        Handles mApplication.BeginRequest
```

9

HTTPHANDLERS AND HTTPMODULES

Listing 9.12   Continued

```
        mApplication.Context.RewritePath(_
            mApplication.Request.ApplicationPath + "/webform1.aspx")
    End Sub
End Class
```

It doesn't matter what you type in as a URL, because as long as it ends in .aspx, you will see the content of Webform1.aspx in the browser, even though the typed-in URL is persisted in the address bar of your browser. Figure 9.3 shows an attempt to browse to a fictitious URL and the resulting page that shows WebForm1.aspx.

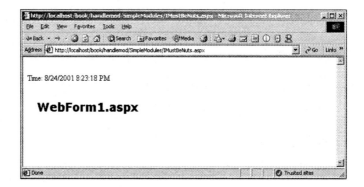

Figure 9.3
The result of typing in a fictitious URL with the RewritePath module in place.

HttpHandlers

Whereas HttpModules are designed to participate in the processing of a request, HttpHandlers are designed to be the endpoint for the processing of a request. As mentioned earlier, an HttpHandler provides a way to define new page processors that handle new types of programming models. Table 9.1 shows the HttpHandlers provided by ASP.NET.

Table 9.1   Built in ASP.NET HttpHandlers

HttpHandler	Purpose
PageHandlerFactory	Processes .aspx pages.
WebServiceHandlerFactory	Processes .asmx XML Web services.
HttpForbiddenHandler	Yields an error message indicating that a type of page is not in service. By default all .asax, .vb, .cs, .ascx, .config, .csproj, .vbproj, .webinfo files are mapped to this in machine.config.

TABLE 9.1 Continued

HttpHandler	*Purpose*
StaticFileHandler	Delivers any page that isn't specifically mapped, such as .html, .htm, and .jpg.
TraceHandler	Shows the page containing all of the trace output.

ASP.NET provides different handlers for ASP.NET pages and Web services. Each knows how to handle the files associated with the extension appropriately. HttpHandlers don't have to be backed by files, however. ASP.NET allows the HttpHandler to provide the entire response to a request. Listing 9.13 shows a very simple HttpHandler that displays a Hello World type of page.

LISTING 9.13   Hello World from an HttpHandler

```
Public Class SimpleModule
    Implements IHttpHandler


    Sub ProcessRequest(ByVal context As HttpContext) _
        Implements IHttpHandler.ProcessRequest
        Dim Response As HttpResponse = context.Response

        Response.Write("<HTML><BODY>")
        Response.Write("Hello from SimpleModule")
        Response.Write("</BODY></HTML>")
    End Sub

    ReadOnly Property IsReusable() As Boolean _
        Implements IHttpHandler.IsReusable
        Get
            Return True
        End Get
    End Property
End Class
```

This code implements the IHttpHandler interface, which describes only one method and one property. The IsReusable property lets ASP.NET know if it can reuse an instance of an HttpHandler or if it needs to re-create it from scratch each time. The ProcessRequest() method is called to do the work of the HttpHandler. In our simple handler, we output a very trivial HTML page that writes a message to the screen.

To get this simple handler to work, you need to do two things. First, you need to add a new application mapping to map an extension to ASP.NET. This mapping is required to make sure that IIS calls ASP.NET when it receives a request for a page with that extension. Without the mapping, ASP.NET is never invoked, and unless the HttpHandler happens to have a matching page, you will receive a 404 Not Found error.

To add a new application mapping, perform these steps in the Internet Services Manager.

1. Select the application root of your application in Internet Services Manager.
2. Open the Property page.
3. Select the Directory tab.
4. Click the Configuration button.
5. Select the App Mappings tab.
6. Click the Add button and create an application mapping to `aspnet_isapi.dll` for the extension you are interested in. For this example, define the extension as .hello.

The next step is to modify the web.config or machine.config files to map the extension to the class you have created. The `<httpHandlers>` section of web.config defines the handlers that ASP.NET will load. By adding a single line like the following:

```
<add verb="GET" path="*.hello" type="handlers.SimpleHandler, handlers" />
```

ASP.NET will now call your HttpHandler whenever a page with the extension .hello is called. Note the verb attribute. This indicates for which HTTP/1.1 verbs the action will be performed. Valid verbs include GET, PUT, and POST. If you want to handle any type of request for that URL, you can use a wildcard of *.

After all these steps are complete, whenever the user types a URL ending in .hello at any path within the application root, SimpleHandler will get called. If no files exist in the application root, all of the following URLs are valid:

- `http://localhost/book/handlemod/handlers/junk/asdfa/asdfas/WebForm1.hello`
- `http://localhost/book/handlemod/handlers/WebForm1.hello`
- `http://localhost/book/handlemod/handlers/.hello`

The resulting output is the very simple HTML page provided by my handler.

Dynamic Reporting

The next sample is going to do something a little more involved, combining SQL and XML. SQL Server 2000 is able to output data as XML and XSL, making a powerful combination.

Let's write an HttpHandler that handles a new file extension, .xsql. In this case there will actually be physical .xsql files on disk. These files are just the XSL templates that should be applied to the XML output from SQL Server. Our handler will expect each request to these files to include a SQL parameter. This parameter indicates the query that should be run and then merged with the XSL template. This combination allows us to run any SQL that can be output as XML and dynamically bind it to an XSL template. It's a pretty powerful concept.

Let's take a look at the code in the HttpHandler first. Listing 9.14 shows the SqlHandler.

LISTING 9.14 SqlHandler Transforms XML SQL Queries from SQL Server with XSL Templates

```
Public Class SqlHandler
    Implements IHttpHandler

    Sub ProcessRequest(ByVal context As HttpContext) _
        Implements IHttpHandler.ProcessRequest
        Dim fs As System.IO.FileStream
        Dim cn As System.Data.SqlClient.SqlConnection

        Try
            ' Get the SQL string
            Dim strSql As String = context.Request.Item("SQL")

            ' Setup a db connection
            cn = New System.Data.SqlClient.SqlConnection(_
                "SERVER=localhost;UID=sa;PWD=;DATABASE=pubs;")
            ' Open the connection
            cn.Open()
            ' Create a command
            Dim cmd As New System.Data.SqlClient.SqlCommand(strSql, cn)
            ' Get a data reader reference
            Dim dr As System.Data.SqlClient.SqlDataReader
            ' Execute the sql
            dr = cmd.ExecuteReader()

            ' Get a buffer
            Dim strBuff As New System.Text.StringBuilder(_
                "<?xml version=""1.0"" encoding=""utf-8"" ?> " + vbCrLf)
            ' Encapsulate with root element
            strBuff.Append("<results>")
            ' Get all rows
            While (dr.Read())
```

LISTING 9.14   Continued

```vb
            strBuff.Append(dr.GetString(0))
        End While
        ' Add ending element
        strBuff.Append("</results>" + vbCrLf)
        ' Close the connection
        cn.Close()
        ' Load XML into document
        Dim xd As New System.Xml.XmlDocument()
        ' Load document with results
        xd.LoadXml(strBuff.ToString())

        ' Attempt to open the file
        fs = New System.IO.FileStream(context.Request.PhysicalPath, _
            IO.FileMode.Open)
        ' Load it into a navigator
        Dim xpn As New System.Xml.XPath.XPathDocument(_
            New System.Xml.XmlTextReader(fs))

        ' Close the file
        fs.Close()

        ' Create a transform
        Dim xslt As New System.Xml.Xsl.XslTransform()
        xslt.Load(xpn)

        ' Transform it to the output stream
        xslt.Transform(xd.CreateNavigator(), Nothing, _
            context.Response.Output)


    Catch e As Exception

        ' send an error message
        context.Response.Write(_
            "<body><html>Invalid xsql query<Br>Message: " + _
            e.Message + "</html></body>")
        Return
    Finally
        If Not cn Is Nothing Then
            cn.Close()
        End If
```

LISTING 9.14 Continued

```
        If Not fs Is Nothing Then
            fs.Close()
        End If
    End Try

End Sub

ReadOnly Property IsReusable() As Boolean _
    Implements IHttpHandler.IsReusable
    Get
        Return True
    End Get
End Property
End Class
```

Right at the beginning, wrap this code in a try/catch block. If any part of the code fails, it will write an error message back to the user indicating that a problem occurred with the query and including the exception text.

Next, grab the SQL parameter from the request object and use it to run a query against SQL Server. The HttpHandler expects that the SQL query includes the "for xml auto, elements" clause. Next the HttpHandler retrieves all the data from the query using a DataReader. The HttpHandler prepends and appends a root element because SQL Server does not create a unique root element by default. The HttpHandler reads only the first column because the for xml clause causes SQL Server 2000 to return a 1 column by N row result, in which each row contains a portion of the string 2033 characters or less in length. So, concatenate these fragments using a StringBuilder. Again, because strings are immutable, concatenation operations are expensive, requiring copying the string around in memory. For something like this where there could be a large number of concatenations, a StringBuilder makes more sense—it's very efficient to append text using a StringBuilder.

After all the data is loaded into the StringBuilder, go ahead and load it into an XMLDocument to prepare it for transforming. The next step is to load the actual XSL template. This was the URL that caused the HttpHandler to fire in the first place. Get its physical path using the PhysicalPath property of the request object, and then open it with a FileStream and load it into an XpathDocument via an XMLTextReader. Finally, an XSLTransform object is created, the XSL is loaded into it, and the transformation is performed. Pass the Response.Output property

9

HttpHandlers AND HttpModules

to the Transform method. This is a stream, which is one of the possible outputs for the Transform method.

Now we also need an XSL template. Listing 9.15 shows a generic XSL template that takes some XML and formats it as a table.

LISTING 9.15   The XSL Template Used to Format the Output

```
<?xml version="1.0" encoding="UTF-8" ?>
<xsl:stylesheet xmlns:xsl="http://www.w3.org/1999/XSL/Transform"
    xmlns:msxsl="urn:schemas-microsoft-com:xslt" version="1.0">
    <xsl:template match="/">
        <xsl:apply-templates select="/*" />
    </xsl:template>
    <xsl:template match="/*">
        <html><body>
        <Table WIDTH="100%" BORDER="1" topmargin="0" leftmargin="0"
                    cellpadding="0" cellspacing="0">
            <xsl:for-each select="./*">
                <tr>
                    <xsl:for-each select="./*">
                        <td> 
                                                <xsl:value-of select="." />
                                            </td>
                    </xsl:for-each>
                </tr>
            </xsl:for-each>
        </Table>
        </body></html>
    </xsl:template>
</xsl:stylesheet>
```

This template is generic XSL that could be used for almost any query. Before we can test these two items (Listing 9.14 and Listing 9.15), we have to add the .xsql application mapping in Internet Service Manager. As noted previously, this routes requests for .xsql files to ASP.NET. We also need to add an entry in web.config to map requests for .xsql files to SqlHandler. Finally, we can run the code. We need to specify a URL of the following form:

```
http://localhost/book/handlemod/handlers/tableviewer.xsql?sql=select%20*%20from
%20authors%20for%20xml%20auto,%20elements
```

This includes the path to our XSL template as well as the URL-encoded SQL that we want it to run. The query contained in the preceding URL yields the output shown in Figure 9.4.

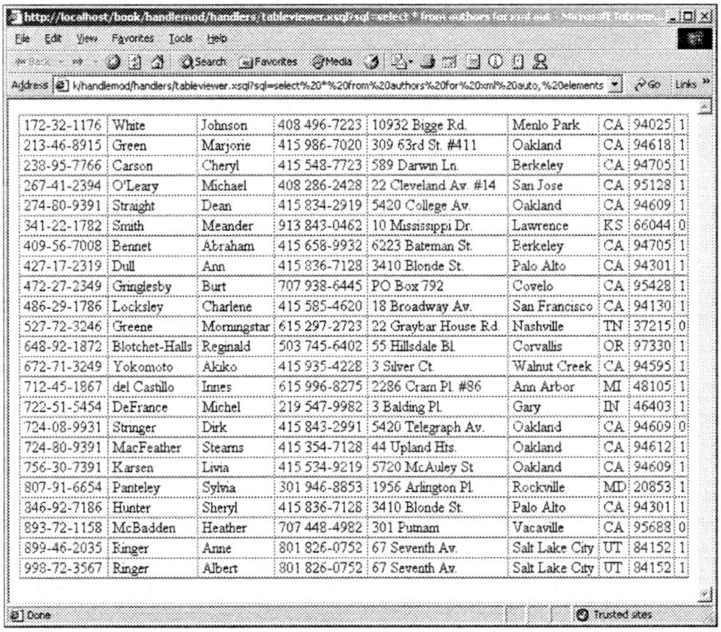

172-32-1176	White	Johnson	408 496-7223	10932 Bigge Rd.	Menlo Park	CA	94025	1
213-46-8915	Green	Marjorie	415 986-7020	309 63rd St. #411	Oakland	CA	94618	1
238-95-7766	Carson	Cheryl	415 548-7723	589 Darwin Ln.	Berkeley	CA	94705	1
267-41-2394	O'Leary	Michael	408 286-2428	22 Cleveland Av. #14	San Jose	CA	95128	1
274-80-9391	Straight	Dean	415 834-2919	5420 College Av.	Oakland	CA	94609	1
341-22-1782	Smith	Meander	913 843-0462	10 Mississippi Dr.	Lawrence	KS	66044	0
409-56-7008	Bennet	Abraham	415 658-9932	6223 Bateman St.	Berkeley	CA	94705	1
427-17-2319	Dull	Ann	415 836-7128	3410 Blonde St.	Palo Alto	CA	94301	1
472-27-2349	Gringlesby	Burt	707 938-6445	PO Box 792	Covelo	CA	95428	1
486-29-1786	Locksley	Charlene	415 585-4620	18 Broadway Av.	San Francisco	CA	94130	1
527-72-3246	Greene	Morningstar	615 297-2723	22 Graybar House Rd.	Nashville	TN	37215	0
648-92-1872	Blotchet-Halls	Reginald	503 745-6402	55 Hillsdale Bl.	Corvallis	OR	97330	1
672-71-3249	Yokomoto	Akiko	415 935-4228	3 Silver Ct.	Walnut Creek	CA	94595	1
712-45-1867	del Castillo	Innes	615 996-8275	2286 Cram Pl. #86	Ann Arbor	MI	48105	1
722-51-5454	DeFrance	Michel	219 547-9982	3 Balding Pl.	Gary	IN	46403	1
724-08-9931	Stringer	Dirk	415 843-2991	5420 Telegraph Av.	Oakland	CA	94609	0
724-80-9391	MacFeather	Stearns	415 354-7128	44 Upland Hts.	Oakland	CA	94612	1
756-30-7391	Karsen	Livia	415 534-9219	5720 McAuley St	Oakland	CA	94609	1
807-91-6654	Panteley	Sylvia	301 946-8853	1956 Arlington Pl.	Rockville	MD	20853	1
846-92-7186	Hunter	Sheryl	415 836-7128	3410 Blonde St.	Palo Alto	CA	94301	1
893-72-1158	McBadden	Heather	707 448-4982	301 Putnam	Vacaville	CA	95688	0
899-46-2035	Ringer	Anne	801 826-0752	67 Seventh Av.	Salt Lake City	UT	84152	1
998-72-3567	Ringer	Albert	801 826-0752	67 Seventh Av.	Salt Lake City	UT	84152	1

FIGURE 9.4

The output from our SqlHandler.

Page Counter Handler

Graphical page counters were all the rage early on during the evolution of the Web, but it wasn't easy to create the images dynamically in ASP until now. The next example is an HttpHandler that can be called inside an image tag in any page, like this:

```
<img src="PageCounter.cntr">
```

As long as the HttpHandler is mapped, the path is irrelevant. Upon execution, the HttpHandler looks at the referrer to determine what page it is being displayed in. The referrer is used as the key of an internal hash table that contains the current page view count. (If you were to move this structure into production, you would need a more durable storage location than just a private hash table.) After the page view has been looked up, it is time to go to work. We get a new 1-pixel bitmap just so we can get a graphics object. Because we are doing this code in an HttpHandler, there is no "paint" method that comes with a pre-created object for us. By creating a 1-pixel bitmap, we can then obtain a graphics object for the bitmap. Next, we create a font. In this case, we are using a Verdana 14-point font, but the font specifics could be passed on the command line to dynamically select a font.

Everything is now in place to measure the page count string. After we know the measurements, it is time to create a new bitmap of the appropriate size. The bitmap is cleared, anti-aliasing is turned on, and the string is drawn into the new bitmap. We convert the bitmap to a GIF using the Save method. The final step is to stream it to the `Response.Output` stream after setting the ContentType to image/gif. Listing 9.16 shows the HttpHandler.

LISTING 9.16   A Page Counter HttpHandler That Dynamically Generates Page Count GIF Files

```
Public Class PageCounter
    Implements System.Web.IHttpHandler

    ' Object to hold our counters
    Private PageCounter As New System.Collections.Hashtable()

    Sub ProcessRequest(ByVal context As HttpContext) _
        Implements IHttpHandler.ProcessRequest
        Dim iPageCount As Integer = 1
        Dim strUrl As String = context.Request.UrlReferrer.ToString()
        Dim strPageCount As String

        ' Do we have this url in the counter yet
        If PageCounter.Contains(strUrl) Then
            ' Get the page count
            iPageCount = PageCounter(strUrl) + 1
            ' Get Page Count
            strPageCount = iPageCount.ToString()
            ' Store the page count
            PageCounter(strUrl) = iPageCount

        Else
            ' init the page count
            PageCounter.Add(strUrl, 1)
            ' Set the page count to 1
            strPageCount = iPageCount.ToString()
        End If

        ' Create a minimum bitmap to get a graphics object to use
        ' in measuring our string
        Dim b As Bitmap = New Bitmap(1, 1)
        ' Get a graphics
        Dim g As Graphics = Graphics.FromImage(b)
        ' Create a font
        Dim f As Font = New Font("Verdana", 14)
```

LISTING 9.16   Continued

```
' Measure the string so we know how wide to make it
Dim s As SizeF = g.MeasureString(strPageCount, f)

' Create the proper size bitmap
b = New Bitmap(CInt(s.Width), CInt(s.Height))
' Get the graphic again
g = Graphics.FromImage(b)
' Clear the background of the graphic to white
g.Clear(System.Drawing.Color.White)
' Indicate that we want the text antialiased
g.TextRenderingHint = System.Drawing.Text.TextRenderingHint.AntiAlias

' Draw the page count on the bitmap
g.DrawString(strPageCount, f, _
    New SolidBrush(System.Drawing.Color.Black), 0, 0)
g.Flush()

' Output the graphic
context.Response.ContentType = "text/gif"
b.Save(context.Response.OutputStream, _
    System.Drawing.Imaging.ImageFormat.Gif)
End Sub

ReadOnly Property IsReusable() As Boolean _
    Implements IHttpHandler.IsReusable
    Get
        Return True
    End Get
End Property
```

```
End Class
```

The end result is an image in the page containing the count of how many times the page has been viewed.

Dynamic Handler Assignment

In some cases, you might want to dynamically determine at runtime the appropriate HttpHandler to call for handling a particular request. .NET provides a Factory design pattern that allows you to create a Factory that is responsible for creating the appropriate HttpHandler to deal with the request. This gives you some additional flexibility in creating HttpHandlers. You could look inside an associated file to determine which handler should be called.

The Factory pattern also provides a way for you to potentially pre-create a number of handlers and hand them to ASP.NET when it requests one, without the overhead of creating one each and every time.

Let's look at an example. Listing 9.17 shows a class that implements IHttpHandlerFactory. This class looks for an argument passed as part of the URL. If the value of this argument is "Chris", the ChrisHandler is returned to ASP.NET to handle the request. If the value of the argument is "Jeffrey", the JeffreyHandler is returned.

LISTING 9.17 A Sample HttpHandlerFactory That Returns Different Handlers Based on the name Parameter

```
Public Class HandlerFactory
    Implements IHttpHandlerFactory


    Function GetHandler(ByVal context As HttpContext, _
        ByVal requestType As String, ByVal url As String, _
        ByVal pathTranslated As String) As IHttpHandler _
        Implements IHttpHandlerFactory.GetHandler
        ' Check the name property
        If context.Request.Item("Name") = "Chris" Then
            ' If it's Chris return chris
            Return New ChrisHandler()
        Else
            ' Else return Jeffrey
            Return New JeffreyHandler()
        End If

    End Function

    ' required to implement the interface
    Sub ReleaseHandler(ByVal handler As IHttpHandler) _
        Implements IHttpHandlerFactory.ReleaseHandler

    End Sub
End Class


' The chris handler
Public Class ChrisHandler
    Implements IHttpHandler

    Sub ProcessRequest(ByVal context As HttpContext) _
        Implements IHttpHandler.ProcessRequest
```

LISTING 9.17   Continued

```
        context.Response.Write("<html><body>Chris</body></html>")
    End Sub

    ReadOnly Property IsReusable() As Boolean _
        Implements IHttpHandler.IsReusable
        Get
            Return True
        End Get
    End Property
End Class

' The jeffrey handler
Public Class JeffreyHandler
    Implements IHttpHandler

    Sub ProcessRequest(ByVal context As HttpContext) _
        Implements IHttpHandler.ProcessRequest
        context.Response.Write("<html><body>Jeffrey</body></html>")
    End Sub

    ReadOnly Property IsReusable() As Boolean _
        Implements IHttpHandler.IsReusable
        Get
            Return True
        End Get
    End Property
End Class
```

The Chris and Jeffrey handlers just write a simple document with the name Jeffrey or Chris.

Class Reference

This section provides a quick interface reference to the key objects described in this chapter. Space constraints prevent us from documenting every object in the .NET framework in this book, so for the sake of brevity and conciseness, we include only the most important objects here. For more information on the other objects in the .NET framework, consult the .NET Framework Reference online help file.

HttpApplication

Member of System.Web

Assembly: System.Web.dll

Represents the top-level class or root object for ASP.NET. Almost everything to do with processing a request in ASP.NET hangs off of this class. This class is responsible for raising events during request processing.

Properties

Application	Context	Modules
Request	Response	Server
Session	Site	User

Methods

AddOnAcquireRequestStateAsync	AddOnAuthenticateRequestAsync
AddOnAuthorizeRequestAsync	AddOnBeginRequestAsync
AddOnEndRequestAsync	AddOnPostRequestHandlerExecuteAsync
AddOnPreRequestHandlerExecuteAsync	AddOnReleaseRequestStateAsync
AddOnResolveRequestCacheAsync	AddOnUpdateRequestCacheAsync
CompleteRequest	Dispose
Equals	GetHashCode
GetType	GetVaryByCustomString
Init	ToString

Events

AcquireRequestState	AuthenticateRequest	AuthorizeRequest
BeginRequest	EndRequest	PostRequestHandlerExecute
PreRequestHandlerExecute	PreSendRequestContent	PreSendRequestHeaders
ReleaseRequestState	ResolveRequestCache	UpdateRequestCache

IHttpModule

Member of `System.Web`

Assembly: `System.Web.dll`

This is the abstract class that all HttpModules must inherit from for ASP.NET to properly load them.

Methods

Init	Dispose

EventLog

Member of `System.Diagnostics`

Assembly: `System.dll`

This class provides everything needed to interact with the event logs.

Static Methods

CreateEventSource	Delete	DeleteEventSource
Exists	GetEventLogs	LogNameFromSourceName
SourceExists	WriteEntry	

Properties

Container	EnableRaisingEvents	Entries
Log	LogDisplayName	MachineName
Site	Source	SynchronizingObject

Methods

BeginInit	Clear	Close
CreateObjRef	Dispose	EndInit
Equals	GetHashCode	GetLifetimeService
GetType	InitializeLifetimeService	ToString
WriteEntry		

Events

Disposed	EntryWritten

SmtpMail

Member of `System.Web.Mail`

Assembly: `System.Web.dll`

This class is a wrapper for CDONTS, the simple SMTP server that is optionally installed with Windows 2000.

Static Properties

SmtpServer

Static Methods

Send

9

HTTPHANDLERS
AND
HTTPMODULES

IHttpHandler

Member of System.Web

Assembly: System.Web.dll

This is the abstract class that all HttpHandlers must implement.

Properties
IsReusable

Methods
ProcessRequest

Building User Controls and Server Controls

IN THIS CHAPTER

Many server-scripting environments, including ASP.old, made it difficult to reuse the code that composes Web-based user interfaces. The most common option for creating reusable code is the *server-side include (SSI)*. With SSIs, you create an external file containing HTML and/or server script that can be referenced, or included, from any other file in your Web application.

SSIs are adequate and are supported on many types of server environments (including both ASP.old and ASP.NET) across different platforms. But the server-side include is a harsh mistress, quick to anger. One problem is that the SSI doesn't provide any standard functionality, only a way for including code functionality from an external file. That means that the way you access code in a given SSI may be totally different from the way you access code in another. Also, code in SSIs typically is not accessible from any language (the language of the SSI must be the language of your main page), and making a change in an SSI that's referenced from multiple files frequently causes code in linked files to break.

This paucity of options for code reuse is in stark contrast to development environments such as Visual Basic and Java, which both have a rich library of user-interface controls that developers can access in the form of reusable objects. (In general, presenting code in the form of objects ensures that the code is consistent and easy to understand; it also keeps the developer who uses the code from having to know much of anything about how the code works internally.)

ASP.NET adds support for several new kinds of reusable user-interface objects (including server controls and HTML controls), all of which were introduced in earlier chapters. This chapter discusses how to create your own user-interface objects.

ASP.NET enables you to create two types of custom user-interface objects in Web forms programming:

- User control—This control is an evolution of the functionality traditionally provided by server-side includes. With user controls, you can easily create a bit of user-interface functionality that is based on easily maintained script. But unlike SSIs, Web forms user controls are fully object oriented, supporting properties, methods, and events.

- Custom server control—This control is a type of .NET component that also provides Web forms user-interface functionality, but in a way that takes advantage of the full spectrum of programmability features available in the .NET component development model. These features include inheritance of .NET UI component base classes, a powerful complexity-management tactic that prevents you from having to reinvent the wheel when creating custom components.

We discuss how to create both types of controls in this chapter. Because user controls are far easier to develop and are probably more commonly encountered, we'll cover those first.

Working with User Controls in Web Forms Applications

When you're interested in reusing a piece of user-interface functionality in an ASP.NET application, but you don't want to expose yourself to the full brunt of a precompiled server control, you can create a user control. User controls are simple to build in ASP.NET script and don't require the precompilation that server controls do.

To create a user control, you typically start with a basic HTML representation of the user interface you want. This is a convenient feature of user controls. It means you can use whatever HTML editing control you're most comfortable with to do the lion's share of control development.

For example, suppose you're building an information portal application in which search functionality is a key feature. You want to have a Search dialog box on every page of your application. To implement this, you can create a Search dialog box user control. The HTML representation of the control is shown in Listing 10.1.

LISTING 10.1 Initial HTML Representation of the Search Dialog Box User Control

```
<table width="250" border="0" cellpadding="3" cellspacing="0">
  <tr>
    <td bgcolor="#000066"><font color="#FFFFFF">Search</font></td>
  </tr>
  <tr>
    <td align="center" bgcolor="#CCCCCC" height='75px'>
      <table width="98%" border="0">
          <tr>
            <td>Text:</td>
            <td>
              <input type="text" name="textfield">
            </td>
            <td>
              <input type="submit" name="Submit" value="Go">
            </td>
          </tr>
        </table>
      </td>
    </tr>
</table>
```

You should notice a few important things about the HTML representation of this user control. First, notice that the HTML header tags (things such as <HTML>, <HEAD>, and <BODY>) are missing. This is the case because this control is intended to be the component of an existing page, not a page that stands alone. You should not include these tags when building a user control.

Next, notice that although this HTML contains form elements such as a text box and button, it does not contain an actual <FORM> tag. This is because the containing page is where the form tag should reside; form tags don't belong in user controls themselves.

Finally, user controls are always saved using the .ascx file extension. Giving your controls an .ascx extension easily identifies the code as a user control and prevents the Web server from serving up the file. You can verify this by attempting to navigate to a file with an .ascx extension—the server will refuse to send it directly in the browser. Rather than navigating to them directly, user controls will be rendered only in the context of a hosting page, as we'll demonstrate later in this chapter.

A Search dialog box such as this one could be useful in many Web applications. If you were to use this bit of HTML again and again in different places, you would want to have some high-level programmatic control over its behavior. For example, you would definitely want to be able to specify the text displayed in the title bar and the Search prompt, as well as specify other cosmetic aspects such as the background color of the title bar and body of the control.

You can provide programmers who use your control the capability to change these values programmatically by exposing them as user-control properties. We'll describe how that works in the next section.

In addition to saving the control as a file with an .ascx extension, your user control can contain an additional element—a Control directive. This directive is similar to the Page directive that appears at the start of ASP.NET pages, but it contains special settings that are relevant to user controls.

The Control directive supports a subset of the attributes supported by the Page directive (described in Chapter 3, "Page Framework"). The attributes supported by the Control directive are the following:

- AutoEventWireup
- ClassName
- CompilerOptions
- Debug
- Description
- EnableViewState
- Explicit
- Inherits
- Language
- Src

- Strict
- WarningLevel

You use these settings nearly identically to the way you use them for pages; see Chapter 3 for more information on what they do and how they work.

The Inherits and Src attributes refer to code-behind functionality for the control itself. This enables you to separate code functionality from a user control the same way you do for a page. Code behind is also discussed in Chapter 3.

You'll notice that the Trace attribute is missing from the list of attributes found on the list of Control directives. The Trace attribute is not a part of the Control directive because trace mode functionality is controlled by the entire page and cannot be limited to a specific user control. For more information on tracing, see Chapter 4, "Debugging ASP.NET Applications."

Adding Properties to a User Control

You can give developers the capability to programmatically change elements of your user control by exposing certain elements of the control as public properties. By doing this, you enable customization of the control at a high level, without forcing developers to manually hack the HTML that composes your control.

To do this, you replace hard-coded HTML elements in your control with references to public variables or (preferably) property procedures. Listing 10.2 shows an example of the Search dialog box created in the previous section, this time with a property procedure for a TitleBarText property.

LISTING 10.2   Search Dialog Box with a TitleBarText Property

```
<SCRIPT runat='server'>
  Private strTitleBarText As String

  Public Property TitleBarText As String
    Get
      Return strTitleBarText
    End Get

    Set
      strTitleBarText = Value
    End Set
  End Property

</SCRIPT>
```

LISTING 10.2   Continued

```
<table width="250" border="0" cellpadding="3" cellspacing="0">
  <tr>
    <td bgcolor="#000066"><font color="#FFFFFF"><% =TitleBarText %></font></td>
  </tr>
  <tr>
    <td align="center" bgcolor="#CCCCCC" height='75px'>
      <table width="98%" border="0">
        <tr>
          <td>Text:</td>
          <td>
            <input type="text" name="textfield">
          </td>
          <td>
            <input type="submit" name="Submit" value="Go">
          </td>
        </tr>
      </table>
    </td>
  </tr>
</table>
```

The three things that changed in this version of the control are the inclusion of a private variable, mstrTitleBarText, to store the value of the title bar text, a property accessor function
called TitleBarText, and a render block (shaded) in the middle of the HTML representation of
the control.

When you include this code in the control, the HTML representation of the control will be different, depending on how the programmer of the containing page chooses to set these properties. For an example of the finished product, see the section "Programming a User Control in a
Page," later in this chapter.

It's common for controls such as this Search control to incorporate other properties to alter the
appearance and behavior of the control. Your controls will probably contain properties for fore-
ground and background color, height and width, and so on. These properties are very easy to
implement in user controls with the techniques demonstrated here.

Programming a User Control in a Page

To use a user control in an ASP.NET Web forms page, you must first include a Register directive at the top of the page and then create a tag that represents an instance of that control, as
you do with the other intrinsic ASP.NET Web forms controls.

Listing 10.3 gives an example of a typical Register directive for the Search user control we created in the previous section.

LISTING 10.3   Example of a Minimal Register Directive Referencing a User Control in a Page

```
<%@ Register TagPrefix="MyControl"
             TagName="Search"
             Src="search.ascx" %>
```

Three attributes are required in the Register directive. The TagPrefix attribute gives your control a unique namespace so that its name doesn't collide with other controls that may have similar names. This prefix comes in handy when you need to use two types of controls, written by different authors but both coincidentally named Search, on the same page. However, rather than using the generic tag prefix MyControl, you should use a tag prefix that identifies yourself or your company. That way, a namespace collision between your control and someone else's will be less likely.

The TagName attribute provides a name that identifies your control class. Note that this is different from the name of the instance of the control you use to manipulate the control programmatically.

Finally, the Src attribute indicates where the source file (.ascx) of your user control is stored. This file does not have to be in the same directory as the page; it can be in a subdirectory.

After you've registered your control for use in a page, you can create an instance of the control using the same tag-based syntax you use for any other kind of Web form control in ASP.NET. For example, if the Register directive for your Search control looks like the previous example (in Listing 10.3), a tag that would create an instance of the control on an ASP.NET Web form looks like this:

```
<MyControl:Search id='Search1' runat='server' />
```

As with all Web form controls, you should ensure that your control tags are placed inside an ASP.NET form (that is, a FORM tag that contains the runat="server" attribute). If you don't do this, your control won't be executed. Also, as with other types of Web forms controls, you can assign default properties to the control two ways: in the tag itself or in the Page_Load event procedure (or both).

For example, suppose you're using the Search user control in an application that enables users to search an online personnel database. In this case, you might want to set certain properties of the user control in code to reflect the purpose of the search. Listing 10.4 provides an example.

10

BUILDING USER
CONTROLS AND
SERVER CONTROLS

LISTING 10.4   Example of a Custom User Control Utilized in an ASP.NET Web Form

```
<%@ PAGE language='VB' debug='true' trace='false' %>
<%@ REGISTER TagPrefix='MyControl' TagName='Search' Src='search.ascx' %>

<HTML>
<HEAD>
<TITLE>
ASP.NET Page
</TITLE>
</HEAD>

<SCRIPT runat='server'>
  Sub Page_Load(Sender As Object, e As EventArgs)
    Search1.TitleBarText = "Personnel Search"
  End Sub
</SCRIPT>

<BODY>

<FORM runat='server'>
<MyControl:Search id='Search1' runat='server' />
</FORM>
</BODY>
</HTML>
```

In this example, the TitleBarText property is set in the page's Page_Load event procedure. But it could just as well have been set in the declaration tag for the control itself, like so:

```
<MyControl:Search id='Search1'
                  TitleBarText='PersonnelSearch'
                  runat='server' />
```

There's really no difference between the two techniques. Which one you use depends on your preference and whether the property setting is known when you author the page. If the property setting isn't known (that is, the property is derived from a calculation), you'll need to assign it in code.

Adding Methods to Your User Control

You can add methods to your user control the same way you add properties to controls. To add a method, you simply create a public function or subroutine in the SCRIPT tag contained in your user control.

For example, suppose you want the page programmer to be able to show an Advanced Search dialog box. To enable this, you might provide a ShowAdvanced method in your Search control. Listing 10.5 shows an example of a new version of the Search control that provides this functionality.

LISTING 10.5   Search Control with ShowAdvanced Method to Provide Extended Features

```
<SCRIPT runat='server'>
  Private strTitleBarText As String

  Public Property TitleBarText As String
    Get
      Return strTitleBarText
    End Get

    Set
      strTitleBarText = Value
    End Set
  End Property

  Public Sub ShowAdvanced()
    ' Public (control method)
    Advanced.Visible = True
  End Sub

</SCRIPT>

<table width="250" border="0" cellpadding="3" cellspacing="0">
  <tr>
    <td bgcolor="#000066"><font color="#FFFFFF">
      <% =TitleBarText %>
      </font></td>
  </tr>
  <tr>
    <td align="center" bgcolor="#CCCCCC" height='75px'>
      <table width="98%" border="0">
        <tr>
          <td>Text:</td>
          <td>
            <input type="text" name="textfield">
          </td>
          <td align="center">
            <input type="submit" name="Submit" value="Go">
          </td>
        </tr>
      </table>
```

LISTING 10.5 Continued

```
      </td>
    </tr>
    <tr id='Advanced' visible='False' runat='server'>
      <td align="center" bgcolor="#CCCCCC" height='40'>
        <asp:checkbox id="ShowContractors" value="1" runat="server" />
        Show contractors</td>
    </tr>
</table>
```

The Advanced Search functionality is provided through an HTML server control, a table row control called Advanced. The Visible property of this control is set to `false` by default, but calling the ShowAdvanced method of the control sets it to `true`. In addition to displaying the row, all the controls contained in the row are automatically displayed as well. You could include code in ShowAdvanced to do other interesting work, such as setting defaults for the Advanced Search controls and so forth.

To call this method, the page programmer calls the Show method in the hosting page:

```
<SCRIPT runat='server'>
  Sub Page_Load(Sender As Object, e As EventArgs)
    Search1.TitleBarText = "Personnel Search"
    Search1.ShowAdvanced
  End Sub
</SCRIPT>
```

The simplicity of this code highlights an important benefit of user controls (and componentized code in general)—adding new functionality to a component does not typically require that programmers who use that component make significant changes in their code to adapt to the new functionality. If you don't want to use the Search control's new functionality, simply leave it out of your method call.

Handling Events from a User Control

Your user control can handle events that are generated by controls contained by the user control. For example, you may choose to encapsulate Search functionality within the Search control itself. To do this, you write a handler for the event that kicks off the search, inserting any code you want in the event handler.

This version of the Search control demonstrates how to handle internal system events. For this example, when the user clicks the OK button, the button's Click event is handled by the Search_Click event procedure, which then kicks off the actual search. We haven't talked about doing database queries yet (we get to that in Chapter 12, "Creating Database Applications with ADO.NET"), so we'll stub out the "real" search results with a label control. Listing 10.6 provides an example of the Search control.

LISTING 10.6   Version of the Search Control That Handles an Internal Event

```
<SCRIPT runat='server'>
  Event DoSearch(SearchText As String)

  Private strTitleBarText As String

  Public Property TitleBarText As String
    Get
      Return strTitleBarText
    End Get

    Set
      strTitleBarText = Value
    End Set
  End Property

  Sub Search_Click(Sender As Object, e As EventArgs)
    SearchResults.Text = "Search results for '" & _
SearchText.Text & "' go here."
  End Sub

</SCRIPT>
<table width="250" border="0" cellpadding="3" cellspacing="0">
  <tr>
    <td bgcolor="#000066"><font color="#FFFFFF">
      <% =TitleBarText %>
      </font></td>
  </tr>
  <tr>
    <td align="center" bgcolor="#CCCCCC" height='75px'>
      <table width="98%" border="0">
        <tr>
          <td>Text:</td>
          <td> <asp:textbox id='SearchText' runat='server' /> </td>
          <td align="center"> <asp:button id="GoSearch"
onClick='Search_Click' text="Go" runat='server' />
          </td>
        </tr>
      </table>
    </td>
  </tr>
</table>
<br>
<asp:label id='SearchResults' runat='server' />
```

Note that you don't have to handle the Click event of the button if you don't want to. Because the user control exists on a form in an ASP.NET page, the control will generate a round trip to the server when its Go button is pressed. You can then handle the Search functionality in the hosting page if you didn't already handle it inside the control. There's no right way to accomplish this division of labor; encapsulating the Search functionality in the control makes the control simpler to use, but less flexible, because the programmer of the hosting page would have to change the control if she wanted to change the Search functionality.

> **NOTE**
>
> Although you can handle events internally in a user control, you cannot *raise* events from a user control to the containing page. To do this you need to create a full server control. The discussion of server control creation begins in the next section.

Creating Server Controls

In the previous sections you learned how to create user controls. User controls are a fast and easy way to create reusable user-interface elements in ASP.NET, and they serve as a more structured and richer alternative to server-side includes. However, user controls don't take full advantage of the .NET component model. As a result, they are somewhat limited in terms of functionality.

User controls are compiled automatically in the background, just as ASP.NET pages are. The first time your page is accessed in the browser, the page and any user controls on that page are compiled. After the first compilation, the page and user controls are recompiled only if you change their source code.

In contrast, server controls must be compiled and deployed to the Web server ahead of time. Although this may seem like a bit of a pain, you can actually automate much of the compilation process ahead of time using the command-line compiler and a Windows batch file. This is the tactic we'll use in this chapter.

> **NOTE**
>
> In Visual Studio .NET, when you create a new project and select Web Server Control, VS .NET creates an actual server control project for you (in contrast to a user control). To create a user control in the development environment, you first create an ASP.NET Web Application and then add a user-control file to the project.

Creating a Basic Server Control

You create the most basic kind of compiled server controls by following these steps:

1. Create a class that inherits from System.Web.UI.Control.

2. Override the Render method of the inherited Control class.

3. Optionally, add any properties, methods, or events that are appropriate to your control's functionality.

4. Optionally, give your control the capability to store and retrieve state using the State object.

As an example, we'll start with a control whose content is completely static—literally, a "Hello, world" example. From there, we'll build more sophisticated and useful controls that have properties, methods, and events you can set programmatically.

> **NOTE**
>
> The properties, methods, and events of the System.Web.UI.Control class are listed at the end of Chapter 3.

The first step is to create a class contained in a namespace that inherits System.Web.UI.Control and overrides the Control class's Render method. Listing 10.7 shows an example.

LISTING 10.7 "Hello World" Server Control Example

```
Imports System.Web.UI     ' Contains HtmlTextWriter and Control classes

Namespace MyExample

  Public Class HelloWorld
    Inherits Control

    Protected Overrides Sub Render(Output As HtmlTextWriter)
      Output.Write("<B>Hello world!</B>")
    End Sub

  End Class

End Namespace
```

After writing the code, the next step is to compile this code into a .NET component DLL and deploy it into the Web application directory. You can compile this code with the command line compiler. The command is

```
vbc helloctrl.vb /t:library /out:helloctrl.dll /r:System.dll /r:System.Web.dll
```

When you compile this control, you must reference the libraries System.dll and System.Web.dll because they contain .NET framework libraries used in your code. The System.Web.dll library is required by every server control because it contains the Control base class from which ASP.NET server controls inherit. This namespace also contains the HtmlTextWriter class that is passed in to the Render method; as you can see from the code listing, this class is used by your code as a way to send HTML data to the browser.

> **NOTE**
>
> For now, we've intentionally glossed over the details of how command-line compilation works in .NET. You can find more detailed information on how to use the command-line compiler to create your components in the next section.

Compiling this code produces a binary, helloctrl.dll, which should be copied to a \bin subdirectory under a Web application directory to be accessible from an ASP.NET application in that directory.

The final step is to create an ASP.NET page that references this control and invokes it. Listing 10.8 shows a minimal example of such a page.

LISTING 10.8 ASP.NET Page That References the Custom "Hello World" Server Control

```
<%@ PAGE language='VB' debug='true' trace='false' %>
<%@ REGISTER TagPrefix='Jeffrey' Namespace='MyExample' Assembly='helloctrl' %>

<HTML>
<HEAD>
<TITLE>
Hello World Server Control
</TITLE>
</HEAD>

<BODY>

<FORM runat='server'>
  <Jeffrey:HelloWorld id='Hello1' runat='server' />
```

LISTING 10.8 Continued

```
</FORM>

</BODY>
</HTML>
```

The Register directive is crucial here; it's what makes the page aware of the control contained in the external library. Like the user controls we discussed earlier in this chapter, the REGIS-TER tag contains a TagPrefix attribute; this attribute is an arbitrary text name you give to distinguish your controls from like-named controls on the page. As you can see in the code example, we used the TagPrefix "Jeffrey"; the same tag prefix is used when referencing the control on the page.

The Register directive for a precompiled server control also contains two attributes not found in user-control registrations. The Namespace attribute references the control's namespace; it must be the same as the namespace you declared when you constructed the server control.

Finally, the Assembly attribute points the page to the name of the assembly in which the component class resides. This should be the filename of the compiled DLL, without the .DLL filename extension. Remember that for the page to find the DLL, the DLL must be copied to a \bin subdirectory beneath the Web application directory.

Assuming everything is in place, when you navigate to this page in the browser, you should be able to see the "Hello World" text emitted by the overridden Render method of the HelloWorld control. You can, of course, replace this simple HTML with any text you want by altering the output of the Render function and then recompiling and redeploying the server control.

Before we go into more detail on the more sophisticated features of server controls, we'll take a brief detour and cover the general steps involved in creating and deploying .NET components. Because server controls are a type of .NET component, it's important to have a basic understanding of how components are built in .NET.

Compiling Your Control as a .NET Component

Because server controls are a type of .NET component, they must be compiled separately from the ASP.NET page that hosts them. You can do this in a number of ways. You may choose to build and compile your control in Visual Studio .NET, which is certainly okay. However, we prefer to compile our .NET components manually, using the command-line compiler. Although this takes a bit longer to set up, you may find that it's faster in the long run. It certainly gives you more control over what's going on, at any rate, and will probably prove to be more enlightening in terms of how your source code gets turned into a .NET component.

You may have created COM components in previous versions of Visual Studio or Visual Basic. The theory behind components in .NET is similar, although the implementation is different (in our opinion, component-based development is easier in many ways in .NET than it was in COM). Any .NET code can be packaged as an independently compiled component as long as the code contains a namespace and at least one public class.

Creating .NET Components Using the Command-Line Compiler

The first step to compiling a component using the command line is to add the location of your compiler to your computer's PATH variable. In Windows 2000 you do this by opening the System Control Panel, clicking the Advanced tab, clicking the Environment Variables button, and altering the PATH variable located in the System variables panel. A number of semicolon-delimited paths should already be in the PATH variable; you'll need to add something like

```
%SystemRoot%\Microsoft.NET\Framework\v1.0.2914
```

to the end of whatever's there. Ensure that you separate the original path and the Microsoft .NET directory string with a semicolon. Note that the location and name of the .NET framework compilers will almost certainly be different on your machine, depending on which version and build of .NET you're using. If you're in doubt as to which PATH setting to append, use Windows Explorer to do a search for the file vbc.exe and use whatever directory that file is located in. The objective here is simply to provide a way for you to get to vbc.exe from a command line without having to type the path to it every time you compile.

> **NOTE**
>
> You should be able to find compilers for at least three languages in the .NET directory; vbc.exe is the Visual Basic compiler, csc.exe is the one for C#, and jsc.exe is used for applications creating in JScript, Microsoft's implementation of JavaScript. You can also see a number of DLLs that compose the .NET framework in this directory—files such as System.dll, System.Web.dll, System.Data.dll, and so forth.

After you've appended the location of the .NET compilers to your PATH setting, you can open a command window by selecting Start, Run, and then typing **cmd** into the Run dialog box. After the command window appears, you can test to make sure everything works by typing **vbc | more** into the command window. If everything worked correctly, the numerous parameters for the Visual Basic compiler will appear in the window.

To compile a class to a component using the command-line compiler, you must specify that the compiled output (the "target") should be a component rather than a conventional executable. When compiling with vbc, you do this using the command-line switch /target:library. The output of a build that uses the switch /target:library is a .NET component contained in a familiar DLL file.

Listing 10.9 shows an example of one of the smallest possible chunks of code that can be compiled into a .NET component.

LISTING 10.9   Example of a Namespace and Class That Can Be Compiled into a .NET Component

```
Namespace HelloComponent

  Public Class Hello

    Public Function SayHello() As String
      Return "Hello, world!!!"
    End Function

  End Class

End Namespace
```

Note that this component is contained by a namespace and contains a single public function, SayHello, which returns a hard-wired text string.

Assuming that this code is contained in a file called hello.vb, you could compile this class to a .NET component called hello.dll by using the following command line:

```
vbc hello.vb /target:library /out:hello.dll
```

You can see that compiling components is fairly straightforward, as long as you keep things simple. The tricky part with command-line compilation of components has to do with ensuring that you've included references to all the external libraries used by your component. For example, if your code uses classes found in the System.Data namespace (including subnamespaces such as System.Data.SqlClient), the command you use to build your component must contain a reference to the component System.Data.dll, or the build will fail because the compiler won't be able to find the external libraries your code refers to.

Therefore, when compiling, you must include references to external libraries using the /r switch. Your command line can have as many /r switches as it needs. For example, if your component references the System.Data and System.Xml namespaces, the command line you use to compile your component might look like this:

```
vbc mysrc.vb /out:mycomp.dll /target:library
/r:System.Data.dll /r:System.XML.dll
```

More options are available in the command-line compiler, but these are all you'll need to know to get your server controls to compile.

10

BUILDING USER CONTROLS AND SERVER CONTROLS

Sooner or later you'll notice that your command-line compilation statements will become long and unwieldy. This is particularly the case when your project comprises many source files or when your project contains more than one or two references to external libraries. In this case, you'll probably want to automate the build process. A common way to accomplish this is by creating a batch file. Listing 10.10 shows an example of a batch file that compiles a .NET component project.

LISTING 10.10   Batch File That Compiles and Deploys a .NET Component Project Automatically

```
vbc mysrc1.vb mysrc2.vb /out:mycomp.dll /t:library /r:System.Data.dll
copy mycomp.dll c:\inetpub\wwwroot\myapp\bin
pause
```

This set of commands, all contained within the text file build.bat, is all that's needed to create and deploy the fictitious mycomp.dll component. Note that two source files are in this project (mysrc1.vb and mysrc2.vb), and we're using the /t abbreviation instead of /target in this example. When the compilation is complete, the batch file copies the newly compiled DLL to c:\inetpub\wwwroot\myapp\bin.

Remember that batch files must end in a .bat or .cmd extension. You can use any text editor (such as the onerous Notepad or the extremely whizzy shareware TextPad) to create them.

Deploying a Component in ASP.NET

Deploying components is much easier in .NET than it was using COM. In .NET, you need only to deploy the component to a \bin directory located beneath your application directory. That's it! No REGSVR32, no shutting down and restarting IIS—none of that jive.

The batch file demonstrated in the previous section also copied the DLL to the Web application's \bin subdirectory after the compiler ran. Copying the file to a directory where it can be tested immediately after compilation is, of course, optional, but it's a handy trick that you'll probably want to use often.

No difference exists between a server control and any other kind of component in .NET, so the technique you use to develop, compile, and deploy server controls is essentially the same that you would use to create middle-tier business-logic components that have no representation in the user interface.

Creating Composite Controls

In the previous section, you saw a simple example of how to create a simple, HTML-based control by overriding the Render method of System.Web.UI.Control. This is a straightforward way to emit a chunk of static HTML.

A *composite control*, on the other hand, is a control that comprises other controls (either HTML controls or server controls). A Search control comprising a text label, a text box, and a button is an example of a composite control. This control would be similar to the Search control described in the section on user controls earlier in this chapter. We will create a new version of this control as a server control in our example.

Composite server controls are a type of ASP.NET server control. You create them essentially the same way as you create server controls, starting by creating a class that inherits from the System.Web.UI.Control class. The technique to create a composite control is slightly different from creating normal server controls, however. Instead of overriding the Render method of System.Web.UI.Control, as you do with normal server controls, you instead override the CreateChildControls method of the Control class. In this method, you add child controls to your control in two ways: by adding instances of existing server control objects to the Controls collection contained by the control object (inherited from the Control base class) and by inserting literal HTML into the control by way of the LiteralControl object. The LiteralControl object is used by ASP.NET for HTML elements that don't require server processing, so make sure that you don't plan on programmatically accessing any of the HTML you create using a LiteralControl.

For example, to build a composite server control similar to the Search user control described earlier in this chapter, you need at least three elements: a text box, a button to submit the search, and a separator to go between the text box and the button. In the user control examples, we used a table for this; for this example, we'll use an HTML nonbreaking space.

Listing 10.11 shows an example.

LISTING 10.11   Creating a Compositional Control by Overriding the CreateChildControls Method of the Control Object

```
Imports System
Imports System.Web.UI
Imports System.Web.UI.WebControls

Namespace MyServerControl

  Public Class Search
    Inherits Control

    Protected Overrides Sub CreateChildControls()
      Dim txt As New TextBox
      Dim btn As New Button

      btn.Text = "Search"
```

Listing 10.11   Continued

```
    Me.Controls.Add(txt)
    Me.Controls.Add(New LiteralControl(" "))
    Me.Controls.Add(btn)
  End Sub

End Class

End Namespace
```

You can compile this code to a file called search.dll by using the following command in a command prompt window:

```
vbc search.vb /t:library /out:search.dll /r:System.dll /r:System.Web.dll
```

By navigating to the page shown in Listing 10.12, you can test how the control appears in the page.

Listing 10.12   Page Created to Host an Instance of the Composite Search Server Control

```
<%@ Register TagPrefix="demo" Namespace="MyServerControl" Assembly="search" %>
<HTML>
<HEAD>
<TITLE>ASP.NET Page</TITLE>
</HEAD>

<BODY>

  <demo:Search id='Search1' runat='server' />

</BODY>
</HTML>
```

If you copy the file search.dll to the Web application's \bin directory and navigate to this page, you should be able to see an instance of the Search control on the page, with a text box and command button.

Notice that within the control code, you can access the properties and methods of the contained controls. In this example, we specified a default text property for the command button (using the assignment statement btn.Text = "Search").

Adding properties and methods to this control is done in the same way you add properties and methods to any class. To do this, you create a public variable or property procedure, or (for methods) a public subroutine or function.

In this example, we'll provide access to the Text property of the Search control. In this version of the control, the public Text property of your Search control just provides access to the Text property contained in the child TextBox control. The TextBox control does the work of storing and retrieving the text. (In object-oriented programming, the term for handing off an operation to a related or contained control is *delegation*.)

Listing 10.13 shows an example of using delegation to store and retrieve the Text property of the Search control within the Text property of the child TextBox control.

LISTING 10.13   Using Delegation to Provide Access to the Text Property of a Child Control

```
Imports System
Imports System.Web.UI
Imports System.Web.UI.WebControls

Namespace MyServerControl

  Public Class Search
    Inherits Control

    Private txt As TextBox

    Public Property Text() As String
      Get
        EnsureChildControls()
        Return txt.Text
      End Get

      Set
        EnsureChildControls()
        txt.Text = Value
      End Set

    End Property


    Protected Overrides Sub CreateChildControls()
      Dim btn As Button

      txt = New Textbox
      btn = New Button

      btn.Text = "Search"
      txt.Text = "Testing this."
```

Listing 10.13   Continued

```
        Me.Controls.Add(txt)
        Me.Controls.Add(New LiteralControl(" "))
        Me.Controls.Add(btn)
    End Sub


    End Class

End Namespace
```

In this version of the Search control, the TextBox control is defined at the class level rather than inside the CreateChildControls subroutine, as in the previous example. This extends the child control's lifetime to that of the class so we have an opportunity to access its Text property after it's created. You can see in the Text property procedure that the Text property of the contained TextBox control can be stored and retrieved. But in each case, there's a call to a function called EnsureChildControls() in there. A call to this function (actually a method of the Control base class) is required whenever you reference a property of a child control in a composite server control. This must be done because the page is loaded asynchronously; without an explicit call to EnsureChildControls, it's possible that your code will attempt to access a property of a child control that has not yet been rendered by the browser.

Delegating to child controls is useful when your control is a composite control comprising two or more types of controls or when the number of properties of a child control you want to expose is limited. But what happens when you want to create a specialized type of existing server control? You may want your control to have most of or all the properties and methods of the existing control, plus a few additional members (or overridden members). You certainly would not want to write custom accessors for the seventy-plus members of the base TextBox class. In this case, you'll instead want to use inheritance to create your server control, subclassing an existing control to use its functionality.

Subclassing Existing Server Controls

In the previous section you saw an example of a composite control built from several existing controls. But we identified a problem—if you want to expose a large number of properties of a child control, you have to write a large number of property accessor functions that enable the page to get to the properties of the contained control.

Inheritance provides an alternative to containing an instance of a control and delegating to its members using accessor functions. A control that inherits from an existing control is said to be *subclassed* from that control.

You can create customized subclassed versions of existing ASP.NET server controls using inheritance, without writing tons of code. Through inheritance, you can use the existing control as a base class, adding new members or overriding existing members to provide enhanced functionality.

The technique for doing this is similar to creating any server control. But instead of inheriting from System.Web.UI.Control, you instead inherit from whichever control you're interested in subclassing. Because all server controls ultimately inherit from System.Web.UI.Control, your subclassed control still satisfies the requirement that all server controls inherit from the abstract Control class.

For example, suppose you want to provide a custom text box that provides a large number of default values. You don't want to have to code these defaults every time you use the control, and you know you're going to use this kind of control again and again in the construction of your site, so creating a custom control that inherits from the basic TextBox control makes sense.

To accomplish this, you create a class that inherits from the System.Web.UI.WebControls.TextBox control, overriding the property of the text box, supplying your own formatting defaults in the object constructor. Listing 10.14 shows an example.

LISTING 10.14 CustomTextBox Control That Contains a Set of Custom Formatting Defaults

```
Imports System
Imports System.Drawing
Imports System.Web.UI
Imports System.Web.UI.WebControls

Namespace MyServerControl

  Public Class CustomText
    Inherits TextBox

    Public Sub New()
      MyBase.BackColor = Color.CornflowerBlue
      MyBase.Text = "Can I get this one in cornflower blue?"
      MyBase.Font.Name = "Verdana"
      MyBase.Font.Size = FontUnit.XSmall
      MyBase.Width = Unit.Pixel(300)
    End Sub

  End Class

End Namespace
```

You can compile this control using the command line:

```
vbc CustomText.vb /t:library /out:CustomText.dll /r:System.dll
/r:System.Web.dll /r:System.Drawing.dll
```

You can see that this code imports a namespace we haven't used before; the System.Drawing namespace is used to set a background color for the control. As a result, the assembly System.Drawing.dll must also be included in your compilation command.

The customized default properties for the text box are set in the control's constructor; you can specify any properties you want by using MyBase to indicate that you want to change a property derived from the base TextBox class. (The quotations are all from the movie *Fight Club*; I got sick of using "Hello, world" all the time.)

Because it inherits from the standard Web forms TextBox control, the subclassed CustomText control has all the properties, methods, and events of the normal TextBox control. In addition to using inherited properties, you could override properties, as well.

To demonstrate how the inherited Text property works, you can deploy the compiled control assembly to the Web server's \bin directory and navigate to a page that instantiates the control. Listing 10.15 shows a page that puts the control through its paces.

Listing 10.15   ASP.NET Page That Uses an Instance of the Subclassed CustomText Control

```
<%@ Page language='vb' debug='true' trace='false' %>
<%@ Register TagPrefix="demo" Namespace="MyServerControl"
Assembly="CustomText" %>

<SCRIPT runat='server'>

  Sub Change_Click(Sender As Object, e As EventArgs)
    CustomText1.Text = "...because waste is a thief."
  End Sub

</SCRIPT>

<HTML>
<HEAD>
<TITLE>ASP.NET Page</TITLE>
</HEAD>

<BODY>
```

LISTING 10.15 Continued

```
<FORM runat='server'>
  <demo:CustomText id='CustomText1' runat='server' /><BR>
  <asp:button runat='server' text='The First Rule of Fight Club'
id='Change' onClick='Change_Click' />
</FORM>

</BODY>
</HTML>
```

You should be able to see when this page loads that the text box is an unappealing cornflower blue color with the font and text properties set as specified in the control's constructor code. By clicking the button, the control's Text property is set to the value specified in the Change_Click event procedure.

Events in the Life of a Server Control

Five events are fired by every ASP.NET server control. These events are inherited from the server control's base class, System.Web.UI.Control; you typically handle these events to perform initialization tasks related to the control and the data it displays.

The sequence of events raised by a server control are listed in Table 10.1.

TABLE 10.1   Events Raised by System.Web.UI.Control in Custom Server Controls

Phase	Description	Found In
Init	Instructs the control to set its default property values. These values are retained for the life of the HTTP request.	Control class
LoadViewState	View state information is loaded into the appropriate properties of the control.	Control class
LoadPostData	Process information from the incoming form.	IPostBackDataHandler interface
Load		Control class
RaisePostDataChanged	Generate events to reflect difference.	IPostBackDataHandler interface
RaisePostBackEvent		IPostBackEventHandler interface

10

TABLE 10.1   Continued

Phase	Description	Found In
PreRender	Triggered just before the control is sent to the client.	Control class
Unload		Control class

You will often find it useful to write code to respond to these events in your server control's lifetime. To handle these events, you override the corresponding "On" method (OnInit, OnLoad, OnDataBinding, and so forth) provided by the Control base class.

Binding Controls to Data

The ASP.NET controls you create can be bound to data. By enabling data binding, you can make it easy for application developers to use your control in database applications.

You provide support for data binding in your application by overriding the OnDataBinding method provided by System.Web.UI.Control, the base class of your control.

You set the data source consumed by your control by assigning a data object to the DataSource property of the control. If you're working with relational data, the data source can be a DataSet or DataReader object (introduced in Chapter 12); but you can also bind your control to a .NET array or collection object. Because we haven't talked about relational data yet, we'll use an array in our example; it'll make things a bit simpler at any rate.

Generating Postback in Server Controls

As we discussed in Chapter 3, *postback* is the process of sending a form to the Web server for processing. When this happens, server script can process the contents of the form and perform useful tasks with the form data; this is the basis of Web applications.

Only two of the server controls provided with ASP.NET generate postback: the Button and ImageButton controls. To generate a postback, your control must emit a chunk of JavaScript code because the process of submitting a form to the server must always be initiated on the client side; a client-side JavaScript is used to perform this in ASP.NET.

But when the control you're using is one you've created yourself, you are responsible for pro-grammatically generating the client-side JavaScript code that kicks off a form postback. To do this, the method that renders your control must include a reference to the GetPostBackEventReference method of the ASP.NET Page object. This method returns the name of a function (generated internally by ASP.NET) that is responsible for submitting the form to the page.

Listing 10.16 shows an example of a simple hyperlink server control that generates a client postback function through a call to GetPostBackEventReference.

Listing 10.16   Hyperlink Control That Can Generate Client-Side Postback of a Form

```
Imports System.Web.UI
Imports System.Collections

Namespace CustomControls
    Public Class MyLinkButton
        Inherits Control
        Implements IPostBackEventHandler

        ' Defines the Click event.
        '
        Public Event Click As EventHandler

        ' Invokes delegates registered with the Click event.
        '
        Protected Overridable Sub OnClick(e As EventArgs)
            RaiseEvent Click(Me, e)
        End Sub

        ' Method of IPostBackEventHandler that raises change events.
        '
        Public Sub RaisePostBackEvent(eventArgument As String)
         Implements IPostBackEventHandler.RaisePostBackEvent
            OnClick(New EventArgs())
        End Sub

        Protected Overrides Sub Render(output As HtmlTextWriter)
            output.Write(("<a  id =""" & Me.UniqueID & _
                """ href=""javascript:" & _
                Page.GetPostBackEventReference(Me) & """>"))
            output.Write((" " & Me.UniqueID & "</a>"))
        End Sub
    End Class
End Namespace

<%@ Register TagPrefix="Custom" Namespace="CustomControls"
Assembly = "CustomControls" %>

<script language="VB" runat=server>
    Private Sub Button_Click(sender As Object, e As EventArgs)
        TextBox.BackColor = System.Drawing.Color.LightGreen
```

LISTING 10.16   Continued

```
        TextBox.Text = "The link button caused postback."
    End Sub
</script>

<html>
<body>
    <form runat=server>
        Here is the custom link button.<br>
        <Custom:MyLinkButton Id = "Link"  OnClick = "Button_Click"
runat=server/>
        <br><br>
        <asp:TextBox id = "TextBox" Text = "Click the link" Width = "200"
            BackColor = "Cyan" runat=server/>
        <br>
    </form>
</body>
</html>
```

Persistence Support

Your control has the capability to store state information that is posted back across round trips to the server. In English, this means that even though the page is destroyed and re-created each time the user submits a form to the server, your controls can maintain the values that users enter into them.

This is accomplished through the encoded postback data. You see this in ASP.NET Web forms programming all the time; if you set up a Web form with a bunch of text boxes and a button, and then fill in the text boxes and click the button to submit the form to the server, you should see that the contents of the text box remain the same, even though the page has been completely torn down and re-created as a result of its round trip to the server.

If the value of one or more of the properties of your control needs to stay the same, you can store the value of that property in the State property of the control. Having a generic way to store state is useful because Web forms controls are created and destroyed each time a page is accessed.

The State property is an object of type StateBag, found in the namespace System.Web.UI. It is a typical collection type, although it doesn't derive from any of the .NET framework collection types. It does, however, implement the interfaces IDictionary, ICollection, and IEnumerable, so you can use it as you would many other types of .NET collection objects.

To demonstrate this property, we'll create a simple counter control that has the capability to store, retrieve, and display a single numeric value. To provide the capability to store and retrieve the value consistently across page reloads, the control will store its property in the state bag collection provided by the Control base class.

Listing 10.17 provides the code for this server control.

LISTING 10.17   Example of a Basic Server Control That Stores Property State

```
Imports System
Imports System.Web
Imports System.Web.UI

Namespace MyExamples

    Public Class Counter
      Inherits Control

        Public Property CurrentValue As Int32
            Get
                Return ViewState("CurrentValue")
            End Get
            Set
                ViewState("CurrentValue") = Value
            End Set
        End Property

        Protected Overrides Sub Render(Output As HtmlTextWriter)
            Output.Write("<table border='1' width='200'><tr>" & _
                         "<td align='center' bgcolor='#FFFF99'>" & _
                         Me.CurrentValue & "</td></tr></table>")
        End Sub

    End Class

End Namespace
```

Simple, simple, simple. You can see from the code example that the ViewState object is a simple key/value pair; the key can be whatever you want, although you'll probably want to give it the same name as the property it stores for simplicity's sake.

To test this control, compile it using the command line:

```
vbc /t:library /out:counter.dll /r:System.dll /r:System.Web.dll counter.vb
```

After it's compiled and copied to the \bin directory, you can test it in a page similar to that shown in Listing 10.18. This page adds two ASP.NET Button controls to increment and decrement the value of your counter control.

LISTING 10.18   Page to Contain the Counter Control

```
<%@ REGISTER TagPrefix="demo" Namespace="MyExamples" Assembly="counter" %>


<SCRIPT runat='server'>

  Sub UpButton_Click(Sender As Object, e As EventArgs)
    Counter1.CurrentValue = Counter1.CurrentValue + 1
  End Sub

  Sub DownButton_Click(Sender As Object, e As EventArgs)
    Counter1.CurrentValue = Counter1.CurrentValue - 1
  End Sub

</SCRIPT>


<HTML>
<HEAD>
<TITLE>ASP.NET Page</TITLE>
</HEAD>

<BODY>

<FORM runat='server'>
  <demo:counter id='Counter1' runat='server' />
  <asp:button id='DownButton' OnClick='DownButton_Click'
text='Down' runat='server' /> 
  <asp:button id='UpButton' OnClick='UpButton_Click'
text='Up' runat='server' />
</FORM>

</BODY>
</HTML>
```

When you load this page, you should be able to see that the Counter control's value is stored each time it's incremented. More importantly, it's displayed properly even if you hit the Refresh button on the browser—and the page designer didn't have to write any code to make that state retrieval happen.

You can see that this is the case if you rewrite the CurrentValue property, commenting out the lines of code that persist data to the state bag and instead storing the data in a private variable, as classes normally would be stored. Listing 10.19 shows an example of this.

LISTING 10.19   Rewritten CurrentValue Property, Demonstrating Lack of State Persistence

```
Public Property CurrentValue As Int32
        Get
             ' Return ViewState("CurrentValue")
             Return _CurrentValue
        End Get
        Set
             _CurrentValue = Value
             ' ViewState("CurrentValue") = Value
        End Set
      End Property
```

If you try this, don't forget to recompile counter.dll using the command line shown in the previous example. You should not have to make any changes to your page to use the new version of this control.

When your page uses this version of the control, the control does not have the capability to increment and decrement as it did previously. It can increment or decrement only once. This means the control can display only the values of zero (the first time the page is loaded), 1 (when the increment button is clicked), or –1 (when the decrement button is clicked). This problem occurs because, in the absence of state persistence, the control's CurrentValue property is reinitialized to zero every time the page is loaded. So, for example, when you click the increment button, the form is first submitted to the server, destroying the page and the control along with it. The side effect is that the control's CurrentValue property is set to zero. Then the event procedure for the increment button is run, setting the property to 1. But in the absence of persistent state, the control's property can never be incremented to 2 again, because when the page reloads, the control will be destroyed and reinitialized to zero before the incrementing code has a chance to run.

As you take advantage of persistent property state, remember that a cost is associated with storing and retrieving state. Every time your control stores state information, that information is encoded and sent over the Internet from the client to the server and back again. The encoding process makes it easier for ASP.NET to handle your data, but it also has the side effect of making the postback data itself larger. Hence, postback will slow down your application significantly if you overuse it.

Also remember that state information that is passed back and forth between client and server isn't encrypted, so it isn't secure. The information is *encoded*, but that isn't the same as encryption; it won't keep hackers' grimy mitts off your data.

NOTE

Ultimately, if your Web application passes sensitive information from client to server in any form, you should consider transferring the information using a Secure Socket Layer (SSL) connection. This way, it doesn't matter whether the postback information is encrypted, because under SSL, *all* the information that passes between client and server is encrypted. (There is a cost in terms of performance and configuration hassle associated with this, however, so plan carefully when you want to secure specific forms or pages.)

Creating Templated Server Controls

A *templated control* is a type of server control in which the appearance of the control is provided by the page designer in the form of script. The compiled control itself does not contain any user-interface information, only abstract display logic.

You create a templated control the same way you create normal server controls. Templated controls must implement the INamingContainer interface (introduced earlier in this chapter). Remember that this interface is a marker interface and has no members; therefore, it doesn't require any code to implement.

Building Validation Controls

You can build controls that have the capability to validate user input in Web forms. Such controls, called validators, are simply a type of ASP.NET server control.

NOTE

ASP.NET comes with a set of validation controls you can use to ensure that user input in Web forms controls is valid. Among these is a CustomValidator control that enables you to use any validation function you want. Before embarking on creating a new validation control from scratch, you may want to first determine whether the CustomValidator control will suit your needs.

Validation controls are discussed in Chapter 12.

Taking Advantage of Rich Clients

ASP.NET server controls have the capability to tailor their output to the capabilities of the client. In the case of present-day Web applications, this capability enables you to write applications that take advantage of features, such as Dynamic HTML, that are supported by only the most advanced browsers, without your having to either write your pages twice or restrict your user base to a particular browser (usually Internet Explorer). This is called *uplevel/downlevel rendering*.

Uplevel/downlevel rendering is a nice feature that can result in performance increases in situations such as client-side data validation (discussed in Chapter 12), and the server controls you design yourself can also take advantage of uplevel/downlevel rendering functionality in ASP.NET the same way that ASP.NET's own server controls do.

> **NOTE**
>
> When Microsoft documentation refers to a "rich client," it's really talking about Internet Explorer 5.0 running on Windows. When it talks about an "uplevel browser," it's talking about the same thing. Conversely, when it's talking about a "downlevel browser," it's talking about every browser except Internet Explorer (including, but not limited to Netscape Navigator).
>
> I don't like using Netscape if I don't have to, particularly to test Web sites I'm developing, because it doesn't seem to run as fast as Internet Explorer. If you want to test uplevel/downlevel functionality but don't want to use Netscape, you have an alternative. The Opera browser is fast, lightweight, aggressively W3C-standards-compliant, and free, if you don't mind looking at a few advertisements while you browse (you can get an ad-free version of Opera by paying a registration fee). It's great for testing Web applications when you need an alternative to Internet Explorer. Download Opera from http://www.opera.com.

The functionality to provide uplevel/downlevel rendering is a feature of the HtmlTextWriter object, which is passed as an argument to the Render method of the Control class.

Supporting Designers in Custom Server Controls

If you want developers to be able to work with your server controls in visual development environments such as Visual Studio .NET, you should add support for visual designers to your control. A designer is a package of information that determines how your control interacts with the development environment when a developer is working with it.

An important distinction exists between the way a control behaves when it's being used by a developer in a tool such as Visual Studio .NET—known as *design time*—and the way a control executes in a running application, known as *runtime*. This distinction will be familiar to you if you've created ActiveX controls in previous versions of Visual Basic or Visual C++.

Using XML

IN THIS CHAPTER

What Is XML?

Here's a problem you've probably faced before. A customer or colleague comes to you asking for help working with an application that was written five years ago. Nobody who originally worked on the application still works for the company; the original developer died in a bizarre gardening accident some years back. The customer wants you to write a Web-based reporting system to handle the data emitted by this dinosaur application.

You now have the unenviable task of figuring out how this thing works, parsing the data it emits, and arranging that data in some recognizable format—a report.

Let's assume that the developer of the original application attempted to make it easy on you by expressing the data in some standardized format—maybe one in which elements within rows of data are separated from each other by a designated character, such as a comma or a tab. This is known as a *delimited* format. Listing 11.1 demonstrates a comma-delimited document.

LISTING 11.1 A Comma-Delimited Document

```
Jones,Machine Gun,401.32,New York
Janson,Hand Grenade,79.95,Tuscaloosa
Newton,Artillery Cannon,72.43,Paducah
```

However, a few problems occur with the delimited format. First, what happens if the data itself contains a comma or a tab? In this case, you're forced to use a more complicated delimiter—typically a comma with data enclosed in quotation marks. That different documents can use different delimiters is a problem in itself, though. There's no such thing as a single universal parse algorithm for delimited documents.

To make it even more difficult, different operating systems have different ideas about what constitutes the end of a line. Some systems (such as Windows) terminate a line with a carriage return and a line feed (ASCII 13 and 10, respectively), whereas others (such as Unix) just use a line feed.

Another problem: What *is* this data? Some of it, such as the customer's name and the item, is obvious. But what does the number 401.32 represent? Ideally, we want a document that is *self-describing*—one that tells us at a glance what all the data represents (or at least gives us a hint).

Another big problem with delimited documents: How can you represent related data? For example, it might be nice to view all the information about customers and orders in the same document. You can do this with a delimited document, but it can be awkward. And if you've written a parser that expects the first field to be the customer name and the fourth field to be the product name, adding any new fields between them breaks the parser.

11

Internet technology mavens realized that this scenario is frighteningly common in the world of software development—particularly in Internet development. XML was designed to replace delimited data, as well as other data formats, with something standard, easy to use and to understand, and powerful.

Advantages of XML

In a networked application, interoperability between various operating systems is crucial; the transfer of data from point A to point B in a standard, understandable way is what it's all about. For tasks that involve parsing data, then, using XML means spending less time worrying about the details of the parser itself and more time working on the application.

Here are some specific advantages of XML over other data formats:

- XML documents are easily readable and self-describing—Like HTML, an XML document contains tags that indicate what each type of data is. With good document design, it should be reasonably simple for a person to look at an XML document and say, "This contains customers, orders, and prices."

- XML is interoperable—Nothing about XML ties it to any particular operating system or underlying technology. You don't have to ask anyone's permission or pay anyone money to use XML. If the computer you're working on has a text editor, you can use it to create an XML document. Several types of XML parsers exist for virtually every operating system in use today (even really weird ones).

- XML documents are hierarchical—It's easy to add related data to a node in an XML document without making the document unwieldy.

- You don't have to write the parser—Several types of object-based parser components are available for XML. XML parsers work the same way on virtually every platform. The .NET platform contains support for the Internet-standard XML Document Object Model, but Microsoft has also thrown in a few XML parsing widgets that are easier to use and that perform better than the XML DOM; we'll cover these later in this chapter.

- Changes to your document won't break the parser—Assuming that the XML you write is syntactically correct, you can add elements to your data structures without breaking backward compatibility with earlier versions of your application.

Is XML the universal panacea to every problem faced by software developers? XML won't wash your car or take out the garbage for you, but for many tasks that involve data, it's a good choice.

At the same time, Visual Studio .NET hides much of the implementation details from you. Relational data expressed in XML is abstracted in the form of a DataSet object. XML schemas (a document that defines data types and relationships in XML) can be created visually, without writing code. In fact, Visual Studio .NET can generate XML schemas for you automatically by inspecting an existing database structure.

So why learn XML? In the .NET framework, XML is very important. It serves as the foundation for many of the .NET technologies. Database access is XML based in ADO.NET. Remote interoperability, known as XML Web services or SOAP, is also XML based. It is true that many of the implementation details of XML are hidden inside objects or inside the Visual Studio .NET development environment. But for tasks such as debugging, interoperability with other platforms, performance analysis, and your own peace of mind, it still makes sense for you as a .NET developer to have a handle on what XML is, how it works, and how it is implemented in the .NET framework.

XML Document Structure and Syntax

XML documents must adhere to a standard syntax so that automated parsers can read them. Fortunately, the syntax is pretty simple to understand, especially if you've developed Web pages in HTML. The XML syntax is a bit more rigorous than that of HTML, but as you'll see, that's a good thing. There are a million ways to put together a bogus, sloppy HTML document, but the structure required by XML means that you get a higher level of consistency; no matter what your document contains, the rules that govern how an XML document can be parsed are the same.

Declaration

The XML declaration is the same for all XML documents. An XML declaration is shown in Listing 11.2.

LISTING 11.2   XML 1.0 Declaration

```
<?xml version="1.0"?>
```

The declaration says two things: This is an XML document (duh), and this document conforms to the XML 1.0 W3C recommendation (which you can get straight from the horse's mouth at `http://www.w3.org/TR/REC-xml`). The current and only W3C recommendation for XML is version 1.0, so you shouldn't see an XML declaration that's different from what's in Listing 11.2. But you might in the future, when the specification is revised into new versions.

> **NOTE**
>
> A W3C recommendation isn't quite the same as a bona fide Internet standard, but it's close enough for our purposes.

The XML declaration, when it exists, must exist on the first line of the document. The declaration does not have to exist, however; it is an optional part of an XML document. The idea behind a declaration is that you may have some automated tool that trawls document folders looking for XML. If your XML files contain declarations, it'll be much easier for such an automated process to locate XML documents (as well as to differentiate them from other marked-up documents, such as HTML Web pages).

Don't sweat it too much if you don't include a declaration line in the XML documents you create. Leaving it out doesn't affect how data in the document is parsed.

Elements

An *element* is a part of an XML document that contains data. If you're accustomed to database programming or working with delimited documents, you can think of an element as a column or a field. XML elements are sometimes also called *nodes*.

XML documents must have at least one top-level element to be parsable. Listing 11.3 shows an XML document with a declaration and a single top-level element (but no actual data).

LISTING 11.3   A Simple XML Document with a Declaration and a Top-Level Element

```
<?xml version="1.0"?>
<ORDERS>
</ORDERS>
```

This document can be parsed, even though it contains no data. Note one important thing about the markup of this document: It contains both an open tag and a close tag for the <ORDERS> element. The closing tag is differentiated by the slash (/) character in front of the element name. Every XML element must have a closing tag—lack of a closing tag will cause the document to be unparsable. The XML declaration is the only part of an XML document that does not require a closing tag.

This is an important difference between XML and HTML. In HTML, some elements require close tags, but many don't. Even for those elements that don't contain proper closing tags, the browser often attempts to correctly render the page (sometimes with quirky results).

XML, on the other hand, is the shrewish librarian of the data universe. It's not nearly as forgiving as HTML and will rap you on the knuckles if you cross it. If your XML document contains an element that's missing a close tag, the document won't parse. This is a common source of frustration among developers who use XML. Another kicker is that, unlike HTML, tag names in XML are case sensitive. This means that <ORDERS> and <orders> are considered to be two different and distinct tags.

Elements That Contain Data

The whole purpose of an XML element is to contain pieces of data. In the previous example, we left out the data. Listing 11.4 shows an evolved version of this document, this time with data in it.

LISTING 11.4   An XML Document with Elements That Contain Data

```
<?xml version="1.0"?>
<ORDERS>
  <ORDER>
    <DATETIME>1/4/2000 9:32 AM</DATETIME>
    <ID>33849</ID>
    <CUSTOMER>Steve Farben</CUSTOMER>
    <TOTALAMOUNT>3456.92</TOTALAMOUNT>
  </ORDER>
</ORDERS>
```

If you were to describe this document in English, you'd say that it contains a top-level ORDERS element and a single ORDER element, or node. The ORDER node is a child of the ORDERS element. The ORDER element itself contains four child nodes of its own: DATETIME, ID, CUSTOMER, and TOTALAMOUNT.

Adding a few additional orders to this document might give you something like Listing 11.5.

LISTING 11.5   An XML Document with Multiple Child Elements Beneath the Top-Level Element

```
<?xml version="1.0"?>
<ORDERS>
  <ORDER>
    <DATETIME>1/4/2000 9:32 AM</DATETIME>
    <ID>33849</ID>
    <CUSTOMER>Steve Farben</CUSTOMER>
    <TOTALAMOUNT>3456.92</TOTALAMOUNT>
  </ORDER>
  <ORDER>
    <DATETIME>1/4/2000 9:32 AM</DATETIME>
    <ID>33856</ID>
    <CUSTOMER>Jane Colson</CUSTOMER>
    <TOTALAMOUNT>401.19</TOTALAMOUNT>
  </ORDER>
  <ORDER>
    <DATETIME>1/4/2000 9:32 AM</DATETIME>
    <ID>33872</ID>
```

LISTING 11.5 Continued

```
    <CUSTOMER>United Disc, Incorporated</CUSTOMER>
    <TOTALAMOUNT>74.28</TOTALAMOUNT>
  </ORDER>
</ORDERS>
```

Here's where developers sometimes get nervous about XML. With a document like this, you can see that there's far more markup than data. Does this mean that all those extra bytes will squish your application's performance?

Maybe, but not necessarily. Consider an Internet application that uses XML on the server side. When this application needs to send data to the client, it first opens and parses the XML document (we'll discuss how XML parsing works later in this chapter). Then some sort of result— in all likelihood, a tiny subset of the data, stripped of markup—will be sent to the client Web browser. The fact that there's a bunch of markup doesn't slow down the data transfer significantly.

At the same time, there is a way to express data more succinctly in an XML document, without the need for as many open and closing markup tags. You can do this through the use of attributes.

Attributes

An *attribute* is another way to enclose a piece of data in an XML document. An attribute is always part of an element; it typically modifies or is related to the information in the node. In a relational database application that emits XML, it's common to see foreign key data expressed in the form of attributes.

For example, a document that contains information about a sales transaction might use attributes as shown in Listing 11.6.

LISTING 11.6 An XML Document with Elements and Attributes

```
<?xml version="1.0"?>
<ORDERS>
  <ORDER id="33849" custid="406">
    <DATETIME>1/4/2000 9:32 AM</DATETIME>
    <TOTALAMOUNT>3456.92</TOTALAMOUNT>
  </ORDER>
</ORDERS>
```

As you can see from the example, attribute values are always enclosed in quotation marks. Using attributes tends to reduce the total size of the document (because you don't need to store open and close tags for the element). This has the effect of reducing the amount of markup at the expense (in some cases) of readability. Note that you are allowed to use either single or double quotation marks anywhere XML requires quotes.

This element/attribute syntax may look familiar from HTML, which uses attributes to assign values to elements the same way XML does. But remember that XML is a bit more rigid than HTML; a bracket out of place or a mismatched close tag will cause the entire document to be unparsable.

Enclosing Character Data

At the beginning of this chapter, we discussed the various dilemmas involved with delimited files. One of the problems with delimiters is that if the delimiter character exists within the data, it's difficult or impossible for a parser to know how to parse the data.

This problem is not confined to delimited files; XML has similar problems with containing delimiter characters. The problem arises because the de facto XML delimiter character (in actuality, the markup character) is the left angle bracket, also known as the less-than symbol. In XML, the ampersand character (&) can also throw the parser off.

You've got two ways to deal with this problem in XML: Either replace the forbidden characters with *character entities* or use a CDATA section as a way to delimit the entire data field.

Using Character Entities

You might be familiar with character entities from working with HTML. The idea is to take a character that might be interpreted as a part of markup and replace it with an escape sequence to prevent the parser from going haywire. Listing 11.7 provides an example of this.

LISTING 11.7   An XML Document with Escape Sequences

```
<?xml version="1.0"?>
<ORDERS>
  <ORDER id="33849">
    <NAME>Jones &amp; Williams Certified Public Accountants</NAME>
    <DATETIME>1/4/2000 9:32 AM</DATETIME>
    <TOTALAMOUNT>3456.92</TOTALAMOUNT>
  </ORDER>
</ORDERS>
```

Take a look at the data in the NAME element in the code example. Instead of an ampersand, the & character entity is used. (If a data element contains a left bracket, it should be escaped with the < character entity.)

When you use an XML parser to extract data with escape characters, the parser will automatically convert the escaped characters to their correct representation.

Using CDATA Elements

An alternative to replacing delimiter characters is to use CDATA elements. A CDATA element tells the XML parser not to interpret or parse characters that appear in the section.

Listing 11.8 demonstrates an example of the same XML document from before, this time delimited with a CDATA section rather than a character entity.

LISTING 11.8   An XML Document with a CDATA Section

```
<?xml version="1.0"?>
<ORDERS>
  <ORDER id="33849">
    <NAME><![CDATA[Jones & Williams Certified Public Accountants]]></NAME>
    <DATETIME>1/4/2000 9:32 AM</DATETIME>
    <TOTALAMOUNT>3456.92</TOTALAMOUNT>
  </ORDER>
</ORDERS>
```

In this example, the original data in the NAME element does not need to be changed, as in the previous example. Here, the data is wrapped with a CDATA element. The document is parsable, even though it contains an unparsable character (the ampersand).

Which technique should you use? It's really up to you. You might prefer to use the CDATA method because it doesn't require altering the original data, but it has the disadvantage of adding a dozen or so bytes to each element.

Abbreviated Close-Tag Syntax

For elements that contain no data, you can use an abbreviated syntax for element tags to reduce the amount of markup overhead contained in your document. Listing 11.9 demonstrates this.

LISTING 11.9   An XML Document with Empty Elements

```
<?xml version="1.0"?>
<ORDERS>
  <ORDER id="33849" custid="406">
    <DATETIME>1/4/2000 9:32 AM</DATETIME>
    <TOTALAMOUNT />
  </ORDER>
</ORDERS>
```

You can see from the example that the TOTALAMOUNT element contains no data. As a result, we can express it as <TOTALAMOUNT /> instead of <TOTALAMOUNT></TOTALAMOUNT>. It's perfectly legal to use either syntax in your XML documents; the abbreviated syntax is generally better, though, because it reduces the size of your XML document.

Accessing XML Data Using .NET Framework Classes

Now that you've seen how to create an XML document, we get to the fun part: how to write code to extract and manipulate data from an XML document using classes found in the .NET frameworks. There's no one right way to do this; in fact, before .NET came along, two predominant ways were used to parse an XML document: the XML Document Object Model (DOM) and Simple API for XML (SAX).

An implementation of the XML DOM exists in the .NET framework. However, in this chapter we'll primarily focus on .NET's own XML handlers, such as the `XmlNodeReader`, `XmlTextReader`, and `XmlTextWriter` objects. These objects are the standard .NET way to access XML data; they provide a good combination of high performance, .NET integration and ease of programming. But you should know about the other ways to deal with XML, too—particularly because the specialized .NET reader and writer objects are designed to interact with the Internet-standard DOM objects. So for the remainder of this chapter, we'll include brief examples of how to work with the DOM model, as well.

About Simple API for XML (SAX)

Simple API for XML (SAX) was designed to provide a higher level of performance and a simpler programmability model than XML DOM. It uses a fundamentally different programmability model. Instead of reading in the entire document at once and exposing the elements of the document as nodes, SAX provides an event-driven model for parsing XML.

SAX is not supported in .NET—yet. In fact, it's not even an official Internet standard. It's a programming interface for XML that was created by developers who wanted an XML parser with higher performance and a smaller memory footprint, especially when parsing very large documents.

If you are currently writing applications using SAX and want to use SAX in your .NET applications today, you can do so by using the MSXML 3.0 COM library through the COM interoperability features in .NET.

> **NOTE**
>
> Although it is not yet supported in the .NET framework, SAX is supported in Microsoft's COM-based XML parser implementation. For more information on this tool, see http://msdn.microsoft.com/xml/.

Using the XML Document Object Model

The XML Document Object Model (DOM) is a programming interface used to parse XML documents. It was the first programming interface provided for XML by Microsoft; XML DOM implementations are available that target other languages and other operating systems.

The original Microsoft XML DOM implementation is COM based, so it is accessible from any COM-compliant language. The XML parsers in .NET are, naturally, accessible from any .NET-compliant language.

The XML DOM does its magic by taking an XML document and exposing it in the form of a complex object hierarchy. This kind of hierarchy may be familiar to you if you've done client-side HTML Document Object Model programming in JavaScript or VBScript. The number of objects in XML DOM is fairly daunting; no fewer than 20 objects are in the base implementation, and then the Microsoft implementation adds a number of additional interfaces and proprietary extensions.

Fortunately, the number of objects you need to work with on a regular basis in the XML DOM is minimal. In fact, the XML DOM recommendation segregates the objects in the DOM into two groups: *fundamental classes* and *extended classes*. Fundamental classes are the ones that application developers find most useful; the extended classes are primarily useful to tools developers and people who like to pummel themselves with detail.

The fundamental classes of the XML DOM as implemented in the .NET framework are XmlNode, XmlNodeList, and XmlNamedNodeMap. These classes, as well as the parent XmlDocument class, are illustrated in Figure 11.1.

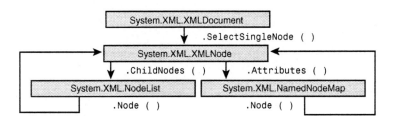

FIGURE 11.1
Fundamental XML DOM objects.

Note that the XmlDocument object is technically an extended class, not a fundamental class, because it inherits from XmlNode. We're including discussion of it in this chapter because it's kind of tricky to do useful stuff in XML without it. The class adds some useful file- and URL-handling capabilities to XmlNode.

> **NOTE**
>
> The XmlNode and XmlDocument classes are found in the System.Xml namespace. The XmlDocument class inherits from System.Xml.XmlNode. A reference to the classes, properties, and methods introduced in this chapter is included at the end of this chapter.

In general, to work with an XML document using the Document Object Model, you first open the document (using the .Load() or .LoadXML() method of the XmlDocument object). The .Load() method is overloaded and can take any one of three arguments: a string, a System.IO.TextReader object, or a System.Xml.XmlReader object.

The easiest way to demonstrate how to load an XML document from a file on disk is to pass the .Load() method a string. The string can either be a local file on disk or a URL. If the string is a URL, the XmlDocument retrieves the document from a Web server. This is pretty handy; it makes you wish that every file-handling object worked this way.

For most of the examples in this chapter, we'll use a small XML file on disk called books.xml. Listing 11.10 contains the full contents of books.xml.

LISTING 11.10   The Full Contents of the books.xml Document Example

```
<BOOKS>
  <BOOK>
    <TITLE>VB.NET Developer's Guide To ASP.NET, XML and ADO.NET</TITLE>
    <AUTHOR id='101' location='San Francisco'>Jeffrey P. McManus</AUTHOR>
    <AUTHOR id='107' location='Seattle'>Chris Kinsman</AUTHOR>
  </BOOK>
</BOOKS>
```

Listing 11.11 shows an example of how to load this XML document from disk using an XmlDocument object.

LISTING 11.11   Loading a Local XML File Using the XmlDocument's .Load() Method

```
<%@ Import Namespace="System.Xml" %>

<SCRIPT runat='server'>
Sub Page_Load(Sender As Object, e As EventArgs)
  Dim xd As New XmlDocument()
  xd.Load(Server.MapPath("books.xml"))
  Response.Write (xd.OuterXml)
  xd = Nothing
End Sub
</SCRIPT>
```

This code works for any XML document accessible to the local file system. Listing 11.12 demonstrates how to load an XML document via HTTP from a remote Web server.

LISTING 11.12   Loading an XML File That Resides on a Web Server

```
<%@ Import Namespace="System.Xml" %>

<SCRIPT runat='server'>
  Sub Page_Load(Sender As Object, e As EventArgs)
    Dim xd As New XmlDocument()
    xd.Load("http://www.myserver.com/books.xml")
    Response.Write (xd.OuterXml)
    xd = Nothing
  End Sub
</SCRIPT>
```

As you can see, the syntax is nearly identical whether you're loading the file from the local file system or over HTTP. Both examples are extremely simple; they demonstrate how easy it is to open and view an XML document using the DOM. The next step is to start doing things with the data in the document you've retrieved.

> **NOTE**
>
> Don't use the DOM—or any of the other XML-reading techniques demonstrated in this chapter—to read the Web application configuration file config.web. The ASP.NET page framework provides an object that is used specifically for retrieving configuration from config.web—the GetConfig method of the HttpContext object, found in the System.Web namespace. For more information on how this works, see Chapter 6, "Configuration and Deployment."

Viewing Document Data Using the XmlNode Object

After you've loaded a document, you need some way to programmatically visit each of its nodes to determine what's inside. In the XML DOM, several ways exist to do this, all of which are centered around the XmlNode object.

The XmlNode object represents a node in the XML document. It exposes an object hierarchy that exposes attributes and child nodes, as well as every other part of an XML document.

When you've loaded an XML document to parse it (as we demonstrated in the previous code examples), your next step usually involves retrieving that document's top-level node. Use the .FirstChild() property to do this.

Listing 11.13 shows an example of retrieving and displaying the name of the top-level node in the document using .FirstChild().

LISTING 11.13   Loading a Local XML File Using the XmlDocument's .Load() Method

```
<%@ Import Namespace="System.Xml" %>

<SCRIPT runat='server'>
Sub Page_Load(Sender As Object, e As EventArgs)
  Dim xd As New XmlDocument()
  xd.Load(Server.MapPath("books.xml"))
  Response.Write (xd.FirstChild.Name)

  xd = Nothing
End Sub
</SCRIPT>
```

The code demonstrates how the .FirstChild() property returns a XmlNode object with its own set of properties and methods. In the example, we call the .Name() property of the XmlNode object returned by .FirstChild().

You can do more useful and interesting things with the XmlNode object. One common operation is drilling down and retrieving data from the ChildNodes object owned by XmlNode. Two features of ChildNodes make this possible: its status as an *enumerable class*, and the InnerText property of each child node.

Enumerable classes implement the .NET IEnumerable interface. This is the same interface definition that arrays, collections, and more complex constructs such as ADO.NET DataSets support. (You may think of ChildNodes as just another collection, but in .NET, Collection is a distinct data type.)

When an object supports IEnumerable, it exposes functionality (through a behind-the-scenes object called an enumerator) that enables other processes to visit each of its child members. In the case of ChildNodes, the enumerator lets your code visit the object's child XmlNode objects. The For Each...Next block in Visual Basic is the construct most commonly used to traverse an enumerable class. Listing 11.14 shows an example of this.

LISTING 11.14   Traversing the Enumerable ChildNodes Class

```
<%@ Import Namespace="System.Xml" %>

<SCRIPT runat='server'>
Sub Page_Load(Sender As Object, e As EventArgs)
  Dim xd As New XmlDocument
```

LISTING 11.14   Continued

```
Dim ndBook As XmlNode
Dim nd As XmlNode

xd.Load(Server.MapPath("books.xml"))
ndBook = xd.FirstChild.Item("BOOK")

For Each nd In ndBook.ChildNodes
  If nd.Name = "AUTHOR" Then
    Response.Write("The author's name is " & nd.InnerText & "<BR>")
  End If
Next
End Sub
</SCRIPT>
```

In this code example, the For Each...Next loop goes through the set of XmlNode objects found in ChildNodes. When it finds one whose Name property is AUTHOR, it displays the node's value. Note that for the books.xml file example, two author names appear because the book example has two authors.

Note also that the value contained in an XML node is returned by the InnerXml() property in .NET, not by the .text property as it was in the COM-based MSXML library. Making a more granular distinction between a simple text property versus inner and outer text or inner and outer XML gives you a greater degree of power and flexibility. Use the outer properties when you want to preserve markup; the inner properties return the values themselves.

With the few aspects of the XmlDocument and XmlNode objects we've discussed so far, you now have the ability to perform rudimentary retrieval of data in an XML document using the DOM. However, looping through a collection of nodes using For Each...Next leaves something to be desired. For example, what happens when your book node contains a set of 50 child nodes, and you're interested in extracting only a single child node from that?

Fortunately, .NET provides several objects that enable you to easily navigate the hierarchical structure of an XML document. These include the XmlTextReader and the XmlNodeReader object described in the next few sections of this chapter.

Using the XmlDataReader Object

The XmlDataReader object provides a method of accessing XML data that is both easier to code and potentially more efficient than the full-blown XML DOM. At the same time, the XmlDataReader understands DOM objects in a way that lets you use both types of access cooperatively.

> **NOTE**
>
> `XmlDataReader` is found in the System.Xml namespace. It inherits from
> `System.Xml.XmlReader`, an abstract class. A reference to the classes, properties, and
> methods introduced in this chapter is included at the end of this chapter.

If you've used the XML DOM in the past, the `XmlDataReader` will change the way you think about XML parsing in general. The `XmlDataReader` doesn't load an entire XML document and expose its various nodes and attributes to you in the form of a large hierarchical tree; that process causes a large performance hit as data is parsed and buffered. Instead, think of the `XmlDataReader` object as a truck that bounces along the road from one place to another. Each time the truck moves across another interesting aspect of the landscape, you have the ability to take some kind of interesting action based on what's there.

Parsing an XML document using the `XmlDataReader` object involves a few steps. First, you create the object, optionally passing in a filename or URL that represents the source of XML to parse. Next, execute the `.Read` method of the `XmlDataReader` object until that method returns the value `False`. (You'll typically set up a loop to do this so that you can move from the beginning to the end of the document.)

Each time you execute the `XmlDataReader` object's `Read` method, the `XmlDataReader` object's properties are populated with fragments of information from the XML document you're parsing. This information includes the type of the data the object just read and the value of the data itself (if any).

The type of data is exposed through the `XmlDataReader` object's `NodeType` property. The value of data retrieved can be retrieved in an untyped format through the `.Value()` property of the `XmlDataReader` object. It can also be retrieved in a typed format through such properties as `.ReadDateTime()`, `.ReadInt32()`, `.ReadString()`, and so forth.

Most of the time, the `NodeType` property will be `XmlNodeType.Element` (an element tag), `XmlNodeType.Text` (the data contained in a tag), or `XmlNodeType.Attribute`.

Listing 11.15 shows an example of how this works. The objective of this example is to retrieve the title of a book from an XML file that is known to contain any one of a number of nodes pertaining to the book itself.

LISTING 11.15   Extracting a Book Title Using the `XmlTextReader` Object

```
<%@ Import Namespace="System.Xml" %>
<SCRIPT runat='server'>
```

LISTING 11.15   Continued

```
Sub Page_Load(Sender As Object, e As EventArgs)
    Dim xr As New XmlTextReader(Server.MapPath("books.xml"))
    Dim bTitle As Boolean

    While xr.Read()
      Select Case xr.NodeType
        Case XmlNodeType.Element
          If xr.Name = "TITLE" Then
            bTitle = True
          End If

        Case XmlNodeType.Text
          If bTitle Then
            Response.Write("Book title: " & xr.ReadString)
            bTitle = False
          End If
      End Select
    End While
End Sub
</SCRIPT>
```

The example opens the XML file by passing the name of the XML file to the constructor of the XmlDataReader object. It then reads one chunk of the document at a time through successive calls to the XmlDataReader object's Read method. If the current data represents the element name "TITLE", the code sets a flag, bTitle.

When the bTitle flag is set to True, it means "Get ready, a book title is coming next." The book title itself is extracted in the next few lines of code. When the code encounters the text chunk, it extracts it from the XML document in the form of a string.

Note that the values XmlNodeType.Element and XmlNodeType.Text are predefined members of the XmlNodeType structure. You can set up more involved parsing structures based on any XML element type found in the DOM if you want. For example, if you included a case to process the element type XmlNodeType.XmlDeclaration, you could process the XML declaration that appears (but that is not required to appear) as the first line of the XML document.

As you can see from these examples, a beautiful thing about XML is that if the structure of the document changes, your parsing code will still work correctly, as long the document contains a TITLE node. (In the previous code example, if for some reason the document contains no book title, no action is taken.) So the problems with delimited data that we discussed at the beginning of this chapter go away in the new world of XML parsing.

The `XmlDataReader` works well both for large and small documents. Under most circumstances (particularly for large documents), it should perform better than the XML DOM parser. However, like the DOM, it too has its own set of limitations. The `XmlDataReader` object doesn't have the capability to scroll—to jump around among various areas in the document. (If you're a database developer, you can think of an `XmlDataReader` as being analogous to a cursorless or forward-only resultset.) Also, as its name implies, the `XmlDataReader` object permits you only to read data; you can't use it to make changes in existing node values or add new nodes to an existing document.

Writing XML Data Using the XmlTextWriter Object

You can create an XML document using any text editor. Similarly, you can create an XML document programmatically using any object capable of writing to a file. For example, the `TextWriter` class, found in the namespace System.IO, is often used for general-purpose generation of text files. Because XML files are normal text files containing markup tags and a specific, defined structure, you could use a `TextWriter` object to create XML files.

However, the `XmlTextWriter` object provides some advantages over creating XML files with a general-purpose object such as `TextWriter`. The main benefit of using `XmlTextWriter` is that it can validate the XML you generate as you write. The class also has a number of useful features, such as the ability to specify and apply formatting, delimiter, and encoding modes automatically.

> **NOTE**
>
> `XmlTextWriter` is found in the System.Xml namespace. It inherits from `System.Xml.XmlWriter`, an abstract class. A reference to the classes, properties, and methods introduced in this chapter is included at the end of this chapter.

To get started creating XML documents with the `XmlTextWriter` class, you must first create an instance of the class. `XmlTextWriter` has three constructors that enable you to create an instance of the object given an existing `TextWriter` or `Stream` object, but it's likely that the most common form you'll use is the constructor that takes a filename and an encoding type. In the code examples in this section, we use the encoding type UTF-8, which is the default. You denote this encoding type using the enumerated value Encoding.UTF8.

Now you're ready to write data to the `XmlTextWriter` object using its methods. To create elements in the document, you use one of the 12 WriteElement methods exposed by the object (the `WriteElementString` method will probably be the one you use most frequently).

Listing 11.16 shows an example that demonstrates how to create a minimal version of the books.xml file using these methods.

LISTING 11.16   Creating a Minimal XML Document Using the XmlTextWriter Object

```
<%@ Import Namespace="System.Xml" %>
<SCRIPT runat='server'>

Sub Page_Load(Sender As Object, e As EventArgs)
  Dim xw As New XmlTextWriter(Server.MapPath("books2.xml"), Encoding.UTF8)
  Try
    With xw
      .WriteStartDocument()
      .WriteStartElement("BOOK")
      .WriteElementString("TITLE", "VB.NET Developer's Guide")
      .WriteEndDocument()
      Response.Write("Your file has been written.")
    End With
  Catch ex As Exception
    Response.Write("Exception: " & ex.Message)
  Finally
    xw.Flush()
    xw.Close()
  End Try

End Sub
</SCRIPT>
```

Normally we don't include exception-handling code in our brief code examples (mainly because we're lazy sods, but also because they sometimes detract from the point of the code example). But in this case, we've included a handler to emphasize that it's important to handle exceptions in code that creates or modifies files. If you fail to include an exception handler in file-handling code, it's easy to make a mistake that prevents a file from being closed properly, for example, which is a bad thing.

In the previous example, you can see that we first begin by creating the XmlTextWriter object, passing it a filename and encoding scheme. We then call the WriteStartDocument method to begin working with the document. This has the side effect of sending an XML declaration to the document. Calling WriteStartDocument is required when using the XmlTextWriter, even though XML itself does not require that a declaration entity be present in a document.

Next we create the root node of the document with a call to the WriteStartElement method. The simplest form of WriteStartElement takes a single string argument—the name of the node to create. This is the form of the method we've used in our example.

Next, we insert a node underneath the root node with a call to `WriteElementString`. The form of `WriteElementString` we're using here lets us pass two strings: a node name and contents of the node.

When we're done with the document, we call the `WriteEndDocument` method to close the root node and then call the `Flush` and `Close` methods to finish the process of committing the file to disk. When this code is executed, it produces the file shown in Listing 11.17.

LISTING 11.17   XML Document Produced by Previous Code Example

```
<?xml version="1.0" encoding="utf-8"?>
<BOOK><TITLE>VB.NET Developer's Guide</TITLE></BOOK>
```

This is adequate (it's parsable), but the formatting leaves something to be desired. If you want line breaks and indented child nodes in your document, you must set the `Formatting` property of the `XmlTextWriter` document to the enumerated value `Formatting.Indented`.

To create attributes associated with nodes, use one of the `XmlTextWriter` object's typed `WriteAttr` methods or the untyped `WriteAttribute` method.

Navigating and Updating Documents Using the `XmlNodeReader` Object

So far in this chapter, you've seen two distinct ways to access XML data—the XML Document Object Model and the `XmlDataReader` object—provided by the .NET framework. Both have their advantages and drawbacks. A third alternative exists: `XmlNodeReader`.

In many ways, the `XmlNodeReader` object represents the best of all worlds. It provides a simpler programmability model than the `XmlDocument` object, yet it integrates with the standard DOM objects nicely. In fact, in most cases when you're working with XML data in .NET, you'll typically create a `XmlNodeReader` by creating a DOM `XmlDocument` object first.

> **NOTE**
>
> The `XmlNodeReader` class is found in the System.Xml namespace. It inherits from System.Xml.XmlReader, an abstract class. A reference to the classes, properties, and methods introduced in this chapter is included at the end of this chapter.

Listing 11.18 shows an example of creating a `XmlNodeReader` object from an existing `XmlDocument` object that has been populated with data.

LISTING 11.18 Creating a XmlNodeReader Object from an XmlDocument Object

```
<%@ Import Namespace="System.Xml" %>
<SCRIPT runat='server'>

Sub Page_Load(Sender As Object, e As EventArgs)
  Dim xd As New XmlDocument()
  Dim xn As XmlNodeReader = New XmlNodeReader(xd)
  ' Code to work with the XmlNodeReader goes here
End Sub
</SCRIPT>
```

Navigating Through the Document Using the XmlNodeReader Object

After you've created and populated the XmlNodeReader, you can use it to move through the document programmatically. You do this by placing calls to the XmlNodeReader's Read method, which iterates through the document one element at a time. Listing 11.19 demonstrates this.

LISTING 11.19 Using the XmlNodeReader Object to Traverse an XML Document

```
<%@ Import Namespace="System.Xml" %>
<SCRIPT runat='server'>

Sub Page_Load(Sender As Object, e As EventArgs)
  Dim xd As New XmlDocument()
  xd.Load(Server.MapPath("books.xml"))
  Dim xn As XmlNodeReader = New XmlNodeReader(xd)

  Do While xn.Read()
    Response.Write(xn.Name & " - " & xn.Value & "<BR>")
  Loop

End Sub
</SCRIPT>
```

This is another example of how repeated calls to the Read method control the looping structure—the same way you use the Read method of the XmlTextReader object (discussed earlier in this chapter). Because Read returns True when it successfully navigates to a new element and False when no more data is left to traverse to, it's easy to set up a While loop that displays all the data in the document.

You've seen that navigating though an XML document using the XmlTextReader and XmlNodeReader objects' Read method works well enough. But if the process of repeatedly executing the Read methods to blast through a document seems a little weak to you, you're right.

Reading elements makes sense when the structure of a document is known, but how do you go directly to a node when you know the name of the node and can be reasonably sure that the node exists? And how do you get rid of the inelegant process of calling MoveToChild repeatedly to drill down to the place in the document where useful data exists?

Fortunately, there is another object that provides a number of more sophisticated techniques for drilling into the document hierarchy using an XML query technology known as XPath. We'll discuss this object in more detail in the next few sections.

Using XPath Queries to Retrieve XML Data

XPath is a standard that defines a syntax for retrieving data from an XML document. You can use XPath query syntax to retrieve data from an XML document without having to traverse the entire document. In .NET, you do this using the XPathDocument and XPathNavigator objects.

NOTE

The XPathDocument and XPathNavigator objects are members of the System.Xml.XPath namespace. A complete listing of the members of the XPathDocument and XPathNavigator objects is given in the reference section at the end of this chapter.

XPath syntax is described in more detail in the section "Querying XML Documents Using XPath Expressions" later in this chapter.

To begin performing XPath queries, you start by creating an XPathDocument object. This object is analogous to the XmlDocument object. You can use its constructor or its Load method to open an XML file on disk.

After you've created an XPathDocument object, you use the object's CreateNavigator method to create an instance of the XPathNavigator object. The XPathNavigator object is responsible for performing the actual XPath query of the document; it returns an iterator (an instance of System.Xml.XPath.XPathNodeIterator) that you can use to access each of the elements returned by the query. (If you're familiar with cursor-based database programming, you can think of the XPathNodeIterator as a type of cursor.)

The Select method of the XPathNavigator object enables you to filter and retrieve subsets of XML data from any XML document. You do this by constructing an XPath expression and passing the expression the Select method of the XPathNavigator object. An XPath expression is a compact way of querying an XML document without going to the trouble of parsing the whole thing first. Using XPath, it's possible to retrieve very useful subsets of information from an XML document, often with only a single line of code.

Listing 11.20 shows a very simple example of using an XPath expression passed to the Select method to move to and display the title of the first book in the document books.xml.

LISTING 11.20   Using the Select Method of the XPathNavigator Object to Retrieve a Subset of Nodes

```
<%@ Import Namespace="System.Xml" %>
<%@ Import Namespace="System.Xml.XPath" %>
<SCRIPT runat='server'>

    Sub Page_Load(Sender As Object, e As EventArgs)
      Dim xpd As XPathDocument = New XPathDocument(Server.MapPath("books.xml"))
      Dim nav As XPathNavigator = xpd.CreateNavigator()
    Dim iterator as XPathNodeIterator = nav.Select("BOOKS/BOOK/AUTHOR")

      While (iterator.MoveNext())
        Response.Write(iterator.Current.Value & "<BR>")
      End While

      End Sub

</SCRIPT>
```

When the Select method in this example is executed, you're telling the XmlNavigator object to retrieve all the AUTHOR nodes owned by BOOK nodes contained in the BOOKS root node. The XPath expression "BOOKS/BOOK/AUTHOR" means "all the authors owned by BOOK nodes under the BOOKS root node." Any AUTHOR nodes in the document owned by parent nodes other than BOOK won't be retrieved, although you could construct an XPath expression to retrieve AUTHOR nodes anywhere in the document regardless of their parentage.

The product of this operation is a *selection*, a subset of XML nodes that can then be manipulated independently of the main document. You can traverse the selection using the XPathNodeIterator object returned from your call to the Select method of the XPathNavigator object. After you have an iterator, you can retrieve and display the data from the selected nodes.

Manipulating the Current Node Using the XPath Iterator's Current Property

In the previous example, you saw that you could query an XML document using the XmlNavigator object. The product of this query was an iterator object, an instance of XPathNodeIterator, that enabled you to access the value of each of the nodes returned in the XPath query one at a time.

When you retrieve data in this manner, you may need to further manipulate each node. For example, rather than simply accessing the value of a node, you may need to retrieve an attribute associated with the node. You can do this by using the Current property of the XPathNodeIterator object. This property, an instance of an XPathNavigator object, contains a rich set of properties and methods for manipulating properties of an XML node retrieved by an XPath query.

The AUTHOR nodes of the books.xml file contain two attributes: id and location. After you've moved to an AUTHOR node, you can display the values of these attributes by using the GetAttribute method of the Current object. Listing 11.21 shows an example of this.

LISTING 11.21   Using the Current Property to Extract the Value of Attributes on a Node

```
<%@ Page debug="true" %>
<%@ Import Namespace="System.Xml" %>
<%@ Import Namespace="System.Xml.XPath" %>
<SCRIPT runat='server'>

    Sub Page_Load(Sender As Object, e As EventArgs)
      Dim xpd As XPathDocument = New XPathDocument(Server.MapPath("books.xml"))
      Dim nav As XPathNavigator = xpd.CreateNavigator()
    Dim iterator as XPathNodeIterator = nav.Select("BOOKS/BOOK/AUTHOR")

      While (iterator.MoveNext())
        Response.Write(iterator.Current.Value)
        Response.Write(" ID: " & iterator.Current.GetAttribute("id", "") &
➥"<BR>")
      End While

    End Sub

</SCRIPT>
```

Changing Values in an XML Document

In addition to navigating in an XML document using the various objects described in this chapter, you can also use the XML DOM to make changes in an XML document. Using DOM objects, you can:

- Insert a node into the document
- Remove a child node
- Change the value of an element

To insert a node, you use the InsertAfter or InsertBefore methods of the XmlNode object. These methods take two parameters: the new child node to insert and a reference to an existing node. The location of the existing node determines where the new node should go.

Listing 11.22 shows an example of how to insert a new book into the books.xml document using the `InsertAfter` method of the `XmlNode` object.

LISTING 11.22   Inserting a New Item into the Document Using the `InsertAfter` Method

```
<%@ Page debug="true" %>
<%@ Import Namespace="System.Xml" %>
<%@ Import Namespace="System.Xml.XPath" %>

<SCRIPT runat='server'>
  Sub Page_Load(Sender As Object, e As EventArgs)
        Dim xd As New XmlDocument()
        xd.Load(Server.MapPath("books.xml"))
        Dim root As XmlNode = xd.DocumentElement    ' BOOKS

    ' Insert BOOK element
        Dim elemBook As XmlElement = xd.CreateElement("BOOK")
        root.InsertAfter(elemBook, root.FirstChild)

        xd.Save(Server.MapPath("output.xml"))

        Response.Write("Open the file output.xml to view the results.")
  End Sub

</SCRIPT>
```

This code loads the XML document from disk and then adds a node using the `InsertAfter` method. It then saves the file to disk using the filename output.xml.

The contents of output.xml is the same as books.xml, but with a blank BOOK node included. However, a book is actually composed of at least two nodes: a BOOK node and a child TITLE node. To insert the child TITLE node, you can use the AppendChild method of the BOOK node, as shown in Listing 11.23.

LISTING 11.23   Inserting a New Child Node Using the `AppendChild` Method

```
<%@ Page debug="true" %>
<%@ Import Namespace="System.Xml" %>
<%@ Import Namespace="System.Xml.XPath" %>

<SCRIPT runat='server'>
  Sub Page_Load(Sender As Object, e As EventArgs)
        Dim xd As New XmlDocument()
        xd.Load(Server.MapPath("books.xml"))
        Dim root As XmlNode = xd.DocumentElement    ' BOOKS
```

LISTING 11.23   Continued

```
' Insert BOOK element
    Dim elemBook As XmlElement = xd.CreateElement("BOOK")
    root.InsertAfter(elemBook, root.FirstChild)

' Insert TITLE element beneath the book
    Dim elemTitle = xd.CreateElement("TITLE")
    elemTitle.InnerText = "MY TITLE"
    elemBook.AppendChild(elemTitle)

    xd.Save(Server.MapPath("output.xml"))

    Response.Write("Open the file output.xml to view the results.")
End Sub

</SCRIPT>
```

This code is the same as Listing 11.23, except that it contains an additional call to the AppendChild method of the BOOK node to add an associated TITLE child node.

You can see from the previous two listings that changes to a document using the DOM change only the in-memory representation of the object, not the way the document is stored on disk. If you want to persist the changes to disk, you must use the Save method of the Xm1Document object. Therefore, to save the changes you made to the document, you execute the Save method of the Xm1Document object that created the document.

Querying XML Documents Using XPath Expressions

XPath is a set-based query syntax for extracting data from an XML document. If you're accustomed to database programming using Structured Query Language (SQL), you can think of XPath as being somewhat equivalent to SQL. But as with so many analogies between relational and XML data, the similarities run out quickly. XPath provides a different syntax that supports the retrieval of hierarchical data in an XML document.

> **NOTE**
>
> The XPath syntax is a World Wide Web Consortium (W3C) recommendation. You can get more information about XPath from the W3C site at http://www.w3.org/TR/xpath. Information on the Microsoft XML 3.0 (COM) implementation of XPath is at http://msdn.microsoft.com/library/psdk/xmlsdk/xslr0fjs.htm.

XPath enables you to extract data from an XML document using a compact expression, ideally with a single line of code. It's generally a more concise way to extract information buried deep within an XML document. (The alternative to using XPath is to write loops or recursive functions, as most of the examples used earlier in this chapter did.) The compactness of XPath can come at a price, however: readability. Unless you're well versed in the XPath syntax, you may have trouble figuring out what the author of a complicated XPath expression was trying to look up. Bear this in mind as you use XPath in your applications.

Although the complete XPath syntax is quite involved (and beyond the scope of this book), you should know about certain commonly used operations as you approach XML processing using the .NET framework classes. The three most common XPath scenarios are

* Retrieving a subset of nodes that match a certain value (for example, all the orders associated with customers)
* Retrieving one or more nodes based on the value of an attribute (such as retrieving all the orders for customer ID 1006)
* Retrieving all the parent and child nodes where an attribute of a child node matches a certain value (such as retrieving all the customers and orders where the Item attribute of the order node equals 'Tricycle')

To make it easy to experiment with different kinds of XPath expressions and see how they retrieve different sections of the XML document, we've created an ASP.NET page that enables you to input an XPath query that is then applied against the books.xml document. We'll use this page as a way of demonstrating various XPath techniques in this section. Listing 11.24 shows a complete listing of this page.

LISTING 11.24 The XPath Query Page Used to Test XPath Queries Against the books.xml File

```
<%@ Import Namespace="System.Xml" %>
<%@ Import Namespace="System.Xml.XPath" %>
<SCRIPT runat='server'>

  Private Sub btnQuery_Click(ByVal sender As System.Object,
ByVal e As System.EventArgs)
        Dim xd As New XmlDocument()
        Dim nd As XmlNode
        Dim nl As XmlNodeList

        xd.Load(Server.MapPath("books.xml"))
        txtOutput.Text = ""

        nl = xd.SelectNodes(txtXPath.Text)
```

LISTING 11.24   Continued

```
        For Each nd In nl
            txtOutput.Text &= nd.OuterXml
        Next
    End Sub

</SCRIPT>

<HTML>
    <HEAD>
        <title>ASP.NET XPath</title>
    </HEAD>
    <body>
        <form runat="server">
            XPath Expression:<br>
            <asp:TextBox id="txtXPath"
                        Text="BOOKS/BOOK/AUTHOR"
                        TextMode="MultiLine"
                        Rows="3" Width="200" runat="server" />
            <asp:Button id="btnQuery"
                        OnClick="btnQuery_Click"
                        Text="Query" Runat="server" /><br>
            <asp:TextBox id="txtOutput"
                        TextMode="MultiLine"
                        Rows="15" Width="400" runat="server" />
        </form>
    </body>
</HTML>
```

This page contains two sections, the XML- and XPath-processing code contained in the btnQuery_Click event procedure and the HTML and ASP.NET server controls that enable the user to interact with the code. The page works by letting the user type in an XPath expression, which is then executed against the books.xml document. The results from the XPath query are placed into the output text box called txtOutput.

You can see how this page works by typing **/BOOKS** into the XPath Expression box. If everything works correctly, the output shown in Listing 11.25 should appear in the Results box.

LISTING 11.25   Results of a Simple XPath Query

```
<BOOKS>
  <BOOK>
    <TITLE>VB.NET Developer's Guide To ASP.NET, XML and ADO.NET</TITLE>
    <AUTHOR id="101" location="San Francisco">Jeffrey P. McManus</AUTHOR>
```

LISTING 11.25   Continued

```
        <AUTHOR id="107" location="Seattle">Chris Kinsman</AUTHOR>
      </BOOK>
    </BOOKS>
```

When you run the code on your own machine, you'll probably notice that the XML is run together without any spaces or line breaks; we've inserted them here for readability.

NOTE

A shortcut exists to retrieve the root node of a document, and the shortcut doesn't even require you to know the name of the root node. The XPath expression /* will always retrieve the root node of a document (and, by extension, all the descendants of the root node).

This kind of query is interesting, but less than useful. It simply returns the entire contents of the document, and we could have done that with much less code. More interesting is XPath's capability to selectively filter information based on criteria that you specify.

In an earlier code example, you saw an example of a more sophisticated XPath query that retrieved author information based on the author's ID. Listing 11.26 shows an example of this query again, with the expected output in the XPath query page listed next.

LISTING 11.26   Using XPath to Retrieve an Author Given a Particular ID

```
XPath Query Expression: /BOOKS/BOOK/AUTHOR[@id = "107"]
<OUTPUT>
  <AUTHOR id="107" location="Seattle">Chris Kinsman</AUTHOR>
</OUTPUT>
```

Note that this expression will retrieve multiple instances of a given author in a case where a document contains multiple books with the same author. Listing 11.27 shows an example.

LISTING 11.27   Using XPath to Retrieve Multiple Instances of the Same Author

```
Source Document:
<BOOKS>
  <BOOK>
    <TITLE>VB.NET Developer's Guide To ASP.NET, XML and ADO.NET</TITLE>
    <AUTHOR id="101" location="San Francisco">Jeffrey P. McManus</AUTHOR>
    <AUTHOR id="107" location="Seattle">Chris Kinsman</AUTHOR>
```

Listing 11.27   Continued

```
  </BOOK>
  <BOOK>
    <TITLE>How to Pluck a Purdue Chicken</TITLE>
    <AUTHOR id="107" location="Seattle">Chris Kinsman</AUTHOR>
  </BOOK>
  <BOOK>
    <TITLE>My Life Among the Baboons</TITLE>
    <AUTHOR id="107" location="Seattle">Chris Kinsman</AUTHOR>
  </BOOK>
</BOOKS>


XPath Query Expression: /BOOKS/BOOK/AUTHOR[@id = "107"]/parent:*

<BOOK>
  <TITLE>VB.NET Developer's Guide To ASP.NET, XML and ADO.NET</TITLE>
  <AUTHOR id="101" location="San Francisco">Jeffrey P. McManus</AUTHOR>
  <AUTHOR id="107" location="Seattle">Chris Kinsman</AUTHOR>
</BOOK>
<BOOK>
  <TITLE>How to Pluck a Purdue Chicken</TITLE>
  <AUTHOR id="107" location="Seattle">Chris Kinsman</AUTHOR>
</BOOK>
<BOOK>
  <TITLE>My Life Among the Baboons</TITLE>
  <AUTHOR id="107" location="Seattle">Chris Kinsman</AUTHOR>
</BOOK>
```

The parent:* clause added to the end of the XPath expression in this example tells the query to retrieve the data as well as the parent node. Rather than just returning the same author three times, as it would if we'd specified only /BOOKS/BOOK/AUTHOR[@id = "107"], we instead get the author node and the BOOK parent node, which makes more sense.

If you change the query expression to /BOOKS/BOOK/AUTHOR[@id = "101"]/parent:* then only one book is retrieved (the book authored by author 101, McManus).

If you were interested in retrieving only one instance of the AUTHOR node, you could use the XmlNodeReader's SelectSingle method (rather than Select method). This ensures that you retrieve only the first instance of the data.

You can combine multiple query criteria using AND and OR logic. For example, to retrieve all the book authors who live either in San Francisco or Seattle, use the expression shown in Listing 11.28.

LISTING 11.28   Using OR in an XPath to Query Based on Multiple Search Criteria

```
XPath Query Expression:
BOOKS/BOOK/AUTHOR[@location="Seattle" or @location="San Francisco"]
<AUTHOR id="101" location="San Francisco">Jeffrey P. McManus</AUTHOR>
<AUTHOR id="107" location="Seattle">Chris Kinsman</AUTHOR>
<AUTHOR id="107" location="Seattle">Chris Kinsman</AUTHOR>
<AUTHOR id="107" location="Seattle">Chris Kinsman</AUTHOR>
```

This query retrieves both authors because each one fits one or the other criterion. Kinsman is retrieved three times because his name is associated with three books in the list. Any book authors located in Saskatoon would be excluded from the resultset.

Now suppose you want to exclude nodes, perhaps by returning all the authors who don't live in Seattle. Listing 11.29 shows an example of an expression that does this, as well as the expected output.

LISTING 11.29   Using XPath to Exclude Nodes Based on the Value of Attributes

```
XPath Query Expression:  /BOOKS/BOOK/AUTHOR[@location != "Seattle"]
<AUTHOR id="101" location="San Francisco">Jeffrey P. McManus</AUTHOR>
```

As you can see, the inequality operator != is the way you use XPath to retrieve all the nodes that do not have the location attribute of "Seattle".

You can also perform greater-than and less-than comparisons using this technique. The XPath expression /BOOKS/BOOK/AUTHOR[@id > 105] retrieves all authors whose id attribute is greater than 105.

In addition to querying on attributes, you can also query on the text contained in nodes. A good example of a node that contains text in the books.xml document is the TITLE node, contained beneath the BOOK node in our hierarchy.

Listing 11.30 shows an example of a query that retrieves the books in which the TITLE node contains specific text.

LISTING 11.30   Retrieving a Specific TITLE Node by Querying on Its Text

```
XPath Query Expression:
/BOOKS/BOOK/TITLE[. = "How to Pluck a Purdue Chicken"]/parent:*
<BOOK>
  <TITLE>How to Pluck a Purdue Chicken</TITLE>
  <AUTHOR id="107" location="Seattle">Chris Kinsman</AUTHOR>
</BOOK>
```

The dot (.) operator is XPath-ese for "right here."

There is another way to retrieve all the books whose title matches a given text string without using the parent:* expression. You can instead include the parameter element in square brackets. Listing 11.31 shows an example of this syntax, retrieving all the TITLE nodes (and their parent BOOK nodes) given a specific title you specify.

LISTING 11.31   Retrieving a Specific BOOK Node by Querying on the Text Found in the Book's TITLE Node

```
XPath Query Expression:
/BOOKS/BOOK[TITLE = 'How to Pluck a Purdue Chicken']
<BOOK>
  <TITLE>How to Pluck a Purdue Chicken</TITLE>
  <AUTHOR id="107" location="Seattle">Chris Kinsman</AUTHOR>
</BOOK>
```

Comparing this XPath expression—and the response it generates—to the query we ran in the previous example illustrates the difference between requesting a node and requesting its parent and all its descendents. In this example we're saying, "Give me the books whose TITLE text matches the following title." In the previous example, the request was, "Give me the TITLE nodes whose text matches the following title." It's a subtle distinction, but important as you delve into getting XPath to work for you.

This section doesn't represent a complete discussion of how to use XPath queries to retrieve data from existing XML documents. However, it should get you on the right path. XPath represents a whole minilanguage with additional functions and operators; for more information on the remaining details, consult the .NET framework documentation or (if you're desperate and/or have trouble getting to sleep at night) the W3C XPath recommendation.

Defining and Validating XML with Schemas

Whenever you use or manipulate data, you need to have a way of answering certain questions about that data. Is an Invoice ID stored as a text value or a numeric value? Is a phone number limited to 10 digits? For that matter, can a person have more than one phone number? What happens if the person has none?

All these questions have to do with the concepts of data definition and validation. Application developers have historically embedded validation logic in application code. Sophisticated designs can encapsulate validation logic in various ways, but in most cases, the data definition and validation logic aren't accessible to processes outside of your application. This defeats the purpose of XML on a number of levels. Remember that XML is designed to be interoperable and human readable. When you commit validation logic to code, you've almost inherently made the validation logic inaccessible to other processes that might come along later. It is, in essence, a black box. The concept of encapsulating data validation in a class is a good and useful thing, but if other developers can't easily access your data design from outside sources, it may not be as useful to them.

A way exists to express and validate data designs expressed in XML. This is done through a standard descriptive format referred to as XML schemas (sometimes abbreviated XSD). Because the various .NET tools provide good support for XML schemas, we'll devote some time to discussing how schemas work, how to build them, and what you can do with them in your Internet applications.

About Document Type Definitions (DTDs)

The first technology used for validating XML structures was known as Document Type Definition (DTD). By linking a DTD document to an XML file, you can ensure that the XML document contains valid data types and structure.

The problem with DTDs is that they have limitations with respect to the things they can do. One glaring limitation is that DTDs can't define data types of elements that appear in a document.

But the most damning implication of using DTDs to validate XML is that DTDs are written using a syntax that is completely removed from that of XML itself; if you want to validate your data using the DTD format, you must ascend a learning curve.

A good example of a DTD is the DTD for XML itself, which resides at `http://www.w3.org/XML/1998/06/xmlspec-v21.dtd`. By looking at this DTD, you can get a sense for how different the syntax of DTD is. Indeed, the response of many developers who had to use DTDs in the early days of XML was, "Couldn't we use XML syntax to define the structure of an XML document?"

Microsoft chose to use a more evolved document definition technology for XML in the .NET universe—the XML schema. The most important benefit of XML schemas is that you can write an XML schema using the XML syntax you presumably already know. For these reasons, this chapter focuses on schemas rather than DTDs.

NOTE
The Visual Studio .NET development environment gives developers a graphical way to build XML schemas and contains little or no support for DTDs. You can certainly use DTDs with XML data in the .NET framework; you just won't get much help from the tools.

Before we proceed, it's worth noting that you're never required to validate the XML documents that you use in your application development; XML documents can live out their whole lives without ever knowing or using an XML schema. However, it's a good idea to validate them for the sake of consistency. In addition, certain tools (including Visual Studio .NET) use XML schemas in various interesting and useful ways. Having a handle on what an XML schema is and how it works will give you a leg up on using these tools.

> **NOTE**
>
> The official W3C documentation on XML schemas comes in three parts: a primer, which as of this writing runs 73 printed pages, and two sections that document the schema specification in detail. The whole thing starts at http://www.w3.org/XML/Schema.

About XML Data-Reduced Schemas

The COM-based Microsoft XML implementation that existed before the arrival of the .NET framework used a syntax known as XML Data-Reduced (XDR) schemas. Confusingly, the Microsoft documentation refers to XDR as "XML Schemas," even though that's really a different, albeit related, syntax from that provided by the W3C. The .NET tools support both the XDR and W3C way of expressing schemas, but Visual Studio .NET follows the W3C schema syntax, so you'll likely see the W3C syntax used in .NET applications more often.

We are including this section on XDR schemas so that you can identify and understand the difference between XDR and W3C XML schemas, and as a way to make it easier for users of the MSXML library who are moving to the .NET framework to migrate their applications. Also, because the XML-handling objects in the .NET framework can process XDR-validated documents, it's possible that you will need to use XDR at some point, even though it's being superseded by the W3C schema format.

Listing 11.32 shows an example of a complete XDR schema definition.

LISTING 11.32   Example of an XDR Schema

```
<Schema xmlns="urn:schemas-microsoft-com:xml-data"
        xmlns:dt="urn:schemas-microsoft-com:datatypes">

  <ElementType name='TITLE' content='textOnly' />

  <AttributeType name='IDType' dt:type='integer' />
```

LISTING 11.32   Continued

```
<ElementType name='AUTHOR' content='textOnly'>
  <attribute type='IDType' />
</ElementType>

<ElementType name='BOOK' content='mixed'>
  <element type = 'TITLE' />
  <element type = 'AUTHOR' />
</ElementType>

</Schema>
```

The example begins with a Schema node, to indicate that this is the start of a schema. The two xmlns attributes refer to external schema documents; the first one is for XML itself, the second one is for the data types defined by the Microsoft data types defined for use in XDR schemas.

The ElementType nodes in the schema document form the definition of the nodes that compose the document. In this example, you can see two types of ElementTypes defined; a simple type (containing no child nodes, such as TITLE) and a complex type (containing child nodes and/or attributes, such as BOOK). We'll discuss simple and complex types in more detail in the section "Understanding Simple and Complex Types" later in this chapter.

> **NOTE**
>
> The Microsoft reference on XDR schemas is at http://msdn.microsoft.com/xml/ reference/schema/start.asp. Another useful Microsoft link is the XML Schema Developer's Guide, located at http://msdn.microsoft.com/xml/xmlguide/ schema-overview.asp.
>
> This reference material was created to document the behavior of the MSXML parser found in Internet Explorer 5.0. It may not have direct applicability to XML applications that you build using the .NET tools (use the W3C specification for XML schemas you build in .NET). Note, again, that when Microsoft refers to "XML Schema," it may be referring to either XDR schemas or W3C-style XML schemas. In general, what you get in the .NET tools are true W3C XML schemas.

This section is intended to give you the briefest example of an XDR schema so you can understand what an XDR schema looks like. Because the Visual Studio .NET uses the more recent W3C recommendation for XML schemas, however, we'll spend the rest of this section discussing the W3C syntax for XML document definition and validation.

> **Note**
>
> Using a tool that comes with the .NET framework SDK, you can convert existing XDR schemas to the W3C format described in the next section. Known as the XML Schema Definition Tool (xsd.exe), this command-line tool can also create basic schemas from existing XML files and build ADO.NET classes in Visual Basic.NET or C# from existing schemas.

Creating W3C XML Schemas

A W3C XML schema is conceptually similar to an XDR schema, but has a number of implementation differences. Because XML schema is on its way to becoming an Internet standard, it's better to use the W3C standard format because you can expect a better level of interoperability as the standard propagates. Fortunately, the new XML-handling tools included in the .NET framework and Visual Studio .NET tend to use the newer W3C versions of technologies such as schemas, so you'll have lots of help when building applications that are designed to be Internet standard and interoperable.

Our objective in this section is to perform a very simple validation on a simple XML document. Because the W3C XML schema language is a very complex syntax that could warrant a short book of its own, in this section we'll cover only the basics of XML schema—particularly, how to create a schema that validates an XML document using the XML-handling objects in the .NET framework classes.

Listing 11.33 shows the document we'll be validating in this section.

Listing 11.33   Simplified book.xml Document

```
<BOOK isbn="1234567890">
  <TITLE>Little Red Riding Hood</TITLE>
  <AUTHOR>Dave-Bob Grimm</AUTHOR>
</BOOK>
```

As you can see, this is a greatly simplified version of the books.xml document we've used in examples throughout this chapter. Rather than containing an unlimited number of books, this document contains only a single book, so it might be used in situations where one software process hands off book information to another.

Like XDR schemas, W3C schemas are generally linked to external files that provide the basic definition of what a schema is. As a result, the W3C-compliant schemas you create will typically begin with a reference to the standard W3C schema definition (known as the schema of schemas). The W3C schema definition gives your schema access to basic data types and structures you'll need to construct schemas to define and validate your XML documents. This basic definition is shown in Listing 11.34.

LISTING 11.34   W3C Schema Definition Boilerplate

```
<?xml version="1.0"?>
<xsd:schema xmlns:xsd="http://www.w3.org/2001/XMLSchema">

<!-- Your schema definition goes here -->

</xsd:schema>
```

This is a boilerplate definition that you'll probably include in most, if not all, of your XML schema documents. (Note that the XML schema-editing function provided by Visual Studio .NET generates a slightly different boilerplate schema definition; what you see here is more streamlined.)

This boilerplate provides the same basic function as the initial definition of the XDR schema shown in a previous example, but it provides a different basic schema type and associates it with the xsd namespace. This means that you'll often see elements of a W3C schema prefixed with the xsd namespace; this is done to prevent namespace collisions between elements defined by the xsd schema definition and elements in your documents with the same name.

The next step to defining your own W3C schema is to define the data types that can appear in your document. To do this, you must have a handle on simple and complex data types in XML and how the W3C XML schema defines them.

Understanding Simple and Complex Types

As you know, an XML document is inherently hierarchical. Every XML document is composed of nodes that can contain child nodes, nested as deeply as necessary to represent a given data structure. When you're authoring an XML schema, you need to be able to make a distinction between simple and complex types. A complex type is defined as any node that has children or attributes; a simple type has no children or attributes. For example, in the book.xml document used as an example in Listing 11.33, BOOK is a complex type because it contains two child elements, AUTHOR and TITLE, as well as an attribute, isbn. AUTHOR, on the other hand, is a simple type, because it contains nothing but a text string (the name of the book's author).

The distinction between simple and complex types becomes important when building XML schemas because the two types are described in different ways in the schema format. In XML schema authoring, it's common to define the simple types first and the complex types later because the complex types are almost invariably built on the simple type definitions.

Listing 11.35 shows an example of a schema with a simple type definition.

LISTING 11.35   W3C Schema Containing a Definition for a Simple Type

```
<?xml version="1.0"?>
<xsd:schema xmlns:xsd="http://www.w3.org/2001/XMLSchema">

  <xsd:simpleType name="ISBNType">
    <xsd:restriction base="xsd:string">
      <xsd:maxLength value="10"/>
    </xsd:restriction>
  </xsd:simpletype>

</xsd:schema>
```

The first few lines of this schema definition are the same as the previous example; they refer to the external master schema maintained by the W3C that defines basic data types and so forth.

The xsd:simpleType node contains the definition for a simple type called ISBNType. You can see from the definition that this type contains a restriction, which provides additional information about the data type and (optionally) the nature of the data that this data type supports. In this case, ISBNType is declared to be a string that can have a maximum length of 10 characters. (Note that although ISBN stands for International Standard Book Number, an ISBN can contain alphabetic characters in addition to numbers, so we declare it to be a string type.)

Be careful typing the names of attributes such as maxLength in your XML schema definitions. As with all XML elements, the elements of an XML schema are case sensitive.

You don't have to define named types in your XML schemas. The advantage is reusability—after you've defined a named type, you can reuse it anywhere you like in the schema definition (or refer to the schema from another schema and reuse it that way). When used in this way, XML schemas behave a bit like class definitions.

After you've created a type definition, you can declare that your document will contain elements of this type. Listing 11.36 shows an example of a schema containing a reference to the ISBNType simple type.

LISTING 11.36   W3C Schema Containing an Element Definition That Refers to a Type Definition

```
<?xml version="1.0" ?>
<xsd:schema xmlns:xsd="http://www.w3.org/2001/XMLSchema">
    <xsd:element name="ISBN" type="ISBNType"></xsd:element>
    <xsd:simpleType name="ISBNType">
        <xsd:restriction base="xsd:string">
            <xsd:maxLength value="10" />
```

LISTING 11.36 Continued

```
        </xsd:restriction>
    </xsd:simpleType>
</xsd:schema>
```

The element definition indicates that XML documents based on this schema will contain an element named ISBN. The type definition for this element is the ISBNType type created in the previous section.

This schema would be sufficient if we were interested only in creating XML documents containing lists of ISBN numbers. But the book information we're working with contains much more than that—we need to transmit the title and author of the book as well. To do this, we'll need to modify our schema to include a new complex type, called BookType, that defines TITLE and AUTHOR elements, as well as an isbn attribute. The isbn attribute is defined as an ISBNType, which means it takes on the properties of that type definition; it's a string data type with a maximum length of 10 characters.

Listing 11.37 shows another version of the schema, this time with a more complete definition of the BookType type. This time, we've added TITLE and AUTHOR types to the BookType.

LISTING 11.37 W3C Schema Containing a Complex Type That Refers to a Simple Type

```
<?xml version="1.0" ?>
<xsd:schema xmlns:xsd="http://www.w3.org/2001/XMLSchema">
    <!-- Element definition -->
    <xsd:element name="BOOK" type="BookType"></xsd:element>

    <!-- Complex type definition -->
    <xsd:complexType name="BookType">
        <xsd:all>
            <xsd:element name="TITLE" type="xsd:string" />
            <xsd:element name="AUTHOR" type="xsd:string" />
        </xsd:all>
        <xsd:attribute name="isbn" type="ISBNType" />
    </xsd:complexType>

    <!-- Simple type definition with restriction-->
    <xsd:simpleType name="ISBNType">
        <xsd:restriction base="xsd:string">
            <xsd:maxLength value="10" />
        </xsd:restriction>
    </xsd:simpleType>
</xsd:schema>
```

This version of the schema completes the complex type definition BookType by adding two elements: TITLE and AUTHOR. Both elements are defined as conventional strings with no special validation logic attached. The <xsd:all> element indicates that two or more child elements can appear in any order beneath the parent element. If you need to specify that the child elements should appear in a particular order, use <xsd:sequence> instead of <xsd:all>.

The big change in this final version of the schema is the addition of the BOOK element definition. Because the type of book was defined previously as a complex type, this section is very straightforward; all we need to do is reference the BookType complex type.

You'll notice, too, that this version of the schema contains comments; comments in XML are syntactically identical to comments in HTML. You should include comments in any XML file you create wherever there's a chance that somebody who comes along later might misunderstand what's going on in your document.

Validating Documents Using W3C Schemas

To validate an XML document using a schema, you first create the schema and then link the schema to an XML document defined by the schema. When an XML parser processes a document that is linked to a schema, the parser will first download the schema document(s) associated with that file. If the file fails to conform with any of the rules specified in the schema, the parser will complain (and in most cases refuse to proceed).

Schemas are often contained in a file separate from the XML data file. This enables you to change the schema definition without having to slog through the data itself. By placing a schema file in a location accessible through the Internet, any file anywhere can access and utilize the data structure and validation rules found in the schema.

In addition to linking XML documents to schemas, schemas themselves can be linked to other schemas. This gives you the capability to build progressively more sophisticated schemas based on more basic schema definitions created in the past.

After you've created an XML schema and linked it to an associated XML data document that implements the schema, you should test it to ensure that it does what you want. Because Internet Explorer understands XML and can render XML in the browser, you can use Internet Explorer 5.0 or later to determine whether your XML document parses. To do this, simply load the file into Internet Explorer using the URL text box or by using the File, Open menu command.

As with any XML parser, Internet Explorer automatically downloads the schema definition when it encounters an XML document that is linked to a schema. After the file and the external schemas are downloaded, the browser then attempts to parse the document. If parsing is successful, Internet Explorer displays the document. If it's unsuccessful, it usually gives you an error message in the browser.

Problems with XML rendering and parsing in a validated context usually stem from one of two problems: the document is not well formed (meaning the document is lacking an end tag for a node, for example), or the document is invalid (according to the validation rules defined in the schema file).

XML parsers almost invariably reject documents that are not well formed; whether they reject invalid documents depends on the tool you use to handle the document. For example, an XmlTextReader object will not throw an error when it reads an invalid XML document, but the XmlValidatingReader object will. The XmlValidatingReader object is introduced in the next section, "Using .NET Framework Objects to Validate XML Schemas."

> **NOTE**
>
> You should watch out for a couple of things when working with XML document validation with schemas. First, make sure your computer has a connection to the Internet when you load a validated document, because schemas must typically access other dependent schemas, and the way that's most commonly done is by downloading them over the Net.
>
> Next, remember that XML is case sensitive—uppercase and lowercase matter. Spelling an element name BOOK in one place in the document and then attempting to refer to something called Book or book later will cause problems.

Using .NET Framework Objects to Validate XML Schemas

Earlier in this chapter, we discussed how to read a document using the XmlTextReader object provided by the .NET framework. You can use an XML schema to validate a document when reading a document using the .NET framework. To do this, you use the XmlValidatingReader object.

> **NOTE**
>
> The XmlValidatingReader class is found in the System.Xml namespace. Like the XmlTextReader object described earlier in this chapter, XmlValidatingReader inherits from System.Xml.XmlReader. A reference to the classes, properties, and methods introduced in this chapter is included at the end of this chapter.

Because they both inherit from the same base class, the XmlValidatingReader object works similar to the XmlTextReader object. To validate a document using the XmlValidatingReader

object, set the object's `Validation` property to one of the values enumerated in
`System.Xml.ValidationType`. The `Validation` property can be set to one of these values:

- `ValidationType.None` (no validation)
- `ValidationType.DTD` (use a document type definition for validation)
- `ValidationType.Schema` (use an XSD schema)
- `ValidationType.XDR` (use an XDR schema)
- `ValidationType.Auto` (infer one of the preceding values)

The value `ValidationType.Auto` tells the `XmlValidatingReader` object to infer which type of
schema to use based on what the document contains. This means that it's possible for no validation to occur when using the `Auto` type—if the XML document does not actually contain a
link to a schema or DTD and the validation type is set to `Auto`, no validation will occur. For
this reason, it's a good idea to explicitly set the validation type (if you know what it's going
to be).

If the XML document does not contain a link to a schema, you can add a link to a schema programmatically. Do this by using the Add method of the Schemas collection contained by the
`XmlValidatingTextReader` object.

After you set the validation type and assign a schema, you must then write code to actually
perform the validation. This is similar to the code you write. Listing 11.38 shows an example
of this.

LISTING 11.38   XML Validation Subroutine Using the `XmlValidatingReader` Object

```
<%@ Import Namespace="System.Xml" %>
<%@ Import Namespace="System.Xml.Schema" %>
<SCRIPT runat='server'>

    Sub Page_Load(Sender As Object, e As EventArgs)
        Dim tr As New XmlTextReader(Server.MapPath("book-invalid.xml"))
        Dim vr As New XmlValidatingReader(tr)

        vr.ValidationType = ValidationType.Schema
        vr.Schemas.Add(nothing, Server.MapPath("book.xsd"))

        While vr.Read()
                Response.Write("[" & vr.Name & "]" & vr.Value & "<BR>")
                If vr.NodeType = XmlNodeType.Element Then
                    While vr.MoveToNextAttribute()
                            Response.Write("[" & vr.Name & "]" & vr.Value &
➥"<BR>")
```

LISTING 11.38   Continued

```
                    End While
                End If
            End While
        End Sub

</SCRIPT>
```

This code throws an error when it encounters an element of the document that violates the schema. The code will fail because it parses a version of book.xml that contains a validation error (an ISBN that is too long).

Raising errors when XML schema validation rules are broken is fine, but you may want a more granular level of control over how the document is validated, in addition to richer information on where validation errors were encountered. To do this, you can cause the XmlValidatingReader object to raise events when it encounters validation problems in the documents it parses.

To handle the events raised by an XmlValidatingReader object, you must create an event-handling procedure in your code and use the AddHandler statement to associate the events raised by the XmlValidatingReader object with your event-handling procedure. Listing 11.39 shows an example of this.

LISTING 11.39   Responding to Validation Events Raised by the Validate Subroutine

```
<%@ Import Namespace="System.Xml" %>
<%@ Import Namespace="System.Xml.Schema" %>
<SCRIPT runat='server'>

    Sub Page_Load(Sender As Object, e As EventArgs)
        Dim tr As New XmlTextReader(Server.MapPath("book-invalid.xml"))
        Dim vr As New XmlValidatingReader(tr)

        vr.ValidationType = ValidationType.Schema
        AddHandler vr.ValidationEventHandler, AddressOf ValidationHandler
        vr.Schemas.Add(nothing, Server.MapPath("book.xsd"))

        While vr.Read()
            Response.Write("[" & vr.Name & "]" & vr.Value & "<BR>")
            If vr.NodeType = XmlNodeType.Element Then
                While vr.MoveToNextAttribute()
                    Response.Write("[" & vr.Name & "]" & vr.Value &
➥"<BR>")
```

LISTING **11.39**   Continued

```
                        End While
                    End If
            End While
    End Sub

    Public Sub ValidationHandler(sender As Object, args As ValidationEventArgs)
        Response.Write("<P><B>Validation error</B><BR>")
        Response.Write("Severity: " & args.Severity & "<BR>")
        Response.Write("Message: " & args.Message & "<BR>")
    End Sub
```

```
</SCRIPT>
```

You can see that the validation-handling procedure is a standard event handler assigned to the XmlValidatingReader with a call to the AddHandler statement. When a validation-handling procedure is assigned to the XmlValidatingReader in this way, the reader will issue calls to the validation-handling procedure whenever it encounters a validation error in the document.

> **NOTE**
>
> Because the ValidationEventHandler object is a member of the System.Xml.Schema object, you should import this namespace at the beginning of any code that uses the XmlValidatingReader object. To do this, use this page directive:
>
> ```
> <%@ Import Namespace="System.Xml.Schema" %>
> ```

You can test your validation code by changing the XML document that the page parses. Do this by altering the constructor of the XmlTextReader object in the code: book.xml should be valid, whereas book-invalid.xml will cause the validation event handler to be triggered. (Remember in our schema definition earlier in this chapter, we defined an ISBN data type to be an alphanumeric string of no more than 10 characters.)

Creating XSD Schemas in Visual Studio .NET

You can use Visual Studio .NET to create XSD schemas, often without writing code. Visual Studio .NET provides a visual drag-and-drop interface for creating schemas; it supports IntelliSense and instant syntax checking, as you'd expect with any other kind of code you would write in Visual Studio.

To create an XSD schema in Visual Studio .NET, begin by creating a Web application project. Next, add an XSD file to the project by right-clicking the project in the Solution Explorer, and then selecting Add, Add New Item from the pop-up menu. Finally, from the Add New Item dialog box, choose XSD Schema.

The XSD schema designer looks similar to the other server-side designers in Visual Studio .NET—it's a blank page. At the bottom of the page are two tabs, labeled Schema and XML. These tabs enable you to easily switch back and forth between visual and code views of the schema; you can create the schema either by dragging and dropping schema definition objects onto the page or by editing the code directly.

You can add a definition to the schema visually in one of two ways: by right-clicking the page, selecting Add from the pop-up menu, and choosing a schema member, or by choosing a schema member from the toolbox. (The Visual Studio .NET toolbox has a whole section devoted to the elements, attributes, simple and complex types, and other members of an XML schema definition.)

Editing Schema-Validated XML Files in Visual Studio .NET

Visual Studio .NET enables you to edit XML files with the same color coding and syntax checking you'd expect from any other kind of code you edit in Visual Studio. If you use Visual Studio .NET to edit an XML file that is defined by an XSD schema, you gain a bonus bene-fit—IntelliSense support. This means that for an XML document that is defined by an XSL schema, Visual Studio .NET will provide drop-down lists of valid elements and attributes as you edit the XML document.

Creating Schemas from Data Sources Using Visual Studio .NET

Visual Studio .NET has the capability to create XML schemas automatically from a data source. This means that you can set up a database and Visual Studio will reverse engineer the structure of the database into XML schemas.

Because this function is tightly coupled to VS .NET's data access features, we'll cover it in Chapter 12, "Creating Database Applications with ADO.NET."

Processing XML Documents Using Style Sheets

In the previous sections, you saw how to create a schema to define and validate the structure of an XML document. One of the reasons to use schemas is to make your applications more flexi-ble and easier to maintain by disassociating the definition of an XML document from the data found in that document. XML also provides a technology that enables you to define how a given document should be displayed, in a way that is similarly disassociated from the data doc-ument itself. This technology is known as XML style sheets, or XSL.

Like XML schemas, XSL style sheets are themselves XML documents, so you don't have to learn a whole new set of data structures to use XSL. However, you will have to ascend a bit of a learning curve as you come to understand the tags and attribute settings offered by XSL.

In addition to defining rules for how XML documents are displayed and formatted, style sheets also perform another interesting and useful function. They can define rules for transforming one type of XML document into another. This process is known as a *transformation*. The subset of the style sheet language that is responsible for transformations is known as XSLT.

The capability of style sheets to define the display of an XML document and to perform transformations are somewhat different, so we'll cover them separately in this section, starting with transformations.

> **NOTE**
>
> Like the other XML technologies covered in this chapter, we won't cover every aspect of XSL here, only the basics and techniques for integrating XSL into ASP.NET applications using the XML-handling objects found in the .NET framework. For more information on XSL, see the W3C site for XSL located at http://www.w3.org/Style/XSL/. A link to the current (as of this writing) recommendation on XSLT is located at http://www.w3.org/TR/xslt.

Transforming XML Documents Using Style Sheets

No matter what kind of data you have, eventually it will need to be converted for use in some other context. This is the case even with a "universal" data format such as XML. Just because the data is in XML format doesn't mean that every XML-aware software process will be able to consume that data meaningfully. In many cases the document you've defined will need to be changed, or transformed, so that it can be consumed by some other program. This is where the XML Style Sheet Transformations (XSLT) come in.

XSLT is based on the idea that a set of rules (known as a *style sheet*) can be applied to an XML document (known as the *source tree*) and produce another XML document (known as the *result tree*).

For example, suppose you're a bookseller running a point-of-sale software application that exports information about books in a form similar to that shown in Listing 11.40.

LISTING 11.40   Bookseller's Hypothetical Output

```xml
<?xml version="1.0"?>
<STOCK>
  <BOOK isbn="0805062971" ti="Fight Club" au="Chuck Palahniuk" />
  <BOOK isbn="0751320005" ti="Eyewitness Travel Guides: London" />
</STOCK>
```

This system might export a list of books sold on a daily basis. This list could be sent to one or more publishers' fulfillment systems, which would then automatically restock your shelves with fresh copies of these books to sell to your clamoring customers.

The tricky part here lies in getting your point-of-sale system to talk to the publisher's automated order system. The publisher might expose an XML schema that lets you know exactly what structure an inbound XML document needs to have to be valid, but how do you get the XML emitted by your point-of-sale system to arrange itself so that it's acceptable to the publisher's order system?

To answer this question, let's start by illustrating what a book order might look like in the publisher's hypothetical order system. Listing 11.41 shows such a document.

LISTING 11.41   Publisher's Hypothetical Input

```xml
<?xml version="1.0"?>
<ORDER custid='10459' date='2001-03-19'>
  <BOOK isbn="0805062971">
    <TITLE>Fight Club</TITLE>
  </BOOK>
  <BOOK isbn="0751320005">
    <TITLE>Eyewitness Travel Guides: London"</TITLE>
  </BOOK>
</ORDER>
```

As you can see, most of the information provided by the point-of-sale system is used in the publisher's ordering system, but the structure of the document is different. First, the publisher's system requires that you add your customer ID and order date as an attribute of the ORDER node. Next, the title of the book is expressed as a child node of the BOOK node rather than as an attribute. Finally, the author name is discarded (because the publisher can look up the author name, if needed, given the ISBN number that uniquely identifies all books).

It's true that you could write complicated parsing code (possibly using XML DOM objects or other XML-handling objects found in the .NET framework) that transforms the structure of your data document to the structure required by the publisher's system. But such code would likely be inefficient and difficult to maintain. If the publisher's requirements changed at some point in the future, you'd have to go in and hack your export code so that your exported data would continue to conform to their requirements. Instead, transforming the data using XSLT means that you have a much smaller body of code to contend with.

To get you started, we'll include a few minimal examples of XSLT transformations in this chapter and give you pointers on how to perform XSLT transformations programmatically using the XML-handling objects found in the .NET framework classes.

First, consider a document called stock.xml that contains output from the hypothetical point-of-sale application we mentioned earlier. To transform this document into a structure you can use, you first create an XSLT style sheet and then associate that sheet with the document.

Creating a Style Sheet to Transform Data

You use the XslTransform class to transform an XML document from one format to another. Transformations done using XSLT can convert XML files from one XML structure to another or convert an XML file to a different format entirely (such as HTML).

> **Note**
>
> The XslTransform class is found in the System.Xml.Xsl namespace. A reference to the classes, properties, and methods introduced in this chapter is included at the end of this chapter.

To transform an XML document, you first create an XSLT style sheet that determines how the input document will be transformed. You then associate the style sheet with the input document (typically using the Load method of the XslTransform object).

Creating an XSLT Style Sheet

An XSLT style sheet is an XML document that specifies how to convert, or transform, another XML document. As with the other XML applications we've discussed in this chapter, such as XSD schemas and XPath queries, XSLT has its own syntax but is ultimately built on an XML framework.

XSLT style sheets typically begin with a stylesheet declaration and a matching expression. The matching expression is an XPath query that determines which elements of the source document you want to convert. If you want to convert the entire source document, you use the expression match="/".

After you've determined the elements you want to convert, you then create a template to perform the transformation. This is similar to template-based programming in ASP.NET; you hard-code the way you want your output to appear and then include XSL expressions that control how the data is merged with the template.

Listing 11.42 shows an example of a simple style sheet that takes the books.xml data file and transforms it into an HTML table.

LISTING 11.42   An XSLT Style Sheet That Converts an XML Document into an HTML Document

```
<?xml version="1.0" encoding="UTF-8" ?>
<xsl:stylesheet version="1.0" xmlns:xsl="http://www.w3.org/1999/XSL/Transform">
  <!-- 'match' attribute is an XPath expression -->
<xsl:template match="/">
 <HTML>
 <BODY>
     <TABLE border="1" cellspacing="0" cellpadding="3">
        <TR>
        <TD bgcolor='#CCCCCC'><B>Title</B></TD>
        <TD bgcolor='#CCCCCC'><B>Author</B></TD>
      </TR>
      <xsl:for-each select="BOOKS/BOOK">
            <TR>
        <TD>
              <xsl:value-of select="TITLE" />
            </TD>
        <TD>
              <xsl:value-of select="AUTHOR" />
            </TD>
      </TR>
      </xsl:for-each>
          </TABLE>
 </BODY>
 </HTML>
</xsl:template>
</xsl:stylesheet>
```

You can see the <xsl:stylesheet> heading at the beginning of the style sheet, as well as the <xsl:template> element that marks the beginning of the template. In the body of the template are HTML markup tags, looping constructs (for-each), and functions that extract the value from XML nodes and insert them into the output of the transformation (value-of). There are a number of other operations similar to for-each and value-of in XSLT; however, you can perform the vast majority of XSLT transformations with these two links.

To see the effect this style sheet has on the XML document, you can create a link from the XML file to the style sheet (described in the next section) and then view the XML file in Internet Explorer.

Associating a Document with a Style Sheet

To link an XML stylesheet to an XML document, you use a processing instruction that is similar in syntax to the optional XML declaration. Listing 11.43 shows an example of how to link an XML file to an XSL style sheet.

LISTING 11.43 Version of the books.xml File Containing a Link to the books.xsl Style Sheet

```
<?xml version="1.0"?>
<?xml:stylesheet type="text/xsl" href="books.xsl"?>
<BOOKS>
  <BOOK>
    <TITLE>VB.NET Developer's Guide To ASP.NET, XML and ADO.NET</TITLE>
    <AUTHOR id="101" location="San Francisco">Jeffrey P. McManus</AUTHOR>
    <AUTHOR id="107" location="Seattle">Chris Kinsman</AUTHOR>
  </BOOK>
  <BOOK>
    <TITLE>How to Pluck a Purdue Chicken</TITLE>
    <AUTHOR id="107" location="Seattle">Chris Kinsman</AUTHOR>
  </BOOK>
  <BOOK>
    <TITLE>My Life Among the Baboons</TITLE>
    <AUTHOR id="107" location="Seattle">Chris Kinsman</AUTHOR>
  </BOOK>
</BOOKS>
```

When you view this file in Internet Explorer 5.0 or later, you should be able to see the data formatted as an HTML table.

Note that if a hard-coded link to the style sheet exists in the XML document, you do not need to write ASP.NET code to perform the transformation—as long as you're viewing the XML file in Internet Explorer and the style sheet file is where the link element says it should be, the XML data should be transformed.

Note, too, that it is legal to include multiple xsl-style-sheet instructions in a given XML document. The XSL specification dictates that when multiple style sheets exist, they're interpreted one at a time, one after the other.

Programmatically transforming the document on the server using .NET code requires a bit more effort, however; this is discussed in the next section.

Performing XSL Transformations Programmatically

You may find yourself in a situation where you want to apply an XSL transformation to a given XML file, but you can't or don't want to hard-code a link to the style sheet in the XML document. Perhaps the file is streamed to your application via HTTP, or it resides in a file system in a read-only state. In this case, you must associate the XSL style sheet with the XML data programmatically.

After you have the data and the XSL style sheet, programmatically transforming an XML document is quite easy. To do this, you use the `XslTransform` object, first loading the XSL style sheet using the Load method and then transforming the XML data using the Transform method. Listing 11.44 shows an example of how this works.

Listing 11.44 Programmatically Transforming an XML File Using an XSL Style Sheet and the `XslTransform` Object

```
<%@ Page debug="true" ContentType="text/xml" %>
<%@ Import namespace="System.Xml" %>
<%@ Import namespace="System.Xml.XPath" %>
<%@ Import namespace="System.Xml.Xsl" %>

<SCRIPT runat='server'>

  Sub Page_Load(Sender As Object, e As EventArgs)
    Dim xslt As New XslTransform()
    Dim xpd As New XPathDocument(Server.MapPath("books.xml"))

    xslt.Load(Server.MapPath("books.xsl"))
    xslt.Transform(xpd, Nothing, Response.OutputStream)

  End Sub

</SCRIPT>
```

It just happens that we chose to stream the output of the transformation to the OutputStream of the Response object (thereby sending the data immediately to the browser). If you choose, you can use one of the many overloaded versions of the Transform method to stream the output to a file or to an `XmlReader` object for further processing.

Editing XSLT Files Using Visual Studio .NET

You can use Visual Studio .NET to create and edit XSLT documents. To do this, simply right-click a Web project, select Add from the pop-up menu, and choose Add New Item from the submenu. Then, from the dialog box, select XSLT File. Give the file a name and click the Open button, and a blank XSLT document will be created. Visual Studio .NET will create the boilerplate definition of your XSLT document, including a link to the W3C namespace for XSLT located at `http://www.w3.org/1999/XSL/Transform`.

You'll need to be careful with one thing when using Visual Studio .NET to create and edit XSLT style sheets—testing XSL by loading the XML document into Internet Explorer (as described in the section "Validating Documents Using W3C Schemas" earlier in this chapter) won't work with the XSLT boilerplate generated by Visual Studio .NET. This is because Internet Explorer versions 5.0 and 5.5 (the current version as of this writing) support an earlier revision of the XSL recommendation. Specifically, Internet Explorer 5.x requires a link to the older version of the W3C namespace for XSL located at `http://www.w3.org/TR/WD-xsl`. Internet Explorer 6.0 works fine with the default XSLT schema supplied by Visual Studio .NET.

Fortunately, however, the XML-handling objects in the .NET framework support the current revision of XSLT, so you can use the XSLT editor in Visual Studio .NET to perform server-side transformations as described in the previous section, "Applying Style Sheets Programmatically Using .NET Framework Classes."

Class Reference

This section provides a quick interface reference to the key objects described in this chapter. Space constraints prevent us from documenting every object in the .NET framework in this book; for the sake of brevity and conciseness, we include only the most important objects here. For more information on the other objects in the .NET framework, consult the .NET Framework Reference online help file.

Inheritance Relationships

This chapter covers the classes used to handle XML in the .NET framework. The following sections provide a brief reference to the properties, methods, and events provided by those classes.

Figure 11.2 shows the inheritance relationship between the objects described in this chapter.

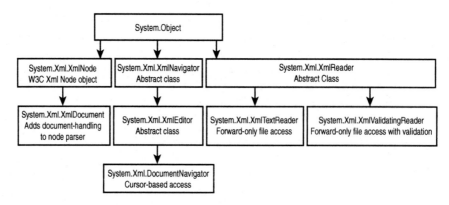

FIGURE 11.2

Inheritance relationships between proprietary .NET XML handler classes.

ValidationEventArgs Class

Member of System.Xml.Schema. Not inheritable.

A ValidationEventArgs object is passed by the ValidationEventHandler delegate used by the XmlValidatingReader object.

Properties

ErrorCode	Message	Source

Methods

Equals	GetHashCode	MemberwiseClone
Finalize	GetType	ToString

XmlDocument Class

Member of **System.Xml**.

The XmlDocument object represents the top-level object in the XML DOM hierarchy. You can use it to read and write any element of an XML document, as well as to retrieve an XML document through the local file system or over HTTP.

Properties

Attributes	InnerText	NextSibling
BaseURI	InnerXml	NodeType
ChildNodes	IsReadOnly	OuterXml
DocumentElement	Item	OwnerDocument
DocumentType	LastChild	ParentNode
FirstChild	LocalName	Prefix
HasChildNodes	Name	PreviousSibling
Implementation	NamespaceURI	Value

Methods

AppendChild	CreateTextNode	InsertBefore
Clone	CreateWhitespace	Load
CloneNode	CreateXml Declaration	LoadXml
CreateAttribute	Equals	MemberwiseClone
CreateCDataSection	Finalize	Normalize
CreateComment	GetElementById	PrependChild

CreateDocumentFragment	GetElementsBy TagName	RemoveAll
CreateDocumentType	GetEnumerator	RemoveChild
CreateElement	GetHashCode	ReplaceChild
CreateEntityReference	GetNamespaceOf Prefix	Supports
CreateNavigator	GetPrefixOf Namespace	ToString
CreateNode	GetType	WriteContentTo
CreateProcessing Instruction	ImportNode	WriteTo
CreateSignificant Whitespace	InsertAfter	

XmlNamedNodeMap Class

Member of **System.Xml**.

The XmlNodeList object is used to handle a collection of nodes. It is used in the XML DOM parser model.

Properties
Count

Methods

Equals	GetNamedItem	RemoveNamedItem
Finalize	GetType	SetNamedItem
GetEnumerator	Item	ToString
GetHashCode	MemberwiseClone	

XmlNavigator Class

Abstract class. Member of **System.Xml.** This class serves as the base class for the XmlEditor object.

Properties

AttributeCount	InnerXml	OuterXml
BaseURI	InternalSubset	Prefix
ChildCount	IsDefault	PublicId

Encoding	IsEmptyElement	Selection
HasAttributes	IsReadOnly	Standalone
HasChildren	LocalName	SystemId
HasSelection	Name	Value
HasValue	NamespaceURI	Version
IndexInParent	NameTable	XmlLang
InnerText	NodeType	XmlSpace

Methods

Clone	MoveTo	MoveToLastChild
Compile	MoveToAttribute	MoveToLastSelected
Equals	MoveToChild	MoveToNext
Evaluate	MoveToDocument	MoveToNextAttribute
Finalize	MoveToDocument Element	MoveToNextSelected
GetAttribute	MoveToElement	MoveToParent
GetHashCode	MoveToEntity	MoveToPrevious
GetType	MoveToFirst	MoveToPreviousSelected
HasAttribute	MoveToFirst Attribute	PopPosition
IsSamePosition	MoveToFirstChild	PushPosition
LookupPrefix	MoveToFirst Selected	Select
Matches	MoveToId	SelectSingle
MemberwiseClone	MoveToLast	ToString

XmlNode Class

Member of **System.Xml**.

The XmlNode object represents a single node in the hierarchy of an XML document. It can contain a number of subordinate objects that represent attributes, other nodes, and so forth.

Constructor Example
Properties

Attributes	IsReadOnly	NodeType
BaseURI	Item	OuterXml

ChildNodes	LastChild	OwnerDocument
FirstChild	LocalName	ParentNode
HasChildNodes	Name	Prefix
InnerText	NamespaceURI	PreviousSibling
InnerXml	NextSibling	Value

Methods

AppendChild	GetPrefixOf Namespace	RemoveChild
Clone	GetType	ReplaceChild
CloneNode	InsertAfter	Supports
Equals	InsertBefore	ToString
Finalize	MemberwiseClone	WriteContentTo
GetEnumerator	Normalize	WriteTo
GetHashCode	PrependChild	
GetNamespaceOfPrefix	RemoveAll	

XmlNodeList Class

Member of **System.Xml**.

The XmlNodeList object is a collection that enables you to iterate through a set of child nodes. It is used in the XML DOM parser model.

Properties

Count	ItemOf

Methods

Equals	GetHashCode	MemberwiseClone
Finalize	GetType	ToString
GetEnumerator	Item	
GetNamespaceOfPrefix	RemoveAll	

XmlReader Class

Abstract class. Member of **System.Xml**.

Properties

AttributeCount	IsDefault	NodeType
BaseURI	IsEmptyElement	Prefix
CanResolveEntity	Item	QuoteChar
Depth	LocalName	ReadState
EOF	Name	Value
HasAttributes	NamespaceURI	XmlLang
HasValue	NameTable	XmlSpace

Methods

Close	LookupNamespace	ReadElementString
Equals	*MemberwiseClone*	ReadEndElement
Finalize	MoveToAttribute	ReadInnerXml
GetAttribute	MoveToContent	ReadOuterXml
GetHashCode	MoveToElement	ReadStartElement
GetType	MoveToFirstAttribute	ReadString
IsName	MoveToNextAttribute	ResolveEntity
IsNameToken	Read	Skip
IsStartElement	ReadAttributeValue	ToString

XmlNodeReader Class

Member of **System.Xml**.

The XmlNodeReader object enables you to navigate an XML document using a scrolling cursor model. It inherits from System.Xml.XmlReader, an abstract class.

Properties

AttributeCount	IsDefault	NodeType
BaseURI	IsEmptyElement	Prefix
CanResolveEntity	Item	QuoteChar
Depth	LocalName	ReadState
EOF	Name	Value
HasAttributes	NamespaceURI	XmlLang
HasValue	NameTable	XmlSpace

Methods

Close	MoveToAttribute	ReadInnerXml
Equals	MoveToContent	ReadOuterXml
Finalize	MoveToElement	ReadStartElement
GetAttribute	MoveToFirstAttribute	ReadString
GetHashCode	MoveToNextAttribute	ResolveEntity
GetType	Read	Skip
IsStartElement	ReadAttributeValue	ToString
LookupNamespace	ReadElementString	
MemberwiseClone	ReadEndElement	

XmlTextReader Class

Member of **System.Xml**. Inherits from System.Xml.XmlReader.

The XmlDataReader object provides read-only, forward-only access to an XML document.

Example Constructor
Properties

AttributeCount	Item	Prefix
BaseURI	LineNumber	QuoteChar
CanResolveEntity	LinePosition	ReadState
Depth	LocalName	Value
Encoding	Name	WhitespaceHandling
EOF	Namespaces	XmlLang
HasAttributes	NamespaceURI	XmlResolver
HasValue	NameTable	XmlSpace
IsDefault	NodeType	
IsEmptyElement	Normalization	

Methods

Close	MoveToAttribute	ReadEndElement
Equals	MoveToContent	ReadInnerXml
Finalize	MoveToElement	ReadOuterXml
GetAttribute	MoveToFirstAttribute	ReadStartElement
GetHashCode	MoveToNextAttribute	ReadString

GetRemainder	Read	ResolveEntity
GetType	ReadBase64	Skip
IsStartElement	ReadBinHex	ToString
LookupNamespace	ReadChars	
MemberwiseClone	ReadElementString	

XmlTextWriter Class

Member of **System.Xml**. Inherits from System.Xml.XmlWriter.

The XmlTextWriter object enables you to write XML to a text stream (typically a text file).

The first constructor takes an instance of the TextWriter class or any object that inherits from it (including another XmlTextWriter object). The second form takes an instance of a System.IO.Stream object and an encoding value (one of the members of System.Text.Encoding). The third form takes a string that represents a filename and an encoding value.

Properties

Formatting	Namespaces	XmlLang
Indentation	QuoteChar	XmlSpace
IndentChar	WriteState	

Methods

Close	WriteBinHex	WriteName
Equals	WriteCData	WriteNmToken
Finalize	WriteCharEntity	WriteNode
Flush	WriteChars	WriteProcessing Instruction
GetHashCode	WriteComment	WriteQualifiedName
GetType	WriteDocType	WriteRaw
LookupPrefix	WriteElementString	WriteStartAttribute
MemberwiseClone	WriteEndAttribute	WriteStartDocument
ToString	WriteEndDocument	WriteStartElement
WriteAttributes	WriteEndElement	WriteString
WriteAttributeString	WriteEntityRef	WriteWhitespace
WriteBase64	WriteFullEndElement	

XmlValidatingReader Class

Member of **System.Xml**. Inherits from System.Xml.XmlReader.

The XmlValidatingReader object provides support for reading an XML file using validation. The object supports validation with the DTD, XDR, or W3C XML schema formats.

Constructor Example

The XmlValidatingReader constructor takes an object that inherits from XmlReader as its sole required argument. Two examples of .NET framework objects that inherit from XmlReader are the XmlTextReader object and the XmlValidatingReader object itself. This constructor example shows how to create an XmlValidatingReader object from an XmlTextReader object.

```
xtr = New System.Xml.XmlTextReader("data.xml")
xvr = New System.Xml.XmlValidatingReader(xtr)
```

Properties

AttributeCount	IsEmptyElement	Reader
BaseURI	Item	ReadState
CanResolveEntity	LocalName	Schemas
Depth	Name	SchemaType
Encoding	Namespaces	ValidationType
EntityHandling	NamespaceURI	Value
EOF	NameTable	XmlLang
HasAttributes	NodeType	XmlResolver
HasValue	Prefix	XmlSpace
IsDefault	QuoteChar	

Methods

Close	MoveToContent	ReadEndElement
Equals	MoveToElement	ReadInnerXml
Finalize	MoveToFirstAttribute	ReadOuterXml
GetAttribute	MoveToNextAttribute	ReadStartElement
GetHashCode	Read	ReadString
GetType	ReadAttributeValue	ReadTypedValue
IsStartElement	ReadBase64	ResolveEntity
LookupNamespace	ReadBinHex	Skip
MemberwiseClone	ReadChars	ToString
MoveToAttribute	ReadElementString	

Events

ValidationEventHandler

XmlWriter Class

Abstract class. Member of **System.Xml**.

Properties

WriteState	XmlLang	XmlSpace

Methods

Close	WriteBinHex	WriteName
Equals	WriteCData	WriteNmToken
Finalize	WriteCharEntity	WriteNode
Flush	WriteChars	WriteProcessing Instruction
GetHashCode	WriteComment	WriteQualifiedName
GetType	WriteDocType	WriteRaw
LookupPrefix	WriteElementString	WriteStartAttribute
MemberwiseClone	WriteEndAttribute	WriteStartDocument
ToString	WriteEndDocument	WriteStartElement
WriteAttributes	WriteEndElement	WriteString
WriteAttributeString	WriteEntityRef	WriteWhitespace
WriteBase64	WriteFullEndElement	

Creating Database Applications with ADO.NET

IN THIS CHAPTER

Why a New Object Library for Data Access?

A database *application programming interface* (API) is a software library that programmers use to perform useful work with a database. Prior to Microsoft.NET, many Web developers on the Microsoft platform used a database API called ActiveX Data Objects (ADO), a COM library that enabled access to data sources.

A notoriously cranky lot, database programmers tend to be irked when the database access API they use is changed. This is because so much depends on the database layer operating correctly and efficiently. The situation is exacerbated when the current database API works well and the new API doesn't provide many compelling benefits.

The version of ADO used by application developers prior to Microsoft.NET worked well for building client/server and traditional Web applications. But the world of application development continues to evolve, and this evolution demands that the tools we use evolve with it. For example, you can manipulate a resultset in the absence of a dedicated database connection in both ADO.old and ADO.NET. In contrast, only ADO.NET provides support for a new type of resultset object (the DataSet), which is relatively easy to create, always disconnected, universally available across any data provider, and powerful.

The advent of .NET has opened an opportunity for Microsoft to revisit the design and architecture of all its core APIs with an eye toward making them simpler and more logical. This chapter examines how you can use ADO.NET to perform the common types of database operations that every application needs to perform and how you can take advantage of the new features of the database API to create more effective data-driven applications.

New Features in ADO.NET

Many of the new features in ADO.NET represent gently evolved ways to perform operations that ADO.old programmers have always done, but some features for accessing and presenting data are fairly abrupt departures from what you may be accustomed to. Here is a high-level summary of some of the most important data-access changes of import to an ASP.NET developer.

Support for Disconnected Access and Remoting

ADO.old provided support for sessionless access through the disconnected recordset. To disconnect from a data source in ADO.old, you had to remember to set a specific cursor type and perform a series of magic incantations to make the recordset disconnect from the server. And then, when it was all done, there wasn't any straightforward way for the developer to determine whether the operation actually worked—maybe it was disconnected, maybe not. Disconnected recordsets in ADO.old, were both difficult to test and lacked adequately detailed documentation.

ADO.NET, on the other hand, makes it much easier to retrieve and manipulate disconnected data, including both relational constructs (formed of rows and columns) and hierarchical ones (such as XML documents). It does this through the use of a dedicated, always-disconnected object, the DataSet object, which we'll discuss at length later in this chapter.

XML Support

Although it was possible to express data contained in the ADO.old Recordset object as XML, the process wasn't as straightforward as it might have been. Support for XML was added as an afterthought in ADO.old, and it was supported in an extremely clunky way; in fact, you could argue that ADO.old's XML support was so convoluted that it made sense to use it only in the context of data operability with other ADO data sources. This runs totally counter to the spirit of data interoperability using XML—if the data can't go anywhere, there's really no point in using XML to begin with!

XML support in ADO.NET is provided through the DataSet object. The DataSet can always be rendered as XML with a single method call, and the XML that it renders is structured in a way that's easy to work with, whether you're working within the .NET framework or on some other platform.

Factored Data Access API

Developers liked ADO.old because the number of objects it provided was small and easy to understand. In fact, it was possible to perform most common data operations with a limited knowledge of only two objects: the Recordset and Connection objects.

The architects of ADO.NET have attempted to divide its functionality in a more granular fashion. The objective behind this is to give you more lightweight objects. For example, if you don't need support for advanced features such as disconnected access and remoting via XML, you can use a DataReader object instead of the DataSet object. One unfortunate side effect is that there are more objects to learn. But the real advantage of a well-factored API is better performance and, in the long run, a simpler API. Now you don't have to internalize all the advanced features of ADO.NET until you're ready to use them.

No Support for Server-Side Cursors

A cursor is a software construct that enables your code to step though rows in a resultset one row at a time. There are different types of cursors; some cursors enable you to jump around from one record to another in the resultset with impunity (so-called scrolling cursors). In the Microsoft database cosmology, there are also "forward-only" or "firehose" cursors, which permit you only to move from the beginning of the recordset to the end without moving backward; some database programming purists argue that a cursor that does not scroll is not really a cursor at all.

In addition to scrolling or forward-only, cursors can reside in memory on the server or on the client. (For the purposes of this discussion, a middle-tier machine or a machine that provides access to data via Web services can be considered a client, too. Basically, any machine that is not the database server can be considered a client in this respect.) A server-side cursor allows you to perform server processing on the server without marshaling more results than you need to the client. Because marshaling data over the network can require a lot of time, database programmers sometimes turn to server cursors to perform processing for certain types of operations on database platforms (such as Microsoft SQL Server) that support them.

The problem with server-side cursors is that they consume resources on the server and provide only single-row access; server-side cursors don't support batch cursors.

In the meantime, one workaround is to embed server-side cursor functionality in a stored procedure, and then call that stored procedure using the normal ADO.NET techniques for calling stored procedures (described later in this chapter). The drawback of this workaround is that you must write your stored procedure in whatever language your database server uses. (This language is Transact-SQL if you're using Microsoft SQL Server.)

Scenarios for Using ADO.NET

One of the most common questions developers ask when attacking a new API is how to do the most basic operations that they are accustomed to performing with the perfectly good API that they already use. Table 12.1 gives an example of some of the most common scenarios for database access and describes the approach you take to implement them in ADO.NET.

TABLE 12.1   Common Database-Access Scenarios with ADO.NET

Scenario	Steps to Perform
Retrieve read-only data from a database	Open a connection; create a command object; create a DataReader object
Retrieve data from a database in read/write mode	Open a connection; create a data adapter; assign commands for selecting, reading, writing, and updating to the data adapter; fill the DataSet
Display the results of a query in a Web Forms control	Open a connection; create a data adapter; create a DataSet object; fill the DataSet; bind the control to a DataView object contained by the DataSet
Manipulate query results as XML	Open a connection; create a data adapter; create a DataSet object; send XML from the DataSet to an XmlTextReader via a call to the DataSet's ReadXml method

TABLE 12.1   Continued

Scenario	Steps to Perform
Retrieve a single (scalar) value from a query or stored procedure	Open a connection; create a command object; call the ExecuteScalar method of the command object
Execute a stored procedure that inserts, updates, or deletes data	Open a connection; create a command object; call the ExecuteNonQuery method of the command object

The remainder of this chapter describes how to perform these operations in detail.

Connecting to a Database

In ADO.NET, as in many object-based data-access APIs, you use a *connection object* to establish a connection with a database. In the ADO.NET SQL Server provider, the object is called SqlConnection; in the OLE DB provider, it's cleverly called OleDbConnection. Both objects are conceptually identical, although their implementation details differ slightly. The main difference between the two objects has to do with the syntax of the connection string. The connection string is required to tell the object how to get to the database that you're interested in.

> **NOTE**
>
> The SqlConnection class is a member of the System.Data.SqlClient namespace. The OleDbConnection class is a member of System.Data.OleDb namespace. A full list of members of both namespaces can be found in the reference section at the end of this chapter.

To connect to a SQL Server database using the SqlConnection object, use code like that shown in Listing 12.1.

LISTING 12.1   Opening a Connection Using the SQL Server Provider

```
<% @Page language='vb' debug='true' %>
<% @Import namespace='System.Data' %>
<% @Import namespace='System.Data.SqlClient' %>

<SCRIPT runat='server'>

  Sub Page_Load(Sender As Object, e As EventArgs)
    Dim cn As SqlConnection
    cn = New SqlConnection("server=localhost;uid=sa;pwd=;database=pubs;")
    cn.Open()
```

LISTING 12.1 Continued

```
    Response.Write("Opened connection to " & cn.Database & "<BR>")
    Response.Write("SQL Server version " & cn.ServerVersion)
  End Sub

</SCRIPT>
```

This code opens the connection, displays information about the connection status, and closes the connection. (You may need to change the server, database, uid, or pwd parameters of the connection string in this code to match the configuration of your system.)

As in ADO.old, one of the most important steps to establishing a connection is providing adequate and accurate information in the connection string that you pass to the connection object. For SQL Server, this information almost invariably includes a server name, database name, user ID, and password; additional settings can appear in the connection string, depending on your configuration and which database you are using.

ADO.old veterans will note that the syntax of the ADO.NET connection string is identical to that of ADO.old's Connection object; this is one of the few areas where the techniques you use of ADO.old and ADO.NET intersect.

To do the same thing using the OLE DB provider, use the code shown in Listing 12.2.

LISTING 12.2 Opening a Connection Using the OLE DB Provider

```
<% @Page language='vb' debug='true' %>
<% @Import namespace='System.Data' %>
<% @Import namespace='System.Data.OleDb' %>

<SCRIPT runat='server'>

  Sub Page_Load(Sender As Object, e As EventArgs)
    Dim cn As OleDbConnection
    cn = New OleDbConnection("provider=SQLOLEDB;server=localhost;" & _
"uid=sa;pwd=;database=pubs;")
    cn.Open()
    Response.Write("Opened connection to " & cn.Database & "<BR>")
    Response.Write("SQL Server version " & cn.ServerVersion)
  End Sub

</SCRIPT>
```

This should produce the same result that the previous example produced.

This OLE DB version of the code differs only slightly from the SQL Server version of the code. It imports the System.Data.OleDb namespace instead of System.Data.SqlClient, and it uses an OleDbConnection object instead of a SqlConnection. The connection string is also different: The OleDbConnection object requires a provider= clause to specify the type of OLE DB data source you want to use.

The capability to specify different OLE DB providers in the connection string is a powerful feature; it means that you can use ADO.NET to gain access to OLE DB and ODBC data sources today, even if the database vendors don't yet support Microsoft.NET with providers of their own. If you can get to a data source using ADO.old, you can get to it using the ADO.NET OLE DB provider.

After you're done with your connection object, you should close it using its Close method. This will free up the computational resources devoted to that connection. In addition, you should handle any exceptions that are thrown by the Open method whenever you attempt to open a database connection.

Listing 12.3 contains a more complete example of opening a connection to a data source in ADO.NET, including explicit use of the Open and Close methods and error handling. Note that the structure of the error handler is such that the Close method is executed only if the Open method is successful.

LISTING 12.3   Opening a Database Connection with Error Handling

```
<% @Page language='vb' debug='true' %>
<% @Import namespace='System.Data' %>
<% @Import namespace='System.Data.SqlClient' %>

<SCRIPT runat='server'>

  Sub Page_Load(Sender As Object, e As EventArgs)
    Dim cn As SqlConnection
    cn = New SqlConnection("server=localhost;uid=sa;pwd=;database=pubs;")

    Try
      cn.Open()
      Response.Write("Opened connection to " & cn.Database & "<BR>")
      Response.Write("SQL Server version " & cn.ServerVersion)
      cn.Close()
    Catch sx As SqlException
      Response.Write("Connection failed: " & sx.Message)
    End Try
  End Sub

</SCRIPT>
```

The easiest way to test this code is to do something to make your connection string invalid, such as change the server name to a server that doesn't exist, or get rid of the connection string entirely. If the connection works, you'll see the name of the database and version of the server. (Note that SQL Server 2000 is considered to be SQL Server version 8.0 for versioning purposes.) If it fails, you'll get the error message contained in the Message property of the SqlException object.

Running Queries

After you have a connection to a data source, you can retrieve data from it by executing a query. The results of a query are stored in one of the ADO.NET data objects, typically either a DataReader or a DataSet object. The type of object can differ, depending on how you intend to work with the data.

This is in contrast to ADO.old, which invariably returned data in the form of a Recordset object. In ADO.NET, several objects can contain data. Table 12.2 summarizes these objects.

TABLE 12.2   Summary of Data-Containing Objects in ADO.NET

Object	Description
DataSet	Read/write; connectionless; contains one or more DataTable objects with relationships defined in a collection of DataRelation objects; supports filtering and sorting; supports automatic serialization to XML; contains an object (the DataView) that can be bound to data-aware ASP.NET Web forms controls
DataReader	Read-only; connection-based; supports scrolling forward only
DataTable	Contained by the DataSet; contains sets of rows and columns
DataColumn	Contained by the DataSet object; defines the schema (structure) of a DataTable
DataRow	Contained by the DataSet object; stores the data in an individual row

As you can see, the DataSet object supports far more features than the DataReader. But as with all benefits in technology, there are trade-offs in terms of programming complexity and performance. The key is to understand when it's most appropriate to use the various options available to you; these issues will be discussed in the next few sections of this chapter.

About the SqlDataReader Object

You can use the SqlDataReader object to execute queries and retrieve data from a data source. You typically use the SqlDataReader object in situations where you want to get a small quantity of data and display it quickly. If you're interested in retrieving and manipulating larger sets of data or you want to perform actions such as updating and deleting records, you will need to use a data command object or the DataSet object, discussed later in this chapter.

> **NOTE**
>
> The SqlDataReader class discussed in this section is a member of the System.Data.SqlClient namespace. The OLE DB provider equivalent of this class is called OleDbDataReader; it is found in the System.Data.OleDb namespace. A full list of members of the SqlDataReader class can be found in the reference section at the end of this chapter.

The SqlDataReader is the rough equivalent of the read-only, forward-only Recordset object found in ADO.old. To create a SqlDataReader, you begin by creating a connection to the database and then executing a command that returns data. Using command objects to execute commands against data sources is discussed in the next section.

Executing Commands Using Command Objects

ADO.old provides the ADO Command object to execute commands against data sources. The ADO Command object can execute queries that retrieve data; it can also execute commands that insert, update, or delete data (these commands are referred to as *data-manipulation commands*). Finally, command objects can also execute stored procedures, which are bits of data-access code stored on the server.

ADO.NET, in contrast, gives you two ways to execute commands against data sources: the command object and the data adapter. The ADO.NET Command object is conceptually similar to the ADO.old Command object; it's used when you want to execute a quick command against a data source. The ADO.NET data adapter, in contrast, is used when you need to perform more involved operations against the back end—those operations that might have required a cursor in ADO.old.

Data adapters are also useful when you need to marshal a complex or hierarchical set of data remotely. Because they are based on XML, you could (in theory) remote the DataSet to another platform (one that does not contain a .NET implementation), manipulate the data—including making inserts and updates, and then remote the DataSet back to the .NET server. Putting this to work in practice would pose challenges (it would depend on the quality of tools available on the non-.NET platform), but the promise of standard XML makes it possible.

Ultimately, think of a command object as a way to manipulate data on the server or to return a data reader. The data adapter, in contrast, is the way to create a DataSet object, which establishes communication between the DataSet object and a specific data source.

In this chapter, we'll start simply, using the data reader and command objects first, and then move on to the more complex and feature-rich data adapter and DataSet objects.

Executing Text-Based Select Commands Using a Data Reader Object

A *text-based command* is a command that is constructed in your code at runtime. Commands are expressed in a query language that your data source can understand; this is typically (although not necessarily) Structured Query Language, or SQL.

Text-based commands are in contrast to *stored procedures*, which are defined ahead of time and reside on the server. (We'll discuss how to call stored procedures later in this chapter.) Text-based commands can perform selects (commands that retrieve data) or data manipulation (commands that insert, update, or delete data).

You can use a text command to retrieve a data reader object. Listing 12.4 shows an example of a text-based command that executes a select query (using a SqlCommand object) and returns a SqlDataReader object.

LISTING 12.4   Executing a Text Command That Returns a SqlDataReader Object

```
<% @Page language='vb' debug='true' %>
<% @Import namespace='System.Data' %>
<% @Import namespace='System.Data.SqlClient' %>

<SCRIPT runat='server'>

  Sub Page_Load(Sender As Object, e As EventArgs)
    Dim cn As SqlConnection
    Dim cm As SqlCommand
    Dim dr As SqlDataReader
    Dim strSQL As String

    cn = New SqlConnection("server=localhost;uid=sa;pwd=;database=pubs;")
    strSQL = "SELECT TOP 10 au_fname, au_lname FROM authors"
    cm = New SqlCommand(strSQL, cn)

    ' ** Open connection
    Try
      cn.Open()
    Catch sx As SqlException
      Response.Write("Connection failed: " & sx.Message)
    End Try

    ' ** Execute command
    dr = cm.ExecuteReader()
```

LISTING 12.4   Continued

```
Do While dr.Read()
  Response.Write(dr.GetString(0) & " " & dr.GetString(1) & "<BR>")
Loop

cn.Close()

End Sub
</SCRIPT>
```

This code example builds on the ADO.NET connection object examples used in Listing 12.1. It adds a SqlCommand object that retrieves the first and last names of the first ten authors in the pubs database. It also includes a SqlDataReader object that stores the information retrieved by the query.

> **NOTE**
>
> The SqlCommand class discussed in this section is a member of the System.Data.SqlClient namespace. The OLE DB provider equivalent of this class is called OleDbCommand; it is found in the System.Data.OleDb namespace. A full list of members of the SqlCommand class can be found in the reference section at the end of this chapter.

You can see from the code that the SqlDataReader object is initially created with a call to the ExecuteReader method of the SqlCommand object. If you're familiar with ADO.old, this pattern may be familiar to you—you can return an ADO Recordset object through a call to the Execute method of the ADO.old Command object as well.

After you have successfully created the SqlDataReader object, you can traverse the reader by executing its Read method in a loop. The Read method returns a `true` or `false` value depending on whether any data is readable; when you reach the end of data, the object returns `false`.

> **NOTE**
>
> The way that data reader objects in ADO.NET retrieve data can be contrasted to the somewhat awkward method that ADO.old employed to retrieve field values from a Recordset object—in ADO.old, you typically set up a `While` loop with a call to the MoveNext method inside the loop. If you forgot to include a call to the MoveNext method, your loop became infinite, and you kicked yourself for making a silly mistake. (You may have guessed that one of the authors of this book commits this error more frequently than he would like.)

As you work with data reader objects, remember that the data they store is read-only and forward-only. You can't make changes to the data returned by the data reader object (at least not through the data reader itself), and you can't jump around in the resultset like you can with a cursor-based resultset. However, the data reader is among the best-performing methods of all the data access methods in ADO.NET. As a result, data reader objects are useful in situations where you want to display or export data quickly without complex code or repeated interaction with the data source.

Executing Stored Procedures That Return Data

A stored procedure is a small chunk of code that is embedded in a database server. Stored procedures are commonly used in database applications because they execute more efficiently than database commands constructed on-the-fly. They also serve to separate data access code from business logic, which can be helpful for managing change and complexity in a database application.

> **NOTE**
>
> This section describes how to call stored procedures, but does not cover how to create them (that would require another whole book). Fortunately, such books have already been written. Two good books on writing stored procedures in SQL Server are *Transact-SQL Programming* (O'Reilly) and *The Guru's Guide to Transact-SQL* (Addison Wesley). However, note that as of this writing, neither of these books covers recent changes in Transact-SQL introduced in SQL Server 2000. They're still great for learning both basic and advanced T-SQL programming and contain examples that demonstrate at least 90% of the operations you're ever likely to perform as a T-SQL programmer.

You can call stored procedures from ADO.NET using an ADO.NET command object (OleDbCommand in the OLE DB provider or SqlCommand in the SQL Server provider). You can also specify a stored procedure as one of the four commands in a data adapter object. The four commands that are possible as data adapter object properties are SelectCommand, UpdateCommand, InsertCommand, and DeleteCommand.

Most stored procedures take parameters; for example, a stored procedure that performs a reporting and aggregation function might take a begin date and an end date as parameters. Similarly, a procedure to return information about a given customer or a given order would typically take a customer ID or order ID as one of its parameters. Parameterization enables you to limit the amount of data returned by the stored procedure.

We'll discuss stored procedures that take parameters later in this chapter. For now, we'll start simply and call a parameter-free stored procedure in the Northwind database. The name of this procedure is "Ten Most Expensive Products" and, not surprisingly, it is a SELECT procedure that should always return 10 rows of data.

In the SQL Server provider, the connection object is called SqlConnection; in the OLE DB provider it is called OleDbConnection. Both objects work essentially the same way, but for our examples in this section, we'll use the SQL Server command object. The most common SqlConnection constructor takes two arguments: a command in the form of a string and a connection object. Executing a command that selects records produces a SqlDataReader object that you can then use to display information.

Calling a stored procedure that returns data is similar to executing a text command that returns data. To call a stored procedure, you first create a connection and a command object, and then set the command object's CommandType property to the enumerated value CommandType.StoredProcedure.

Listing 12.5 shows an example of how to execute a query and retrieve data by calling a stored procedure using a SqlCommand and SqlDataReader object.

LISTING 12.5 Calling a Simple Stored Procedure Using the SqlCommand Object

```vb
<% @Page language='vb' debug='true' %>
<% @Import namespace='System.Data' %>
<% @Import namespace='System.Data.SqlClient' %>

<SCRIPT runat='server'>

  Sub Page_Load(Sender As Object, e As EventArgs)
    Dim cn As SqlConnection
    Dim cm As SqlCommand
    Dim dr As SqlDataReader

    cn = New SqlConnection("server=localhost;uid=sa;" & _
pwd=;database=Northwind;")
    cm = New SqlCommand("Ten Most Expensive Products", cn)
    cm.CommandType = CommandType.StoredProcedure

    ' ** Open connection
    Try
      cn.Open()
    Catch sx As SqlException
      Response.Write("Connection failed: " & sx.Message)
    End Try

  ' ** Execute command
  dr = cm.ExecuteReader()
```

LISTING 12.5   Continued

```
Do While dr.Read()
  Response.Write(dr.GetString(0) & " " & dr.GetDecimal(1) & "<BR>")
Loop

cn.Close()

End Sub

</SCRIPT>
```

This code again modifies Listing 12.4, which demonstrates executing a text command and retrieving a SqlDataReader object. In addition to setting the CommandType property of the SqlCommand object to CommandType.StoredProcedure, we also replace the command text with the name of the stored procedure ("Ten Most Expensive Products"). This user-defined stored procedure returns two columns of data: the name of the product and a column called UnitPrice. The data type of the UnitPrice column is of the currency data type (called "money" in SQL Server parlance) but is expressed as a decimal data type in .NET because that's how .NET deals with currency data. As a result, we use the GetDecimal method of the SqlDataReader object to extract prices from each row.

Passing Parameters to Stored Procedures

Just like function calls and subroutines in your code, most stored procedures take parameters. When you call a stored procedure that has one or more parameters, you must supply values for those parameters in code before you execute the stored procedure.

In ADO.NET, you can pass parameters to stored procedures in two ways. To pass parameter values, you can either include the parameter as part of the command itself (this is known as the *inline* method of passing parameters), or you can use the Parameters collection of the connection object. (This technique is syntactically closer to the ADO.old method of passing stored procedure parameters, but requires a bit more code than the inline approach.)

Like the previous examples, calling a command requires a connection object and a command object that are appropriate to the provider you're using. As we've been doing throughout this chapter, we'll stick with the SQL Server objects, SqlConnection and SqlCommand.

For our stored procedure, we'll use the SalesByCategory stored procedure in the Northwind database. This is a fairly simple select procedure that requires a single parameter: a product category (a string value found in the list of product categories in the Categories table), examples of which include Beverages, Produce, and Seafood.

Listing 12.6 shows how to pass a parameter to a stored procedure using the Parameters collection contained by the Command object.

LISTING 12.6 Calling a Parameterized Stored Procedure Using the Parameters Collection of the SqlCommand Object

```vb
<% @Page language='vb' debug='true' %>
<% @Import namespace='System.Data' %>
<% @Import namespace='System.Data.SqlClient' %>

<SCRIPT runat='server'>

  Sub Page_Load(Sender As Object, e As EventArgs)
    Dim cn As SqlConnection
    Dim cm As SqlCommand
    Dim dr As SqlDataReader
    Dim sp As SqlParameter

    cn = New SqlConnection("server=localhost;uid=sa; _
pwd=;database=Northwind;")
    cm = New SqlCommand()
    cm.Connection = cn
    cm.CommandType = CommandType.StoredProcedure
    cm.CommandText = "SalesByCategory"

    ' ** Add parameter and parameter value
    sp = cm.Parameters.Add(New SqlParameter("@CategoryName", _
SqlDBType.NVarChar, 15))
    sp.Value = "Condiments"

    ' ** Open connection
    Try
      cn.Open()
    Catch sx As SqlException
      Response.Write("Connection failed: " & sx.Message)
    End Try

  ' ** Execute command
  dr = cm.ExecuteReader()

  Response.Write("<B>" & sp.Value & "</B><BR>")
  Do While dr.Read()
    Response.Write(dr.GetString(0) & " " & dr.GetDecimal(1) & "<BR>")
  Loop
```

LISTING 12.6   Continued

```
cn.Close()

End Sub

</SCRIPT>
```

This version of the code uses the Add method of the Parameters collection contained by the SqlCommand object, cm. By adding this object to the command object's Parameters collection and then setting its Value property to the value you want to supply to the parameter, you tell the stored procedure which category of data to retrieve.

Note that the Add method used in the example takes a SqlParameter object as an argument. You can use several other constructors for the SqlParameter, depending on how much information you want to specify about the parameter. However, in most cases, the constructor we used (specifying the parameter name, data type, and size) will be the one you use most frequently. Note that the values for SQL Server data types are found in the enumeration System.Data.SqlClient.SqlDbType. All the SQL Server 2000 data types are found in this enumeration (including SqlDbType.BigInt, the 64-bit integer, and the Unicode types NChar, NText, and NVarChar).

With SQL Server, it's actually not necessary to use the Parameters collection to supply a parameter to a stored procedure. In fact, you can call any SQL Server stored procedure using the EXEC keyword. The syntax of EXEC is

```
EXEC procname [param1], [param2] ...
```

where procname is the name of the stored procedure. Parameters, if any, are passed in a comma-delimited list following the name of the stored procedure.

Listing 12.7 shows an example of using EXEC to call a parameterized stored procedure. As in the previous example, the resultset of the stored procedure is returned in the form of a SqlDataReader object.

LISTING 12.7   Calling a Parameterized Stored Procedure

```
<% @Page language='vb' debug='true' %>
<% @Import namespace='System.Data' %>
<% @Import namespace='System.Data.SqlClient' %>

<SCRIPT runat='server'>

  Sub Page_Load(Sender As Object, e As EventArgs)
    Dim cn As SqlConnection
```

LISTING 12.7   Continued

```
    Dim cm As SqlCommand
    Dim dr As SqlDataReader

    cn = New SqlConnection("server=localhost;uid=sa; _
pwd=;database=Northwind;")
    cm = New SqlCommand()
    cm.Connection = cn
    cm.CommandText = "EXEC SalesByCategory 'Beverages'"

    ' ** Open connection
    Try
      cn.Open()
    Catch sx As SqlException
      Response.Write("Connection failed: " & sx.Message)
    End Try

  ' ** Execute command
  dr = cm.ExecuteReader()

  Do While dr.Read()
    Response.Write(dr.GetString(0) & " " & dr.GetDecimal(1) & "<BR>")
  Loop

  cn.Close()

  End Sub

</SCRIPT>
```

It's important to note here that an EXEC call is technically a text command that calls a stored procedure, rather than a "pure" stored procedure call (as in the previous code example). Because an EXEC call is a text command, we get rid of the line of code that specifies that the command is a stored procedure by setting the CommandType property of the command object.

Also, when using EXEC to call a stored procedure, parameters must be passed in the order they're declared in the stored procedure itself (a potential deal-killer if you don't have access to the stored procedure source code). Also, make sure to delimit non-numeric values (including date/time values) with single quotes; numeric values don't need to be delimited.

Executing Commands That Do Not Return Data

ADO.NET command objects have a special method for calling commands that do not retrieve data. This is an ADO.NET concept that does not specifically exist in ADO.old; it presumably exists for performance reasons, because a procedure that does not return data can be managed slightly more economically than one that does.

Examples of commands that don't return data include most data manipulation commands (including inserting, deleting, and updating records) as well as certain types of administrative commands in SQL Server.

You call a stored procedure that does not return data using the ExecuteNonQuery method of the connection object. Listing 12.8 shows an example of this.

LISTING 12.8   Executing a Nonquery Command

```
<% @Page language='vb' debug='true' %>
<% @Import namespace='System.Data' %>
<% @Import namespace='System.Data.SqlClient' %>

<SCRIPT runat='server'>

  Sub Page_Load(Sender As Object, e As EventArgs)
    Dim cn As SqlConnection
    Dim cm As SqlCommand
    Dim dr As SqlDataReader
    Dim strSQL As String

    cn = New SqlConnection("server=localhost;uid=sa;pwd=;database=pubs;")
    strSQL = "INSERT INTO authors " & _
             "(au_id, au_fname, au_lname, contract) " & _
             "VALUES ('123-45-6789', 'Chris', 'Kinsman', 0)"
    cm = New SqlCommand(strSQL, cn)

    ' ** Open connection
    Try
      cn.Open()
    Catch sx As SqlException
      Response.Write("Connection failed: " & sx.Message)
    End Try

    ' ** Execute command
    cm.ExecuteNonQuery()
    cn.Close()

  End Sub

</SCRIPT>
```

Note that executing this code will not display anything in the browser; you'll need to run a query against the Authors table to determine whether the insert actually worked. Later in this chapter, we'll construct a user interface that enables you to easily do this.

This code inserts a new author into the Authors table in the pubs database. It starts by constructing a SQL INSERT command, storing it in the string variable strSQL. This command contains the minimum amount of information required to insert a new author (the contract and au_id fields require non-null values). Aside from the syntax of the SQL command itself and the call to the ExecuteNonQuery method of the SqlCommand object, this code is nearly identical to the examples of commands we've demonstrated earlier in this chapter.

Executing Stored Procedures That Return Scalar Values

Most queries return resultsets, which are similar to arrays comprising one or more rows and one or more columns. In ADO.old these were called Recordsets; in ADO.NET, results typically are stored in an object such as a data reader or DataTable.

It is possible, however, to run a query that returns a single value. Such values are known as *scalars*, and they can be retrieved using the ExecuteScalar method of the ADO.NET command object.

As with the ExecuteNonQuery method discussed in the previous section, the idea behind ExecuteScalar is to give you additional options for executing commands that presumably perform better than returning the results in the form of a data reader or other object.

NOTE

You'll notice that when describing ADO.NET methods such as ExecuteNonQuery and ExecuteScalar, we use the word *presumably* a lot when describing their performance benefits. Doing a scientific performance analysis of the relative performance benefits of these various methods isn't our intention and isn't really within the scope of this book. At any rate, you'll want to examine the various methods for retrieving data in real-world scenarios before committing to a particular technique.

Listing 12.9 shows an example of using the ExecuteScalar method to retrieve a single value from the Northwind database.

LISTING 12.9 Using ExecuteScalar to Retrieve a Single Value from the Database

```
<% @Page language='vb' debug='true' %>
<% @Import namespace='System.Data' %>
<% @Import namespace='System.Data.SqlClient' %>

<SCRIPT runat='server'>
```

Listing 12.9 Continued

```
Sub Page_Load(Sender As Object, e As EventArgs)
   Dim cn As SqlConnection
   Dim cm As SqlCommand
   Dim dr As SqlDataReader
   Dim strSQL As String

   cn = New SqlConnection("server=localhost;uid=sa; _
pwd=;database=Northwind;")
   strSQL = "SELECT Count(CustomerID) FROM Customers"
   cm = New SqlCommand(strSQL, cn)

   ' ** Open connection
   Try
     cn.Open()
   Catch sx As SqlException
     Response.Write("Connection failed: " & sx.Message)
   End Try

   ' ** Execute command
   Response.Write("The number of customers is: " & cm.ExecuteScalar())

   cn.Close()

   End Sub

</SCRIPT>
```

This code prepares a SQL command that returns a single value and submits it to the server using the ExecuteScalar method of the SqlCommand object. The ExecuteScalar method returns whatever value was returned by the command.

Using Data Adapters to Retrieve and Manipulate Data

In database programming, it's common to retrieve data and then perform other actions on the data (such as inserting new data, updating existing data, and deleting data). Often an application will need to take different actions based on the results of one or more queries or stored procedure calls.

In ADO.old, this can be accomplished through the use of a cursor. A cursor-based approach is expensive, however, because it implies a persistent connection to the data source. ADO.old does support a batch-update model whereby the developer can retrieve data, perform updates, and then reconnect to the data source and commit the updates in one operation (known as a batch).

The .NET vision of scalable, disconnected data access demands a different approach, however. The .NET DataSet requires a sessionless, cursorless approach. To provide access to retrieving, inserting, updating, and deleting records in a single object without the use of cursors or persistent connections, ADO.NET provides the *data adapter* object.

Data adapters

- Are similar to command objects, except they can contain four separate commands (one each for select, insert, update, and delete).
- Can be used to create always disconnected DataSet objects. DataSets can be serialized as XML and bound to Web Forms controls.
- Decouple data-manipulation code from the data itself, making the data easier to remote and the data manipulation code easier to maintain and reuse.

NOTE

In Beta 1, data adapters were called DataSetCommand objects. The term *data adapter* was adopted to avoid confusion between the DataSet (which contains the data) and the object that produces the data set. Additionally, the term *DataSetCommand* implied that the data adapter's sole purpose is to create a DataSet object, which isn't strictly the case.

Each ADO.NET provider has its own data adapter object. In the SQL Server provider, the data adapter is named SqlDataAdapter; not surprisingly, in the OLE DB provider, the data adapter class is called OleDbAdapter.

The implementation details of the data adapter may vary slightly from one provider to the next, but the basic purpose of the data adapter is the same across all providers: Data adapters provide a connectionless method to engage in rich interaction with data sources. By rich interaction, we are talking about operations that go beyond the simple requests and display of data. If all you need to do is retrieve data and display it, you shouldn't be using a data adapter; use a data reader instead. Data readers are described in the "About the DataReader Object" section of this chapter.

Although each ADO.NET provider has its own data adapter, DataSet objects created by different adapters are the same; DataSets are totally interoperable across providers. This is an important aspect of ADO.NET's interoperability story; it provides a standard way to express relational or hierarchical data that can be manipulated in any language, on any platform.

The ultimate objective of a Web database application is to present data to the user and permit users to manipulate data in interesting ways in the browser. The next few sections will introduce data adapters and demonstrate the various things you can do with them in ASP.NET applications. To demonstrate the power and flexibility of the data adapter, we'll first need to take a detour and discuss the principles of building a database-driven user interface in ASP.NET.

Displaying Query Data in the Browser

Earlier code listings in this chapter gave several examples of displaying data in a Web browser using calls to Response.Write. This is basically the same way you send output data to the browser in ASP.old. However, with ADO.NET and ASP.NET Web Forms controls, you have new options that provide better structure and maintainability, as well as more powerful features.

One of these features is browser-based *data binding*. Data binding refers to the process of automatically mapping the fields in a database to the user interface. Performing data binding automatically is handy because it relieves the developer from having to write a large amount of tedious code associated with retrieving and displaying data.

The concept of data binding got a bad rap among Visual Basic developers for a number of valid reasons. Data binding promised the capability to create a rich database user interface with a minimum of coding. Simplicity was the objective.

But this simplicity came at a price. Thick-client data-bound applications typically ran slowly, consumed a persistent database connection resource whether or not they were doing any work, and were difficult for programmers to code against because much of the underlying data-access functionality was encapsulated in the form of an object (the Data control) that exposed a painfully limited set of properties, methods, and events associated with data operations. If you were interested in building a certain type of data browser application and performance wasn't an issue, data binding worked well. But if you needed to build anything more sophisticated than a simple data browser, binding to a Data control was problematic at best.

Data binding in ASP.NET is different from the data-control-centric, connection-based vision of thick-client VB.old. First, because it's based on the inherently disconnected DataSet object, data binding in ASP.NET does not consume a persistent connection to the database server. Next, the problems involving a "no-code" solution aren't a problem in ASP.NET, because ASP.NET data binding doesn't use black-box abstractions like the VB.old Data control.

The next few sections discuss the objects and techniques involved in data binding in ASP.NET and give you some examples describing how to put data binding to work in your applications.

Creating a DataSet Object Using a Data Adapter

You can use a DataSet in conjunction with a data adapter object to retrieve data from a database in a manner similar to the DataReader example in Listing 12.4. Although you might not use this code to display data in this way in a real application, dumping the contents of a query into a DataSet and then into the browser is a useful stepping stone on the way to data binding with Web Forms controls (which we'll discuss next).

Listing 12.10 shows a very simple example of a database select query using the SqlDataAdapter and a DataSet object.

LISTING 12.10   Using the SqlDataAdapter and the DataSet Object to Display Query Results

```vb
<% @Page language='vb' debug='true' %>
<% @Import namespace='System.Data' %>
<% @Import namespace='System.Data.SqlClient' %>

<SCRIPT runat='server'>

  Sub Page_Load(Sender As Object, e As EventArgs)
    Dim cn As SqlConnection
    Dim da As SqlDataAdapter
    Dim ds As DataSet
    Dim strSQL As String

    strSQL = "SELECT TOP 10 au_fname, au_lname FROM authors"
    cn = New SqlConnection("server=localhost;uid=sa;pwd=;database=pubs;")
    da = New SqlDataAdapter(strSQL, cn)

    ' ** Open connection
    Try
      cn.Open()
    Catch sx As SqlException
      Response.Write("Connection failed: " & sx.Message)
    End Try

    ' ** Fill DataSet
    ds = New DataSet()
    da.Fill(ds, "Authors")

    ' ** Display data
    Dim Author As DataRow
    For Each Author In ds.Tables("Authors").Rows
      Response.Write(Author("au_fname").ToString() & " " & _
```

LISTING 12.10   Continued

```
                                 Author("au_lname").ToString() & "<BR>")
        Next

        cn.Close()

    End Sub

</SCRIPT>
```

You can see in this example, the SqlDataAdapter object is created from a SqlConnection object; this is similar to the way we created the basic SqlConnection object earlier. To build a DataSet object from the SqlDataAdapter object, we declare and instantiate the DataSet and then pass the DataSet to the Fill method of the SqlDataAdapter. (The second parameter passed to the Fill method gives the resultset a name.)

Executing the fill method executes the SELECT query; at this point, we can start accessing the data through the Rows collection contained by the (one and only) table contained by the DataSet.

This example is similar to some of the data reader examples from earlier in this chapter, but with more complexity and more code. Fear not; this is just the first example and doesn't scratch the surface of what the DataSet can accomplish.

One of the big differences you can see between the behavior of the DataSet and the data reader object is that the DataSet has a Tables collection that contains DataTable objects. The capability to contain multiple tables in a single object (potentially containing relationships defined by one or more DataRelation objects) is one of the defining characteristics of the DataSet objects. We'll take a look at the power of multiple tables in a single DataSet in Listing 12.14.

For now, it might be worthwhile to look at more efficient and structured ways to display data on the page. Outputting HTML to the browser using a loop containing calls to Response.Write works fine, but if you're interested in doing anything more complicated than displaying row-by-row data with line breaks, you will want a more powerful display technique. Fortunately, ASP.NET provides this in the form of data-bound Web Forms controls, which we'll discuss in the next section.

Binding a DataView Object to Web Forms Controls

You can display data in an ASP.NET Web Forms page by using data binding. To use data binding, you begin by executing a select command with a data adapter. This produces a DataSet object that contains a collection of DataTable objects; each DataTable contains a DataView object that can be connected to any Web Forms control capable of binding to data (including many HTML server controls).

To perform the actual data binding after the DataSet is created, you first set the Web Forms control's DataSource property to a DataView object contained by the DataSet, and then use the DataBind method of the ASP.NET Page object to initiate binding. This method, typically called in the Page object's Load event, serves to connect the user interface control(s) on the page with the DataSet object(s) you've created.

Listing 12.11 takes the code from the previous example and amends it to display its output in a Web Forms DataGrid control.

LISTING 12.11   Displaying Query Data in a Web Forms DataGrid Control

```vb
<% @Page language='vb' debug='true' %>
<% @Import namespace='System.Data' %>
<% @Import namespace='System.Data.SqlClient' %>

<HTML>
<SCRIPT runat='server'>

  Sub Page_Load(Sender As Object, e As EventArgs)
    Dim cn As SqlConnection
    Dim da As SqlDataAdapter
    Dim ds As DataSet
    Dim strSQL As String

    strSQL = "SELECT TOP 10 au_fname, au_lname FROM authors"
    cn = New SqlConnection("server=localhost;uid=sa; _
pwd=;database=pubs;")
    da = New SqlDataAdapter(strSQL, cn)

    ' ** Open connection
    Try
      cn.Open()
    Catch sx As SqlException
      Response.Write("Connection failed: " & sx.Message)
    End Try

    ' ** Fill DataSet
    ds = New DataSet()
    da.Fill(ds, "Authors")

    ' ** Display data
    With DataGrid1
      .DataSource = ds.Tables("Authors").DefaultView
      .DataBind()
    End With
```

Listing 12.11   Continued

```
   cn.Close()

 End Sub

</SCRIPT>

<BODY>

  <ASP:datagrid id='DataGrid1' runat='server' />

</BODY>
</HTML>
```

Nothing is really new here except for the changes in the "display data" section of the code. This time we simply assign the DefaultView property (a DataView object) of the Authors table (a DataTable object) to the DataSource property of the DataGrid control, which we named DataGrid1. You should be able to see that the ASP:datagrid definition in the HTML section of the code doesn't specify any property settings for the DataGrid control other than its ID, so all the defaults are in place. The result is a plain vanilla HTML table, outputted to the browser.

Binding Other Objects to Web Forms Controls

Web Forms controls can be bound to any object that implements the System.Collections.IEnumerable or System.Collections.ICollection interfaces. The DataView object supports the IEnumerable interface, which is why it can be bound to ASP.NET server controls. You can also build your own .NET classes that implement one of these interfaces if you're interested in binding custom classes to ASP.NET Web Forms controls.

Creating your own classes for data binding is beyond the scope of this book, but it is pretty easy to see how an existing class can be bound to an ASP.NET control. The ArrayList class (found in System.Collections) is a perfect candidate to use as a guinea pig to see how this works; ArrayList is simple to work with and implements both IEnumerable and ICollection.

Listing 12.12 shows an example of how to bind a DataGrid control to an ArrayList object.

Listing 12.12   Binding a DataGrid Control to an ArrayList Object

```
<% @Page language='vb' debug='true' %>
<% @Import namespace='System.Collections' %>

<HTML>
<SCRIPT runat='server'>
```

LISTING 12.12   Continued

```
Sub Page_Load(Sender As Object, e As EventArgs)
   Dim al As New ArrayList()
   al.Add("Alaska")
   al.Add("Alabama")
   al.Add("California")
   al.Add("Kentucky")

   ' ** Display data
   With DataGrid1
      .Datasource = al
      .DataBind()
   End With

   End Sub

</SCRIPT>

<BODY>

   <ASP:datagrid id='DataGrid1' runat='server' />

</BODY>
</HTML>
```

The technique to bind the DataGrid control shown here is the same as the methods shown earlier in the chapter to bind to relational data; as far as the DataGrid control is concerned, no difference exists between different types of bindable objects. As long as the object supports IEnumerable or ICollection, it can be displayed through binding.

Note that data readers (the SqlDataReader and OleDbDataReader classes) support the IEnumerable interface and can therefore be bound to Web Forms controls as well.

Expressing a DataSet as XML

One of the advantages of retrieving data with a DataSet is that a DataSet can be accessed at t he object level (through the collection of DataTable and DataRow objects contained by the DataSet) or on a raw XML level. The capability to process a DataSet as XML means that you can easily transfer a DataSet to other platforms that don't explicitly support Microsoft.NET or work with the DataSet with XML tools (whether or not they're explicitly built to support .NET).

You can use the GetXml method of the DataSet object to extract XML data from the result of a query. By setting the ContentType Page directive to text/xml, it's possible to see the XML output directly in the browser window.

As with many Web-based XML examples, Listing 12.13 works best when you use Internet Explorer 5.0 or later; Internet Explorer has support for parsing and displaying XML directly in the browser window.

Listing 12.13 shows an example of outputting a query in XML format to the browser window using this technique.

LISTING 12.13   Sending Query Results to the Browser Window Using XML

```
<% @Page ContentType='text/xml' language='vb' debug='true' %>
<% @Import namespace='System.Data' %>
<% @Import namespace='System.Data.SqlClient' %>

<SCRIPT runat='server'>

  Sub Page_Load(Sender As Object, e As EventArgs)
    Dim cn As SqlConnection
    Dim da As SqlDataAdapter
    Dim ds As DataSet
    Dim strSQL As String

    strSQL = "SELECT TOP 10 au_fname, au_lname FROM authors"
    cn = New SqlConnection("server=localhost;uid=sa;pwd=;database=pubs;")
    da = New SqlDataAdapter(strSQL, cn)

    ' ** Open connection
    Try
      cn.Open()
    Catch sx As SqlException
      Response.Write("Connection failed: " & sx.Message)
      Exit Sub
    End Try

    ' ** Fill DataSet
    ds = New DataSet()
    da.Fill(ds, "Authors")

    ' ** Display data
    Response.Write(ds.GetXml())

    cn.Close()

  End Sub

</SCRIPT>
```

Instead of simply dumping XML to the browser window, you can also assign the XML output of a DataSet object to one of the XML-manipulating objects in the .NET framework. To do this, you pass an XmlDataReader object to the ReadXml method of the DataSet object. You can then manipulate the XmlDataReader object as you would any other XML document, including sending it to a file or passing it to another process.

> **NOTE**
>
> The XmlDataReader object is one of the objects that the .NET framework provides for reading XML. For more information on how the XmlDataReader works, see Chapter 11, "Using XML."

Implementing Strongly Typed Data Objects Using Inheritance

One of ADO.NET's much-vaunted features is support for *strongly typed* DataSets. With strong typing, the field data is always returned and handled in its native data format (such as a string or integer), in contrast to a Variant (in VB6 and VBScript) or a generic object type.

Strong typing is a good thing because it reduces the amount of overhead imposed by more generic data types such as Variant. Strong typing also moves your code away from the cumbersome coding syntax imposed by ADO.old. In ADO.old (as well as the precursor data object models DAO and RDO), you typically retrieved data in the form of a Recordset object that contains a Fields collection. The Fields collection is a set of key/value pairs that enables you to retrieve a value from the recordset by specifying a field name as a key into the collection, like this:

```
rs.Fields("FirstName").Value = "Steve"
```

The key (in this example, "FirstName") isn't known by the code until runtime. Its data type is never known; ADO.old always returns field values as Variants. This causes a couple of problems. First, a performance overhead is associated with Variants; it's always more expensive to pass weakly typed variables around.

More frustrating, though, is remembering the names of database fields. When you're writing code to retrieve a value out of a keyed collection whose membership is not determined until runtime, you, the programmer, get no help. It's easy to forget or misspell the names of members in a collection. In the case of the ADO.old Recordset object, programmers frequently find themselves digging up the database schema as a reference. If the names of fields in the recordset don't match the code (possibly as a result of field aliasing in a view, or perhaps because the schema representation itself doesn't correspond to reality for some reason), your code breaks.

With a strongly typed DataSet, on the other hand, you can use syntax that looks like this:

```
ds.FirstName = "Steve"
```

The code syntax here is cleaner and supports IntelliSense in development environments such as Visual Studio .NET. This means that you can refer to the members of a DataSet object without having to manually look up the table's schema each time you need to refer to its fields. This is syntactically much tidier than the way ADO.old exposed members of recordsets.

Strongly typed DataSets aren't technically a feature of ADO.NET at all. They're really a feature of inheritance in Microsoft.NET. You can use Visual Studio .NET's code-generation capabilities to build a child class that inherits from System.Data.DataSet, but it's easy enough to hand code your own. It's a good exercise, at any rate, so we'll take a stab at it in the next example.

Begin by defining a class to define the properties of the Author object. Ordinarily we'd use behind-the-scene code or a separately compiled component to do this for maintainability and reusability purposes, but for this example, we'll define it in the ASP.NET page along with our data presentation. The code to do this is shown in Listing 12.14.

LISTING 12.14   A Class That Inherits from DataSet and Provides Property Accessors

```
<SCRIPT runat='server'>
  Class Author
    Inherits DataSet

    Public Property ID() As String
      Get
        Return Me.Tables(0).Rows(0)("au_id").ToString()
      End Get

      Set
        Me.Tables(0).Rows(0)("au_id").ToString()
      End Set
    End Property

    Public Property FirstName() As String
      Get
        Return Me.Tables(0).Rows(0)("au_fname").ToString()
      End Get

      Set
        Me.Tables(0).Rows(0)("au_fname").ToString()
      End Set
    End Property
```

LISTING 12.14   Continued

```
Public Property LastName() As String
  Get
    Return Me.Tables(0).Rows(0)("au_lname").ToString()
  End Get

  Set
    Me.Tables(0).Rows(0)("au_lname").ToString()
  End Set
End Property

End Class
```

You can see that this is a pretty straightforward class. It assumes that the class has been initialized (it generates an error if a property is accessed before the database is queried). In addition to retrieving properties, the class also enables you to assign an ID, a first name, and a last name to the Author object. There's no facility for saving data after it's been written to the properties; if needed, you could write this code using the patterns we've discussed earlier in this chapter.

Listing 12.15 shows the remainder of the code in this page. This is the code that initializes and outputs data using the class.

LISTING 12.15   Initializing and Displaying Data from the Class

```
Sub Page_Load(Sender As Object, e As EventArgs)
  Dim cn As SqlConnection
  Dim da As SqlDataAdapter
  Dim au As New Author
  Dim strSQL As String

  strSQL = "SELECT au_id, au_fname, au_lname " & _
"FROM authors WHERE au_id = '427-17-2319'"
  cn = New SqlConnection("server=localhost;uid=sa;pwd=;database=pubs;")
  da = New SqlDataAdapter(strSQL, cn)

  ' ** Open connection
  Try
    cn.Open()
  Catch sx As SqlException
    Response.Write("Connection failed: " & sx.Message)
  End Try

  ' ** Fill DataSet
  da.Fill(au, "Authors")
```

LISTING 12.15 Continued

```
' ** Display data
With DataGrid1
  .Datasource = au.Tables("Authors").DefaultView
  .DataBind()
End With

  ' ** Now demonstrate the might of the inherited DataSet
  Label1.Text = "The ID of this author is " & au.ID & _
" and the last name is " & au.LastName

  cn.Close()

End Sub


</SCRIPT>
```

This code performs the same initialization as the previous examples that use the DataSet object by itself. The important difference is the line of code near the end; instead of extracting fields from the DataSet object in the form au.Fields("au_id"), you can simply use au.ID. This is much easier and clearer and provides better performance.

A name describes the process of translating relational data into data that maps cleanly to a paradigm involving objects, properties and methods—it's called *object-relational mapping*. As you evaluate the best way to perform object-relational mapping, bear in mind that many ways exist to do it, and different methods will work better in some situations than in others.

Some object programming purists scratched their heads when they first saw the inheritance-based method of object-relational mapping in .NET; they argued that it broke the object-oriented principle of encapsulation by allowing programmers to access the DataSet object that the business object inherits. For example, in this model, nothing keeps you from doing an end-run around the property accessor and assigning a bogus value to au: Tables(0).Rows(0)("au_id") instead of au.ID. This may not seem like a big deal (it may seem like a benefit at first blush), but if the property accessor contains validation logic that must not be circumvented, it can cause serious problems.

In COM programming prior to .NET, it was common to use a different object programming tactic known as *containment* to perform object-relational mapping. In containment, you have better encapsulation because the data (possibly contained in the form of a recordset, DataSet object, or XML document) is private. Because the data can't be accessed directly by the programmer, there's less chance of the programmer doing something unexpected or inconsistent with the data.

There's no reason why you can't implement a containment model for object-relational mapping in .NET. In fact, in many ways, the design is simpler than an inherited model. Listing 12.16 shows an example of this.

LISTING 12.16   Example of Containment-Based Object-Relational Mapping

```
<%@ PAGE language='VB' debug='true' trace='false' %>
<% @IMPORT namespace='System.Data' %>
<% @IMPORT namespace='System.Data.SqlClient' %>

<HTML>
<HEAD>
<TITLE>
ASP.NET Page
</TITLE>
</HEAD>

<SCRIPT runat='server'>
  Public Class Author
    Private cn As SqlConnection
    Private da As SqlDataAdapter
    Private ds As DataSet
    Public ConnectionString As String

    ' *** TODO: Uncomment constructors
    Public Sub New()
      ' ** Default constructor; do nothing
    End Sub

    Public Sub New(strConnect As String, ID As String)
      Dim strSQL As String
      cn = New SqlConnection(strConnect)
      ds = New DataSet()
      strSQL = "SELECT au_id, au_fname, au_lname " & _
"FROM authors WHERE au_id = '" & ID & "'"
      da = New SqlDataAdapter(strSQL, cn)

      ' ** Open connection
      Try
        cn.Open()
      Catch sx As SqlException
        ' ** TODO: Return exception to calling function
      End Try
```

LISTING 12.16 Continued

```
    ' ** Fill DataSet
    da.Fill(ds, "Authors")
    cn.Close()

End Sub

Public Property ID() As String
  Get
    Return ds.Tables(0).Rows(0)("au_id").ToString()
  End Get

  Set
    ds.Tables(0).Rows(0)("au_id").ToString()
  End Set
End Property

Public Property FirstName() As String
  Get
    Return ds.Tables(0).Rows(0)("au_fname").ToString()
  End Get

  Set
    ds.Tables(0).Rows(0)("au_fname").ToString()
  End Set
End Property

Public Property LastName() As String
  Get
    Return ds.Tables(0).Rows(0)("au_lname").ToString()
  End Get

  Set
    ds.Tables(0).Rows(0)("au_lname").ToString()
  End Set
End Property

End Class

Sub Page_Load(Sender As Object, e As EventArgs)
  Dim strCn = "server=localhost;uid=sa;pwd=;database=pubs;"
  Dim au As New Author(strCn, Request.QueryString("ID"))

  Label1.Text = "The first name of this author is " & _
               au.FirstName & _
               " and the last name is " & au.LastName
```

LISTING 12.16   Continued

```
  End Sub

</SCRIPT>

<BODY>

  <ASP:label id='Label1' runat='server' />

</BODY>
</HTML>
```

This page requires a query string as a parameter. To test it, you'll need to include the query string parameter in the browser URL when you navigate to it. A query string parameter that should work (based on data that exists in the default pubs database) is

```
http://localhost/contain.aspx?ID=722-51-5454
```

(This assumes that you have placed the file contain.aspx in the root directory on the local machine. If not, you'll need to adjust the URL accordingly.)

A number of interesting differences exist between this example and the previous, inheritance-based code. In this example, the Author class doesn't inherit from the DataSet class; instead, the Author class contains a private instance of a DataSet object that is created at the time an Author object is instantiated. Because this DataSet is private, its properties and methods aren't exposed by the Author class. This provides a higher level of data protection for the members of the class. But in doing this, we lose an important feature—the capability to configure the DataSet's connection to the database. If you can't assign a connection string, populating the object with data will be tricky, to say the least.

The containment-based version of Author solves this problem by using a constructor. (This is implemented in VB .NET classes through the use of the New subroutine.) Using constructors makes it easy for developers to create and initialize objects in one fell swoop; it's a common tactic in object-relational mapping.

If for some reason, supplying the connection string in the constructor isn't sufficient—perhaps the object needs to retrieve data from one data source or another based on information that isn't available at the time it is created, for example—you could supply a ConnectionString property in the Author object. This gives you, the developer, the capability to assign whatever connection string she wants on an ad-hoc basis.

The moral of the story is, just because you *can* use inheritance in .NET doesn't mean that you have to. Ultimately, in the real world you'll likely see a combination of containment and inheritance in your .NET object designs. You should understand and recognize both patterns in code and have a sense as to why you'd use one or the other in the data-driven applications you create.

Creating Web Forms for Data Entry

Now that you have a sense of how to retrieve and manipulate data using ADO.NET, you'll need to have a strategy for building user interfaces in ASP.NET to access database functionality.

Like other Web-programming paradigms, the process of inserting or updating data through a Web browser typically involves constructing an HTML form that contains an array of input controls. The user inserts or changes values in the controls on the form and then submits the form to the Web server. The server passes the form contents to a script that then forms the actual data operation.

Listing 12.17 shows a simple example of an ASP.NET page that facilitates data entry.

Listing 12.17   Simple Data-Entry Form

```
<% @Page language='vb' debug='true' trace='false' %>
<% @Import namespace='System.Data' %>
<% @Import namespace='System.Data.SqlClient' %>

<SCRIPT runat='server'>
  Sub Page_Load(Sender As Object, e As EventArgs)
    If Page.IsPostBack Then
      Dim cn As SqlConnection
      Dim cm As SqlCommand
      Dim strSQL As String

      cn = New SqlConnection("server=localhost;uid=sa;pwd=;database=pubs;")
      strSQL = "INSERT INTO authors " & _
               "(au_id, au_fname, au_lname, contract) " & _
               "VALUES ('" & txtID.Text & "', '" & _
               txtFirstName.Text & "', '" & _
               txtLastName.Text & "', '" & _
               ChkToInt(chkContract) & "')"
      cm = New SqlCommand(strSQL, cn)

      ' ** Open connection
      Try
        cn.Open()
      Catch sx As SqlException
        Response.Write("Connection failed: " & sx.Message)
      End Try

      ' ** Execute command
      Trace.Write("Command: " & cm.CommandText)
      cm.ExecuteNonQuery()
      cn.Close()
```

LISTING 12.17   Continued

```
      ' ** Clear form for next item
      txtID.Text = ""
      txtFirstName.Text = ""
      txtLastName.Text = ""
      chkContract.Checked = False
    End If
  End Sub

  Function ChkToInt(chk As CheckBox)
    If chk.Checked Then
      Return 1
    Else
      Return 0
    End If
  End Function

</SCRIPT>

<html>
<head>
<title>ASP.NET Data Entry</title>
</head>

<body bgcolor="#FFFFFF" text="#000000">
<FORM runat='server'>
  <table width="300" border="0">
    <tr>
      <td>ID: </td>
      <td>
        <asp:textbox id="txtID" runat='server' />
      </td>
    </tr>
    <tr>
      <td>First Name: </td>
      <td>
        <asp:textbox id="txtFirstName" runat='server' />
      </td>
    </tr>
    <tr>
      <td>Last Name:</td>
      <td>
        <asp:textbox id="txtLastName" runat='server' />
      </td>
    </tr>
    <tr>
      <td>Contract:</td>
```

LISTING 12.17 Continued

```
      <td>
        <asp:checkbox id="chkContract" runat='server' />
      </td>
    </tr>
  </table>
  <p>
    <asp:button id="btnSave" text="Save" runat='server' />
  </p>
</FORM>
</body>
</html>
```

This page takes the code used to perform a nonquery command (introduced earlier in this chapter) and attaches a simple user interface to it. Although it is minimal, the pattern set by this example, in Listing 12.8, forms the basis of a great deal of Web-based data entry forms in ASP.NET.

The Page_Load event procedure performs the work involved in inserting the data into the database. Note that the data is sent to the database only if the IsPostBack property of the Page object is true. There's no point sending data to the database unless there's something to send. Note, too, that we explicitly cleared the contents of the controls on the form after inserting the data (this circumvents ASP.NET's default view state behavior).

The only other tricky thing on this page is the ChkToInt function. This function takes the Checked value returned by the CheckBox control and converts it into the 1 or 0 value required by SQL Server.

Two problems occur with this page—both related to validation. If the user enters an author with the same ID as an existing author, she will get an error. You can get around this problem by catching the SqlException that is thrown when the ExecuteNonQuery method is reached.

The next problem is less straightforward: how to ensure that the user actually enters valid data for the ID, first name, and last name fields. It happens that ASP.NET provides some powerful and flexible components for dealing with this problem. We'll cover them in the next section.

Performing Validation

Every software application should have code that ensures that data entered by users is valid. Web applications are no different.

In ASP.old, developers typically embedded validation logic in pages that also contained display logic; separating validation logic from presentation logic was tricky, but it was possible. If you were interested in performing a simple validation, such as making sure that a given text box contains a value between 1 and 10, the template-based design of ASP.old practically forced you to embed that validation code on the same page.

Incorporating client-side validation adds a new level of complexity to this problem. Because client-side validation is commonly done using JavaScript (for cross-browser compatibility), this forced you to embed code written in two very different languages in a single page. Madness!

ASP.NET solves this problem by creating language-neutral objects for performing validation. These come in the form of Web Forms server controls—validation objects that accept generic rules pertaining to the most common types of data validation. These objects are tightly integrated with the Page object so that when a Web form is submitted to the server, the validation object can communicate to the Page object that the field it validates has not passed the validation rule.

ASP.NET provides six validation objects:

- The `RequiredFieldValidator` control
- The `CompareValidator` control
- The `RangeValidator` control
- The `RegularExpressionValidator` control
- The `ValidationSummary` control
- The `CustomValidator` control

To perform validation, you create the Web form as you normally would and then attach validation controls to the input controls in the form. This is done by setting the validation control's ControlToValidate property. You can also validate a control against a variable or constant value instead by setting the validation's ValueToCompare property. You then assign validation parameters where appropriate. (Some validation controls, such as `RequiredFieldValidator`, don't need extra validation parameters.)

When the page is submitted to the server, the validation rule contained by the validation control is applied. Validation controls are invisible until their validation rules are violated; if the validation rule fails, an optional error message is displayed. Your code must provide a way to deal with the situation where a validation rule is violated. You can programmatically inspect the IsValid property of the Page object to quickly determine whether one or more validation controls were violated. For complex pages with many validation controls, you can also provide a list of all validation violations on the page; in fact, ASP.NET provides a special object (the `ValidationSummary` control) to perform this function.

Eight controls that can be associated with validation controls, shown next, ship with ASP.NET.

HTML controls:

- `HtmlInputText`
- `HtmlTextArea`
- `HtmlSelect`
- `HtmlInputFile`

Server controls:

- `TextBox`
- `ListBox`
- `DropDownList`
- `RadioButtonList`

To keep the examples simple, in this section we'll perform validation against the TextBox server control exclusively. Also, to make these examples more brief and easier to understand, we won't bother including the actual data access code in the validation examples here; we'll assume that you'll include code similar to that described earlier in this chapter to perform the actual database operation required to get your data into the database.

Validation controls work by generating DHTML and JavaScript for browsers that support them, and performing round trips to the server for browsers that do not. This greatly increases the efficiency of validation, ensuring that forms that contain bad data aren't sent across the network. The best part of this feature is that you don't have to learn JavaScript to make this client-side validation happen; validation controls can emit the appropriate JavaScript code automatically.

The next few sections describe how to use each validation control in more detail.

Validating for Required Fields

Required field validation forces the user to enter a value in the validated control. It's one of the easiest validators to implement because it doesn't require a separate property assignment to determine what the validation rule is. If a `RequiredFieldValidator` is attached to a control, the field is required and the page isn't valid unless the user puts something in the field.

Listing 12.18 shows an example of the `RequiredFieldValidator` control in action.

LISTING 12.18   Requiring a Field Using the `RequiredFieldValidator` Control

```
<HTML>
<HEAD>
<SCRIPT language="VB" runat="server">
```

LISTING 12.18 Continued

```
Sub SaveBtn_Click(Sender As Object, e As EventArgs)
    If Page.IsValid Then
        lblOutput.Text = "Record saved."
    Else
        lblOutput.Text = ""
    End If
End Sub
</SCRIPT>
</HEAD>

<BODY>
<FORM runat="server">

<asp:textbox id=TextBox1 runat=server />

        <asp:RequiredFieldValidator id="RequiredFieldValidator2"
            ControlToValidate="TextBox1"
            Display="Static"
            Width="100%" runat=server>
            Please enter your name.
        </asp:RequiredFieldValidator>

        <asp:Button id=Button1 text="Save" OnClick="SaveBtn_Click" runat=server
/>
        <asp:label id='lblOutput' runat='server' />
</FORM>
</BODY>
</HTML>
```

As you can see from the code, this mode of validation is pretty straightforward—just specify the control you want to validate in the RequiredFieldValidator's ControlToValidate property, and then check to see if the page is valid in an event procedure attached to a control that submits the form (in this case, the button called Button1).

One of the main objectives of client validation is to catch bad input before your application performs expensive trips across the network. This example demonstrates how ASP.NET handles this; if you enter bad data, the page will not be submitted to the server.

You might find it useful to see how this validation is performed "under the hood" of the browser. To see the client code generated by the validation control, navigate to this page and create a validation error by clicking the button without typing anything into the text field. Watch the browser as the error is generated; you should notice that no progress bar is at the bottom of the window to indicate a jump across the network, and the page displays the error message instantly, without having to reload.

Next, use the View Source command to take a look at the HTML code generated by the ASP.NET page. As you scroll through the code, you should be able to see a reference to a JavaScript file called WebUIValidation.js. This file resides on the server (in a directory called \aspnet_client under the IIS root directory) but is downloaded and executed on the client side when a validation control is present in a Web form. The JavaScript function named RequiredFieldValidatorEvaluateIsValid is called when you use a `RequiredFieldValidator` control (analogous functions exist for the other types of validators). By viewing the script file WebUIValidation.js, you can see how they work. The one for required field validation is monumentally trivial—it's listed in Listing 12.19.

LISTING 12.19   Client-Side Validation for Required Field Function

```
function RequiredFieldValidatorEvaluateIsValid(val) {
    return (ValidatorTrim(ValidatorGetValue(val.controltovalidate)) !=
_ValidatorTrim(val.initialvalue))
}
```

This function uses a lot of verbiage to accomplish a simple task—figuring out whether a value is there. If it's there, the function returns `true`; if not, it returns `false`. Of course, this isn't so complicated that you couldn't have written it yourself, but it's nice that this kind of code is abstracted behind the validator control so that you don't have to think in two languages just to perform simple validation.

Comparison Validation Using the `CompareValidator` Control

Comparison validation examines the value of a control and compares it against the value of another control's property, a variable, or a constant. To use `CompareValidator`, you must specify three things: the control to validate, the control (or value) to compare it to, and an operator (one of the equality or inequality types).

As an example of this, suppose you're building a Web form that gives your employees pay raises. The important validation rule with a pay raise calculation is: don't accidentally give your employees a pay cut! You can use a `CompareValidator` control with the greater-than operator to ensure that this is the case. Listing 12.20 shows an example.

LISTING 12.20   Performing Comparison Validation in a Data Entry Form

```
<HTML>
<HEAD>
<TITLE>
Pay Raise Calculator
</TITLE>
<SCRIPT language="VB" runat="server">
```

LISTING 12.20 Continued

```
    Sub SaveBtn_Click(Sender As Object, e As EventArgs)
        If Page.IsValid Then
            lblOutput.Text = "The new pay rate is: " & txtNewRate.Text
        Else
            lblOutput.Text = ""
        End If
    End Sub

</SCRIPT>
</HEAD>

<BODY>
<FORM runat="server">

Current Rate:<asp:textbox id=txtOldRate text='3000' runat=server /><BR>
New Rate:<asp:textbox id=txtNewRate runat=server />
<asp:Button id=Button1 text="Save" OnClick="SaveBtn_Click" runat=server /><BR>

    <asp:CompareValidator id="CompareValidator1"
        ControlToValidate="txtNewRate"
        ControlToCompare="txtOldRate"
        Type="Double"
        Operator="GreaterThan"
        runat="server">
    You eeeediot! Do not give your employees a pay cut!
    </asp:CompareValidator>

<asp:label id='lblOutput' runat='server' />
</FORM>
</BODY>
</HTML>
```

To understand the relationship between `ControlToValidate`, `ControlToCompare`, and `Operator`, think of the three properties as elements of an expression that looks like this:

`ControlToCompare    Operator    ControlToValidate`

Hence, if `ControlToCompare` is 3000, `ControlToValidate` is 3500, and `Operator` is `"GreaterThan"`, the expression is `true` and the page is valid. If `ControlToValidate` is 0, for example, the expression becomes `false` and the validation fails.

The legal values for the `Operator` property for controls that use them are enumerated in System.Web.UI.WebControls.ValidationCompareOperator and are listed in Table 12.3.

TABLE 12.3 Members of the `ValidationCompareOperator` Enumeration Used in Comparison Validation

Member	Description
DataTypeCheck	Returns true if the two values are the same data type
Equal	Returns true if the two values are equal
GreaterThan	Returns true if `ControlToValidate` is greater than `ControlToCompare`
GreaterThanEqual	Returns true if `ControlToValidate` is greater than or equal to `ControlToCompare`
LessThan	Returns true if `ControlToValidate` is less than `ControlToCompare`
LessThanEqual	Returns true if `ControlToValidate` is less than or equal to `ControlToCompare`
NotEqual	Returns true if the two controls are not equal

The broad range of operators gives you a great deal of flexibility; however, if you need a validation rule that goes beyond what any of the standard validation controls are capable of, you can always turn to the custom validation control, as seen in Listing 12.23.

Range Validation Using the `RangeValidator` Object

Range validation forces the data in a given control to fall within a given numeric range. You specify the numeric range using the control's MinimumValue and MaximumValue properties. As with the `CompareValidator` control, you can also specify a numeric data type on which to base the comparison (using the control's Type property).

Listing 12.21 shows an example of the `RangeValidator` object in action.

LISTING 12.21 Performing Range Validation

```
<HTML>
<HEAD>
<TITLE>
Pay Raise Calculator [Range]
</TITLE>
<SCRIPT language="VB" runat="server">

    Sub SaveBtn_Click(Sender As Object, e As EventArgs)
       If Page.IsValid Then
         lblOutput.Text = "The new pay rate is: " & txtNewRate.Text
       Else
         lblOutput.Text = ""
```

LISTING 12.21   Continued

```
        End If
    End Sub

</SCRIPT>
</HEAD>

<BODY>
<FORM runat="server">

Current Rate:<asp:textbox id=txtOldRate text='3000' runat=server /><BR>
New Rate:<asp:textbox id=txtNewRate runat=server />
<asp:Button id=Button1 text="Save" OnClick="SaveBtn_Click" runat=server /><BR>

    <asp:RangeValidator id="RangeValidator1"
        ControlToValidate="txtNewRate"
        MinimumValue='1000'
        MaximumValue='5000'
        Type="Double"
        runat="server">
    Please enter a value between 1000 and 5000.
    </asp:RangeValidator>


<asp:label id='lblOutput' runat='server' />
</FORM>
</BODY>
</HTML>
```

In this example, we revisit the pay raise calculator. This time, we want to make sure that our human resources executives aren't too generous or too stingy with our employees. To test this code, navigate to the page and attempt to enter a value less than 1000 or greater than 5000 as a new pay rate. The control will render the page invalid, preventing the data from being processed until you enter a valid amount.

You'll want to make sure that you always provide an error message that clearly informs the user what the valid range is when using a RangeValidator control. If you can, it's even better to let the user know what the valid range is initially, before the user has a chance to make an error.

Validation Using Regular Expressions

Regular expressions are a symbolic minilanguage used for text processing. You can use the RegularExpressionValidator control to apply a regular expression comparison to a value in your form. To do this, you assign the regular expression pattern to the ValidationExpression property of the RegularExpressionValidator control.

For example, suppose you're creating an application that requires users to establish a PIN number when they initially create their account. The rules for your application are that PINs must be composed of a single non-numeric character followed by three numbers. Determining whether a given string is four characters in length is easy in code, but determining whether those digits are numbers or letters may take a bit of doing. Fortunately, it's easy using a regular expression—the expression "\D\d\d\d" matches a string comprising a non-digit character followed by three digits. A comparison based on this expression will reject anything larger or smaller than four characters in length.

Listing 12.22 shows an example of how to perform regular expression validation in ASP.NET using this validation rule.

LISTING 12.22   Performing Validation Based on a Regular Expression Comparison

```
<HTML>
<HEAD>
<TITLE>
Account Creation [RegExp]
</TITLE>
<SCRIPT language="VB" runat="server">

    Sub SaveBtn_Click(Sender As Object, e As EventArgs)
       If Page.IsValid Then
          lblOutput.Text = "Account created!"
       Else
          lblOutput.Text = ""
       End If
    End Sub

</SCRIPT>
</HEAD>

<BODY>
<FORM runat="server">

User ID:<asp:textbox id=txtUserID text='newuser' runat=server /><BR>
PIN:<asp:textbox id=txtPIN runat=server />
<asp:Button id=Button1 text="Save" OnClick="SaveBtn_Click" runat=server /><BR>

    <asp:RegularExpressionValidator id="RegularExpressionValidator1"
        ControlToValidate="txtPIN"
        ValidationExpression="\D\d\d\d"
        runat="server">
    Please enter PIN comprising a non-number followed by three numbers.
    </asp:RegularExpressionValidator>
```

LISTING 12.22   Continued

```
<asp:label id='lblOutput' runat='server' />
</FORM>
</BODY>
</HTML>
```

To test this code, navigate to the page in a browser and attempt to enter an invalid PIN (such as XXXX) into the PIN field. You should be able to see that any combination of characters that does not match the regular expression will cause the validation rule to fail; a valid entry is a string similar to "A599."

> **NOTE**
>
> A full exploration of the syntax of regular expressions is beyond the scope of this book, but they're covered adequately in the .NET framework SDK documentation. The seminal book on regular expressions is Jeffrey E. F. Friedl's *Mastering Regular Expressions* (O'Reilly). The book is geared toward developers writing scripts using the Perl programming language in Unix, but don't let that scare you away—the amount of actual Perl code in the book is very small.

Custom Validation Using the `CustomValidator` Object

You can use custom validation in situations where your validation is too complicated or irregular for the standard validation controls described in this section.

To implement a custom validation rule using the `CustomValidator` control, you must write a custom validator function. The cool thing about `CustomValidator` is that your validation function can reside and execute on either the server side or the client side, or both. (Of course, if cross-browser compatibility is important to you, you will want to write your client-side validation function in JavaScript.) To assign a server-side validation function to a `CustomValidator`, you write a function and assign the name of the function to the ControlValidator's OnServerValidate property. To assign a client-side function, write a client function and assign it to the ControlValidator's ClientValidationFunction property.

To demonstrate this function, we'll return to the PIN example introduced in the previous example. This time, we'll assume that the user created an account and is ready to log in. We want to provide custom validation on the client and server side for the PIN field. On the client side, we want to make sure that the PIN is composed of a letter and three numbers; we will use a regular expression in JavaScript to do this. But you wouldn't want to verify the password using client-side JavaScript, because this technique isn't secure (JavaScript is executed on the client and is visible to the client). So we'll perform the actual verification of the PIN on the server.

Listing 12.23 shows an example of custom validation using server-side validation.

LISTING 12.23   Performing Custom Validation on the Server Side

```
<HTML>
<HEAD>
<TITLE>
Login with PIN [Custom Validation]
</TITLE>

<SCRIPT language="VB" runat="server">

    Sub SaveBtn_Click(Sender As Object, e As EventArgs)
      If Page.IsValid Then
        lblOutput.Text = "Login successful!"
      Else
        lblOutput.Text = ""
      End If
    End Sub

    Sub ServerVerify(Sender As Object, Value As ServerValidateEventArgs)
      ' In a real application, this code would do
      ' a database call or use Active Directory or
      ' something interesting. For this example, no.
      If txtPIN.Text = "A999" Then
        Value.IsValid = True
      Else
        Value.IsValid = False
      End If
    End Sub

</SCRIPT>
</HEAD>

<BODY>
<FORM runat="server">

User ID:<asp:textbox id=txtUserID text='myusername' runat=server /><BR>
PIN:<asp:textbox id=txtPIN runat=server />
<asp:Button id=Button1 text="Save" OnClick="SaveBtn_Click" runat=server /><BR>

    <asp:CustomValidator id="CustomValidator1"
        ControlToValidate="txtPIN"
        OnServerValidate="ServerVerify"
        runat="server">
```

LISTING 12.23   Continued

```
    Invalid PIN number!
    </asp:CustomValidator>

<asp:label id='lblOutput' runat='server' />

</FORM>
</BODY>
</HTML>
```

You can see that the `CustomValidator` is pretty straightforward—to make it work, you set its OnServerValidate property to the name of the function you want to use to perform the validation. Your code then sets the IsValid property of the `ServerValidateEventArgs` object passed into the function to either `true` or `false`, depending on whether the validation logic contained in the function has validated the data.

To create a client-side validation function, you create a validation function and assign its name to the ClientValidationFunction property of the `CustomValidator` control. Your function should take two parameters: source and arguments (this is similar to an event procedure declaration). Within the client validation function, you set the value of arguments.IsValid to `true` or `false`, depending on the outcome of the validation code.

Also, you can write your client-side validation code in VBScript if cross-browser compatibility isn't important to you (that is, you know that every user who uses your Web application will be using some version of Microsoft Internet Explorer).

Note that if you don't want to perform client-side validation for some reason, you can simply omit it, as our code example has done in Listing 12.23.

Providing a Summary of Validation Rule Violations

Summary validation takes the error messages generated by any number of validation controls and displays them in a summary format. The `ValidationSummary` control can display its output inline on the page or in a pop-up message box. Because it has the capability to give the user multiple error messages at once, it's very effective in situations where you have many validation controls on a form.

Listing 12.24 shows an example of how summary validation works.

LISTING 12.24   Displaying a Summary of Validation Errors

```
<HTML>
<HEAD>
<TITLE>
Pay Raise Calculator [Summary]
```

LISTING 12.24   Continued

```
</TITLE>
<SCRIPT language="VB" runat="server">

    Sub SaveBtn_Click(Sender As Object, e As EventArgs)
      If Page.IsValid Then
        lblOutput.Text = "The new pay rate is: " & txtNewRate.Text
      Else
        lblOutput.Text = ""
      End If
    End Sub

</SCRIPT>
</HEAD>

<BODY>
<FORM runat="server">

    <asp:RequiredFieldValidator id="RequiredFieldValidator1"
        ControlToValidate="txtName"
        ErrorMessage="Please enter an employee name."
        runat=server>
    *
    </asp:RequiredFieldValidator>

Employee Name:<asp:textbox id=txtName runat=server /><BR>
Current Rate:<asp:textbox id=txtOldRate text='3000' runat=server /><BR>

    <asp:RangeValidator id="RangeValidator1"
        ControlToValidate="txtNewRate"
        ErrorMessage="Please enter a value between 1000 and 5000."
        MinimumValue='1000'
        MaximumValue='5000'
        Type="Double"
        runat="server">*</asp:RangeValidator>

New Rate:<asp:textbox id=txtNewRate text='12.98' runat=server />

<asp:Button id=Button1 text="Save" OnClick="SaveBtn_Click" runat=server /><BR>

<asp:label id='lblOutput' runat='server' />

<asp:ValidationSummary id='ValidationSummary1' runat='server'
    DisplayMode='BulletList'
    HeaderText='You Committed Serious Data Validation Crimes:'
    ShowSummary='true'
```

LISTING 12.24   Continued

```
    ShowMessageBox='true' />

</FORM>
</BODY>
</HTML>
```

Here we've returned to our pleasant pay raise calculator scenario. This time, we require that the user enter an employee name and a new pay rate (the current pay rate is filled in automatically with a hard-coded value). Two validation controls are on this page: a RequiredFieldValidator attached to the Employee Name field, and a RangeValidator connected to the New Rate field. It would be obnoxious to give users an error message if they failed to enter the employee's name, only to zap them with another error message when they neglect to enter a new pay rate; the validation summary gives them all the applicable error messages at once. To test this, navigate to the page and click the Save button without changing any of the values on the page.

The combination of red asterisks, warning messages on the page, and the message box alert probably makes this the most annoying data entry form in the history of Web programming, but it's really all in the name of science. Certainly your production Web forms will be more tasteful.

Using Multiple Validators

It often makes sense to have multiple validators attached to the same control. For example, if a field is required to be present and to fall within a certain range of values, you might attach both a RequiredFieldValidator and a RangeValidator to the control. There's no trick to this; simply assign as many validators as you need to implement the validation logic you want.

Handling Errors

Errors in ADO.NET are handled the same way as elsewhere in the .NET framework—you can catch exceptions that are thrown by objects involved in connecting to and interacting with the database.

The tricky thing about dealing with errors in data access programming is that so many things can go wrong at various stages in each request. The programmer can phrase the command in a syntactically incorrect way; the network connection can be bad; the database server can be on vacation. So it's useful in database programming to have a rich collection of error messages from every element in every database call.

ADO.old provided this in the form of an Errors collection associated with the database connection object. In ADO.NET, you are given a provider-specific exception object that contains a collection of error messages. Again, the functionality is similar to ADO.old; the only difference is in the implementation details.

In the SQL Server provider, a `SqlException` object is thrown whenever a data access operation fails. This object contains a collection of `SqlError` objects that you can examine in code to determine the full extent of what went wrong with your database call.

If you're interested only in determining whether a particular data access operation succeeded or failed, you need only catch the top-level error. To get a brief error message pertaining to the error, use the Message property of the `SqlException` object. On the other hand, if you want complete and detailed information about what went wrong, you must iterate through the SqlError objects contained in the `SqlException` object (these are exposed through `SqlException` object's Errors collection).

Listing 12.25 shows an example of the simple method of displaying a SQL error.

LISTING 12.25 Displaying a Data-Access Error

```vb
<% @Page language='vb' debug='true' %>
<% @Import namespace='System.Data' %>
<% @Import namespace='System.Data.SqlClient' %>

<HTML>
<SCRIPT runat='server'>

  Sub Page_Load(Sender As Object, e As EventArgs)
    Dim cn As SqlConnection
    Dim da As SqlDataAdapter
    Dim ds As DataSet
    Dim strSQL As String

    strSQL = "SELECT TOP 10 au_fname  FROM authors"
    cn = New SqlConnection("server=localhost;uid=sa;pwd=;database=pubs;")
    da = New SqlDataAdapter(strSQL, cn)

    ' ** Open connection and query
    Try
      cn.Open()
      ' ** Fill DataSet
      ds = New DataSet()
      da.Fill(ds, "Authors")

      ' ** Display data
      With DataGrid1
        .Datasource = ds.Tables("Authors").DefaultView
        .DataBind()
      End With
```

LISTING 12.25 Continued

```
  Catch ex As Exception
    Response.Write("Query failed: " & ex.Message)
  End Try

  cn.Close()

End Sub

</SCRIPT>

<BODY>

  <ASP:datagrid id='DataGrid1' runat='server' />

</BODY>
</HTML>
```

This code intentionally contains an error (the SQL command contains a reference to a field that doesn't exist). To show how the code runs without the error condition, fix the SQL command (the string "SELECT * from authors" will work).

Listing 12.26 provides an example of the more complete way of iterating through the Errors collection to display complete error information.

LISTING 12.26 Using the Errors Collection to Display Rich Error Information

```
' ** Open connection and query
Try
  cn.Open()
  ' ** Fill DataSet
  ds = New DataSet()
  da.Fill(ds, "Authors")

  ' ** Display data
  With DataGrid1
    .Datasource = ds.Tables("Authors").DefaultView
    .DataBind()
  End With

Catch sx As SqlException
  Dim se As SqlError
  For Each se In sx.Errors
    Response.Write("SQL Error: " & se.Message & "<BR>")
  Next
End Try
```

See the reference at the end of this chapter for more information on the properties and methods supported by the `SqlError` object. Also remember that `SqlError` is unique to the SQL Server managed provider in ADO.NET (if you're using the OLE DB managed provider, the analogous class is System.Data.OleDb.OleDbError).

ADO.NET Framework Reference

This section contains a brief reference to the ADO.NET objects mentioned in this chapter. It is not designed to be an exhaustive reference. For complete descriptions, including information on the objects not discussed in this chapter, refer to the .NET framework SDK documentation.

Component Class

Member of System.ComponentModel. Inherits from System.MarshalByRefObject.

The Component object serves as the base class for certain data objects in ADO.NET (such as the connection objects SqlConnection and OleDbConnection).

Properties

Container	Events	
DesignMode	Site	

Methods

Dispose	GetLifetimeService	MemberwiseClone
Equals	GetService	ToString
Finalize	GetType	
GetHashCode	InitializeLifetimeService	

Events

Disposed

DataAdapter Class

Member of System.Data.Common. Abstract class. Inherits from System.ComponentModel. Component.

The DataAdapter class serves as the base class for data adapter implementations in the SQL Server, OLE DB (and potentially other) data providers in ADO.NET.

Note that this is *not* the class you instantiate when you want to access data in ADO.NET; to write data-access code using a data adapter in your applications, use the OleDbDataAdapter, SqlDataAdapter, or other provider-specific data adapter class.

Properties

AcceptChangesDuringFill	Events	Site
Container	MissingMappingAction	TableMappings
DesignMode	MissingSchemaAction	

Methods

CloneInternals	Finalize	InitializeLifetimeService
CreateTableMappings	GetFillParameters	MemberwiseClone
Dispose	GetHashCode	ToString
Equals	GetLifetimeService	Update
Fill	GetService	
FillSchema	GetType	

Events

Disposed

DataSet Class

Member of System.Data. Inherits from System.ComponentModel.MarshalByValueComponent.

Note that the DataSet class is not owned by any particular provider; any ADO.NET data provider is capable of creating a DataSet object, and DataSet objects should interoperate across providers.

Constructor Example

Properties

CaseSensitive	EnforceConstraints	Namespace
Container	Events	Prefix
DataSetName	ExtendedProperties	Relations
DefaultViewManager	HasErrors	Site
DesignMode	Locale	Tables

Methods

AcceptChanges	GetService	OnRemoveTable
BeginInit	GetType	RaisePropertyChanged
Clear	GetXml	ReadXml
Clone	GetXmlSchema	ReadXmlSchema
Copy	HasChanges	RejectChanges
Dispose	HasSchemaChanged	ResetRelations

Methods

EndInit	InferXmlSchema	ResetTables
Equals	MemberwiseClone	ToString
Finalize	Merge	WriteXml
GetChanges	OnPropertyChanged	WriteXmlSchema
GetHashCode	OnRemoveRelation	

Events

Disposed	MergeFailed	PropertyChanged

DataColumn Class

Member of System.Data. Inherits System.ComponentModel.MarshalByValueComponent.

The DataColumn object represents the structure, or schema, of data in a DataTable object. You use the DataColumn object to determine information about the structure of the field (not the data it contains).

This object is contained by the DataSet object and is therefore not provider specific.

Constructor Example

No constructor example.

Properties

AllowDBNull	DataType	Ordinal
AutoIncrememt	DefaultValue	Prefix
AutoIncrementSeed	DesignMode	ReadOnly
AutoIncrementStep	Events	Site
Caption	Expression	Table
ColumnMapping	ExtendedProperties	Unique
ColumnName	MaxLength	
Container	Namespace	

Methods

Dispose	GetHashCode	OnPropertyChanging
Dispose	GetService	RaisePropertyChanging
Equals	GetType	ToString
Finalize	MemberwiseClone	

Events

Disposed

DataRelation Class

Member of System.Data.

The DataRelation object is used to denote the relationship between two DataTable objects.

Constructor Example

No constructor example.

Properties

ChildColumns	ExtendedProperties	ParentTable
ChildKeyConstraint	Nested	RelationName
ChildTable	ParentColumns	
DataSet	ParentKeyConstraint	

Methods

CheckStateForProperty	GetHashCode	ToString
Equals	GetType	
Finalize	MemberwiseClone	

DataTable Class

Member of System.Data.

The DataTable object represents a unit of data arranged as collections of rows and columns. It is contained by the DataSet object and is not provider specific.

Constructor Example

No constructor example.

Properties

CaseSensitive	DesignMode	Namespace
ChildRelations	DisplayExpression	ParentRelations
Columns	Events	Prefix
Constraints	ExtendedProperties	PrimaryKey
Container	HasErrors	Rows
DataSet	Locale	Site
DefaultView	MinimumCapacity	TableName

Methods

AcceptChanges	Finalize	OnColumnChanged
BeginInit	GetChanges	OnColumnChanging
BeginLoadData	GetErrors	OnPropertyChanging
Clear	GetHashCode	OnRemoveColumn
Clone	GetRowType	OnRowChanged
Compute	GetService	OnRowChanging
Copy	GetType	OnRowDeleted
Dispose	HasSchemaChanged	OnRowDeleting
Dispose	ImportRow	RejectChanges
EndInit	LoadDataRow	Select
EndLoadData	MemberwiseClone	ToString
Equals	NewRow	

Events

ColumnChanged	RowChanged	RowDeleting
ColumnChanging	RowChanging	
Disposed	RowDeleted	

MarshalByRefObject Class

Member of System. Abstract class. Inherits from System.Object.

MarshalByRefObject serves as the base class for many of the classes composing an ADO.NET provider.

Properties

Equals	GetLifetimeService	InitializeLifetimeService
GetHashCode	GetType	ToString

Methods

Finalize	MemberwiseClone

MarshalByValueComponent Class

Member of System.ComponentModel. Inherits from System.Object.

MarshalByRefObject serves as the base class for the DataSet object as well as the objects contained by DataSet, including DataColumn, DataTable, DataView, and DataViewManager. In the .NET framework, objects that are remotable are required to inherit from this class.

Properties

Container	Events
DesignMode	Site

Methods

Dispose	GetHashCode	MemberwiseClone
Equals	GetService	ToString
Finalize	GetType	

Events

Disposed

OleDbCommand Class

Member of System.Data.OleDb. Inherits from System.Component.Component.

The OleDbCommand object is used to execute commands (including queries and such operations as data manipulation commands) against a data source.

Properties

CommandText	Container	Parameters
CommandTimeout	DesignMode	Site
CommandType	DesignTimeVisible	Transaction
Connection	Events	UpdatedRowSource

Methods

Cancel	ExecuteScalar	
InitializeLifetimeService		
CreateParameter	Finalize	MemberwiseClone
Dispose	GetHashCode	Prepare
Equals	GetLifetimeService	ResetCommandTimeout
ExecuteNonQuery	GetService	ToString
ExecuteReader	GetType	

Events

Disposed

SqlDataAdapter Class

Member of System.Data.SqlClient. Inherits from System.Data.DataAdapter.

The SqlDataAdapter object is used primarily to create DataSet objects in the SQL Server managed provider. In thick client context, the data adapter can also be used to provide cursorless navigation, filtering, creation, deletion, and updating of data. The OLE DB equivalent is System.Data.OleDb.OleDbDataAdapter.

Constructor Example

No constructor example.

Properties

AcceptChangesDuringFill	Events	SelectCommand
Container	InsertCommand	Site
DeleteCommand	MissingMappingAction	TableMappings
DesignMode	MissingSchemaAction	UpdateCommand

Methods

CloneInternals	Fill	InitializeLifetimeService
CreateObjRef	FillSchema	MemberwiseClone
CreateRowUpdatedEvent	FillSchema	OnFillError
CreateRowUpdatingEvent	Finalize	OnRowUpdated
CreateTableMappings	GetFillParameters	OnRowUpdating
Dispose	GetHashCode	ShouldSerializeTableMappings
Dispose	GetLifetimeService	ToString
Equals	GetService	Update
Fill	GetType	Update

Events

Disposed	RowUpdated
FillError	RowUpdating

SqlDataReader Class

Member of System.Data.SqlClient. Inherits System.MarshalByRefObject.

The SqlDataReader object enables connection-based, fast access to data in the SQL Server managed provider. The OLE DB equivalent to this object is System.Data.OleDb.OleDbDataReader.

Constructor Example

No constructor example.

Properties

Depth	IsClosed	RecordsAffected
FieldCount	Item	

Methods

Close	GetHashCode	GetSqlInt64
CreateObjRef	GetInt16	GetSqlMoney
Equals	GetInt32	GetSqlSingle
Finalize	GetInt64	GetSqlValue
GetBoolean	GetLifetimeService	GetSqlValues
GetByte	GetName	GetString
GetBytes	GetOrdinal	GetType
GetChar	GetSchemaTable	GetValue
GetChars	GetSqlBinary	GetValues
GetData	GetSqlBoolean	IntializeLifetimeService
GetDataTypeName	GetSqlByte	IsDBNull
GetDateTime	GetSqlDateTime	MemberwiseClone
GetDecimal	GetSqlDecimal	NextResult
GetDouble	GetSqlDouble	Read
GetFieldType	GetSqlGuid	ToString
GetFloat	GetSqlInt16	
GetGuid	GetSqlInt32	

SqlConnection Class

Member of System.Data.SqlClient.

The SqlConnection object is used to create and maintain a connection to a data source in the SQL Server managed provider. Its OLE DB provider equivalent is System.Data.OleDb.OleDbConnection.

Properties

ConnectionString	DataSource	ServerVersion
ConnectionTimeout	DesignMode	Site
Container	Events	State
Database	PacketSize	WorkstationId

Methods

BeginTransaction	Equals	InitializeLifetimeService
ChangeDatabase	Finalize	MemberwiseClone
Close	GetHashCode	Open
CreateCommand	GetLifetimeService	ToString
CreateObjRef	GetService	
Dispose	GetType	

Events

Disposed	InfoMessage	StateChange

SqlError Class

Member of System.Data.SqlClient.

The SqlError object is found in the Errors collection contained by the SqlException object. It is designed to provide SQL Server-specific error information. Its OLE DB provider equivalent is the OleDbError class.

Note that this object (and the SqlException object that contains it) is available only when you use the SQL Server managed provider.

Properties

Class	Number	Source
LineNumber	Procedure	State
Message	Server	

Methods

Equals	GetHashCode	MemberwiseClone
Finalize	GetType	ToString

SqlException Class

Member of System.Data.SqlClient. Inherits from System.Exception.

The SqlException object is the object thrown when an error occurs in the ADO.NET SQL Server managed provider. This object contains a collection of SqlError objects that you can use to get detailed information on exactly what caused the data access error.

The equivalent to this class in the OLE DB provider is the OleDbException class.

Constructor Example

This object is typically caught in an exception handler rather than constructed.

Properties

Class	HelpLink	Server
Equals	Hresult	Source
Errors	InnerException	StackTrace
GetBaseException	LineNumber	State
GetHashCode	Message	TargetSite
GetObjectData	Number	ToString
GetType	Procedure	

Methods

Finalize	MemberwiseClone

INDEX

SYMBOLS

S